By David Kipen

The Schreiber Theory: A Radical Rewrite of American Film History

TRANSLATOR

The Dialogue of the Dogs by Miguel de Cervantes

EDITOR

Dear Los Angeles: The City in Diaries and Letters, 1542 to 2018

California in the 1930s: The WPA Guide to the Golden State

San Diego in the 1930s: The WPA Guide to America's Finest City

Los Angeles in the 1930s: The WPA Guide to the City of Angels

San Francisco in the 1930s: The WPA Guide to the City by the Bay

Dear Los Angeles

The City in Diaries and Letters 1542 to 2018

Edited by David Kipen

THE MODERN LIBRARY
NEW YORK

2018 Modern Library Edition

Published in the United States by Modern Library, an imprint of Random House, a division of Penguin Random House LLC, New York.

MODERN LIBRARY and the TORCHBEARER colophon are registered trademarks of Penguin Random House LLC.

Permissions acknowledgments can be found starting on page 554.

LIBRARY OF CONGRESS CATALOGING-IN-PUBLICATION DATA
Names: Kipen, David, author.
Title: Dear Los Angeles: the city in diaries and letters 1542 to 2018 / edited by David Kipen.
Description: First edition. | New York: The Modern Library, [2018] | Includes index.
Identifiers: LCCN 2018018940 | ISBN 9780812993981 | ISBN 9780812993998 (ebook)
Subjects: LCSH: Los Angeles (Calif.)—Civilization. | Los Angeles (Calif.)—Quotations, maxims, etc. | Los Angeles (Calif.)—History—Chronology. | Authors—California—Los Angeles—Anecdotes. | Pioneers—California—Los Angeles—Anecdotes. | Celebrities—California—Los Angeles—Anecdotes.
Classification: LCC F869.L85 K56 2018 | DDC 979.4/94—dc23
LC record available at https://lccn.loc.gov/2018018940

Printed in the United States of America on acid-free paper

modernlibrary.com
randomhousebooks.com

246897531

FIRST EDITION

For my parents, Angelenos by choice,
now even farther west

And for my beloved Colleen, native Bloom
of Lincoln Heights

Los Angeles, give me some of you!

—John Fante, *Ask the Dust*

There it is. Take it.

—"Chief" William Mulholland, dedicating the Los Angeles Aqueduct

Real good documentation, this Californiana crap.

—Thomas Pynchon, *The Crying of Lot 49*

Contents

Preface

This book is a collective self-portrait of Los Angeles when it thought nobody was looking. Joyous, creative, life-giving. Violent, stupid, inhospitable to strangers. Cerebral, melancholy. *Funny.*

What makes L.A. what it is, anyway? What's true of Los Angeles that isn't true of anywhere else? In real estate parlance, look at the comparables. We're a movie town, but so is Mumbai. The weather's nice, but you can't buy a decent windowscraper in Honolulu, either. Yes, we're "so spread out," but have you tried hoofing it across London?

We're the Italy of America—no wait, we're the capital of the Third World—hang on, now we're the Ellis Island of the West. What next? Yesterday's hyperbole is tomorrow's ephemera. If, in some perverse urban version of orienteering, you blindfolded and dropped me in random cities with just a canteen and a compass, would I even recognize L.A. if I landed in it?

It might take a while. To my blinkered, biased eye, no other town scumbles together the best and worst of every other city in the world as profligately as L.A. does. It's Heidelberg next door to Youngstown, hard by Positano. After all, what do Mumbai and Honolulu have in common? Other than L.A.'s resemblance to them, I can't think what. Los Angeles is, for better and worse, the Los Angeles of Los Angeles.

This exceptionalism transcends the old postcard cliché of someone picking an orange and throwing a snowball on the same day. My favorite parlor trick is to ask a transplant what they miss most about where they're from, and then try to come up with a Southern California approximation. It can be done, however dubiously. Nobody need ever feel homesick here—although, over the following pages, plenty of diarists and correspondents have managed it somehow.

Partly this homesickness stems from the natural propensity of visitors here to travel in packs. Too few of them know the natives, or the gone-natives, who could point them toward consolation. The other excuse for homesickness is that a lot of people enjoy it. When I'm out of town, I cherish the occasional pang as much as the next guy. Homesickness reassures us that we're right to live where we do instead of wherever we've temporarily shanghaied ourselves to. Where's my morning *Times*, my Dodgers broadcast, my jacarandas in June, a decent burrito? Only a return ticket away.

—

A reader's first reaction to *Dear Los Angeles* might be, what's with the hiccuping, date-by-date structure? Why not just march out all the entries in straightforward chronology, like *Bartlett's Familiar Quotations* does? Who ever heard of a book that inches forward each day, only to ratchet back overnight, just as far or farther? Is this a daybook or the myth of Sisyphus?

The ungrateful answer is, it wasn't my idea. Teresa Carpenter's delightful *New York Diaries* provided the template. Oh, how I fought this. First I tried the traditional *Bartlett's* approach, from 1542 up to the present, until I realized that we'd be at page 150 before getting to statehood—i.e., to any diarist that a lay reader had actually heard of. Chucking that, I had the bright idea of starting with the fulcrum year of 1935 and zigzagging back and forth in time from there, but the thing read more like a double-crostic than a book. At one point the manuscript even morphed into a coffee table–ready history of the city, complete with elaborate self-amused photo captions that still smirk at me from the depths of my hard drive. (I do miss that shot of Jack Nicholson arriving at the Dorothy Chandler Pavilion, hot off *Chinatown* and with, yes, the Department of Water and Power Building looming up behind him.)

And then it hit me. I could start with January 1 and just work forward one day at a time, complementary trying to juxtapose a few passages for each date. One step forward, two centuries back—the perennial, quixotic spectacle of L.A. forever finding fresh mistakes to make. In that moment, the whole deck of the book started shuffling into place.

I was so excited, it took days for me to realize I'd replicated Teresa's schema all but exactly. I hope she hit upon it more efficiently than I did.

—

The biggest difference between *Dear Los Angeles* and *New York Diaries* is the addition of epistolary writing alongside the diary excerpts. Two reasons for this, the first one easy: I just kept finding such terrific L.A. letters, published or unpublished, from people who, in most cases, didn't keep diaries, that I couldn't bear leaving them out.

The other reason is that Manhattan circa 1609 has an unsporting century-and-a-half head start over Los Angeles in the diary-keeping department. Even allowing for that handicap, New York's ever-endearing self-absorption gives it an unfair advantage. Historically, more New Yorkers' diaries get published, for reasons both justifiable and not. I also suspect that more New Yorkers per capita *keep* a diary. Something has to pass the time there.

Trash-talking aside, I realized that another form of offhand writing had to pick up the slack. Once I incorporated letters (plus a few irresistible scraps of columnizing, tweets, blogs, and the odd oration)—essentially, any kind of L.A. writing with a date on it and no real posterity intended—my feared undersupply of material became a horn of plenty.

Apart from how it's organized, and how letters crashed the diary party, a last unavoidable question to address here is what got in and what didn't. You could spend a lifetime in libraries and archives and barely scratch the surface of what's available. The only constraints are publisher patience and authorial liquidity. Within these parameters, my criteria for including an entry were basically 1) relevance to L.A., and 2) indefensible, undefinable editorial prerogative.

Mostly I liked these entries because they told me something about my city. For reasons hard to quantify, they played off each other in quirky, quarky, covalent ways. Some underscored how far we've come, others how far we still have to go. Ultimately, the entries had a hard time getting in if they didn't make me laugh, or tick me off, or choke me up.

A shamefaced word here about those who didn't make the cut often enough, i.e., poor people, minorities, women, and all the other Angelenos who've lived some fascinating but tantalizingly unrecorded lives. Historic reasons may exist for their relative oblivion. So, probably, do careless, myopic ones on my part. Those forgotten might or might not have cared that this book stints them, but I do, and I apologize for it.

That's why I'm not done yet. Every day, dumpster-loads of family diaries and letters wind up in landfills. Descendants cherry-pick the antiques for estate sales and, regretfully or not, consign the rest to oblivion. Executors of Los Angeles, I implore you: Have pity on the social historians (and beachcombing pseudo-historians) of the future. Half-assed temporary preservation is easier than ever. Haul out your *bubbe*'s Saratoga trunk. Open up your *abuelita*'s closet. Read some of those yellowed notebook pages, those bundled love letters, even some of that "Sent Mail." Then snap pictures of at least a good example or two. If you don't have anywhere else to donate them, email them to me at kipend@gmail.com. I'm working to launch an initiative that'll give your history a home. If you've shelled out for *Dear L.A.,* it's the least I can do.

—

You won't be alone, either. To quote a lyric that Stephen Stills dashed off after the riot on the Sunset Strip, there's something happening here. There always was, but it's not just our secret anymore. Some megacities have started to look upon Los Angeles not as the cautionary bogeyman of old, but as a possible way forward. Resourceful, inventive homegrown scholars, peer-reviewed and otherwise, continue to emerge. Next to their labors, mine look less like research and more like vampirism. Developmentally, the city may finally be entering the mirror stage, starting to recognize its own reflection. Other mirrors, too, may now be called for—the funhouse variety, I hope, not excluded. This is Los Angeles. There's always an alternate route.

Now's the time to shut up and let hundreds of my neighbors get a word in—quick and dead alike, the habitués and the just passing through. L.A. is a mountain lion we only glimpse in shutter-quick flashes. A strong diary entry or letter makes as good a tripwire as any.

Way back when, for a lark, Angelenos used to plant "Now Entering Los Angeles City Limits" signs in faraway places and pose next to them for pictures. L.A. is so big, the joke went, that you could trek to the Himalayas and still never escape. L.A. *had* no limits.

But the joke cracks both ways. A driver only sees an "Entering Los Angeles" sign on the way *in*to town, never the way out. Looked at this way, L.A. is the place Angelenos are forever approaching but can never quite get to. Like the city's most salient, salable feature, you can't look directly at it. On the right day, though, over the shoulder of a frank letter-writer or diarist, you can feel its radiance.

David Kipen, Los Angeles, Cal.

Dear Los Angeles

JANUARY 1

1853

I have not yet seen a gold mine! Few emigrants can say this. Nearly all rush to the mines on their first coming, as if there were no other pursuit worthy of attention. From this mania, however, they are fast recovering. Thus hope is reviving for this part of the country. A great revolution is silently going on.

JUDGE BENJAMIN HAYES

1923

On January the first, 1923, this mighty temple was opened. Since the break of day, surging multitudes had been gathering, filling the streets in every direction, waiting for the doors to open. At 2 o'clock in the afternoon, a scaffolding had been hastily erected in front of the Temple and draped with a great American flag. Loving hands, atremble with eagerness and the excitement of the moment, lifted me to the top of the scaffolding, from which the outside dedication service was held, and from which we read the story of the ancient Temple of Jerusalem.

SISTER AIMEE SEMPLE MCPHERSON

1934

Had awful flood in La Crescenta and Montrose. Many killed and injured and many homes washed away. Rained all Day. Stayed home & Quilted.

G. MCGRAMA

1941

I must really try to keep this journal more regularly. It will be invaluable to me if I do. Because this year is going to be one of the most decisive periods of the 20th century—and even the doings and thoughts of the most remote and obscure people will reflect the image of its events.

That's a hell of a paragraph to start off with. Why are we all so pompous on New Year's Day? Come off it—you're not Hitler or Churchill. Nobody called on you to make a statement. As a matter of fact, what did you actually do?

Last night you . . . went on to the temple, where the Swami, wrapped in a blanket, read aloud from the sayings of Ramakrishna, the Vedas and the Bible, until a quarter past midnight. Then you came home and couldn't sleep, so you reread most of Wells's *First Men in the Moon.*

CHRISTOPHER ISHERWOOD

1985

Where is the life? Where are the people? Even though I know all of the answers, I am still not satisfied by the responses.

A Korean family bought the Ekins house. Yesterday they began to cut down every tree growing in the backyard. Peggy would turn over in her grave. Debby would cry. I was anguished.

What a city! Widen the streets! Tear down the past! Destroy the trees. . . .

I'm having trouble building up the energy and commitment I need to form a committee to save 50's architecture.

Oi.

AARON PALEY

JANUARY 2

1848

I will now give an account of Col Fremonts proceedings out here as well as the difficulty he had with Col Mason. . . .

Col M said—Sir when I send for an officier whom I rank and command I expect him to obey me—Why did you not come Sir when I sent for you—I have a mind to put you under arrest Sir

—Col F replied my business was closed with you Sir was my reason for not comeing

—Col Mason immediately said—I want none of your insolence Sir

—Col Fremont [said], that is a term applied to a menial Sir and I hope you will wave your rank and give me an opportunity to wipe it out

—Col M answered within the hour Sir—at the same time telling him that double barrel shot guns must be the weapons

—some delay however occurred in sending the challenge and Mason had time to think of what he was doing and he sent a letter to Fremont asking that it might be put off for a while.

LIEUTENANT JOHN MCHENRY HOLLINGSWORTH

1932

Dinner in Santa Monica. Home in Rolls Royce. Jolly, futile, childish fun.

DAWN POWELL

JANUARY 3

1929

The Santa Monica Mountains are not big, as mountains run, but they are very picturesque. That is proven by the Lasky Ranch. Driving past that ranch yesterday we saw motion-picture sets for a cliffdwellers' settlement, a Belgian village, a western mining town and a water-front scene, each in what seemed its natural setting. And doubtless those hills and valleys, chocolate-drop peaks and corrugated canyons have been seen by motion-picture patrons all over the world. It made us think of the two ex-doughboys talking of the trees of France. "Did they have any eucalyptus up in the war zone?" one asked. "I never saw any," said the other, "but I notice in all the big war pictures the roads are lined with 'em."

We have seen tropical jungles which could not compare with the hillsides of the Malibu range, which are covered with chemise brush tall as a man and so thick that you couldn't even shoot a gun through it for more than fifty yards. Deer and coyotes can hardly penetrate except along broken paths . . . coveys of quail have to alight along the roadside in order to find open ground enough to spread out on, and continually whirr into the air before one's approaching motor.

Lee Shippey

1935

The hills are all intensely green, and from my window I awake to look at snow-capped mountains. The air is very gentle and the sunlight is brilliant and warm. . . .

Mother says that I may buy a flute. . . . Mother's being on the newspaper makes it possible for her to get tickets for anything she wants to go to, so that I will be able to attend any concerts there are that I want to. I want to go to the Philharmonic whether I like the programs or not, because I think it is very necessary to hear as much music as I can.

I am also enjoying the records Henry gave me. I have a phonograph, not a very good one, but it goes around.

JOHN CAGE

1979

Bad December, including week in hospital just before Christmas for exhaustion. The usual tests; no new discoveries. Am now on oxygen all night, with portable machine for daytime use. Spent New Year's Eve with K.H. and children at hotel in Death Valley, vast expanse of nothing that has less of anything than any tourist resort in the world—less water (indeed, no water at all), fewer flora and fauna (unless you count the coyote and the kangaroo rat), fewer hotels and buildings of interest (e.g. handful of very vestigial ghost towns and the unimpressive pseudo-Spanish mansion called Death Valley Scotty's Castle), less of everything attractive to the civilised mind except heat, of which there is far too much (the average summer temperature is around 120 degrees F). We drive back through ghastly company towns run by chemical firms and by the US navy's weapons research department. Death Valley is minimal tourism, a gigantic natural monument to the theory that less is more. Query: Why is it that all man-made objects in the States—especially cars, trains, aircraft and modern buildings—look like outsize toys?

KENNETH TYNAN

JANUARY 4

1928

It is precisely a week ago that we suffered a fright with Miguelito. He was crossing the street nearby when he was hit by a car. Even though it was not serious, it wasn't without consequences, for the car passed over him and dragged him a good stretch. It seems that perhaps he will come out of it with only slight bruises and contusions that have kept him in bed for a couple of days. He now gets around with a bit of a limp, somewhat like don Cuco.

Lola did go through a terrible ordeal. Since I wasn't there when it all happened, she went out to see what was going on and there she found only his shoes and was told that her boy had been carried away dead and had been taken to the hospital. And so she returned with his shoes in hand and with her heart in pieces. We immediately telephoned to find out which hospital they had taken him to so we could go see him when a man arrived with him very much alive.

Dolores Venegas, to her family

1928

I wish I could see you. It has been many years since we saw each other. We are very happy because dad has a store. . . . [W]hen I was going to buy tortillas I was struck by a car that dragged me about 10 blocks. My dad is thinking how we can return and be together again with my aunt Anita and with all of you.

José Miguel Venegas, to his family

1985

I can't make the city what I want it to be. And I can't stop wishing it were something else. I cannot. Nor have I ever really accepted it.

So, San Francisco again emerges as the compromise?

But no, that's not really where my thoughts are going. . . .

For now, I feel homeless. Not here inside my room, but almost everywhere else in the city. I feel like a tourist. Not a resident. But I have all of these déjà-*vus*.

AARON PALEY

JANUARY 5

1776

The converted Indians of this mission . . . appear to be gentle, friendly and of good hearts. The men are of medium stature, the women being somewhat smaller, round-faced, flat-faced, and rather ugly. The costume of the men in heathendom is total nakedness, while the women wear a bit of deer skin with which they cover themselves, and likewise an occasional cloak of beaver or rabbit skin, although the fathers endeavor to clothe the converted Indians with something as best they can.

The method which the fathers observe in the conversion is not to oblige anyone to become a Christian, admitting only those who voluntarily offer themselves, and this they do in the following manner: Since these Indians are accustomed to live in the fields and the hills like beasts, the fathers require that if they wish to be Christians they shall no longer go to the forest, but must live in the mission, and if they leave the Ranchería, as they call the little village of huts and houses of the Indians, they will go to seek them and will punish them. With this they begin to catechize the heathen who voluntarily come, teaching them to make the sign of the cross and other things necessary, and if they persevere in the catechism for two or three months and in the same frame of mind, when they are instructed they proceed to baptise them.

If any Indian wishes to go to the mountain to see his relatives or to hunt acorns, they give him permission for a specified number of days. As a rule they do not fail to return, and sometimes they come bringing some heathen relative, who remains for the catechism, either through the example of the others or attracted by the pozole, which they like better than their herbs and the foods of the mountain; and so these Indians are usually caught by the mouth.

FATHER PEDRO FONT

1853

Jan. 5: Gardening all these days. The flowers transplanted last month all flourishing; seeds sown last month coming up, pink, poppy, larkspur; peas and turnips sown middle of December coming up finely. On the 2d, Sunday, we walked to the hills and transplanted a few of the wild yellow violet. A large congregation at church, an unusual number of men, perhaps the effect of good resolutions at the beginning of the year. . . .

Mr. Barker spent six months at the Tejon trading with the Indians who . . . reside there. These, he says, were not engaged in the hostilities on the Four Creeks in 1850–1851. As a proof of their present friendship, I may state that some two weeks ago they took a band of horses from some Sonorians that had Stolen them and delivered them up to their owner here. They say that one of the Sonorians was [the notorious outlaw] Joaquin Murrieta.

JUDGE BENJAMIN HAYES

1860

Tomas, an Indian, was sentenced to be executed on the 27th day of September last, but escaped from jail just prior to that day. He was subsequently re-taken, and on the 4th day of December I appointed the 31st of January for his execution. He had in cold blood killed his wife and daughter at the Tejon Reservation, to which place he belonged. . . .

On the morning of the day of execution, a strong feeling began to pervade the community in reference to this prisoner . . . expressing the opinion that his mind appeared to be not above idiocy, or that he was insane. An application being made to me, under our statute, I gave an order concurring in the summons by the Sheriff of a jury of twelve persons, to determine upon his supposed insanity. Accordingly by 2 p.m. the inquisition was concluded; and the jury found him to be sane—contrary to my expectation, and, as it seemed to me, to the expectation and wishes of a large number of the people who were in attendance.

A feeling of awe appeared to rest upon society—of doubt and fear—lest this poor man after all should have been found guilty originally when insane, or executed in that state, even if his conviction was right. I confess I could not help now and then participating in this solemn feeling of all around me. The *Los Angeles Star* gave the following brief account of this execution:

EXECUTION.—On Tuesday last, a miserable, imbecile looking creature, Tomas, an Indian, was executed in the jail yard, for the murder of his mother and wife.

Judge Benjamin Hayes

1942

At around four, the doorbell rang. It was two neatly dressed Americans about thirty years of age. They said, "There is something we want to ask Aoki."

. . . I called Sachiko and told her, "Go get Father from Mr. Onodera's place."

Sachiko said, "Okay." And in her cheerful way as usual, she took off, walking like she was jumping sideways, so I hurriedly ran down the front stone steps and caught up with her and in rapid Japanese told her, "They are FBI. Father is going to be investigated, so keep that in mind." She said, "What?" And the little girl's face that was always shining white with health suddenly went pale and turned blue, and with tears in her eyes, she took off running!

After a short while, my husband came home; and with my husband, we sat at a table facing the two Americans.

The two Americans rose slightly and said, "This is who we are." And they opened their coat and showed us their FBI badges and let loose their first arrow of questions.

Aoki Hisa

1977

Read a magazine quiz, compiled by experts on geriatric subjects, which purports to predict your life expectancy on the basis of your answers to questions about habits and general way of life. I answer with scrupulous accuracy and discover that I shall be dead in May.

Kenneth Tynan

JANUARY 6

1931

Here in Pasadena it is like Paradise. Always sunshine and clear air, gardens with palms and pepper trees and friendly people who smile at one and ask for autographs.

Albert Einstein

JANUARY 7

1861

It has now rained about seventy hours without cessation—for forty hours of that time, over twenty consecutive, it has rained like the hardest thundershower at home. No signs of clearing up yet—fire out by the rains, provisions getting rather scarce—one meal per day now. But our tent is dry—we have it well pitched, and in a dry place.

I have been studying Spanish, writing up letters, notes, etc. I have written thirteen letters, or about eighty pages, during this rain, to be mailed when we can get to town, but it will be a number of days, for the streams will be impassable. Lucky we did not stay up in the canyon Friday night as they wanted us to, we could not have got down yet. I never saw such rains before.

William H. Brewer

1932

Impossible to keep track of time or anything out here—life slips pleasantly out of your control almost at once.

Dawn Powell

2017

People in LA are deathly afraid of gluten. I swear to god, you could rob a liquor store in this city with a bagel.

Ryan Reynolds

JANUARY 8

1827

Last night there was a great fandango or dance among the Spanyards. They kept it up till nearly day light from the noise. The women here are very unchaste; all that I have seen and heard speak appear very vulgar in their conversation and manners. They think it an honnour to ask a white man to sleep with them; one came to my lodgings last night and asked me to make her a blanco Pickanina, which, being interpreted, is to get her a white child, and I must say that for the first time, I was ashamed, and did not gratify her or comply with her request, seeing her so forward.

HARRISON ROGERS

1964

Came upon Los Angeles by bus at night.... Ah the crazy hotels, crazy streets, sad signs of America—Jesus Saves!—Tom's Tattoo—"The Electric Rembrandt"—Snooker Parlor—"Acres of Autos"—Hotel Small—Ice Rink—Greyhound—Los Angeles Street—TV in Rooms—EAT—Barber & Beauty Supply—Pawn Shop—"Shave Yourself"—

... And lonely the hotel doors, gaping. And lonely the lobbies, lonely the beds! ... Forever & ever ... Lonely the lunchrooms, lonely the cars running in the streets! Lonely Los Angeles, lonely world! ...

Sure are a lot of defeated people in this here America....

I go to midnight burlesque show—the Morosco—original standup comedian in baggy pants & strippers bumping & grinding to staccato drum rolls—in pink spotlight which also catches face of drummer drumming in orchestra pit just below stripper on apron of stage—he looking up at her to synchronize his drumbeats with the movement of her pelvis, boom boom, bump bump, now jerking spasmodically, her face detached from the whole scene, having nothing to do with her body, trying to get as far away from it as possible. . . .

The Girl with the 56-Inch Bust grinds her final bump into the curtain, her lost face finally hidden in it as in a huge brown bedsheet. I am alone in the balcony with the spotlight projectionist. Smoke rises from the seats below as in an Inferno. The house lights come on.

LAWRENCE FERLINGHETTI

2008

It's Kaiser Permanente. It's an HMO mundo we inhabit (digo, those of us even lucky enough to *have* health coverage), so I won't know anything for up to ten days, can you believe it?

SUSANA CHÁVEZ-SILVERMAN

JANUARY 9

1890

Rode on a burro, first time. Liked it.

CHARLOTTE PERKINS GILMAN

1917

I am still firmly convinced that to change Tarzan, even though the change made a better story of it, would be to ruin it for the million or so people who have read the story.

EDGAR RICE BURROUGHS, to his agent

1957

So much emphasis was laid on the foreign fate of our pictures that some of us left [the] meeting with an impression that was both erroneous and discouraging. The domestic results were either dismissed lightly or in some cases not even mentioned. It is all very well to make the point that musical pictures fare badly as a rule in foreign language countries, but the argument was pressed so far the other evening that I, for example, came away with the bewildered impression that *The King and I* was a failure. All I heard was that Burma, Pakistan, and Rangoon didn't care for it.

NUNNALLY JOHNSON

JANUARY 10

1847

Crossing the plain, we encamped, about two o'clock p.m., in the mouth of a *cañada,* through which we ascend over a difficult pass in a range of elevated hills between us and the plain of San Fernando, or Couenga [Cahuenga]. Some forty or fifty mounted Californians exhibited themselves on the summit of the pass during the afternoon. They were doubtless a portion of the same party that we met several days ago, just below San Buenaventura. A large number of cattle were collected in the plain and corralled, to be driven along to-morrow for subsistence. Distance 10 miles.

EDWIN BRYANT

1888

The boy is growing and talks now remarkably well. He remarked the other day—when told to be careful or he would break his neck—"I don't want to break my neck—I wouldn't break it for any 'mount of money."

Mary had quite a sore throat—& the other night Ruth & I kept both babies all night. We had a circus—had to take both in bed—at the same time. The boy [the future General George S. Patton, Jr.] is fearful as a bed-fellow. I had just as soon sleep with a mule.

George Patton

1939

Re: "GONE WITH THE WIND"

JUST a word about the beginning. To suggest the romance of the old South immediately I should suggest borrowing from the trailers. Under the turning pages of the book I'd like to see a two or three minute montage of the most beautiful pre-war shots imaginable and played over it I'd like to hear the Stephen Foster songs right off the bat. I'd like to see young men riding, Negros singing, long shots of a barbecue, shots of Tara and Twelve Oaks and carriages and gardens and *happiness* and gaiety.

F. Scott Fitzgerald, to David O. Selznick

JANUARY 11

1847

I have been engaged all day arranging my Hospital. I have not heard any thing that is going on, everything seems quiet, the citizens of the place do not so far as I can discover manifest very friendly feelings—Nothing heard from Fremont, last night there was a devil of a row from the men, liquor the cause of it all—although every precaution had been taken. An Indian was found dead this morning—how killed I do not know.

Dr. John S. Griffin

1847

Emerging from the hills, the advance party to which I was attached met two Californians, bareheaded, riding in great haste. They stated that they were from the mission of San Fernando; that the Californian forces had met the American forces under the command of General Kearny and Commodore Stockton, and had been defeated after two days' fighting; and that the Americans had yesterday marched into Los Angeles.

Edwin Bryant

1933

I have just consumed a stack of wheats & a mug of mocha in this place [the Brown Derby restaurant]. The weather is very hot: yesterday went out in a motor boat from Balboa harbour. Have lectured three times & addressed several classes; have driven a Ford and got stuck in a snow drift. The trees are full of oranges.

T. S. Eliot

1935

Life has been hectic and the sky beautifully cloud-filled, sunlight and then beautiful shower-baths. Palm trees and acacias in bloom and all sorts of things I took for granted for too long. I feel bristling with spontaneity.

John Cage

JANUARY 12

1847

This morning two Californian officers, accompanied by . . . Pico, who marched with us from San Luis Obispo, came to the mission to treat for peace. A consultation was held and terms were suggested, and, as I understand, partly agreed upon, but not concluded.

Edwin Bryant

1847

In virtue of the aforesaid articles, equal rights and privileges are vouchsafed to every citizen of California, as are enjoyed by the citizens of the United States of North America.

Doña Bernarda Ruiz de Rodriguez,
amending the Treaty of Cahuenga

1968

Power corrupts the corruptable [*sic*].

Octavia E. Butler

JANUARY 13

1847

We continued our march, and encamped near a deserted rancho at the foot of Couenga [Cahuenga] plain. Soon after we halted, the Californian peace-commissioners appeared, and the terms of peace and capitulation were finally agreed upon and signed by the respective parties. . . .

The next morning a brass howitzer was brought into camp, and delivered. What other arms were given up I cannot say, for I saw none. Nor can I speak as to the number of Californians who were in the field under the command of Andres Pico when the articles of capitulation were signed, for they were never in sight of us after we reached San Fernando. Distance 12 miles.

EDWIN BRYANT

1958

The glory that was old Siam will soon vanish from the hills of West Los Angeles.

Medieval castles will tumble and antique oriental temples will fall.

Mansions and gardens will be ravaged like Atlantis.

Whole communities will perish without a trace.

Lakes and rivers will dry up and jungles will be swept away.

The instruments of this doomsday will be neither war, famine, death nor pestilence.

It will be wrought by the bulldozer and the ax.

It will be the end of a make-believe world—the 176-acre, false-front world of film sets on the famed 20th-Century-Fox lot.

Its doom was sounded last week by the studio's announcement that this portion of the 284-acre lot will be razed and cleared to make way for a $400 million complex of steel and concrete towers to be known as Century City.

JACK SMITH

1993

OK, so we were called into the [Menendez trial] courtroom one last time—it was standing room only—and the judge thanked us for our service and declared it a mistrial. It was all really kind of sad.

Hazel Thornton

JANUARY 14

1847

Drenched with rain and plastered with mud, we entered the "City of the Angels," and marched through its principal street to our temporary quarters. We found the town, as we expected, in the possession of the United States naval and military forces under the command of Commodore Stockton and General Kearny, who, after two engagements with six hundred mounted Californians on the 8th and 9th, had marched into the city on the 10th. The town was almost entirely deserted by its inhabitants.

Edwin Bryant

1949

[Talent agent Herman] Citron arrived with Montgomery Clift, with whom we discussed the story, selling him the idea at last, or so we think. As he left Billy [Wilder] said, "He might be any pimply messenger boy on the lot" and so he might.

Charles Brackett

JANUARY 15

1770

We set out with a guide from this village and traveled until we came to another small one in about a league and a half. From there we took another guide who led us in a northeasterly direction. A little farther on he turned east. We climbed a long and steep hill, from whose summit we made out the valley of Santa Catalina [San Fernando]. We descended to it, and, traveling to the southeast, arrived, late, at [Encino], where we camped on the 7th of August. The march covered six and a half leagues.

FRAY JUAN CRESPI

1971

This morning the sheets are twisted and the pillows lie on the floor. Perhaps I shall get up and drive over the mountains to find myself sitting in a field of clover.

LIZA WILLIAMS

JANUARY 16

1770

We now proceeded with a better knowledge of the country and, knowing where we were going, we discussed the direction we had to follow with greater certainty; besides this, the mountains furnished us points and determined places which served as landmarks to ascertain our position.

MIGUEL COSTANSÓ

1954

[The British actress] Gracie Fields seems to feel about Los Angeles very much as I do: that it has become a grotesque and impossible place for a human being to live in.

Raymond Chandler, to his publisher

1982

E. and I went into town. (such a funny perspective being in the Valley—anyways—today was the first time I went "over the hill"). . . .

I think this time in L.A. I can finally get past all of the shit from my past and just accept L.A. for what it is.

You can't expect any more from this town. And there are advantages. In short, I finally do fully understand the reasoning and motivation behind moving to L.A. . . .

I have good ideas (take a gas station and rehab it into a café/gallery. Who knows?).

Aaron Paley

JANUARY 17

1769

We set out from the place in the morning, and as soon as we entered the plain we saw a bare chain of mountains covered with snow, which we descried on entering the valley of Santa Clara; from the hills we also saw the Porciúncula River. We crossed the plain in a southeasterly direction, arrived at the river, and forded it, observing on its sands rubbish, fallen trees, and pools on either side, for a few days previously there had been a great flood which had caused it to leave its bed.

FRAY JUAN CRESPI

1876

At daylight we stopped in San Fernando cañon for breakfast, and of all the meals in California, for meanness, that was the champion. The mutton—they don't eat much else—was so tough that it was beyond the powers of human grinders to masticate it. I gave it up.

D. L. PHILLIPS

1882

I hear the San Juan paper is out—but my *Atlantic* has not arrived—& if you will believe it, I can't buy one in this place....

Whoever will come & and live a year on this coast, can make a book of romance which will live: It is a tropic of color and song. It is real pain to have to skim over it flying, as I do. —

HELEN HUNT JACKSON, to her editor

1960

I am, of course, the Robert Rich who wrote the original story and screenplay of a simple—if not simple-minded—little film called *The Brave One*, for which young Rich was awarded an Oscar. He hasn't got it yet, and neither have I. However, it's just as well, for although those statues look like gold, I'm told they're nothing but pot-metal inside....

[T]he only woman I ever married is still at my side. She brings in extra money as a photographer, so we eat well and love each other rather more than we did on that day twenty-two years ago when each confronted the other, with justifiable suspicion.

DALTON TRUMBO, to an editor

JANUARY 18

1847

We left the Puebla this morning. . . . Our hearts were heavy and forebodings of misfortune not wanting. . . .

It is nothing but my sense of duty as an officer that compels me to take the trip—A great majority of the men have as good as no shoes—some none at all—already they begin to complain of sore feet—a falling house it is said, will be deserted by the rats—so with us—Some of the servants refused to accompany the officers—upon whom they had been in attendance. Commodore Stockton said that he did not consider that peace was made with these people until they complyed with the terms of their treaty—that they had rendered up their arms. This they have not done—nor do they evince any disposition so far as I have heard—of doing so. They do not carry themselves as a people conquered or even overpowered—On the contrary they boast of having compelled us to make terms, and there is not an American who had been resident in the country but expects another revolution.

Dr. John S. Griffin

1935

There was a little open space the other day: I was walking and thinking of you in Ojai, and open space of country, and suddenly I knew what wildness was. I hissed and grunted and found myself expanding with a big heart 'til for a moment I was out of my mind and only tremendously alive.

I did not know you were wildly intoxicating. And now I have only very present memories. Life has been short, has only begun. And I can see in the corner your eyes, never turned away. And your hair is some kind of a promise, I don't know of what, perhaps that it will reach your shoulders and that I may bury myself in it.

Perhaps I am satisfied that you, who I know are a fragment, you are entirely another's. And yet, these days you are always with me.

It is late and I am tired and I love you and want to be with you.

I am sure there is something unexplainably and mysteriously sacred about the Valley, something including evil.

JOHN CAGE, to Pauline Schindler

1939

We are getting more and more murals in our public buildings. Now if we can just increase the proportion of morals to keep up with the murals everything will be grand.

LEE SHIPPEY

JANUARY 19

1856

And it further appearing by satisfactory proof to the judge here, that all of the said persons of color are entitled to their freedom, and are free and cannot be held in slavery or involuntary servitude, it is therefore argued that they are entitled to their freedom and are free forever. . . .

Given under my hand as judge of the First Judicial District Court of the State of California, on the 19th day of January, A.D. 1856, at the City of Los Angeles.

JUDGE BENJAMIN HAYES

1858

I walked through a beautiful garden & vineyard this afternoon. In the garden orange & lemon trees hung full of fruit. Fine cabbage, peas in bloom & many other vegetables. Pinks & flowers were to be seen on every side. The day warm and pleasant. Fig trees. This man can truly say that he can sit under his own vine & fig tree.

James Gillespie Hamilton

1971

Your review filled me with joy, as your earlier letter did. I have been able to encourage other writers, but never until now have the tables been turned so blessedly on me. To you I can confess that I left the academic world to write popular fiction in the hope of coming back by underground tunnels and devious ways into the light again, dripping with darkness. You encourage me to think that there was some strange merit in this romantic plan.

Ross Macdonald, to Eudora Welty

JANUARY 20

1868

My Dear Mary: —By my drinking to excess, and gambling also, I have involved myself to the amount of about three thousand dollars which I have borrowed from time to time from friends and acquaintances [under] the promise to return the same the following day, which I have often failed to do. To such [an extent] have I gone in this way that I am now ashamed to meet my fellow man on the street; besides that, I have deeply wronged you as a husband, by spending my money instead of maintaining you as it becomes a husband to do. Though you have [never] complained of my miserable conduct, you nevertheless have suffered too much. I therefore, to save you from farther disgrace and trouble, being that I cannot maintain you respectably, I shall end this state of thing this very morning. . . .

If I write these few lines, it is to set you [right] before this wicked world, to keep slander from blaming you in [any] manner whatever. Now, my dear beloved, I hope that you will pardon me. . . . It is time to part, God bless you, and may you be happy yet, your husband Damien Marchesseault.

MAYOR DAMIEN MARCHESSEAULT, in his suicide note

1880

Respected Mr. & Mrs. Cohn,

On this day of so much joy for you and your family, allow us to join our humble congratulations and sincere wishes to those of your many friends on the occasion of the marriage of your dear child and [the] good young man whom providence has destined for her. May the God of Abraham, of Isaac and Jacob bless their union and be with them.

May she be amiable to her husband as Rachel, wise as Rebecca, long lived and fruitful as Sarah. May both, to your joy, see their children's children unto the third and fourth generation, filled with all the blessings which we invoke upon them, as well as upon you.

BISHOP FRANCIS MORA

1938

Oh, Joe, can't producers be wrong? I'm a good writer—honest.

F. SCOTT FITZGERALD, to a director

1940

It is as if you tipped the United States up so all the commonplace people slid down here into Southern California.

FRANK LLOYD WRIGHT

2018

"Girls just wanna have fun-damental human rights," "I've seen better cabinets at Ikea," "We are girlcotting this presidency," and "Donald Trump uses [reviled Microsoft Word font] Comic Sans" were a few of my favorite posters at the women's march in downtown LA. Everyone was fired up, empowered, and sick of Donald Trump's s**t. The rally was full of positive energy and support for women of all races, religions, sexualities, classes, and origins. The speakers discussed political and social rights, and there was live music! After, my friend and I walked through downtown to buy plants. I bought a little air plant in a glass container. As an environmental science major, I should really be better at not killing plants, but honestly I always forget to water them. My little air plant, that I named Sheldon, only needs to be watered once every two weeks though, so I should be able to keep the little guy alive for awhile. Plus, everytime I water him I'll remember the women's march. This country definitely isn't perfect, but there are a lot of great people here that I trust to keep the country growing.

JULIA CAMPBELL

JANUARY 21

1861

That portion of our party which went to the Lighthouse had the good fortune to see the shot from a boat . . . and the chase, first up, then down the coast. In their excitement, they thought the run was four miles. Capt. C, who was the lucky shot, says not more than three-fourths of a mile, when the flurry ended in death; he brought in the whale that same night. Often, however, it sinks and does not rise. . . .

Both these companies employ chiefly Indian hands, at $15 per month. The work is measurably light, and the Indians well content with this pay, better than they can get at any other kind of employment.

Capt. Packard considers that he has done well, but thinks the large number of ships that will come here next season on hearing of the success of his venture will seriously interfere with the proceeds of those who operate on land and will soon destroy the whales.

Judge Benjamin Hayes

1939

It rained glorious rain all day.

Ray Bradbury

1957

I woke a little late and reread Orson's rewrite of *Touch of Evil.* It now lacks only good dialogue to make it a really meritable script. The makeup test was a great success. Bud Westmore made me look so acceptably Mexican they're cutting the covering lines about my not being. Orson thinks a moustache is in order; if I start today I can just make it. We also had a Mexican tailor begin work on a suit, which will help.

Charlton Heston

1982

We saw a meteor falling to Earth.

It was close to the surface. A few hundred yards—no more. A bright wide vertical swath of white light.

I stood on top of the mountain at Beverly Glen. I could see the snow on the San Gabriel mountains, the mountains of Simi Valley, Catalina Island and Palos Verdes. It was a stunning spectacle—as high as possible—the city stretching around me—reaching upwards.

Aaron Paley

2006

I had a book talk and signing Thursday evening at the Los Feliz library, so I departed lovely Mar Vista early to beat the crush. To be more precise, I pulled out of the Starbucks at Barrington and National, fortified with caffeine for the Santa Monica Freeway, right about 4:30. Ten minutes into the trip, my editor at *Los Angeles* Magazine called. She had just left Wilshire and Ogden, headed for Altadena via surface streets. We chatted about gossip, did some serious work and compared traffic notes. Mine was flowing smooth and easy, so I decided to keep it simple and barrel straight up Vermont. With luck I'd get an hour at Fred 62 to collect my thoughts.

Her drive was a grind, hammered by buses and short lights. We had time to discuss a story and dissect the day's headlines. I'm not sure when we realized what might be coming. In retrospect, perhaps we should have given it the reverence you afford a perfect game in baseball and let the feat go unmentioned until it was official. But we didn't. She began to call off the street names. Catalina slipped past. "Can you see El Pollo Loco?"

I could. As I rolled north on Vermont, she idled three cars back from the red light on eastbound Olympic. "Oh look," she reported. "There's a bicycle behind you."

Two Angelenos passing in the sprawl, our paths intersecting in time and space and the ether of cell phone technology.

KEVIN RODERICK

JANUARY 22

1885

I am gaining very slowly and walking, and I'm still on crutches, and I fear likely to be so for months. But if one must be helpless I know of no place in the world where one can bear it better than in Southern California. The hills are already green, as velvet, the barley many inches high, and some volunteer patches in full head, larks and linnets singing all along the roads, and all sorts of flowers in full bloom in the gardens; nevertheless it is cool enough to make a fire welcome, indeed needful, at night and in the morning; the perfection of weather.

I hope you have read my story *Ramona* and become converted by it (if you needed conversion) on the Indian question. I have, in this book, flung my last weapon! If this does not tell, I know nothing more to do. In my *Century of Dishonor* I tried to attack people's consciences directly, and they would not listen. Now I have sugared my pill, and it remains to be seen if it will go down.

HELEN HUNT JACKSON, to her editor

1989

Dear former President Reagan,

Welcome back to Los Angeles, to be sure from a design and development point of view, a very different Los Angeles from the one in which you and Nancy once lived.

In your waning days as president, one of your more popular lines was to ask people whether they were better off now than they were 8 years ago. No doubt a select portion of L.A.'s population is, judging from the over-subscription of the pricey-per-plate testimonials honoring you; the sizes and costs of the custom-designed houses rising here like souffles.

SAM HALL KAPLAN

JANUARY 23

1930

Of all the Christbitten places and businesses in the two hemispheres this one is the last curly kink on the pig's tail. And that's without prejudice to D. W. Griffith. I like him and think he's good. But, Jesus, the movies!

STEPHEN VINCENT BENÉT

1936

I do not look forward to their [my children's] future with pleasure, not even with confidence. I see only war and taxes.

HAMLIN GARLAND

1987

While driving through Beverly Hills with Julie today, saw an RTD bus pulled over next to some park. The driver was outside practicing his golf swing *with a club.* Only in Beverly Hills. Also walked by Andy Rooney shooting a piece in Westwood. Weird Thursday morning.

Carolyn Kellogg

JANUARY 24

1826

Some of the men are kept employed [breaking] wild horses. Daniel Ferguson, one of our men, when leaving the mission on the 18th hid himself, and we could not find him; the corporal who commands at the mission promised to find him, and send him on to us. But I expect we shall not see him again. The weather continues fine.

Harrison Rogers

1940

While I was seated and drinking a boy brought a piece of paper on which was written: "Mr. Dreiser—would you honor me by having a drink with me—John Stemtuck" or some such name. My near reading sight is not much without eye glasses and they weren't handy. Anyhow, without thinking more about it (I took it to be from a total stranger—someone not known to me in any way) I decided, if you please, to go over and be as pleasant as possible and get it over with.

How it came off, what you thought (and now I am wondering) I can only guess. Somewhere along the way I must have stuck the note in my pocket and forgotten it. And I know now (perhaps 6 weeks later) that you did not trouble to enlighten me. And right you were. But what a boor you must have taken me to be!

And today, 6 weeks later, I'm regretting it all so much. I'm so truly sorry for myself. For today I upset my ink well and spilled ink on a crumpled piece of paper lying on my desk. How it got there I don't know. Anyhow I picked it up to throw it into the waste basket. . . .

And then—Christ—what a dunce! The one man I've been truly wanting to meet since I read *Of Mice and Men,* not to mention your beautiful and powerful *Grapes of Wrath.* And there I sat and then walked away without saying anything!—trashy formalities. My God!

Well, anyhow, here I am. And that is my story. And tears won't collect and bottle spilled milk. But maybe they'll dissolve the righteous and yet mistaken opinion you're holding concerning me. I hope so. For, although you've met me, you're still the one man I want to meet—and talk to—and will—your gracious and far-reaching charity permitting—

THEODORE DREISER, to John Steinbeck

2009

Mis dreams. Bubbling up, también—con el tarry viscosity and regularity de ese *glug glug glug* que se escucha at the La Brea Tar Pits—from the primeval swamp *sine qua non:* el subconsciente. My dream/journal. Working on, working *out* tantas cosas.

SUSANA CHÁVEZ-SILVERMAN

JANUARY 25

1962

2457 Folsom St.
Boyle Heights

I wish I had time to tell you some of my latest dreams. . . . I hope you dig this, man!!! I am going to try this on my own. . . . by the time I get to Hanford I may be forced to take a hard look at the situation and decide to latch on to the dear old paycheck for all its worth and continue here in the little office and really enjoy it. What I need is an accomplice to go along with me.

Cesar Chavez, to his mentor

2004

Whenever I come to L.A. I feel as though I have left my real world and stepped into a parallel universe. It is familiar the way a movie is but the lawns are greener, the colors of the bougainvillea more intense, the sun glinting off windshields seems brighter and people wear clothes I've only seen on TV.

Last night we attended a Hollywood party for cast and crew to celebrate the five Golden Globe nominations *Lost in Translation* received. I learned about the party at the last minute. . . .

At midnight there was a stir as Bill Murray and his wife arrived directly from a European flight. Bill is in Wes Anderson's film *The Life Aquatic,* shooting in Rome. When I greeted Bill I'd forgotten how tall he is, how far he had to bend down to kiss me on the cheek, and I stumbled backwards. It was the first time I'd seen him with grey hair and a beard. He introduced me to his wife. I'd heard he was very devoted to his family. I asked her about her children. She said, "We have six boys. Two boys seventeen and nineteen from Bill's previous, ah, earlier marriage and four ages two to ten." Her eyes grew dark and I thought I saw pain in them as she took a big gulp of wine. I imagined how difficult it could be, home with four school-aged children while your charismatic actor husband is being catered to on a movie location in Rome.

As the evening wound down and we walked out through the big carved door I was glad to be alone with just Francis.

ELEANOR COPPOLA

JANUARY 26

1847

This morning the Indians were busy in burying their dead.

HENRY STANDAGE

1932

My Constance Bennett scenario wasn't passed by the Constance Bennett section of R.K.O. They had about twenty stories to choose from and they chose another. As a matter of fact, I am learning a tremendous lot of what is required in motion pictures, not only the angles but the interests that the public want, and when I get back I'll be able to give British Lion a real ripsnorter. . . .

At twelve o'clock to-day I presented myself at the Biltmore Hotel to address the Los Angeles Advertising Club. There were about two hundred people present—one of the biggest gatherings they have had since Will Rogers addressed them, and Will is a star turn.

I talked upon "Crime and the Law," and my speech was broadcast. I discovered this after I had got down there, and it was a little disconcerting.

EDGAR WALLACE

JANUARY 27

1940

We didn't reply to those last letters of yours and Ruth's out of a combination of growing desperation and the mañana fever that grips one after being out here a few weeks; though strictly speaking there is no such thing out here as a few weeks, it's just one lifeless eternity.

S. J. PERELMAN

1977

Life is cloudless here in every sense.

KENNETH TYNAN

JANUARY 28

1940

This part of California seems to me completely loathsome, but I like San Francisco.

ALEXANDER WOOLLCOTT

1947

I have been led by strange ways indeed, and in my youth could never have dreamed that I would spend my latter days as an American on this palm-grown coast. But at bottom destiny has always been well-disposed to me, and I cannot but marvel at the way the individual always triumphs over the general, wins through against circumstances. I live here and do my work as I used to in Munich's Herzogpark, and my "de-Germanization," to use Nietzsche's word, has not progressed very far after all. On the contrary, I find that in these happier foreign parts I have become all the more conscious of my Germanism. Especially during the past two and a half years I have been occupied with a novel [*Doktor Faustus*]—or whatever the thing should be called—which I hope to complete within a few days and which is something so utterly German that I have the greatest fears concerning its translatability.

THOMAS MANN

1982

Saw L. at [the Los Angeles County Museum of Art] today. It was very pleasant. He was very helpful. Offered to introduce me to everyone I should meet.

Went across the street to [the Craft and Folk Art Museum] and Edith Wyle was as friendly as a cat. Gave me a personal tour of the annex (I can't believe all the beautiful women in that office—)

AARON PALEY

JANUARY 29

1882

We arrived in Los Angeles at eight this morning and went immediately to the Pico House, which is on the Plaza, or town square, in the lower part of the town. We were hungry and enjoyed a delicious breakfast of fried chicken, eggs, chocolate, strawberries, oranges and griddle cakes. For supper tonight we had hot tamales, made by Mexican women, of beef, corn meal and red peppers, stuffed into a corn husk and then boiled. . . .

The nights of Los Angeles are always cool and one can sleep under blankets the year round. Few persons are troubled with sleepless nights, or wake in the morning feeling more tired than they retired the evening before, which we all know is a common occurrence in the East. . . .

Blizzards or sand storms are rare; the only one of importance took place April 2, 1872, and almost obscured the sun's light. The number of perfect cloudless days averages about two hundred in the year. During the summer the city is favored with a sea breeze in the afternoon, which is very pleasant and relieves the intense heat of the sun. Foliage remains green until several months after the last rain; in fact, the sun does not seem to have the same power that it does east of the Rockies. Sunstrokes are unknown, and there have been but two cases of rabid dogs reported in the whole State of California.

Through East Los Angeles there flows what we in the East would call a brook, but here it is designated as Los Angeles River.

L. Vernon Briggs

1928

Writing is next to impossible—what with the purling of fountains, the drawling of mockingbirds, the roaring of surf, the blazing of movie stars, the barking of dogs, the midnight shakings of geraniums, the cruising of warships, etc., etc. . . .

The peculiar mixtures of piety and utter abandon in this welter of cults, ages, occupations, etc., out here make it a good deal like Bedlam. Retired schoolmarms from Iowa, Kansas and all the corn-and-wheat belt along with millions of hobbling Methuselahs, alfalfa-fringed and querulous, side by side with crowds of ambitious but none-too-successful strumpets of moviedom, quite good to look at. . . .

Our house, a large U with patio and fountain, rambles all over the place, and is almost vertical to the observatory on Mt. Wilson. Plenty of roses, camellias, oleanders, acacias, etc., as well as a good wine-cellar. I've just been interrupted by the butler bringing in a makeshift for champagne, composed of carbonated apple-juice with a sling of gin; so all attempts at epistolary consecutivety are hereby and henceforth abandoned!

HART CRANE

JANUARY 30

1848

I was on guard—It was Sunday and crouds of persons were walking on the heights, the day was beautiful, our band was present playing some beautiful airs I had a visit from a number of ladies among whom was the fair Isadora—I invited them in to the guard room and shewed them all the attention I could

LIEUTENANT JOHN MCHENRY HOLLINGSWORTH

1936

Rollo the Whale is having a picnic off Laguna Beach these days.

Maybe Rollo isn't his name, but it ought to be. He is a jolly, friendly mountain of blubber, coming just as close inshore as he can to play.

He was late arriving this year—he'll turn around and go north again next month—but he's having a grand time while he's here.

Rollo can be seen every day off the rocks of Three Arches. He comes to the top and spouts a huge column of water in the air, flips his tail, threshes around in the sea, dives, reappears and spouts some more.

It is like a fountain with St. Vitus dance. . . .

Ed Ainsworth

JANUARY 31

1867

Up pretty early & baked grub and afterwards we all posted off to town. Passed a few low flat-roofed whitewashed & solitary looking Mexican houses on the right & left. Passed over the Los Angeles river on a narrow foot bridge & followed a very winding street up into the central part of the town. On the right & left were large gardens filled with grape vines, lime trees, oranges & many curious trees that were strange to me. Most of the buildings on this st (Aliso) were Spanish. Even at the business center were a large number of the limed one story, flat-roofed buildings. Most of the merchants were Germans, Jews & Mexicans or Spaniards. Passed up to the P.O. first thing. All letters as they were received were posted in a small book. Didn't find my name. Bill got two.

William Henry Jackson

1937

Since the 9th of November I have been sitting in the most terrible construction mess, with winter storms during which I have to go up on the roof at 4 in the morning to direct the water into another channel so that my gallery does not flood. There's not been such a cold winter like this in 23 years, therefore construction had to be stopped, and that with open doors and walls and windows. I sit with all my earthly belongings in the picture storage room. At the same time there's the lack of trained workmen and everything gets done wrong, so that I, who pay every penny, have to supervise everything, because if one is going to create something, it must happen with intelligence and for that even the gods search here in vain. If I had kept a diary of my contractor's stupidity, no one would believe it. I have no problem dealing with the workers. Then there are my other commitments and playing girl Friday. Am I still alive? Yes. I will survive and my thanks will be the enthusiasm of my friends.

Galka Scheyer

FEBRUARY 1

1928

The notable hour of the day was sunset on the Palos Verdes Hills: not a gorgeous sunset,—but exquisite in rose and grey of water, clouds and hills. I realized how much one misses living in an ugly, squat, city like Glendale, surrounded by box-like abominations in brick,—or worse, stucco and cardboard pretensions.

EDWARD WESTON

1945

Our second preview, which seemed to play better to a sparser and graver audience, but had rather a high percentage of bad cards. We have a stunning picture [*Sunset Boulevard*] which it's going to be hard to get people to see.

CHARLES BRACKETT

FEBRUARY 2

1942

My husband and I went to the Alien Registration Office. There were four policemen on guard. It is only a little after opening hour of eight, but there are many people there. There are Germans and Italians, but Japanese make up the majority.

AOKI HISA

1962

I had dinner last night with the Attorney-General of the United States, Robert Kennedy, and I asked him what his department was going to do about Civil Rights and some other issues. He is very intelligent, and besides all that, he's got a terrific sense of humor. . . . he was the guest of honor and when they asked him who he wanted to meet, he wanted to meet me. So, I went to the dinner and I sat next to him, and he isn't a bad dancer either.

MARILYN MONROE, to her stepson

1962

Marilyn would have been a terrible problem, though I am crazy about her. The studio is beginning to view her as Marat must have regarded the lethally-poised Charlotte Corday. Of course, Marilyn can't help her behavior. She is always in terror. Not so different from you and me, only much prettier!

DOROTHY PARKER

1968

Sent off the letter about the novel contest. Spent the day at Brookside [Park]. . . . Love it enjoy it write it in bursts.

OCTAVIA E. BUTLER

FEBRUARY 3

1861

The nights have been too cold for me to write without bringing on my rheumatism, and my days have been entirely occupied, much of the time with fatiguing travel or field work. Today is lovely again. I am writing this sitting under a tree, minus coat, vest, and hat, thermometer at 80° in shade, and sky as clear as August.

WILLIAM H. BREWER

1911

As regards collaboration, it's not a case of my meeting the wrong kind of person. The point is, I'm the wrong kind of person. It's nobody's fault but mine—this inability to collaborate. . . .

I am on such shaky legs just now, that with interest on mortgages overdue, taxes unpaid, and heavy month's bills coming in from everywhere, I was compelled to flee here to Los Angeles so as to stall off payment for a while. I haven't paid my ranch foreman's salary for three months. I managed to raise the wages for the first of February for the laborers, and they're the only ones that I've paid. . . .

And there's the everlasting hell of it.

JACK LONDON

FEBRUARY 4

1932

At William Gillette's invitation we all saw *Sherlock Holmes,* his play written some forty years ago. It is a good, tense, well-played "yarn" of the detective sort so popular now in book form. Gillette concealed his age amazingly well. He read the lines as well as ever and was heartily cheered at the end of each exciting episode, but when he said, in Holmes' character, "What does it matter? What does anything matter?" I felt he was expressing his own philosophy, and then, a little later, Holmes said, "In a short time nothing will matter." I forecast Gillette's own shortening span of life. This is undoubtedly his farewell to the stage and almost the final year of his life. He is a lonely man. He has no family. No close relatives. He will go back to his hermit life on the Connecticut River and await the sunset.

Hamlin Garland

1976

We have a young Polish student here, Isabel Kierkowska, who is doing a remarkable job. . . . She rose rapidly to the top of her class and is doing wonderfully. She is the kind of student this place is designed for, and for such a student we feel we really make a distinct and unique contribution. Their full scientific potential is developed and stretched to the limit.

To interrupt such a good start and to break so natural a connection between institution and student as we have found here, would mean a tragic loss of human potential.

It has come to my attention that she is having some difficulty in obtaining the necessary exit visa to continue her studies here in the United States. . . . Is there anything you could do to clear up the difficulty with her papers?

RICHARD FEYNMAN, to a friend

FEBRUARY 5

1850

Feb. 5th: Descending through lofty hills, covered, like the plains from the ranch of Chino, with grass and flowers, one obtains his first view of the pueblo of Los Angeles, nearly three miles off; this view, of course, is not complete, but the stranger hastens his steps, and is soon repaid, in a measure, for at least a portion of his toils. . . .

The morning of the 3d, Sunday, brought crowds of people to the church from the neighboring ranchos. I went to Mass; after which witnessed the burial of an Indian who had died the day before. The corpse was interred beneath the floor of the Church. . . .

The whole scene, "American" by the side of "Mexican," (to adopt the language of the day), Indian and white, trader and penitent, gayety, bustle and confusion on the one side and religious solemnity on the other, was singular to me. A beggar at the door, as we sallied out, at the conclusion of the service, struck my attention, although I did not understand the language in which he now chanted and again prayed, as many in passing placed their alms in his hand.

JUDGE BENJAMIN HAYES

1928

We have met some movie actors, attended some studio screenings, etc. And I have had a fair amount of swimming and tennis. (The beaches—Long Beach, Venice, Santa Monica—are really a delight, and I have spent whole days watching the gulls, sandpipers, pelicans in their manoeuvres.) But I am especially enjoying the wealth of reading and music around the house. [His employer Herbert] Wise is buying all the albums of symphonies, quintettes, concertos and what-not on the Victor list. So I'm living on intimate terms with Brahms and Beethoven—the two most exciting of all to me.

HART CRANE

1985

J. took me to this meeting of the inner art sanctum of Los Angeles tonight at Lyn Kienholz's house on Outpost filled with incredible art. . . .

What a funny crew—art people—really good people—but white and affluent—little diversity or scope.

AARON PALEY

FEBRUARY 6

1932

Last week I slipped off a rostrum at the Mayfair and cut my ankle slightly. It is still bothering me, and I had to give it some sort of treatment last night. At ten o'clock to-day an osteopath is calling and treating me for my cold.

I hope to knock off a few articles to-day and start to-morrow on serious work. I have not had any reaction on my scenario yet, but then the executives are recovering from the visit of the bankers, who, thank heaven, have gone back to New York. . . .

At this point the osteopath came, Dr. Bell. Make a note of his telephone number: Gladstone 0875. He gave me a real tossing about—broke my neck twice, broke my feet four times, gave me belly treatment and back treatment, used a vibrator and alcohol and generally left me feeling a better man.

I like him very much, and I've arranged for him to see me twice a week, not because I am ill but because I feel ever so much better after his treatment, which was for a cold and bronc.

He is a youngish-looking man, but he told me he's been thirty-three years in Hollywood and has only once seen a rattlesnake. Before he came I was feeling a little bit dopy, but I am quite gay and bright now.

Edgar Wallace, days before his death

1947

Arrived at Pasadena at 9 a.m. and were met by a car from MGM. We drove for a long time down autobahns and boulevards full of vacant lots and filling stations and nondescript buildings and palm trees with a warm hazy light. It was more like Egypt—the suburbs of Cairo or Alexandria—than anything in Europe. We arrived at the Bel Air Hotel—very Egyptian with a hint of Addis Ababa in the smell of the blue gums. . . .

We unpacked, sent great quantities of clothes to the laundry, bathed and lunched. A well-planned little restaurant, good cooking. We drank a good local wine, Masson's Pinot Noir. We were the only people in the room drinking. Two tables of women with absurd hats. Rested. At 6 sharp we were called on by the two producers Gordon and McGuinness, who were preceded with fine bunches of flowers—with their shy wives. We sat in our bedroom and drank. Conversation difficult. Bed early, after dining without appetite in the restaurant, and slept badly; woke in pain.

EVELYN WAUGH

FEBRUARY 7

1949

Billy and I worked on the home-movies scene until Gloria [Swanson] appeared from Edith Head's, whereupon Billy was really superb, quieting her fears, telling her to stop worrying about the script and let us take the responsibility—kidding and bolstering her at the same time. I think she'll be all right.

CHARLES BRACKETT

1977

I crossed over into the golden years with a great deal of claret and, I think, some degree of grace. Carl and Eve Foreman assembled two dozen assorted friends and when we had the cutting of the cake and the serving of the champagne, Norman Corwin was warm and eloquent, but I've heard him speak twice in the last year at memorial services, which gave me an uncomfortable feeling.

JOHN D. WEAVER, to John Cheever

FEBRUARY 8

1854

The government really desires their good, and not to exterminate them, as malicious and reckless white men have informed them. . . .

I have clothed them coarsely, but comfortably, and on Sunday (work having ceased on Saturday at noon) they seem as happy as it is possible to conceive. To that day I have encouraged them to look as one of pleasure, and for this purpose have instituted among them our own games, in which I have requested and encouraged my white employees to take part; so that on every Sunday we have sometimes two or three hundred playing at bandy and ball with those who during the week are their overseers and instructors in manual labor.

In fact, so happy are my people, that that which I never thought possible has come to pass, and my feelings for this poor race, which at first were merely those of compassion, are rapidly changing into a deep interest in their welfare, and in many instances to a personal attachment.

I have no military force here, and require none; my door has neither been locked nor barred night or day, and yet my feeling of security is as great as though I were surrounded by an armed guard. . . .

I hope to raise these people to believe that God has not created them to live and die as the wolves and beasts of their mountains. Already some faint and indistinct notion that such may be the case appears to have struck their sight; but as yet it is vague and distant, like the first uncertain glimpse of a distant lighthouse. Constantly, they say to me, "We have been asleep a long time. We are just beginning to awake, but our eyes are not yet wide open."

E. F. Beale

1891

We have a cottage on the bluff and I can sit there and feel the enchanting soft freshness of this blue ocean and get that stilled feeling the sea always brings me. There is nothing crude or newly raw about this lovely spot for it was well planted nearly twenty years ago—equal fifty elsewhere—and the broad terrace on the bluff has its wide double avenues of old windswept cypress and eucalyptus trees, where a long mile of firm grass-grown walk can be had. And a hundred feet below the long rollers break on a firm sand beach on which one can drive for many many miles.

To you [John Greenleaf Whittier], SnowBound—at this season, it is hard to realize the June-like beauty of the roses and heliotrope and honeysuckle and fuschias that cover the cottages to the roof, while beds of violets are in full bloom. And yet morning and evening we have wood fires, for beauty and companionship more than necessity.

Jessie Benton Frémont

1944

On Friday at Salka's for tea . . . there was only this sportily dressed woman who was vaguely familiar. I had only noticed that Salka told her our names, but not vice versa, from which I inferred that she must be so famous that she expected us to know who she was anyway. It was only after having this thought that I recognized her as Garbo. She was pleasant and friendly, and stayed for a long time—whereas she normally leaves, out of an almost pathological shyness, any social gathering at which she encounters new faces. She is beautiful . . . very affected and probably not especially intellectual, to put it discreetly—comes across as someone who makes a great effort to live up, at least somewhat, to her own nimbus. Ali Baba waited in the car. He cropped up in the conversation, and Ms. Garbo, who loves Afghans, requested that he be brought in. Now, Salka has three dogs of her own, two highly nervous setters and an enormous German shepherd that had just bitten Ms. Garbo (it bites everyone). But the three monsters were locked away. So Ali was then allowed in. He smelled his colleagues, stormed about like mad—I had never seen him so beside himself—and suddenly, before we knew it, he had lifted his little leg by a bookshelf and made his mark upon a book by Osa Johnson—in the presence of the supposedly most beautiful woman in the world. . . .

THEODOR ADORNO

FEBRUARY 9

1931

They keep writers in little coops out here, on the movie lots, and sometimes it is months before the writers can find out who hired them and why. I was supposed to be writing a picture for Will Rogers, but they changed the plot on me five times in nine days, so I went away, and they didn't even know I had gone away for some time—that was with the Fox Film Corporation—but they were very nice financially: they didn't want what I did, but they paid me $5000 for something I hadn't done. There is a kind of an idea around there that I am still working for them, in some quarters, I believe. Then I went into Paramount one day to sell the movie rights of an old novel of mine, and it seems they got the idea I was working there, so they paid me some money too, and I went on a vacation after that; and now I don't think I have a job, but I don't know, because no one knows anything about anything at all in Hollywood.

But it seems to me that the proper system here is to find out where all the pay windows of all the different studios are, and go around them every now and then and ask if there's a check, and act a little surprised if there isn't; after while maybe there will be. I found in one studio that they were getting ready to shoot a story; fifteen writers had worked on it for ten months; but they found they did not have a script when they started to shoot. So they gave me two weeks pay to write it; I did it in five days, but I think they lost it somehow; anyway, they probably wouldn't use just one script. They need five or six, they shoot a little from one, and a little from another, and so forth—and then they wonder why the picture is kind of disconnected. There are some writers out here who have never had a thing filmed in two years; others turn out a script every two weeks; the ones who never get anything filmed get the most money. George Kaufman's play [*Once in a Lifetime*] is not a burlesque or an exaggeration, it is a sober bit of reporting.

P. G. Wodehouse

1942

Some friends here and I have drafted the enclosed telegram to the President, and would be much obliged if you would sign it. . . .

To Franklin D. Roosevelt

We beg to draw your attention to a large group of natives of Germany and Italy who by present regulations are, erroneously, characterized and treated as "Aliens of Enemy Nationality."

We are referring to such persons who have fled their country and sought refuge in the United States because of totalitarian persecution. . . .

We, therefore, respectfully apply to you, Mr. President, who for all of us represent the spirit of all that is loyal, honest, and decent in a world of falsehood and chaos, to utter or to sanction a word of authoritative discrimination, to the effect that a clear and practical line should be drawn between the potential enemies of American democracy on the one hand, and the victims and sworn foes of totalitarian evil on the other.

THOMAS MANN, to Albert Einstein

FEBRUARY 10

1850

After Mass, there was a public meeting, in reference to schools and on the subject of taxation. I looked in at them awhile, then went to the hills to contemplate the flowers, and enjoy the balmy air that still prevailed as during the last six days. . . .

JUDGE BENJAMIN HAYES

1927

Why this type of women? Why do they all come at once? Here I am, isolated, hardly leaving my work rooms, but they come, they seek me out,—and yield, (or do *I* yield?)

EDWARD WESTON

FEBRUARY 11

1931

Do a group of stories about Los Angelesians in the manner of Joyce's "Dubliners."

CAREY MCWILLIAMS

1933

I am lying in the sun, drinking coffee. Of course I could use the typewriter. For the first time in one solid month it is idle. This is a good day. . . . But I have no intention of trying to explain my book [*To a God Unknown*]. It has to do that for itself. I would be sure of its effect if it could be stipulated that the readers read to an obbligato of Bach. . . .

We are very happy. I need a dog pretty badly. I dreamed of dogs last night. They sat in a circle and looked at me and I wanted all of them. Apparently we are heading for the rocks. The light company is going to turn off the power in a few days, but we don't care much.

JOHN STEINBECK

1948

I hesitate to put down these lines of appreciation as I'm of the belief that there should be little or no traffic at all between the critic and the criticized. If friendly relations exist between the two, the critic, when the time comes around to criticize, invariably leans over backwards in an effort not to be influenced by his personal feelings, and as a result he is more severe than he would want to be otherwise. By the same token, if upon making the acquaintance, the criticized appears a thoroughgoing s.o.b. in the eyes of the critic, he (the critic) in an effort to be fair and unbiased, is generally inclined to give the criticized a break he doesn't deserve. All of which is leading up to this proposal—will you have a drink with me next time I am in New York? In the meantime, thank you very much.

JOHN HUSTON, to James Agee

1952

FOUR YEARS LATER

The review [of his and Huston's *The African Queen*] of course makes me feel very good—both in the simple pleasure of being praised, and, more gratifyingly, because he realizes so much more clearly than most people, what I was trying to do.

James Agee, to his priest

FEBRUARY 12

1957

The blacklist in the American motion picture production industry is enforced by all three branches of the government of the United States. The expansion of American motion picture production throughout Europe has carried the blacklist with it, and writers abroad are now alarmed lest the American policy of suppression be imposed, by sheer weight of financial power, upon countries where such practices are abhorrent.

I have been asked to discuss this matter in very respectable publications in Britain and France, and I consider it my duty to do so. I felt, however, that I was first obliged to make the essential facts known to the head of my own Government, in the hope that relief might be obtained. . . .

My moral obligation being thus fulfilled, I shall proceed in good conscience to warn the intellectuals and artists of Western Europe to resist with all their strength that policy of inquisition, imprisonment, blacklist, and denial of passport which in

America has destroyed hundreds of artists and intimidates all of them.

Dalton Trumbo, to President Eisenhower

1965

First, about the STAR TREK pilot itself. Whether or not this was the right story for a sale, it was definitely a right one for ironing out successfully a thousand how, when and whats of television science fiction. It did that job superbly and has us firmly in position to be the first who has ever successfully made TV series science fiction at a mass audience level and yet with a chance for quality and network prestige too.

We have an opportunity, like "Gulliver's Travels" of a century or more ago, to combine spectacle-excitement for a mass group along with meaningful drama and something of substance and pride. . . .

For the first time I think I see our particular and peculiar medium exactly for what it is. It has been and can be very good—and if someone proves to me they want me to try for that level, I gladly will. On the other hand, without that proof, I intend to aim for safe copies and parallels of existing successes—settle for doing it just two or three percent better than the next guy so that job and profits are always there, and I eat dinner every night at 6:00 p.m. with the children and have two days at home out of every seven to play horseshoes and putter in the garden . . .

Gene Roddenberry, to his agent

FEBRUARY 13

1947

The city is quarter-built, empty building lots everywhere and vast distances. Since the war they have succeeded in spoiling even the climate by inducing an artificial and noxious fog. . . .

The men lunch in wineless canteens. Jovial banter prevails between the hotel servants and the guests, but our insular aloofness is respected. We have trained the waiters in the dining-room not to give us iced water and our chauffeur not to ask us questions. There is here the exact opposite of the English custom by which the upper classes are expected to ask personal questions of the lower.

On Thursday afternoon Gordon proudly showed us his last film—*The Green Years;* it was awful. Mercifully the cinema was provided with push buttons to stop the film, so when Gordon had gone I stopped it. . . .

We met the actor who plays Dr. Watson.

EVELYN WAUGH

1967

THERE IS *ANOTHER* HIGH-RISE APT. GOING UP DIRECTLY ACROSS THE STREET. I am now completely surrounded. I see all these beehives. . . .

Luckily I can't afford to die in such voluptuous candyshit; I will end up in a cardboard box in the hills. I have discovered the last green hills in town—it is just before you hit Huntington Drive on the way to Santa Anita, a turn left off of North Main or North Broadway, I don't know which, anyhow the streets end there, and there it is: these slices of high green hills, tall, and nothing on them, no terrible houses, no terrible people, and I always feel like stopping the '57 and getting out and climbing up there, walking around in it, laying down in the weeds, but no guts, the city has me, the track calls me, but those hills ride inside me as I drive past, and looking at them, it's like vomiting up a whole sick metropolis and I feel better. . . .

2 p.m., 2:05 KFAC symphony now coming on, hope they give me something to lean against this highrise across the way . . . not bad, something offbrand by Haydn, who was a kind of a kool suckass in his time but managed to save some juice.

Charles Bukowski

1991

Late tonight we were walking along the Sunset Strip. The only other pedestrian was a man up ahead dressed in baggy shorts. "If he's walking he's got to be British," my wife said and as we got closer we recognized the [British] pop songster Billy Bragg.

Alexei Sayle

FEBRUARY 14

1924

Formerly we were way out in the country, while now everything is rapidly moving in our direction. . . . With the exception of one or two tracts, everything between us and Los Angeles has been subdivided.

Edgar Rice Burroughs

1949

It is beginning to look like television may soon kill not only the theater and the movies but radio, books, magazines, newspapers, and finally articulate speech and all the processes of ratiocination. Talk of the barbarian invasions—the fifth century was nothing to the 20th.

We had Grace and Edwin [Hubble] staying with us for three days last week. Both in good form, and Edwin full of enthusiasm over the first photographs taken by the two-hundred-inch telescope. The thing does all that was hoped for it, and the first sample shot revealed two entirely new and unsuspected kinds of nebulae, with faint images of nebulae going on and on in undiminished numbers to 1 billion light years into space.

ALDOUS HUXLEY, to Anita Loos

1987

Today I sit on the library lawn in front of Doheny and it's cloudy and I'm cold in my cotton overalls and Tanya's t-shirt. I'm sitting on the green hunting jacket. I have a little cold. I have bruises from the Chili Peppers last night and I kind of have to pee. This is a very normal day. Maybe sometime I'll have a special Valentine's Day. Maybe it'll mean a lot to me. Maybe it's time to walk home.

CAROLYN KELLOGG

FEBRUARY 15

1928

Constance took me for a ride to Beverly Hills and Santa Monica where some very picturesque and costly estates are being built among the hills. It is an astounding development. There is, however, a disturbing effect of unreality in it. It is like a stage setting, something built in a hurry, in a flurry of enthusiasm, of sudden wealth. It suggests the eagerness of those newly rich. Twenty-five years from now this region will look settled but it will still lack the settled quality which I love in old New England. If I were young I might, possibly, find it to my liking because to my interest. I have no future. My task is to record the past.

HAMLIN GARLAND

1941

We got us a cabin in a two by four tourist court. Aircraft boom here make it hard to get shelter. Wont take kids hardly a tall. We househunted 3 days with no luck. Same old tale, How many kids? Sorry the owner's away. No kids. Awful sorry. The god dam silly way they look at you like you'd ought to take your kids off somewhere and tie a grinding stone around their neck and throw them in the river—and then you could pay twice as much as you ought to and rent you a house. I'm a adult and I dont need their bastardly old houses, but my kids do and it is one hell of a thing. You run onto hundreds of folks that feels this same way. Some kind of houses has got to be built for families with kids—the more kids, the bigger bargain you would get.

Have made a few bookings out here already, the APM, People's World Forum, etc., and they are as worked up over the songs of the east coast as they are of their own west coast. It is a good thing to see a feeling so solid from coast to coast and to see the songs of the midwest or the old broke down south as welcome in Seattle, San Diego, Boston, or Houston—; and that is sign that folks are just plain folks everywhere you go, all has been hit hard, went through several political cyclones, been sold out so often that they feel like they've got pimps. . . . the thought is about the same everywhere, because the song on one side of the map is the same on the other side—and when newspapers and radios and records wont carry these songs, nor help these people out, it is good to see the song spread anyhow, like their war scare, only bigger—just like on any other subject, folks has got something to say about it; they might not let on around high society ginks, but the people has got just a plenty to say about every little thing that's said and done that's a leading us down this lonesome road to the war—and of course you know how folks always has pretended to be dumb or blank in the presence of officers of the law that they dont trust or like. With every invention of modern times turned against them, the people sing their song just the same as they ever did. Everywhere you go they tell you they dont believe what you hear on your radio. They point and smile and listen the same as they play cards or pool or checkers, just to have something to pass the time away—as far as soaking up all of this war scare and bloody talk and hooray stuff—, they've had hard luck enough to wake them up and put them away above that stuff—that comes from great big overgrown rich folks. They control everything that's said and done on every single radio. (Everything but the feelings of the people). We'll have some real honest to goodness singing and playing on the air waves some of these days, when the real peoples songs and programs can be broadcasted instead of what we have got now.

Los Angeles and southern California is thickly settled. This little station covers a strip about 100 miles in each direction. It is full of people that work and talk a working man's lingo, no matter what tongue or color; so I thought, beings our program on WABC was overloaded, beings it only come on 3 times a week, beings it didn't ever get released onto a nationwide chain, that it might be better for me to step off out here and take a swing at her six times a week, and cover this country that's so newly settled and where there's a possible chance for alot of new things to get started.

My best regards to all of the gang on Back Where I Come From. Tell them all to set their self down and write me a big long letter.

Take it easy but take it,

Woody Guthrie

1976

Souvenir shops by the thousand, laden with pin-cushions, plastic doilies, worry-beads, and shell necklaces there are; bookshops piled high with Christian Science tracts, plaster replicas of the Madonna, and catechisms bound in *broderie Anglaise* line the streets; but restaurants and laundries there are none. The philosophy, obviously, is that since everyone here is 92 years old, he is practically dead anyway, so why feed him and wash his undies?

S. J. PERELMAN

1991

To get to the airport, LAX, from Sunset Boulevard you just head down Sepulveda Boulevard for about 400 miles. One thing you notice as you crawl down this wide avenue is that as most shops such as greengrocers and butchers have retreated into the shopping malls and supermarkets, their premises on the streets have been taken over by specialist retailers, many seemingly connected with light engineering.

It's much easier to pop out of your house and buy a cone and friction drive variable speed lathe than it is to buy a grapefruit.

ALEXEI SAYLE

FEBRUARY 16

1880

Never before, and not since, when, with Gov. Smith we spent those wonderful eighteen days in Old Egypt, have I seen any such sunlight, transparency and luminousness of atmosphere as characterize the days here in Southern California. They are much alike.

The Indiana settlement is eight or ten miles northeast of Los Angeles. This settlement was started some seven years ago upon virgin land by Indiana people. It is situated directly before the Sierra Madre Mountains, upon an open, undulated plain. Today it is a garden spot. Handsome dwellings rise up amid orange and lemon groves, and occupy a wide expanse of country. Admirably-made roads and churches and school-houses attest the character of the people. A system of water works, carried by iron pipes, spreads through this settlement [Pasadena], affording water for irrigating and other purposes.

E. D. Holton

1943

E. and I went to Cukor's at 4:30, a party for Evelyn Waugh. Ethel Barrymore was pouring, the Reggie Allens and Andrea, Olivia [De Havilland] and Marcus, Constance Collier, Lucille Watson, Garbo—but no Evelyn Waugh till just as E. had decided she wasn't feeling well and wanted to go home, Mr. and Mrs. Waugh came up the steps, very unprepossessing—a bank clerk and his snuffly wife, an ill-favored tailor's dummy with halitosis and a blue-eyed Elsa Lanchester part. I brought E. home and returned to Cukor's. It seems that in my absence Waugh had sent his wife home, dismissed her in a rude way which impressed everyone unpleasantly.

Talked at, or rather sat next to Garbo for some time, stirred by her beauty but bored by her little-girl silliness.

Charles Brackett

FEBRUARY 17

1954

Up to LA where I dig city again, to Woody Herman's band on marquee—Get off bus & down South Main St burdened with all pack and have jumbo beers for hot sun thirst—Go on down to SP railyards, singin, "An oldtime non-lovin hard-livin brakeman," buy wieners and wine in an Italian store, go to yards, inquire about Zipper. At redsun five all clerks go home, yard quiet—I light wood fire behind section shanty and cook dogs and eat oranges & cupcakes, smoke Bull Durham & rest—Chinese new year plap-plaps nearby—at seven I get foolishly on Zipper caboose and talk to rear brakeman as train is made up—BRAM! SLAM! Brakeman struggles to fix mantle and lamp and start coal fire—conductor is Stormy Mason—doesn't bide my papers, order me out of the caboose—train is underway to Santa Barbara

. . . For first time in months, in cold rushing night air of California Golden Coast, uncork wine & drink up—raw, bad, rotgut—but I warm and sing all the way—

Jack Kerouac

1962

Thank you for your champagne.

It arrived, I drank it and I was gayer.

Marilyn Monroe, to the local German consul

FEBRUARY 18

1948

Since I do not intend to alter my behavior in the future, I'm afraid you'll just have to go on hating.

DALTON TRUMBO, to a colleague

1957

Well, we began shooting with a drama I've no doubt Orson planned. We rehearsed all day, lining up a dolly shot covering the entire first scene in Sanchez's apartment. We never turned a camera all morning or all afternoon, the studio brass gathering in the shadows in anxious little knots. By the time we began filming at a quarter to six, I know they'd written off the whole day. At seven-forty, Orson said, "OK, print. That's a wrap on this set. We're two days ahead of schedule." Twelve pages in one take, including inserts, two-shots, over-shoulders; the whole scene in one, moving through three rooms, with seven speaking parts.

CHARLTON HESTON

FEBRUARY 19

1853

On Tuesday of last week we had four weddings, two funerals, one street fight with knives, a lynch court, two men flogged, and a serenade by a callithumpian band; also a fist fight and one man tossed in a blanket. If any of the flourishing up-country towns can hold a candle to that, let them do it forthwith or forever hold their peace.

La Estrella de Los Angeles / The Los Angeles Star

1934

Left home at dinner time.

Edgar Rice Burroughs, leaving his wife

1940

This singular place is an odd haven in which to sit in the sun and read about the boarding of the [Nazi oil tanker] *Altmark.* Kaufman, Hart and Alice Miller, all of whom came out to see the opening, are all quitting their villas [at the Garden of Allah hotel] here today. Rachmaninoff has the next one to mine and begins practicing every morning at dawn. Beyond him are the Charles Laughtons. Beyond them is Robert Benchley. Beyond him is Dorothy Parker. It's the kind of village you might look for down the rabbit-hole. That muted mutter from across the way is just Dame Mae Whitty, rehearsing as the nurse to the impending Juliet of Vivien Leigh and the Romeo of Larry Olivier. Down the street is the charming home of a small Jewish screenwriter who used to be my office boy. He has just bought a Reynolds. It's a mad world, my masters! And always was.

Alexander Woollcott

FEBRUARY 20

1861

I climbed a high ridge, some two thousand feet above camp. Here a stratum of rock comes out filled with large shells in fine preservation. It rises in a ridge, ending in a precipice to the north. In places these fossil shells had been weathered out in immense numbers. The ridge was strewn with them, as thick as any sea-beach I have ever seen. . . .

I cannot describe my feelings as I stood on that ridge, that shore of an ancient ocean. How lonely and desolate! Who shall tell how many centuries, how many decades of centuries, have elapsed since these rocks resounded to the roar of breakers, and these animals sported in their foam? I picked up a bone, cemented in the rock with the shells. A feeling of awe came over me. Around me rose rugged mountains; no human being was within miles of me to break the silence. And then I felt overwhelmed with the magnitude of the work ahead of me. I was at work alone in the field work of this great state, a territory larger than all New England and New York, complicated in its geology.

But the real soon roused me from reveries—I must get back. I was alone, far from camp—grizzlies might come out as the moon came up.

William H. Brewer

1928

Just walk down Hollywood Boulevard someday—if you must have something *out* of uniform. Here are little fairies who can quote Rimbaud before they are 18.

Hart Crane

1934

Came to live at the Garden of Allah, Villa 23.

EDGAR RICE BURROUGHS

1960

From the moment I arrived in America, everyone told me that Los Angeles was horrible, that I would really like SFrancisco but would hate LA, so I had convinced myself that I would definitely like it. And indeed I arrive and am immediately enthusiastic: yes, this is the American city, the impossible city, it's so enormous, and since I only enjoy being in huge cities it is just right for me. It is as long as if the area between Milan and Turin were just one single city stretching north as far as Como and south as far as Vercelli. But the beauty of it is that in between, between one district and the next (they're actually called cities and often they are nothing but endless stretches of villas, big and small), there are huge, totally deserted mountains which you have to cross to go from one part of the city to another, populated by deer and mountain lions or pumas, and on the sea there are peninsulas and beaches that are among the most beautiful in the world. . . .

"Here anyone going on foot will be arrested immediately" was what we jokingly said on arrival in Los Angeles, where there are no pedestrians. In fact, one day I try to go by foot for a stretch through Culver City, and after a few blocks a policeman on a motorbike comes alongside and stops me. I had crossed a street—one that was narrow and deserted, what's more—while the light was at red. In order to avoid the fine—"the ticket"—I explain that I am a foreigner, etc., that I am an absent-minded professor, etc., but he has no sense of humor, makes a lot of fuss and asks a lot of questions because I do not have my passport with me (in America I have noticed—even before this—that documents are totally pointless); he does not give me a ticket, but he keeps me there for a quarter of an hour. A pedestrian is always a suspicious character.

ITALO CALVINO

FEBRUARY 21

1776

We set out from the mission of San Gabriel at half past eleven in the morning.... The land was very green and flower-strewn. The road has some hills and many mires caused by the rains, and for this reason the pack train fell very far behind. At the camp site there is permanent water, though little, and plenty of firewood. On the left at a distance runs the chain of hills which form the Bay of San Pedro.

FATHER PEDRO FONT

1943

Wish you could have seen us playing the Internationale to him in [Samuel Goldwyn's] office—(He said: It's a "steering" tune.)

You deserve some kind of medal—but I'd rather wait till I can pin it on myself...

P.S. Just heard the Strav. Symphony on the air.

AARON COPLAND, to Leonard Bernstein

FEBRUARY 22

1882

Yesterday noon I gave a seven-course dinner at the Cosmopolitan Hotel. . . .

I was at the train to see them off, and there met Mr. Perry and returned with him to call on his daughter. She gave me some violets from her first concert in America last Saturday night, and her picture, and showed me some beautiful jewels which she had purchased in Europe. Mr. Powers left in low spirits, as Velma did not encourage his suit. I went out with Mrs. Voorhees this evening to see a fire.

L. Vernon Briggs

1934

Went to Palm Springs with Florence.

Edgar Rice Burroughs, decamping with his mistress

1935

STRAVINSKI! . . . The evening was pure joy.

This is now music which we have and which is accepted, which does not provoke anger or hysteria or any vulgar objection.

John Cage

FEBRUARY 23

1854

Dined at Roland's, thence home to wife and baby. An Indian girl who used to wash for us came in and sauntered through the garden. After looking round everywhere, she seemed to think there was very little useful in it, asking me, "Why, señor, do you not sow *calabazas* and *zandías*?" What a question for the heart of a florist! In self-defence I appealed to my *chiceros* (peas) but she replied, "There are so few of them!"

JUDGE BENJAMIN HAYES

1874

Benjamin Hayes, formerly district judge at Los Angeles, later a resident of San Diego, and for twenty-five years an enthusiastic collector and preserver of historic data, not only placed me in possession of all his collection, but gave me his heart with it, and continued to interest himself in my work as if it were his own, and to add to his collection while in my possession as if it was still in his. . . . It was the 23d of February that this important purchase was consummated. . . .

It was a hard day's work, beginning at seven o'clock, and during which we did not stop to eat, to catalogue and pack the collection. Taking up one after another of his companion-creations, fondly the little old man handled them; affectionately he told their history. Every paper, every page, was to him a hundred memories of a hundred breathing realities. These were not to him dead facts; they were, indeed, his life.

HUBERT HOWE BANCROFT

1965

Where would I come in? Just before Bunin, Ivan, *The Gentleman from San Francisco*? No? Well. Or Bulosan, Carlos? *America Is in the Heart.*

America is in the balls. America is in the factories. America is in the streets, hustling shines and newspapers, climbing down through skylights to the mother-blossom of the safes. I am the toilet paper wiped against America.

Charles Bukowski

1976

The only chopped-liver known hereabouts is what these cigar-colored retired bank presidents contract from drinking too much bourbon. . . . The octogenarian waitresses in the dining room are ringing their cowbell to indicate that unless I get in there pronto (it's now 6:18 p.m.) I will get no chopped carrot-and-raisin salad. . . . I will have to draw to a close on this melancholy vignette of a man ready to sell his soul for a whiff of a potato *lotkeh.*

S. J. Perelman

FEBRUARY 24

1935

The stores of Los Angeles put on a dollar sale and they played to more money than the races did, and Iowa had a picnic the same day out here and they had more people than the races and the dollar sale combined. . . . With all these going on in one town, I wouldn't worry too much about the country going Bolsheviki.

Will Rogers

1959

This blacklist will not be broken by the triumph of morality over immorality. It will not be broken by the triumph of one organization over another organization. It will only be broken by the sheer excellence of the work of two or three blacklisted writers. Call it talent, call it competence, ability, craftsmanship, or what you will—still in all, that is the only practical weapon for the job. I think we have that weapon, and that within the next few months, or the next year, we shall have to use it. Which is to say that each of us individually, acting in coordination with each other, must very soon use the excellence of our work to compel the use of our names.

DALTON TRUMBO, to a fellow blacklistee

FEBRUARY 25

1853

Frequent rumors reach our city from San Gorgonio, that the Indians are deprived of the use of the water, by Mr. Weaver, and that in consequence they are unable to sow their grain. We hope the rumors may not prove true; for the acts complained of are outrages which may provoke retaliation. The law expressly provides that the Indians shall retain uninterrupted possession of lands they may have occupied for a series of years. Moreover, these Indians are Juan Antonio's Cahuillas, with whom Gen. Bean formed a treaty, pledging the faith of the State that they should not be molested so long as they observed its terms. Thus, to deprive them of any of their former privileges would be a violation of both the law and the treaty, and may lead to serious difficulties.

BENJAMIN DAVIS "DON BENITO" WILSON

1942

Last night, nothing occurred, and morning came. Secretary of Navy Knox announced that an enemy plane flying over Los Angeles was an error. On the other hand, the Department of the Army is saying an enemy reconnaissance plane definitely came. Both departments are publicly engaged in an absurd argument. . . .

It seems the anti-aircraft rounds fired the night before were produced in the 1930s, and one third failed to explode. In the English-language newspaper, there were photos of these useless duds where they had come down on roads and people's yards.

Aoki Hisa

FEBRUARY 27

1926

Have you a little Colt in your home? I have three—a Government Model 45 automatic that I packed for years on Tarzana Ranch and with which I missed every coyote in the Santa Monica mountains at least once until finally The Colonel became so peeved that he bucked me off on top of a mountain and left me to walk home—and another old and rusty six-gun that Bull might have toted in *The Bandit of Hell's Bend.* It bears the serial number 70495. Once, being broke and jobless, I annexed a temporary job as railway policeman in Salt Lake City. It was then that 70495 assisted me materially in running boes [hoboes] off the U.P. passenger trains.

Edgar Rice Burroughs

1939

Los Angeles seems familiar, perhaps because Prince Michael Dimitri Alexandrovitch Obolensky Romanoff is jailed and publicized on the day of my arrival. Prince Mike, who is an agreeable, harmless fellow, is always getting into jail. He was in jail in Wichita when I first met him, about 18 years ago. I have gone to the Tombs in New York to greet him, and if I have time I shall hunt him up in the Los Angeles holdover. . . . He has so many friends that stone walls do not a prison make for him. . . .

In the coffee shop of the Ambassador I have breakfast with Dale Carnegie and his nephew, Pierre, who is attending school here, but lives in Kansas City. Dale and I have offices only a few blocks apart in Manhattan and have been friends for years. But we have to come to California to eat together and have a half hour's chat.

Charles B. Driscoll

FEBRUARY 28

1848

If the Mexicans do not improve very shortly in their War department [Scott] will occupy all the small as well as the principal towns; it will be as well, for really it is time their race is annihilated to make room for better.

Henry Dalton

1852

We left San Pedro after breakfast and reached Los Angeles between two and three o'clock; we would have got there much sooner, but it rained the night before. The road is very good and passes through a beautiful prairie which is covered with clover and flowers. You cannot guess who was our driver—Pete Middleton, of Liberty. He has been here six years, has a Spanish wife and is bootblacker and barber for the town.

The site of Los Angeles is lovely, but the city is very ugly. Most of the houses are built of mud, some are plastered outside, and have a porch around them, looking neat and pretty as any house, but these are few and far between. We are surrounded almost by high green hills. Remove this and place here one of the pretty towns in the States, and I do not think there could be a more lovely spot.

Mrs. Emily Hayes, wife of Judge Benjamin Hayes

1938

At outs with the Schick and preparing to renounce it for the old fashioned lawnmower method. We go down town, where all is wet, and most of the day a fine drizzle is promoting. I do librarying, getting out Aubrey Drury's *California: An Intimate Guide* for the fifth time because no matter how sick it makes me I consider it my duty to read it. To Mays for dinner and evening, and now the drizzle has turned to a downpour. When we leave, crossing Chevy Chase is like one of our hinterland river crossings.

Charis Wilson

1947

It's marvelous: you can see the whole of Los Angeles in the distance, and the sea, and there are big eucalyptus trees and horses and hens—it's countryside and town at the same time. On the table there's an immense basket of oranges and orange-blossom that some unknown admirer sent me. . . .

I've had three fantastic days here. [A mutual friend] has taken me gallivanting about everywhere: to the seaside; to the cemetery, which is extraordinary; into the hills; to Pasadena, etc. I gave lectures at Los Angeles on Tuesday and at Pasadena on Wednesday. . . . The first evening they took me to the Mexican quarter, which is very, very agreeable, and we ate in a restaurant so pretty it would have reduced the Kosakiewitch sisters to tears. The band, the cabaret, the cuisine and the drinks were all Mexican. Afterwards we went to a very pretty nightclub, with good jazz. On the second day we went to a kind of Los Angeles Montparnasse, at the bottom of a canyon beside the sea. There was a French café of the artistic kind with French cuisine, also very agreeable. We made a trip to Venice, to the Luna Park . . . and went on the most terrifying "scenic railway" of my life . . .

Yesterday was cinema day. In the morning I went to the hairdressers and visited the village of Westwood, near where we're living—it's close to Beverly Hills. The village itself is very pretty. We went and picked up [Ivan] Moffat at the studio. [George] Stevens invited us to lunch at Lucey's. . . .

Afterwards, a sumptuous Chinese dinner in the smartest restaurant in Los Angeles—truly the most beautiful setting I've ever been in—a kind of aquarium or Haitian conservatory with the most marvelously pretty and astonishing lights and decor. The consul was host. I drank a monstrous zombie and ate delicious things. . . .

Moffat took us to the very top of a hill from which you can see all Los Angeles at your feet. An immensity of twinkling lights in silence. It was very mild, and we stayed for quite a while smoking cigarettes and gazing. We were very happy. We went to bed at 2 in the morning. . . .

Goodbye, my love. . . . I'd like to live in America with you for a good long while. I live with you all the time, and kiss you with all my might.

Your charming Beaver

SIMONE DE BEAUVOIR, to Jean-Paul Sartre

FEBRUARY 29

1848

Left Los Angeles for Santa Barbara I was ordered by Col Mason on a courtmartial—left on Saturday morning with 18 horses and reached there on Sunday night a distance of 120 mile—staid one week at Santa B—was three days getting back—slept in the woods all night, wolves howling all around me could not sleep, hunted about in the dark for water, found a mud puddle at last drank heartily—had nothing to eat—

LIEUTENANT JOHN MCHENRY HOLLINGSWORTH

1968

There is a growing feeling of urgency. Be assured that there is no false or artificial deadline we face.... reworking some more original work if we don't quite build up enough money. We have decided that we must get the tooth filled and the [gap-toothed *Mad* magazine icon Alfred E.] Newman look wiped out before I go. But I'll forgo the $100 Newman bit if necessary.

OCTAVIA E. BUTLER

1968

A nice expression I just learnt: as queer as a tree full of ducks. (Good titles for trilogy: *A Tree Full of Ducks, Dick's Hatband, The Three-Dollar Bill.*)

Monday morning was foggy. I woke and immediately knew that, for some extraordinary reason, I wanted to reread *The Prisoner of Zenda.* So I did, right through, and most of *Rupert of Hentzau* too. They are a very good demonstration of the supreme importance of narrative viewpoint. *Zenda* is far superior to *Hentzau* chiefly because it is so much more fun to be with Rassendyll than von Tarlenheim. . . .

Cabaret opened in London yesterday and Robin French has heard from Hugh that the notices are very good. *The Daily Mail* tracked down Jean [Ross] as the original of Sally Bowles and she has been interviewed and is being brought to the theater to meet Judi Dench.

CHRISTOPHER ISHERWOOD

MARCH 1

1934

I'm beginning to realize that it's as important to inoculate myself against my family as it is for hay-fever victims to stay away from goldenrod and mimosa. . . . God, if I could swing it, I know I could make a good piece of work.

M.F.K. Fisher

1949

I bought *Point Counter Point* today and read steadily for six hours to finish it. Huxley's prose is so deliciously assured—his observations so gloriously acute, if one glories in the deft exposing of our civilization's emptiness—I found the book very exciting, though—a tribute to my embryonic critical abilities.

Susan Sontag

2004

In the split second between sleeping and waking, before my eyes were opened, I sensed I wasn't at home and felt deep undefined emotions. It was similar to the way I felt for months in 1986 waking up on location in Washington, D.C., each morning, away from home and disoriented, waking after the escape of sleep to the first moment of realizing that Gio was dead. This morning I realized I was in Los Angeles and when I was awake enough to define the emotion it was not pain I remember but happiness. Sofia won an Oscar last night.

Eleanor Coppola

MARCH 2

1905

Joseph B. Lippincott, resident supervising engineer of the Geological Survey, has returned from an official trip to Washington, D.C., whither he was summoned on business connected with reclamation work on the Lower Colorado River and kindred projects. Mr. Lippincott brings word of plans in contemplation by the government for arid-land development.

Los Angeles Times

1938

It's a real flood. And my worst sorrow is that we have no radio on hand and can't [hear] all the minute to minute news. . . .

Santa Monica Canyon is flooded and Santa Monica cut off, as also Malibu Topango [*sic*] and Laurel and most of the canyon places. The lights have taken to going off too, and the radio broadcasts urgent requests for people to stay at home and not to use the telephone except for emergency calls. Neglecting which [advice], when the rain [slows] down to a fine mist we tour out to see a movie, and a very bad one which I suppose serves us right. [There] are sandbags along the store fronts on Brand so the water must have topped the curbs and we hope Central—i.e. Lyons Storage—has better drainage luck, Edward's negative box being on the floor of the ground floor.

Charis Wilson

MARCH 3

1935

The day cleared and the sky was like June, deep blue with great white clouds sailing about. The country is now so beautiful that I should be perfectly content but I am not. I feel separated from my kind. I think I could find them if I went back to New York, but they are either dead or grown indifferent to me. In going back I should carry my added years with me, and I would find them with an equal weight of added age. I should have gained a philosophy which would enable me to find solace in the flowers, birds, clouds and mountains of this marvelous land, but I haven't.

HAMLIN GARLAND

1957

Frank Sinatra made his boyish entrance with not one but three standard Hollywood beauties, as if made to order, so perfect in every detail, "*tirage en série*," that they seemed cut out of *Playboy* covers and advertisements, and I could not distinguish one from the other. His stance was one of pride in his triple conquest.

ANAÏS NIN

MARCH 4

1919

I am stranded here on the edge of the world's backwaters for the next five or six weeks but hope to get to Santa Fe again about the middle of April. This is a great town in which to rest, though, so

I suppose I ought to be satisfied. It looks a good deal like the folders they sell you on the train: "typical" California stuff: orange groves in the fore-ground, middle distance of pine trees, and blue and White Mountains beyond. If I had designed the place, however, I should have left out the palms. They march in single file down either side of the streets, parched and brown and dusty as the Sahara, with their hands clasped above their heads in an everlasting rain-prayer. I should call them a doubtful attraction to the real-estate agent's happy hunting ground. The town's chief attraction is an Airedale pup that lives about a block from where we are. He is the best specimen of his breed that I have ever seen—on a bench or off—this side of the Mississippi. I shall cultivate his acquaintance.

I tried my hand as a propagandist today—converted my barber to Socialism while he was cutting my hair—and was really amazed at the talent I displayed. I merely guided his flow of conversation—which started Republican, and ended redder than Max Eastman. My technique was impeccable.

Yvor Winters

1966

This is a city of plastic paradises wherein one true thing is left, a handmade doughnut.

Liza Williams

1995

My car died today. I don't care. It's gone. I should have known that would happen. It was making all of these noises, but I just kept turning up the radio so I didn't have to hear them and worry. I can be like that with my health too—if I see something wrong with me, I just cover it up, keep going, and try not to think about it.

Amy Asbury

MARCH 5

1927

Arrived home. Mayor's office clogged with divorces. Have to get rid of some of them before we can have any new marriages.

WILL ROGERS

1974

The sun has been shining here. . . .

We are expecting a set of Britannica III any day, because it comes with a fee I got for doing the Los Angeles entry. We have no place to put it. Harriett has been calling a contractor about doing some remodeling. She figures that while everything is in such a high state of confusion, it would be a good time to have work done. It's like having your appendix out while you're under anesthetic for major surgery.

JOHN D. WEAVER, to John Cheever

MARCH 6

1850

Emigrants, when the phrensy of the mines has passed, will be strongly attracted to Los Angeles, the capital of the southern department. It stands inland from San Pedro about eight leagues, in the bosom of a broad fertile plain, and has a population of two thousand souls. The San Gabriel pours its sparkling tide through its green borders. The most delicious fruits of the tropical zone may flourish here. As yet, only the grape and fig have secured the attention of the cultivator; but the capacities of the soil and aptitudes of the climate are attested in the twenty thousand vines, which reel in one orchard, and which send through California a wine that need not blush in the presence of any rival from the hills of France or the sunny slopes of Italy. To these plains the more quiet emigrants will ere long gather, and convert their drills into pruning-hooks, and we shall have wines, figs, dates, almonds, olives, and raisins from California. The gold may give out, but these are secure while nature remains.

William Rich Hutton

1887

Mr. Baker and I went for a turn in the *calesa.* Arcadia and Nana went to Los Angeles and back in the afternoon. They went to the funeral of Estela's baby. They say that small pox is increasing all over Los Angeles. Rather cloudy day. Very low tide all day.

Don Juan Bautista Bandini

MARCH 7

1896

We took the electric cars to Altadena (Mr. and Mrs. Roy Barnhart's home is at this place), thence up to Rubio canon, one of the most picturesque and beautiful canons in the Sierra Madre mountains, where is taken the great cable incline to the hotel among the mountains. On this electric cable incline, in the open "white chariot," we were carried up fourteen hundred feet at an average of 59 per cent. . . .

Immediately upon our arrival, after securing rooms, we went to the white dome of the Lowe observatory. . . . After dinner we watched the search light flash over the cities of Pasadena and Los Angeles, whose electric lights, like stars, contrasted strangely with the world over our heads, which an hour later was shown to us through Professor Swift's superb sixteen-inch refracting telescope. Jupiter and suns were admirably seen and the milky way with its I dare not say how many planets, no one has yet been able to count them. An evening with Music and Readings in honor of Professor Lowe, (who was at the hotel that evening, his magnificent home is on Orange Grove avenue, Pasadena), and the birthday of one of the guests, Miss Stevenson, of England, concluded our first day's stay up in the sky.

LORAINE IMMEN

1936

Dottie [Dorothy Parker] and Alan have acquired a Picasso. It is one of a collection Stanley Rose, the bookseller, showed. I saw it at his place, thinking it and other Picassos singularly ugly. I never really noticed it on the Campbells' mantelpiece till they gestured to it proudly. It led Thornton [Wilder] . . . to quote something [Picasso] said about the wife he is divorcing or has divorced, "When I beat her even her screams were artificial."

Thornton also quoted Gertrude Stein—her explanation of a line which is apparently nonsense, "A rose is a rose is a rose." She claims that poetry was in its beginnings the worship of the noun. In those days a poet could mention a noun and achieve clear beauty. That innocent day is past. Miss Stein claims that when she wrote "A rose is a rose is a rose," for the first time in three hundred years a rose really smelled like a rose on the printed page.

CHARLES BRACKETT

MARCH 8

1851

Be it enacted by the Senate and House of Representatives of the United States of America in Congress assembled, That for the purpose of ascertaining and settling private land claims in the State of California, a commission shall be, and is hereby, constituted . . . it shall be to superintend the interests of the United States.

THE LAND ACT OF 1851

1856

May we be governed by principle, not greed, and be comrades in our republics rather than slaves. We wish to be full members of society, not just props; human beings rather than simple shadows. May the rich not hamper the poor seeking to become rich, nor the poor become rich by stealing from the powerful. May the nobleman respect the common man, and may the common man accept the nobleman. May all governments take on the responsibility of promoting prosperity among the poor and honor among the virtuous, not the opposite.

Clearly, no one person should be of more value than any other because those who partake of excess destroy equality and those who allow excess conspire with those who seek it. Equality is harmony, and thereon rests peace in the Republic. Disrupting equality through excess is out of tune and what was once sweet music becomes simply noise.

Republics should have the same relationship with monarchs as the relationship the land . . . has with the sea. . . . The two are intertwined, but the shoreline provides the land with a way of defending itself against the insolence of the sea, which is constantly threatening it, lapping upon its shores, trying to drown it and drink it up. And the land takes its due on the one hand, and hides on the other. The land, always firm and unmoveable, opposes the rowdiness and perpetual discord of the sea's ever-changing nature. The sea rises up in fury at any gust of wind while the land increases its abundance. The sea is enriched by whatever the land offers her, and the land, with fishing hooks and nets, empties out the sea.

FRANCISCO P. RAMIREZ

1941

I do not yet know all the possibilities of Hollywood, because it's a place where you never see anyone. . . .

We live in a very pretty house, with a rather large garden, built on a hill which overlooks the whole city. It is in Hollywood which, it seems, is not very elegant at all. The high-class people live in Beverly Hills, or further west, towards the sea. The most expensive villas are in Santa Monica. . . .

The streets here are very long. For example, we live at 8150 Hollywood Boulevard. And before you reach us, on our side of the street, there really are 8148 houses. . . .

At the very end of this little area, which is the intersection of Laurel Canyon and Sunset Boulevard, is Schwab's drugstore. One finds everything there, even medicine. They sell cigarettes, bras, newspapers, fountain pens, lingerie, sweets, dishes, wine, and alcohol. There is a huge counter where they serve you strange food. I will not tell you much about the food because I want you to be surprised. Americans cook like little girls playing with their toy plates, making themselves dishes with whatever they can steal from their mothers' kitchens: raw carrots, a piece of chocolate, leftover cauliflower, and some currant jelly. . . .

A few hours from here is a desert as beautiful as the Sahara. A little further are some Indian reservations which, it seems, have not changed. And above all, there remain some entirely Mexican areas which must be wonderful. In the old part of Los Angeles, one can see some far from ordinary characters.

Jean Renoir

MARCH 9

1935

There is no hope here. There is nothing but life as incredible as the place, and to that life and to that place a human becomes inured because nature refuses to let outraged senses and sensations and muscles react after they have been shocked to their limit. Else we should go mad.

So I am growing used to impossible snow-capped mountains, outrageous trees and lush gardens, heaven-blessed atmosphere and evening air impossibly laden with perfume of jasmine and orange blossoms. It is unjust that there should be such beauty in such a childish hellhole.

Eric Knight, to a friend

1968

I wonder if my signs shouldn't be where I can touch them. Contact can be good. Love, Success, Control, Strength, Love.

Octavia E. Butler

MARCH 10

1920

Dear Comrade and fellow-worker Debs:

Just a short letter to let you know that you have a comrade who think[s] of you tho I be an I.W.W. and locked tight into a cold steal sell at Los Angeles Cal. Just for my loyalty to the cause of industrial socialism and for running Red International Book's my bail is twenty five thousand dollars and I don't know just when my trial will be however I am not losing any sleep over it knowing as I do that there are no justice to be gotten from a capitalist court the enemy of the working class and here I am to face them not only as an IWW or Bolshevik but also as a yellow man from the far East where only real bad men can come from.

I am not well today my very life longs for a great big green world where I can breathe fresh air and bath into the warm light of the sun, I trust you are well and strong and will live to see the jail doors swing wide and we go marching on. I am giving this letter to a boy to mail for me who is going to get his freedom today. I hope he will mail it right away. I am yours always

J. W. Nishida, to Eugene V. Debs

1924

Coast road like dead snake in road—Malibu Beach—barbed-wire fence on both sides keeping people out from Mrs. Rindge's Spanish land grant—ridge of rocks like iguanodon's back going down to the sea—California horses and cattle on the tawny hills.

—John Barrymore's wife a soft little doughnut.

Edmund Wilson

1954

I have sampled the waters here briefly, and have reason to believe I shall be able to earn a living. . . . Many of our old friends have given up writing entirely, and turned to other lines of work.

Dalton Trumbo, to a fellow blacklistee

MARCH 11

1938

The Garden of Allah Hotel, Hollywood, California

In the old days, when movies were a stringing together of the high points in the imagination of half a dozen drunken ex-newspapermen, it was true that the whole thing was the director. He coordinated and gave life to the material—he carried the story in his head. There is a great deal of carry-over from those days, but the situation of *Three Comrades,* where Frank Borzage had little more to do than be a sort of glorified cameraman, is more typical of today. A Bob Sherwood picture, for instance, or a Johnny Mahin script, could be shot by an assistant director or a script girl, and where in the old days an author would have jumped at the chance of becoming a director, there are now many, like Ben Hecht and the aforesaid Mahin, who hate the eternal waiting and monotony of the modern job.

This is a necessary evolution that the talkies brought about, and I should say that in seven out of ten cases, your feeling that the director or producer was the great coordinator no longer applies.

F. Scott Fitzgerald, to a journalist

1966

Taix's manufactures a round, flat, hearth-baked sourdough bread. Cradle it on your chest, push it between your breasts, pull it apart and chew on its stretching crust, cheese, butter, taste it. A Mr. Felix makes German pumpernickel. Markets it in cellophane with his Victorian-perfect face on the label. Keep it in the fridge and eat it all week, full of grain, and dark sultry mountain-climbing taste, as though it were the last taste on earth.

I should like to sleep in a bed of Jewish doublewhipped cream cheese.

LIZA WILLIAMS

1968

Didn't read the story tonight, the "King at the hospital" one. . . . Lets work with. I think it can be saved.

OCTAVIA E. BUTLER

MARCH 12

1850

Our town has been some three months infested with a gang of rowdies and gamblers who alike set law and order at defiance. They have rendered the place a very unsafe one for the peaceable inhabitants. . . .

The native population, unaccustomed to our laws, if called on would certainly be led on into excesses that would arouse national hatreds and lead to far worse evils. . . .

Already, in two instances, sectional fights where firearms have been used have taken place between Californians and Americans, and we know not the hour when the difficulties of 1846 may not be renewed.

STEPHEN CLARK FOSTER

1921

I have much work to do—I told you in my last letter, which apparently you did not receive, that I have to supervise for Wright the construction of 19 houses and a commercial building with 40 shops—a $400,000 development. I am still not at home here yet and I have to get used to everything slowly. Later I will try to open my own office. There is enough building here.

RUDOLF SCHINDLER, to Richard Neutra

1929

This is a desert; they have irrigated it physically, but it has never had any intellectual irrigation. . . .

I seriously believe that one thing the matter with the movies is that they are made here. The native fruits have little flavor; the flowers are very self-assertive but not odorous; women who have been here a few years get so dry you would just as soon fuck a wrinkle in the bed-sheet. It is a great place for superficial religious cults, not only the pseudo-Christian, but the pseudo-Buddhist, new-thoughtist, and all the Blah stuff. The beef is stringy, the chickens are tasteless and tough, the fish is bad, the houses are flimsy, the hills are ugly, there is little oxygen in the air, the natives and old residents are all cheap childish crooks with no finish to them, bad crude uninteresting liars; there is neither passion nor reality in this trashy civilization—except, possibly, among the Mexicans, Hawaiians, Japs, Chinese. . . .

P.S. You ought to see my rectum! They are looking into it with tubes and mirrors. I have colitis, neuritis and several other things, besides the heart business. A night nurse and a day nurse to give me suppositories, enemas, and pat my ass. I get a thrill out of it—an old man's senile sexually reminiscent thrill.

P.P.S. There's nothing in tits out here, either. I felt a couple of pairs. No snap.

P.P.P.S. Did you ever get black coffee through your rectum? Great! When I have a sinking spell they jazz up my heart with an enema of black coffee—God damn it, I'm still pretty sick, no heart, no guts, no balls. Don't tell anyone I'm still sick—business reasons.

Don Marquis, to his oldest friend

1953

Dear Ernest:

. . . You continually speak of abuses. What are these abuses? Let's be specific. What has any producer done to create a situation that calls for unionism among the ranks of creative talent? You admit, in your letter, that if all producers were like me there would be no cause for complaint. It is also quite obvious, despite your denials in your letter to me, that your article definitely promises the screenwriters that eventually they will be able to control the screen destinies of the stories they work on. I can imagine nothing that would kill this business any quicker.

Darryl Zanuck, to a screenwriter

1974

Dear Pam,

I apologize for being so rude and thank you for not hitting me.

P.S. Harry Nilsson feels the same way.

John Lennon, to Pam Grier

MARCH 13

1852

The country is beautiful, but I suppose there is no comparison between it now and twenty years ago. The gentleman we visited has been here 22 years. He lives only a mile and a half from the Mission of San Gabriel. This Mission is almost in ruins. The large Church is yet in good repair, but most of the other buildings have fallen down. Twenty years ago, says Mr. White, it was in a flourishing condition, the country all around in cultivation, with several mills and fine orchards of all kinds of fruit. There were about a thousand Indians kept employed, and all happy, the Padres being like fathers to them. Beside the farm, mills, orchards, and vineyards, all kinds of manufactures were carried on immediately at the Mission.

We rode over to it, and it made me sad to see it, after hearing what it had been only a few years since. We visited the orange orchard, a remnant of what it was, yet a pleasant sight, large trees hanging full of fruit, others just blooming and the air filled with the fragrance of the bloom. There are now only about fifty trees; a few years ago there were about five hundred.

Emily Hayes

1941

Los Angeles will be the largest city in the world within 25 years if it provides adequate transportation facilities to help fulfill its destiny.

Jack Frye

1985

The opening is at Grauman's Chinese Theater. There are searchlights and what appear to be a troop of Horse Guards on duty. Close inspection reveals that none of the troops is under sixty. A few passers-by watch the arrival of the celebrities, of which there seem to be only two, Michael York and Michael Caine (who later slags off the film). The audience is not star-studded either and heavily sprinkled with those freaks, autograph-hunters and emotional cripples who haunt the stage doors of American theatres. The British Ambassador now stands up to introduce the evening, but his microphone doesn't work and the audience starts barracking. The producer Mark Shivas, Malcolm Mowbray and myself are sitting in different parts of the cinema, and we are to be introduced to the audience. Mark is introduced first, the spotlight locates him, and there is scattered applause; then Malcolm similarly. When my turn comes I stand up, but since I am standing further back than the others the spotlight doesn't locate me. "What's this guy playing at?" says someone behind. "Sit down, you jerk." So I do. The film begins.

ALAN BENNETT

MARCH 14

1919

The range into which Tarzana runs is very wild. It stretches south of us to the Pacific. We have already seen coyote and deer on the place and the foreman trapped a bob-cat a few weeks ago. Things come down and carry the kids out of the corral in broad daylight. Deeper in there are mountain lion. . . .

I bought a couple of .22 cal. rifles for Hulbert and myself beside my .25 Remington and automatics, so we are going to do some hunting. Jack has an air rifle with which he expects to hunt kangaroo-rats and lions and I am going to get them each a pony. . . . There is plenty of room for a golf course and a mighty sporty one too. Also expect to put in a swimming pool and tennis court.

EDGAR RICE BURROUGHS

1920

A nice, clear day but windy. Helen & I start for Pasadena to see the big hotels—Raymond, Green, Maryland, etc. On my advice we go via Eagle Rock Car to Eagle Rock Park & look for a bus. There is a bus line, but we miss one. Helen becomes pettish & we fight. I call her a "god damned sour dough." She gets nervous after a time & attempts to make up. Along this road which is beautiful we see the Annandale Country Club, a handsome thing. Soon enter Pasadena via a wondrous viaduct.

Then to a restaurant, then to the Hotel Green which is a huge barn, badly furnished. From there we go to the Hotel Maryland, a very different place—almost as good as El Mirasol at Santa Barbara. The hat shop. The Italian & his monkey. I give up 10 cents. We stay till 7 p.m. Then to Renee's in the Hotel Green where we dine. I see a stunning girl there & attract her attention. Helen becomes conscious of it, but says nothing. We walked to the So. Pasadena car & then home. Helen dances naked & in the small tight chemisette which ends in the usual way.

THEODORE DREISER

1942

I did not sleep a wink, and daybreak came. It is raining. It is a spiteful chilling rain, and around ten, even the wind joined in. I went to the California bank to change my husband's savings account over to the children's account. In the afternoon, my younger sister came with her child to express her condolences. I received a chicken last night from one of the callers, so we fried that and we had dinner together. In a disappointed voice, Sachiko said, "Father's not here."

Aoki Hisa

1955

I have been a professional writer for twenty years. That is the way I earn my living. My wife and I feed and house and clothe ourselves and our three children out of money derived from the sale of my writings. I have a place in which I work for which I pay rent. I have money tied up in an electric typewriter which wears out infinitesimally with every word it hammers out. I have capital invested in a desk for the typewriter, and in a chair to sit on. I pay for the heat and light in my workroom. In order to have something to write on, I purchase paper and carbon paper and envelopes, and when I mail a project I purchase the stamps for its transmission. I also pay for and consume, pencils, erasers, ink and other articles in the course of writing, whether I write for nothing or for money.

Dalton Trumbo, to a late-paying editor

1957

Slept late and satisfied and woke to play a little tennis, but no dailies. The main setup tonight was the damndest shot I've ever seen, and that includes our first day's work. After Joe Cotten had finished his cameo scene, we started working on the opening shot of the film: a complicated setup with the Chapman boom moving three blocks, angling down over buildings to inserts, through two pages of dialogue to a car blowing up as I kiss Janet.

The sun came up at six and wrapped our night, but I think we got it. To bed at seven, feeling *great.*

Charlton Heston

MARCH 15

1943

I'm getting on pretty well, but a damn dull life though. I spent Saturday at a friends in the country, on a tremendous big roan Tennessee walking gelding, and feel better for it.

William Faulkner, to his agent

1949

Worked with Billy all day, trying to find scenes for Stroheim and putting back patches Billy had unraveled. Why such indecisiveness should have descended on him I can't understand. Rosy Rosenstein brought in Dick Breen's radio actor, Jack Webb, whom I'd suggested to play Artie in our picture. Billy was enchanted with him.

Charles Brackett

MARCH 16

1964

Los Angeles. Silver-pink towers in honey-coloured air. Palm-trees. Tall trees, a sprout of leaves, and "beards." The great flow of power up and down the freeways, easy and controlled and fast—everywhere this characteristic American mode of moving, a sort of inherent jet-age tempo that you see in the way a young man crosses the street or a chair is designed—even status objects have this laconic muscled flow.

JOHN FOWLES

2007

A couple of things I didn't know (or maybe forgot): Echo Park Lake has a clay bottom. It's a real lake, albeit one that's filled with tap water and rimmed with cement. Also, the lake is leaking. They are not sure where the leak is occurring, but water is leaving.

JENNY BURMAN

MARCH 17

1964

I am luxuriously ensconced in a hotel on the Sunset Strip, with a view south over the whole of LA. The night view is very beautiful, a spill of jewels glittering in limpid air. . . . This is the mad rich woman America; with the courage of her convictions, her rich madness.

JOHN FOWLES

1976

I'm back home and all is well, but things got off to a shaky start at Mt. Sinai when we were waiting in the Admitting Office to be taken to my room, and a young male attendant came in and clamped a plastic ID bracelet around the left wrist of the middle-age woman across from us. She took one look at it and shrieked: "I'm not John Weaver, I'm Mrs. Blumberg." I told her she was about to make medical history, and as they wheeled her away, she said, "Wait till you get my hysterectomy." On the morning of the operation, the nurses forgot to give me a shot to sedate me, so I was wide awake when they wheeled me off to surgery, and while I was lying there waiting for the elevator, I heard the urologist saying, "But Mister Weaver's chart must be here *somewhere*."

There had also been a mix-up about my room the first day, and I insisted on being transferred from the one they had assigned me. When I got to the next room and settled down in bed, a nurse came in with a clipboard, beamed at me and said, "You're Mr. Blatnik?" I'm not sure just what operation I got, Mrs. Blumberg's, Mr. Blatnik's or my own, but I feel great and the surgery was quite painless, with minimal discomfort afterwards.

I've come home to a burst of lovely spring weather, and the orange blossoms outside my work room smell like a Las Vegas wedding chapel. I have to take it easy for another couple of weeks and it will be a while before I'll be able to pose for a Playgirl centerfold. I keep thinking of Mr. Blumberg, and hear him asking, "Darling, what in God's name did they do to you?" And Mrs. Blatnik may be in for some surprises. "*This* is a tonsillectomy?"

JOHN D. WEAVER, to John Cheever

MARCH 18

1845

Called all the people on the ranch, servants and not servants, for the purpose of knowing them. Gave warning to all that did not work to leave the place. Divided the working hands. Gave six to Sr. Benabe for work of the timber, the rest to other occupations on the rancho cleaning the vineyard on the ditch, cutting firewood.

Henry Dalton

1851

SIX YEARS LATER

Acting for myself and in behalf of my fellow citizens of Angeles in your district, I beg to call your attention to the enclosed "Prospectus" for the Publication of the "Los Angeles Star." The necessity and importance of a publication of this description cannot fail to meet the approbation, not only of southern California, but of the honorable party of all the state. I beg therefore to suggest to you the propriety of soliciting from the government an appropriation for the purpose of publishing the laws in Spanish.

Henry Dalton, to Abel Stearns

1949

We have a view of the same little monastery church in the mountains—directly in front of us is the golf course. . . .

The plans enclosed will give you an idea of the furnishings—Fritz Lang drew them up for us, so that we knew exactly where to put every piece of furniture.

Theodor Adorno

1950

I am not doing much of anything. Reading a little, loafing a lot, and writing letters sporadically; I've a lot of them to catch up on. . . . I find that I am relieved of a great tension; if I am driving the jeep down the freeway and begin to think about a tire blowing, in the back of my mind is [the] thought of how I wouldnt really mind dying so much now. There is enough of it there now that they could print it; maybe it wouldnt be quite as good as it will be, but it would be printed.

James Jones

MARCH 19

1930

EVERYTHING HERE IS MOVING ALONG BEAUTIFULLY AND I LIKE IT IMMENSELY.

Horace Liveright

1940

To: Zelda Fitzgerald

Dearest . . . Nothing has developed here. I write these Pat Hobby stories—and wait. I have a new idea now—a comedy series which will get me back into the big magazines—but my God I am a forgotten man. *Gatsby* had to be taken out of the Modern Library because it didn't sell, which was a blow. With dearest love always

F. Scott Fitzgerald

1942

The other day I was talking to a hookey cop who told me that there is more delinquency and more absences due to illness among boys with paper routes and selling papers on the streets. It is not unusual for boys to rise in all weather between 3:30 and

4 a.m. and to return at 7 a.m. Often too ill to attend school, they nevertheless deliver their papers. Before going to school the boys often go back to bed for a short nap. If the mother works, which is often the case, the children sometimes sleep past school time.

I used to stop at the corner of Santa Monica Boulevard and Third Street in Santa Monica to watch a little newsie stationed there. He is a Negro boy who has lost the use of his legs and sits in a wagon with his shrunken helpless feet straight out in front of him. There are four children in his family similarly crippled, due to a nutritional deficiency disease. Often after the newsie sells out his papers he waits for hours until one of his sisters or brothers with sound legs comes to pull him home.

When he gets home to his bedraggled short street with its many slow-moving arrogant flea-bitten dogs and the dirty shacks that overflow children into the street, he is part of the freemasonry of children at play. I have seen twenty or thirty children lined up along the curb, unplanned, casually singing spirituals together, teaching the three and four-year-olds to keep on key. They turn to games, and the crippled newsie is given his turn to be *it.* I have seen people struggling in vain to entertain themselves, and I never watch them without thinking of the Negro kids lined up along the street singing their slow powerful songs, and their dogs scratching, and the wagon-bound newsie not excluded, but one of them.

THEODORE DREISER, to Eleanor Roosevelt

1957

We finished up the scenes in the hotel room and the lobby. They tell me you have to come early to get seats at the studio runnings of our dailies now.

CHARLTON HESTON

1971

We crouched under the lintel, here—here, he said, holding us close under the crossbeam—here is the safest place. The floor rocked and I longed for the walls to fall away, fall away and leave for my eyes a landscape of suspended people each in his box, each in his moment. And we would look at each other across this encapsulated city and recognize each other.

LIZA WILLIAMS

MARCH 20

1927

I was given a party last night—O Jesus! What a party! Drink reveals what a person is made of: drunk, the burgesses lose the thin veneer which hides their crudeness. I don't mind,—it is the WAY in which one is noisy, foolish, amorous. . . .

I tried hard to fit in, but I feel the party thought me stiff, cold, indifferent, and probably were disappointed, for although I knew but two or three who came, they knew of me, from talk,—and pictured me as a gay Don Juan.

I stole away at 1:30, an unpardonable breach of etiquette! I could not stomach the mess longer.

This morning I am consumed by disgust. At least I am not "crudo,"—I only pretended to drink.

EDWARD WESTON

1948

We went to the Academy Awards, which seemed to me more tidily done than I'd ever seen them—sentimentally, folksily, but at least with a care and preparation and consideration for the feelings of everyone. . . . Elia Kazan got the Best Director Award, which he in no way merited, and he hadn't the grace to wear a dinner coat. Social protest, I presume.

CHARLES BRACKETT

1964

If possible, I'd like to stay at the Sheraton because I'm treated well there and they do a good job screening off well-wishers, strangers who claim to be my best friend, kooks who want to assassinate me, and assorted and sundry sycophants who want me to buy oil wells, interest in super markets.

ROD SERLING

MARCH 21

1923

Finally, by paying a fee of two and a half dollars I got a job through a commercial labor agency.

It was a pick-and-shovel, or "mucking" job in Hollywood Hills, where a syndicate of Los Angeles realtors were starting a new and exclusive subdivision called Hollywoodland, intended to appeal specially to movie stars, directors, oil millionaires, high-powered evangelists, wealthy widows, and divorcees from the East. . . . It was the hardest work I have ever done. . . .

I shoveled gravel into huge wheelbarrows, pushed the wheelbarrows and dumped them into trucks from a platform, and rolled boulders from underneath an overhanging wall of rock.... I was in constant terror that a rock might break off the wall and crush me. The quarry was lighted by huge incandescents which cast over the scene weird shadows of trees and moving men. The owls hooted in the holly bushes....

I became acquainted with some of my fellow workers, many of whom were I.W.W., or "Wobblies."

Louis Adamic

1923

Same old Los Angeles, only more beautiful.

It has grown enormously in the years since I was here. Its shops are very fine; its new boulevards magnificent; its skyscrapers, scattered through the city, stand by themselves like great and beautiful towers.... This remains one of the loveliest spots in the world.

When one sees in the suburbs the innumerable homelike stucco or wooden bungalows, small and crowded but often attractive in their architecture and delightfully landscaped, with many flowers and shrubs, one learns to understand a good deal about this strange community. People live so comfortably and easily here that one can appreciate why Los Angeles has been and still is one of the most reactionary of cities.

Oswald Garrison Villard

MARCH 22

1847

Struck tents quite early and resumed our march over this large plain. Cattle seen today also as far as the eye can reach. I fell in the rear today did not reach camp till sun down. Camp'd on the River San Gabriel. Here Gen Kearney and Commodore Stockton fought a battle with the Spaniards. The Americans coming off victorious.

HENRY STANDAGE

1903

Last night 3 robbers attacked an electric car of the L.A. and S.M.—killed a passenger and wounded 4 or 5. They believe one of the malefactors was wounded. 15 or 20 shots were shot and the robbers fled without stealing anything. Clear day and agreeable.

DON JUAN BAUTISTA BANDINI

MARCH 23

1903

Bought a book for a diary in Los Angeles.

DON JUAN BAUTISTA BANDINI

1910

Leo N. Tolstoy,

Sir: Having written a book on the question of "Crime and Criminals," we found that our Investigations forced us to the conclusion that violence and brutality can beget only violence and brutality and that to attempt to suppress crime by such methods is but to make bad infinitely worse.

Asking ourselves who was most closely identified with this conclusion we were unanimously of the opinion that you had inculcated, above all others, year after year and decade after decade, the principles which examination of the facts in the case had driven us to adopt.

It is with the profoundest respect, therefore, that we have ventured to dedicate to you the accompanying volume, entitled, "Crime and Criminals."

We trust you will accept with it the assurance of our most affectionate regard extended across the seas to one whom we recognize as a master worker in a cause that knows no limitations of race or territorial boundaries.

With the deepest respect, we remain,

Griffith J. Griffith

1946

In flying in to Los Angeles, we had snow-capped mountains on either side of us and soft white billowy clouds underneath. It was really a beautiful sight. But the most impressive time to fly in to Los Angeles is at night, when all the lights are on and the city lies below you like a multi-colored heap of jewels.

Eleanor Roosevelt

1988

Met my father for lunch at Nickodell, the old Hollywood restaurant next door to Paramount, around the corner from Beth Olam cemetery where my grandparents are buried. I had Hungarian goulash, the special of the day. Dad had a French dip sandwich. He told me he doesn't expect Mom to live more than five years. He's been reading up on the stats for pancreatic cancer; doesn't look good. I still think she will defy the statistics, though she has been having bouts of unexplained pain, was in terrible condition during Ken's wedding. I asked the waitress if I could take home what was left of my goulash (most of it). It didn't feel like a good time to eat a lot of meat.

We went outside and climbed into Dad's new car which he calls the Mafia Mobile. Surprising, since Dad's not the flashy type. It's a shiny black New Yorker with caramel-colored leather interior and a sunroof and a digital read-out of the compass. Dad said he realized there was no point in waiting to be comfortable. He wants Mom to be comfortable. We drove off to the cemetery. We stood in front of my grandparents' graves in the vault. It was the third anniversary of Grandma's death. We said a silent prayer, then Dad took me upstairs and showed me the empty slots in the marble wall where he and Mother will be entombed. (Encrypted?)

I felt a sob come up then regained my humor, remembered Susan's story about how her dad traded a Cadillac for his tombstone. Remembered the Day of the Dead in Oaxaca, how I felt in the cemetery there, those piles of marigolds, red coxcombs, brass bands. Friendly spirits can be kind to one another.

It was light and airy in the vault and it felt right that my father would want me to see the space he has reserved for himself and my mother for the hereafter. Then it didn't feel odd to be there.

I decided to tell my father that Lloyd and I are going to get married. He didn't have much reaction, which somehow felt ok.

We stopped in front of the grandparents on the first floor before we left; I told Dad I thought Grandma would be happy that I was getting married.

"Tell her," he suggested.

"I already did," I said.

Louise Steinman

MARCH 24

1882

We got word this evening of the death of the poet Longfellow. He died in Cambridge at 3.15 p.m., aged seventy-five. This comes specially near home to me, for I remember meeting him often and hearing him read his poems at the Sunday afternoon musicales.

L. Vernon Briggs

1931

I'm working this week at one of the most generous studios in Hollywood. Thirty or forty cents in stationery means practically nothing at all to this outfit.

Don Marquis, to a friend

MARCH 25

1942

About 100,000 Japanese (incl. American citizens) are being evacuated from the coast here for military reasons. wonderful how humanity pulls through despite all these psychoses and panics. in the office where we too had to register as enemy aliens i saw an old Japanese woman, half-blind, and not looking at all dangerous. she had her companion, a young girl, apologise to the people who were waiting that she was taking so much time to write. everybody smiled: the American officials were very polite.

BERTOLT BRECHT

1946

Here in Los Angeles, Miss Corinne Seeds, principal of the elementary school of the University of California, has helped to start what seems to me a very interesting plan. The names of 3,000 school children in one little town in Holland were secured and already 2,000 have become "adopted friends" of children in the schools of Los Angeles. . . . The children's efforts may have more success than their elders have had in the past, so at least we can applaud their efforts and hope for the future.

Spring is certainly the most delightful time to see the Southern California landscape. The hills and fields are green and I know of no more beautiful beaches anywhere than those along the Pacific. When I come to California at this time of year, I always remember my first visit here. Franklin K. Lane, then Secretary of the Interior, was traveling with us. He loved this state, and early in the morning he would send us huge bunches of flowers, saying that this was the state of flowers and sunshine and he wished our first impression to be of their beauty and of the sweet odor of the orange blossoms. On this visit I've been sent a number of the very decorative paradise flowers, which one does not see as much in the East as out here. I must say that the profusion of little flower marts along the streets adds greatly to the charm of the city. On Saturday I had a chance to walk through Olvera Street, the heart of the Mexican community, and many of my old friends there spoke to me.

Eleanor Roosevelt

MARCH 26

1927

With K. to see Ruth Draper, an actress of unusual ability, who presented an enjoyable evening's entertainment. She has a great vogue, but I came away with not more than a pleasant feeling: I would rather have seen a Chaplin comedy. . . .

I am disgusted this morning for not having slept longer,— I needed to. Probably I overworked yesterday, having made 12 enlargements from as many negatives on an order. It will bring me $120, then I'll sleep better!

Edward Weston

1946

Yesterday afternoon, I drove out to the Junior Auxiliary Jewish Home for the Aged. This home is for both men and women. They have a small hospital, a very charming dining room and auditorium, a small synagogue, and pleasant living quarters.

The old Jewish people there seem to spend most of their time in prayer, and so it was fitting that they should hold their short but moving ceremonies of welcome to me in their synagogue. In these ceremonies, they remembered my husband as their friend and presented me with a gift which will always have value because of the sentiment attached to it.

I could not help being thankful that, in this country, these old people could find a sanctuary in their declining years. A happy contrast to the sad old people that I saw in a Jewish refugee camp in Germany.

ELEANOR ROOSEVELT

1968

God, what I need is a man.

OCTAVIA E. BUTLER

MARCH 27

1848

Received orders to proceed to San Gabriel with a party of 12 dragoons to assist the Alcalde of that place to arrest some horse thieves We proceeded at a rapid rate but the birds had flown—It was my first expedition with dragoons and as I am a volunteer officier, considered it a compliment—I had also an opportunity of seeing a beautiful part of the country and we paid a long visit at Mr [Hugo] Reid's who gave us a fine dinner and I had an opportunity of seeing the fair Dona Maria—she was very polite and gave me a splendid orange—I tried hard to make friends with them all and I think my fine charger dressed off in dragoon trappings and the military appearance of the rider made quite an impression on the fair flower of San Gabriel. . . .

As I stood and looked at this spot—thoughts of home filled

my mind and I could but think of her in the cold grave and of those from whom I was so far distant—I asked myself when I should see home again and walk among the scenes of my youth—I never felt more sad or more dispirited than I did then since I left home—Yes I thought of home and of all those that are dear to me and when I should see them again—I trust it will not be long and that I shall find them all well and happy—

LIEUTENANT JOHN MCHENRY HOLLINGSWORTH

1928

I'm only praying he's still alive, for when I left him in his berth in the "glory-hole" of the "California" last Sat. night he looked as though he were nearing the Pearly Gates. We were held up and beaten by a gang in San Pedro. . . .

I put up quite a fight, but neither of us were in much condition. They all beat it as a car turned on a nearby corner. Both of us robbed of nearly everything, and practically unconscious. After reporting at police headquarters I don't know how I would have got him back to his ship without the help of a sailor friend of mine whom I had run into earlier in the evening while waiting for him. We roused several of his shipmates—and I'm only hoping that his bumps and bruises haven't been any more fatal than mine. I finally had to finish the night in a ward of the Salvation Army Hotel, and it was five o'clock Sunday before I got enough money to get back to Hollywood. On his way back to Frisco I'm hoping to see him again—but not in Pedro!

HART CRANE

1955

I'm really scared about Disneyland. . . . So much I don't know and trying to design and not being sure I'm on the right track.

RUTH SHELLHORN

MARCH 28

1928

You ought to hear Aimee [McPherson] carry on over the radio to get the full blast of her personality. . . . they almost caught her with her shoes off in that "kidnapping" episode.

HART CRANE

1949

Billy and I dined at his house with Audrey [Wilder, *née* Young], who is his "girl," and he and I worked until 10:30. . . . Am I merely deceiving myself when I view his life, upon which the bores and parasites are moving so fast, with a lot of pity for him, and regret for that mind of his which can be so first-rate at best, and so ox-stupid at worst. . . . It was not an evening of inspired work but very useful.

CHARLES BRACKETT

1957

We cleared up quite a night's work . . . finished off Janet in the picture, and got some good cuts in the water and under the bridge for the last scene. The company is tiring a little now, after fifteen straight nights, but they still work well and cheerfully, full of the hope of a good film. [Cinematographer] Russ Metty cooked up a mess of spaghetti in the trailer, which saved us from that dreary catered stuff.

CHARLTON HESTON

MARCH 29

1946

It must be ghastly in Germany, compared to that we really are in paradise, as incredible as that may seem.

THEODOR ADORNO

1979

L.A. is the ultimate expression of the capitalist system in spatial terms.

AARON PALEY

MARCH 30

1867

Off quite early. From the mission took Scott's ranch road to the city. Got into quite a talk with Carl about painting his wagon. May get the job. Arrived at the town at three. Went up to his house & helped him unload, unharness, etc. Has got a gay wife, is as fresh & as plump as a ripe peach. Their greeting made a poor wandering homeless homesick youth like me most awfully blue & heartsick. Went down to the U.S. [Hotel] & booked myself & then out to get shirts & pants, as my appearance in that respect was most awfully dilapidated. Took a bath & shave & put on clean clothes: felt much better. Went to bed early in evening.

WILLIAM HENRY JACKSON

1927

The shells I photographed were so marvelous one could not do other than something of interest. What I did may be only a beginning.

Edward Weston

MARCH 31

1853

California is a bad place to raise children. I suppose it will not always be so. Los Angeles has become somewhat better since I came here.

A Methodist preacher and family have removed here within the last month or two who are trying to civilize the place. His wife has a school, and is liked very much; and he preaches every Sunday. I have never heard him; I believe, he is not considered a very good preacher, but is liked as a man. They also have Sunday School every Sunday.

Americans are beginning to settle here very fast now. . . .

I have just been out visiting. Mr. Hayes and I went to Mr. Wilson's for a walk. Mrs. W. would make us stay to tea. She had some of the nicest biscuit I ever ate, they are made with a patent yeast. I shall not be satisfied until I have some of it. It is a light powder which is sprinkled through the flour and mixed with water. Mr. Hayes has now gone down town on some business. I feel very lonely when he is gone, although he talks but little when he is here. He reads almost constantly and when he is not reading he is in the garden pulling up weeds or transplanting flowers. We will have a great variety of flowers this summer, most of them wild flowers.

Emily Hayes

1858

The men seem to spend their time on horseback, charging around as if they were on business of the greatest importance. They are lazy & indolent, do not so much as raise vegetables or fruit but lounge around half starved, living on poor beef. . . .

From my experience on the road, the settlers are more to be dreaded than the roving banditti. Many years ago a large portion of the valleys have been cultivated which are now not cultivated owing to the scarcity of water for irrigation. It seems that the heavens have been shut up against this people & country & the rain withheld, the earth parched & the streams dried up—caused no doubt from the wickedness of the people.

James Gillespie Hamilton

1906

I went down to the wholesale district, to Lazarus & Milgan, to get an old historical pamphlet, "Historical Sketch of Los Angeles County," 1876 (known as Warner's). Got six copies, fifteen cents each. Someday this will be valuable Californiana.

Olive Percival

1964

Marineland is built on a spare clifftop, a splendidly Roman place a lovely circus tossed to the masses. Tiberius and Nero would have approved of the idea; and made it more "interesting" by substituting sharks for dolphins, and living slaves for dead herrings. . . .

I bought Stephen a baby turtle in Farmer's Market the day before. He insists on carrying it around everywhere with him in a small paper bag. It irritates me that Jud and Suzanne don't forbid it. But they let Stephen do as he likes. If a child does something wrong here the parents keep quiet and send him to the analyst to be "repaired." "Correcting children is a skilled job—they send the children to the man skilled at the job." Suzanne said this approvingly of Californians the other day; I don't absolutely disagree. But it's an easy get-out for parents.

JOHN FOWLES

1987

Yesterday got a ride down to Venice Beach with Barbara (and Emily and Sarah) and Barbara locked the keys in the car. Sarah was down on the beach with her boyfriend and Emily and I were walking down by the shops. And who's filming? *Colors* with Dennis Hopper directing, starring Sean Penn and Robert Duvall, the script that I read and the film Justin might get his SAG card from. I hung out, talked to some people, and to get a better view was an extra. Found out from the real extras that they'd shoot again the following day. We all thought that we'd wrap early so Dennis Hopper could make it to the Academy Awards, but they just finished the scene without him.

So it's today and I come down again and I find out they're filming inside, all done with exteriors for the day, and I walk by Dennis Hopper. . . . he was talking to someone, but I think he watched me walk past, because as I'm coming back past him he kind of looks at me again (red glowing hair can be kind of distracting, I suppose) and I walked up. . . . I said I was sorry about last night but he deserved the nomination for the other movie anyway. . . . I said I thought he was really cool and I just wanted to tell him that. He thanked me and I walked away.

So I sounded like an idiot. But what do you say to someone that you know of and would like to know? . . . I suppose it's best just to be honest and say what you're thinking.

CAROLYN KELLOGG

APRIL 1

1883

Fancy a village of 150 souls—living in houses they have built, on lands they & their ancestors have tilled for 100 years—peach orchards, apricot orchards, wheat fields irrigating ditches—fancy such a community as that, actually being obliged to "remove,"—on account of never having had a title to the land,—the tract in which their village lies having been patented without their knowing it;—I believe they really will have to go—& the U. S. Govt. has little better than desert left to offer them.

My regards to Mrs. Aldrich. I shall bring her an Indian basket.

Yours ever truly

HELEN HUNT JACKSON, to an editor

1940

April 1: *Los Angeles Evening News* and *Daily News* merge to constitute *The News*, a 24-hour newspaper.

The WPA Guide to Los Angeles

APRIL 2

1858

Commenced raining about 2 o'clock had to stop shearing on account of the sheep being so wet.

AUGUSTUS SIMON BIXBY

1957

We finished work with a final dawn shot, of Orson's death, in an overturned chair on a dump heap, and then had a celebrant drink or two in the trailer. Orson and I took along the last magnum of champagne and found a place still open to give us bacon and eggs to go with it. A hell of a picture to work on . . . I can't believe it won't be fine. It was wonderful to loaf tonight, all the same. We had steak and saw Orson's LADY FROM SHANGHAI on TV. It's good, but not as good as ours, I think.

CHARLTON HESTON

1970

I did nothing all day except stare at the ocean and occasionally memorize some irregular Spanish verbs. I am well over half way through the Grammar at the moment and, given a little peace in LA I will have practically finished it by the time we return. I will then go through it again fast and translate the editorials from the most reputable Mexico City papers every day, in the meantime finding some intelligent bilingual Spaniard to make conversation with for an hour a day. . . .

Another worry is that I have temporarily lost all sexual urge which is very frustrating for E. Presumably the terrific change in my body as a result of total abstinence for (now approaching) three weeks, after thirty years of steady and sometimes unsteady drinking is taking its time to reassert itself. When it does come back it will be a vast explosion. If it does come back which it had better had.

RICHARD BURTON

APRIL 3

1943

You must know how to beat fear. If you cannot feel it, you are a moron, an idiot. The brave man is not he who does not know fear; the brave man is he who says to himself, "I am afraid. I will decide quickly what to do, and then I will do it."

WILLIAM FAULKNER, to his nephew

1966

Routine—got up just before 9:30 to watch Superman and Bullwinkle. Forget to mention that in yesterday—cut the lawn. Today bathed, styled hair, got all ready to go to afro club. Club mostly boys. Nice, but while I could follow them easily, I was a damn weak voiced opposition. I appologized [*sic*] too much for calling Costa Rican, African. Made me look prej.

OCTAVIA E. BUTLER

APRIL 4

1901

My house is charming. To tourists it is always pointed out as the "Fremont House" and often Kodacked.

Jessie Benton Frémont

1963

Dear diary: "You open this door with the key of imagination" Quoted from Rod Serling's T.L.Z. I'm living in a sort of twilight zone. . . .

I cried today in spanish after standing infront of the class attempting to give a *lectura* summary. It was such a stupid human thing to do. . . . I don't know what to do about my personality (a fear of people and worms) I can't talk to people the way I want to. They nearly all see a difference in me. They talk to each other, then they talk to me. What's wrong?!! Also, is mother hiding? If so, why? I'm breaking through slowly.

Octavia E. Butler

1968

Just before six, I heard that King has died. Oh fuck them all. How blood-horny this'll make the killers on both sides.

Christopher Isherwood

APRIL 5

1954

I've been reading in columns that there is ill feeling between you boys [Jerry Lewis and Dean Martin] and that there's even a likelihood that you might go your separate ways. I hope this isn't true for you are awfully good together, and show business needs you. I don't mean to imply that either of you couldn't make a living on his own. I am sure you could. But you do complement each other and that's one of the reasons you click so successfully.

I am sure you have had disagreements and arguments, just as all teams, trios and quartets have had since the beginning of the theater. In the heat of working together there's inevitably a nervous tension and frequently it's during these moments that two high-strung temperaments will flare up and slash at each other. There may be nothing to the rumors of your separation. However, if there is any ill feeling or bitterness between you, it will eventually affect your work. If that feeling does exist, sit down calmly together, alone—when I say alone, I mean no agents, no family, no one but you two—sit down alone, and talk it out.

Groucho Marx

1960

We are in Los Angeles where we found a charming house in a blooming canyon full of good butterflies. We live very quietly. My main occupation is a screenplay I am making, but I am also occupied in reading the proofs of my ONEGIN, the proofs of my SONG OF IGOR, and Dmitri's translation of my DAR [*The Gift*].

The screenplay [of *Lolita*] will keep me busy till August or September when we shall sail again for Europe. I feel happy and relaxed in lovely and serene Los Angeles, and we both wish Elena and you could visit us here.

VLADIMIR NABOKOV, to Edmund Wilson

1970

In building, it seems, we must look back to the dear Jews and the rare Latins to learn how to live.

O Children of Israel, come out of Fairfax and old Boyle Heights. Send us your architectural rabbis to lead us from the wilderness of the blacktop and oil drips and gasoline fumes. Open our eyes so we may see. Sit us down so we may rest. Open our mouths so we may talk and eat. . . .

O small towns of Mexico, send us your mariachis to strum at the centers of our plazas to bring the people back, the girls wandering this way, the boys ambling that, the warm rivers running softly over the wide mosaic walks.

Dear Moses, sweet Virgin of Guadalupe, teach us Gentile Protestants how once more to spend an evening that is neither far-traveling and senseless, nor violent, nor sick, nor hidden away from the world in colored but colorless TV. Inhabitants, inheritors of Tel Aviv and Guadalajara, hear me now. The hour grows late. Help, o help. Give us back to ourselves. For what finer gift *is* there in all the world?

RAY BRADBURY

1982

And so my L.A. adventure begins.

I looked at an apartment in Mid-Wilshire—Serrano—I like the area. It's urban. I spent the whole day on the buses and walking around. Bringing all the energy and excitement of San Francisco to this crazy and dispersed city. Hollywood, Fairfax, Wilshire, Downtown, Ventura Blvd. All on the bus. It's all accessible. Sometimes it's a bit frustrating. But it's because one is spoiled by the automobile in this town. . . .

I just bounced around town. I went to Wilshire between Normandie and Western on Lorrain's suggestion. I was just walking the neighborhood when I saw a good looking 20s apartment building. A black man, young—walked out and I asked him if there were vacancies. He said there always were—and that it was a cool place to live.

Aaron Paley

APRIL 6

1896

The first thing I did in the morning was to walk out of the veranda-roof and pick my hands full of La Marque rose-buds, all covered with dew. (Oh! I can never forget the beauty of that moment!) We enjoyed the rose-buds as a centerpiece, heaping them upon the oranges.

Olive Percival

1957

The geographical constriction of L.A. We all live far away from each other and I do not drive. Taxis are inordinately expensive. It takes an afternoon to get to Hollywood to buy paper and a typewriter ribbon.

Anaïs Nin

1970

I went this morning for a final fitting for my dinner jacket for the Oscars tomorrow night. There is apparently an outside chance I might win but I give it no mind or else I shall become morose if I'm a loser. I have now gone over 3 weeks without a drink and never give it a thought, though win or lose tomorrow night it's going to be another test of my will-power, because certainly everybody else will be intoxicated. It's one of those nights. E found her speech for the presentation of the Best Picture Award too sententious and asked if she could re-write it herself, which she did last night so that they can put it onto the idiot boards.

RICHARD BURTON

APRIL 7

1847

A petition was got up in the Battalion, petitioning the officers of the Battalion or Commanders of Cos. for our discharge from the service of the U.S. believing the war to be at an end and our services no longer needed.

HENRY STANDAGE

1930

Galka repelled me at the very start of our acquaintance but now I find myself wishing she would drop in once more before leaving. She is a dynamo of energy. She would wear me out in a few days—but insight of unusual clarity, and an ability to express herself in words, brilliantly, forcefully, to hit the nail cleanly.... She is an ideal "go-between" for the artist and his public.

EDWARD WESTON, on Galka Scheyer

1968

Such a beautiful day, though windy and a bit misty. Out on the bay, the flash of the water-skiers is like an appeal to get on with it, to participate, to live in the moment, to make the scene, to be where the action is. Here I am, sitting up on the balcony with the typewriter plugged in, determined to witness, to record, rather than to run down to the beach and wander around looking for—what? Not sex. This isn't senile silliness even. I was just the same when I was young. The Beach and the Balcony—that's the story of my life.

CHRISTOPHER ISHERWOOD

APRIL 8

1918

Mother went to Appomattox Day picnic in Sycamore Grove. A divine, heavenly, Eden-perfect day. I could not get home before two but then I gardened hard until dark. O, how I love to garden—to forget the uglinesses and disappointments of everyday life!

Saturday Morning, to inaugurate the Third Liberty Loan, bells rang at 6 in the morning and airmen dropped bombs and literature! We did not know the programme and Mother thought it meant a victory but I guessed the real reason (for a wonder) and hastily dressing in the dim light, it was easy to fancy it a German raid—to see how impossible it would be to escape with more than mere life and a night-dress! It made me plan to have my most precious things in a bag, by my bed. But already I'm seeing what a bother that would be.

Olive Percival

1925

The studios pay big salaries to their girls but you certainly earn it. It's no simple matter working for people who are as nervous and temperamental as movie people are. . . .

I met Mr. W. R. Hearst. I didn't know him by sight and had quite a novel introduction. I came rushing through the door with much speed and he was coming out from an inner door and we collided. If he had been about 4 feet shorter than he is, I might have knocked him over. . . . Mr. Hearst is quite tall, but he has such a small voice that you are quite surprised when he opens his mouth. . . .

Vilma Banky has arrived and I like her very much. With good management she ought to be a success. She can't speak English so most of her conversation is by gestures and a word or two here and there.

I'm so happy to be here at the studio that I just wish that all my friends were here too. I like the atmosphere and the hustle and bustle of this life. Everybody but my boss is so nice and friendly—so different from a regular business office. No one but the art director, Mr. Anton Grot, has gotten too friendly yet. Mr. Grot tried once to kiss me but my guess is that he won't try that again.

Valeria Belletti

1949

This afternoon I heard a lecture on "The function of art and the artist" by Anais Nin: she is very startling—pixie-like, other-worldly—small, finely built, dark hair, and much make-up which made her look very pale—large, questioning eyes—a marked accent which I could not label—her speech is over-precise—she shines and polishes every syllable with the very tip of her tongue and teeth—one feels that if one were to touch her, she would crumble into silver dust.

SUSAN SONTAG

APRIL 9

1945

I never found the tar-pits in Los Angeles, but I had a dish of Spam with raisin sauce at the Thrifty Drug Store.

JOHN CHEEVER

1972

Please let's get together for a drink when we are both on the same side of the Los Angeles River.

NORMAN CORWIN, to Rod Serling

1982

David [Hockney] was in a great state of excitement. He has invented a way of juxtaposing multiple Polaroid photographs as part of a subject (which may be a portrait, still life or landscape) so that they produce an effect of many superimposed images of the subject taken from different angles, as with cubism. The remarkable achievement is that the spectator seeing a face which has perhaps three noses and four eyes nevertheless makes a sum in his head of the multiple images and sees a single face correcting the distortion. That D. can produce such unity out of multiple images is due to his unerring eye, which one can judge from seeing him at work making one of these compositions.

He tells me that he has put into photography the dimension of passing through time which it lacks. He attaches importance to the fact that it takes up to three hours for him to make one of these pictures. The three hours through minute transitions in the lighting as well as the observation of things from different angles go into the picture, as they would with a drawing that took the same amount of time. . . .

People kept wandering in and out of the apartment the whole time I was there. David seemed utterly indifferent to them, neutral perhaps, welcoming them as spectators of his new photographs, and listeners to his new spiel about them. Usually David and I got up before anyone else, and David would say mildly: "You would think that someone would have noticed there is no bread and no milk in the house" and I would accompany him to the store.

STEPHEN SPENDER

APRIL 10

1950

I think I will write down my memories of Dylan Thomas now. . . . I'd better record them here, before they get too vague. . . .

As we drove out to Santa Monica, Dylan gradually heightened the steam pressure of his indignation against the English department of UCLA. He also kept pressing me to stop for a drink. This I evaded, because I was afraid he was going to get so high that he wouldn't be able to give his reading. . . .

Lunch was tense. Dylan had had some drinks at my house, and now accepted more—unwillingly as they were offered. The nice clean youngish-oldish blank-faced anxious English teachers sat around, waiting for the volcano to erupt. . . . They had conjured up this dangerous little creature, excited by the dangerousness in his poems, and now that they had him there in the flesh, he terrified and shocked them. . . . It's the attitude of the small boy who would love (he thinks) to have live roaring tigers leap into the room out of his picture books, but who doesn't want to be afraid of them if they appear.

I was nervous too, of course. I felt sure that Dylan would disgrace himself at the reading. But I was entirely wrong. When Dylan got on the platform, no one could have told that he wasn't sober. He gave a masterly performance, not only of his own work, but of Hardy and many others. (I wish I had the program.) The marvellous beauty of his voice in the more serious poems can be heard on records, but I do wish I also had records of his comic reading. He was a brilliant comedian and mimic. The audience loved him—the students, that is.

Christopher Isherwood

1969

This afternoon Gary Bell and I went to Pershing Square (in Los Angeles) to listen to some of the old ladies in sneakers tell us to be prepared to meet our maker. I confess I enjoy rapping with them and usually wind up assured that eternal salvation is beyond my reach.

Later on we came across a group that was into the Indian thing and they were chanting *Hari Krishna Rama Rama,* etc., and I got to talking to one of them, who said their religion simply was to reaffirm love of God regardless of the particular religion and I thought that was fair enough and we hung around enjoying the chanting and sitar music.

Then a priest, probably about fifty-five years old, happened by and got into conversation with one of the group. When he left

I asked what it was about. "He said this was a religion that didn't belong in this country," the young man said. "He said we already had enough religions in this country and that we should go back to India or wherever it was we came from."

Going over the hitters is something you do before each series, and before we went against the mighty Angels, Sal Maglie had a great hint for one of their weaker hitters, Vic Davalillo. "Knock him down, then put the next three pitches knee-high on the outside corner, boom, boom, boom, and you've got him."

Everybody laughed. If you could throw three pitches, boom, boom, boom, knee-high on the outside corner, you wouldn't have to knock anybody down. It's rather like telling somebody if he'd just slam home those ninety-foot putts he'd win the tournament easily.

Jim Bouton

APRIL 11

1939

I hope you like the watch; if not, we'll exchange it. In the meantime, please use it to help me count the minutes.

I adore you forever, darling.

P.S. Kiss the children for me, if you've had mumps. I love you.

Ogden Nash

1946

Spent the morning at the studio in a whirl of wild activity. Billy and I lunched with Leland at Lucey's and talked the chances of a percentage deal. We then came to Billy's and tried to write a simple connective scene and Billy paced up and down moaning that he was unhappy about it and we didn't get far. His desire to have every syllable a laugh has become, to me, pathological and boring.

CHARLES BRACKETT

APRIL 12

1867

Rained all last night and until noon. Cleared up splendidly in p.m. but was quite cool. See nothing of Jim yet in town. Must settle matters soon for cash is getting most derned low. By my foolishness in getting a book to read I am now one bit short of enough to pay for present week's board, so next week I shall again be literally penniless.

WILLIAM HENRY JACKSON

1907

Cousin Lem Graves walked into the office today—he has not been well and he and Cousin Jennie are going to San Diego to rest. They are old people and find Los Angeles far too disturbing. . . . Ordered a new tailored-gown today—a white French worsted with invisible old-blue line in it. It will be charming and wholly impracticable for me, a country resident. But I am very tired of being practical. . . . I ought to have ordered a dark suit—something suitable for Sunday, Monday and all the year around! But I didn't!

Mrs. Foster's luncheon at the California Club yesterday and the matinee-party afterward was a perfectly arranged affair—

quite ideal. . . . Did not think much of the performance of "Candida."

Olive Percival

1963

Dear diary: Mama woke me up this morning to tell me to wash my hair. . . . How can I just sit and resign my body to such a life.

Octavia E. Butler

1966

Volume 1 of the Diary is published!

. . . [The *Los Angeles Times* book critic] Robert Kirsch confirmed my belief that if one goes deeply enough into the personal, one transcends it and reaches beyond the personal.

At the end of this Diary I feel I have accomplished what I hoped to accomplish: to reveal how personal errors influence the whole of history and that our real objective is to create a human being who will not go to war.

Anaïs Nin

APRIL 13

1876

A general flare up in the office. Col. Peel, who was acting editor in the absence of Bassett, had a clash with the management and was relieved. The bone of contention was the newly appointed Board of Public Works and its support by the paper.

Hancock Johnson, the President of the company, then came

to me and gave the editorial charge of the paper into my hands. I employed Hawley as city editor and went into the job with all the energy I could muster but not without some misgivings. This is my first experiment at real editorial work and the opportunity has been thrust upon me almost without a moment's notice.

William Andrew Spalding

1982

HOW I NEVER SAW THE HOLLYWOOD LIBRARY

The Hollywood Library burned down this morning. I was in the neighborhood one evening—about three weeks ago. I was circling the building by chance, wondering what this imposing structure represented. Why was it here? Finally, I came around to the front and read the letters engraved into the stone: "Los Angeles Public Library Hollywood Branch." Oh! The Hollywood Library—it was a tempting 30's classic revival building. I made a mental note to myself to return to the library by day. I was sure the inside would contain details undreamt of to delight my senses.

It burned down this morning.

Not a single book in its collection was saved.

Aaron Paley

APRIL 14

1882

I worked at the Orphans' Home, both yesterday and today. Mamie is giving a concert for the home tomorrow night, and she is training the orphans to sing. Velma also helps to rehearse them. General William T. Sherman arrived this morning to attend the reunion of the Grand Army of the Republic. This evening Mamie and I called upon General Sherman and his daughter, and we met General Poe and Adjutant General Morrill or Morrow. We had a very delightful evening, listening to General Sherman's reminiscences, especially about his famous "March to the Sea." The conversation was interrupted only once, by the arrival of a group of Grand Army men, who marched up to the house and demanded that he come out and speak to them; so he went to the balcony and delivered a short address.

L. VERNON BRIGGS

1934

I now happen to live in both towns, back and forth, and to like certain things in both of them. . . .

The New Yorker transplanted to Los Angeles may in a year or so learn to like the place. . . . He can learn to stay home from banquets where they may discuss "our beloved California." And he will come to enjoy living outdoors, and stepping out into a garden instead of into an elevator.

DON HEROLD

1965

This is to record progress, physical mental and psionic toward my chosen goal. This is my first entry.

Octavia E. Butler

APRIL 15

1867

Went down to corral about 7. Sam came after a while & we made preparations to brand some mules he had sold. Lassoed them quickly, & soon had 'em branded. Were wild devils & gave me a great lurch over the ground, "busting" my breeches & skinning my knees.

William Henry Jackson

APRIL 16

1945

Spoke this evening on station KFI, debating the Japanese question. . . . Later received a threatening phone call from a man who gave his name as A. B. Williams, 4975 Wilshire Blvd. Am noting this for the record.

Carey McWilliams

1945

My first act was to clean the clutter out of the big office and restore it to a state of purity and emptiness reminiscent of the days of [producer] Arthur Hornblow. I don't know whether it was doing so that made me miss the wild young Wilder excessively all day.

CHARLES BRACKETT

1972

Thank you for your marvellous letter about spring in Mississippi—it's spring in California, too, and to the delight of the hummingbirds the bottlebrush in our garden is exploding in red blossoms, and yes, you can see the spring on its way when you look out over the sea, literally on its way, with schools of whales and flights of scoters and Bonaparte gulls and other birds all heading north. . . .

My book such as it is is moving along towards the end of the first draft. I can't vouch for its quality but am simply grateful that I was able to get it written—rewriting is less impossible. Between drafts we'll head north with the Bonaparte gulls, for a week or two.

ROSS MACDONALD, to Eudora Welty

APRIL 17

1848

I have neglected to note down many occurrences of late and this is the first time I have opened my journal for many days—there is however but little stirring. [Kit] Carson is making preperations to leave this country for the United States and we are all grumbling at our hard fate in not being permitted to go with him—We have parades every day, duty is harder now than ever—the battalion paraded in white pants this morning in the publick square and looked well

LIEUTENANT JOHN MCHENRY HOLLINGSWORTH

1928

One fine day last week Henry, Brett, and I packed cameras, paints, lunch, and went to Santa Monica for work and outing. I had grown tired of "still-life," of confinement,—I wanted air and soil. Santa Monica was chosen because of a fine group of sycamore trees

I have printed another of the sycamore tree which I like without question. It is life at first hand. . . .

Perhaps the most fun I have had lately has been in a swimming hole discovered by Cole and Neil. It was reminiscent of Huckleberry Finn, with bonfires, rafts and naked boys. Fed by fresh river water this hole gouged out by steam shovel is deep enough for diving, and much larger than the local swimming tanks. It is hidden from public gaze so no spinster can be horrified by naked boys and men.

EDWARD WESTON

APRIL 18

1847

Singing and remarks by Pres. St. John on the evils arising in the Battalion, to wit: drunkenness, swearing and intercourse with the squaws &c.

HENRY STANDAGE

1949

Today the temperature is about forty-two, the sky is the color of mud, and the walls drip. During the ten days when we were scouting around, we found the sun bright and the sea inviting. We couldn't accept the invitation. We aren't even invited today.

Nothing short of a seal would enter the Pacific today.

ROBERT PENN WARREN, to his editor

1950

I am without the one thing in life that matters to me, which happens to be a small unhappy blonde in Laugharne, Carmarthenshire. Went to Hollywood, dined with Charlie Chaplin, saw Ivan Moffat, stayed with Christopher Isherwood, was ravingly miserable for you my true, my dear, my one, my precious love.

I LOVE YOU XXX

DYLAN THOMAS, to his wife

1955

How far away that night at Sanary seems—the shooting stars and then your wife's accident! A long time during which two individuals grow almost into one organism, whose separation leaves the survivor feeling strangely amputated.

Aldous Huxley, to Lion Feuchtwanger

1962

The remarkable thing is that, despite the explosion of gracious living that has erupted all over the American landscape on the shores of the illimitable river of gold that irrigates all our other-directed life—nothing has changed south of the Tehachapi. It is still all one Blue Plate Special.

Kenneth Rexroth

APRIL 19

1923

A Mr. Allen, Madame Alberti's brother, took me in his car and gave me a ride all about Hollywood, passing in ranks hundreds of the gay little stucco bungalows in the Spanish-Mexican, Italian-Swiss, and many other styles, a conglomeration that cannot be equaled anywhere else on earth I am quite sure. Someone has laid awake nights to think up these queer facades, porches, roofs, and towers. Some were cheery but many were merely curious or petty. Some elaborate places were English or partly Italian with formal gardens and stately trees.

I have never seen so many buildings going up all at one time. There are thousands in process in every direction I looked.

We rode back into the hills where they put their cars into their attics—literally—and have their stump of a house on the edge of the cliffs. Some of it was quite like Italy. A mad era of house building is on. How long it will continue is a question but I see no reason why it should not continue. The whole Middle West wants to come here. It is the only alternative to New York.

HAMLIN GARLAND

APRIL 20

1882

We were indeed sorry to leave such good friends, and the delightful hospitality of Los Angeles. Soon after our train passed Walters, a station on the Southern Pacific Railroad, a terrific sandstorm struck us; double windows and tightly closed doors failed to keep out the dust.

L. VERNON BRIGGS

1901

In the morning went to Los Angeles in the electric car. . . . we went to [the] O'Melveny office in the Baker Block and we tried to arrange the business of lands in Sta Monica and San Vicente. Mr. Jones left the papers for O'Melveny to review them. O'Melveny said he had paid Arcadia's taxes in the amount of $14,000. Jesus Bildaria who died suddenly two days ago was buried. Heard also that Luis Forbes son of Carlos died last night.

DON JUAN BAUTISTA BANDINI

APRIL 21

1945

Spent a weird evening on Aline Hill conferring with [heiress] Aline Barnsdall, about her twenty cocker spaniel dogs and her endless feud with the city of Los Angeles. . . . Then to dinner at Tam o' Shanter.

CAREY MCWILLIAMS

1950

The urgency is so great that I have worked all day and night to get this finished, and have sent a man into town with it, so that no time will be lost. . . .

I am now, like a fiendish machine, starting on another one.

DALTON TRUMBO, to his agent

APRIL 22

1920

Once home (588 N. Larchmont) write various letters & finally work on *Newspaper Days.* At 4 Helen comes. In a kind of wild desperation over not having all the money she wants she has pawned her ring & bought two hats, 1 dress, shoes & some stockings. Her frenzy of delight over her purchases. Wildly describes their beauty. Drunkenness in men & clothes buying in women are kindred passions. It is a kind of debauch. The gleam in her eyes. I cannot complain for the ring is her own. Her beauty in one of the new hats staggers me. We fool around & finally indulge in a fierce round after which I return to work. Am working on the porch this day in the sun.

THEODORE DREISER

1944

I have a considerable talent, perhaps as good as any coeval. But I am 46 now. So what I will mean soon by "have" is "had."

WILLIAM FAULKNER, to his agent

1971

At that time in Watts there was an Italian man, named Simon Rodia—though some people said his name was Sabatino Rodella, and his neighbors called him Sam. He had a regular job as a tile setter, but on weekends and at nighttime, under lights he strung up, he was building something strange and mysterious and he'd been working on it since before my boy was born. Nobody knew what it was or what it was for. Around his small frame house he had made a low wall shaped like a ship and inside it he was constructing what looked like three masts, all different heights, shaped like upside-down ice cream cones.

First he would set up skeletons of metal and chicken wire, and plaster them over with concrete, then he'd cover that with fancy designs made of pieces of seashells and mirrors and things. He was always changing his ideas while he worked and tearing down what he wasn't satisfied with and starting over again, so pinnacles tall as a two-story building would rise up and disappear and rise again. . . .

Mr. Rodia was usually cheerful and friendly while he worked, and sometimes, drinking that good red wine from a bottle, he rattled off about Amerigo Vespucci, Julius Caesar, Buffalo Bill and all kinds of things he read about in the old encyclopedia he had in his house. . . . the local rowdies came around and taunted him and threw rocks and called him crazy, though Mr. Rodia didn't seem to pay them much mind.

CHARLES MINGUS

APRIL 23

1847

I went today to visit an old Spaniard from Spain who had some American papers, also some books from whom I learned a little more of the Spanish language.

HENRY STANDAGE

1867

At half an hour after supper while we were all around the fire joking & making merry Jim came down the road, his horse covered with sweat & reported that he had lost every single head of the horses. He had no sooner relieved Sam than they gave a snort, turned quickly & stampeded, nearly ran over him. Tried to follow them in the darkness & fog, but soon lost them and himself too. Struck the ravine above camp and followed it down until he found us. Concluded that there was not a particle of use to try & follow them that night for we should only lose ourselves in the fog, & with but small probabilities of finding anything, so we all bunked in to prosecute the search in the a.m.

WILLIAM HENRY JACKSON

1925

Today Ronald Colman and Constance Talmadge started on a new picture. I believe it will be called "The Twins." I was on the stage watching them "shoot" a scene and was quite thrilled watching them both act. Ronald is certainly good looking and he's so modest about it that one can't help but like him. Ronald doesn't like Constance at all and I'm wondering if he'll be able to make love to her sincerely. There is no doubt that at some time or other he'll be called upon to do it, as movies are never made without (as they call it here) "heart interest."

. . . Mr. Goldwyn has married Miss Frances Howard. In a way I'm glad because it might make him just a little more gentle and considerate of his secretary. . . .

Last Saturday I was driving through the mountains near Los Angeles and through orange groves. The groves are now in blossom and the odor is almost sickening it is so strong. You can usually smell a grove about a mile before you get to it.

Valeria Belletti

APRIL 24

1942

I asked my sister to tell me the situation in detail as soon as possible if she goes to Santa Anita. Are we going to be confined in a horse track? Until today, we had gone there as a family on a number of occasions to entertain visitors from Japan. . . .

There may be many among the white people who say, "So what? Even horses, there are Arabian horses worth a hundred and fifty thousand dollars which is a lot more than you worthless Japanese. . . ." But we are human beings. Humans are the lord of all primates. Just because we became enemy nationals, we didn't drop in rank to an animal. We have the pride of possessing mystical blood and spiritual depth of the East. Who would have thought that war, war between Japan and America, a war that was planned in a world we had no knowledge of even in our dreams, would get us involved this deeply and cause us to suffer? Crime? Where should we look in ourselves to find our offense for which we must be treated like this?

. . . Evening, I heard Santa Anita stinks with the odor of dead horses, and Owens Valley is a place troubled by terrible whirlwinds of dust clouds.

AOKI HISA

1953

We saw Mary and Richard the other night at the showing of Charlie Brackett's film about the Titanic—Richard [Quine] so Olympianly the great director that he could hardly make himself aware of the existence of ordinary insects like ourselves. . . .

Do you ever plan to come out here? It isn't so bad, after all; so perhaps you'll bring yourself to take the westward plunge. In the meantime this brings you all our love.

P.S. Your picture hangs in my room. It is a constant reminder of you.

ALDOUS HUXLEY, to Anita Loos

APRIL 25

1949

Yesterday we went for a long drive through the blossoms. Last Friday I started teaching a course for the psychoanalytic candidates to great success.

THEODOR ADORNO

1974

April 25. The friction that's been building with the studio for some time came to a head today. I never approved the original ending where my character survived the earthquake. They agreed to a change to accommodate my death in a futile, doomed effort to save my bitchy wife, which seems to me to lend some credibility to a basically implausible story. (An earthquake destroys the whole *city*, this guy with the mean wife and the neat girl friend escapes scot-free, wife killed, neat girl left alive for him while he rebuilds Los Angeles?) Anyway, they kept edging up on me about shooting an alternate ending. I've been at this trade too long not to know better than that. Script approval doesn't help you if you've shot it.

CHARLTON HESTON

APRIL 26

1847

Last night we were called up and ordered to load and fix bayonets, as the Col. had sent word that an attack might be expected from Col. Fremont's men before day. They have been all using all possible means to prejudice the Spaniards and Indians against us by telling them we would take their wives &c. thereby rousing an excitement through the country. The Col hearing that they were intending to come sent us word. They did not come.

HENRY STANDAGE

1928

Since the fleet with its 25,000 gobs has left for Hawaii I have had a chance to recognize the full inconsequence of this Pollyanna greasepaint pinkpoodle paradise.

HART CRANE

1954

I don't like it here. I don't like people here. I like it home (N.Y.). . . . Must I always be miserable? I try so hard to make people reject me. Why? . . . I WANT TO DIE. . . . Wow! Am I fucked up. I got no motorcycle I got no girl. . . . Kazan sent me out here to get a tan. Haven't seen the sun yet. (fog & smog) Wanted me healthy looking. I look like a prune. . . .

Jim {Brando Clift} Dean

JAMES DEAN

APRIL 27

1863

Mr. Banning himself was on board of the vessel at the time of the explosion and was thought to have been dangerously wounded. He sent me word by express to come to his aid at once, whereupon I obtained leave of absence from my superior officer County Clerk Shore and hastened to the spot. O, horrors of horrors! . . .

Of the about fifty persons who happened to be on board but three or four escaped injury, among them the engineer, Clark, and the fireman. The wreck sank immediately.

On my arrival at San Pedro I found my beloved friend and employer unable to concentrate his mind, and I at once realized that I had to take matters into my own hands, which task I did not underrate. . . . In addition to this, the many able hands that lay helpless in death, and the sight of the many noble men whose hearts beat no more actually dazed me.

When I entered the large warehouse, so well known to me, I found it partly turned into a morgue, as more than twelve bodies had already been brought in and stretched out on primitive frames. In some cases it was impossible to recognize them, as even the very features were distorted or torn to pieces. . . . whenever a new body was brought in from the shore and we recognized the well known figure of some honest co-worker, our hearts grew weak and work went on slowly. Then came calls from mourning friends, whose piercing cries would melt the coldest hearts. One by one they finally were laid to rest—and may they rest in peace!

FRANK LECOUVREUR

1982

Everyday I've been taking the bus. The 93 to the 212 to any bus on Wilshire. And I look for the little details in the landscape that provide some solace. They are discontinuous, tiny at times, insignificant features, but my mind ties them together and I see elements of how this city could have some sense of urban continuity and please us aesthetically also.

One thing I've noticed is the two old canary palms that diagonally cut across a corner lot marking the entrance to Universal City. They were well placed. They marked out "gateway." The large billboard "Welcome to Universal City" in black and white was placed directly in front of them. It was very stupid. Considering how marvelously the two palm trees already said the same thing.

It was disturbing this morning to see a crane and crew of workers pulling one of the palm trees out of the ground.

And the other? . . .

It happens so quickly in L.A.

AARON PALEY

APRIL 28

1774

At seven we continued our journey along the little range mentioned, going east-northeast for more than a league, when we descended and finished the range. Then crossing the plain to the east, which lasted for about four leagues, we went three more over broken country in the same direction, making a total of more than eight leagues, arriving after ten hours of travel at five in the afternoon at Porciúncula River, where we camped for the night. As soon as we halted I sent three soldiers to the nearby mission of San Gabriel, in order that the commander of these establishments might be notified of my arrival there in the near future.

JUAN BAUTISTA DE ANZA

1919

I never loved any place in my life as I do this and if anything happens that I don't make a go of it I believe that it would about break my heart.

EDGAR RICE BURROUGHS

APRIL 29

1855

I preached this morning upon the destruction of Sodom and Gomorrah and had I wanted material for supposed scenes in those cities I could have found them in the very scenes now transpiring around me.

THE REV. JAMES WOODS

1992

The intricate framework of the neighborhood collapsed for a few hours. Drawn out onto the streets by a particularly nasty bit of apartment-house arson—not by any means a rarity around here—a crowd coalesced, moved to the supermarkets and, barred from there, into the strip malls that line Vermont Avenue. From the stoop of my building, it seemed like a giant block party, a looters' bacchanalia of new tennis rackets and boom boxes, then of liberated rental tapes from the video store, plastic-wrapped clothes from the dry cleaner and fake palm trees from the furniture store. On Vermont itself, I saw thousands of people out on an illegal shopping spree, cheerfully helping one another maneuver a sofa or a heavy Barcalounger across the busy street. One tired-looking cop drank a cup of coffee and tried not to look anyone directly in the eye. . . . [M]en stood rooftop sentry with Uzis, outlined against the orange sky. It was the first time I can remember being comforted by the sight of armed drug dealers.

JONATHAN GOLD

APRIL 30

1944

I think I have found an apartment, a little cubbyhole but in a quiet, convenient, *not Hollywood* neighborhood, with no yard, etc. But after several years of Rowan Oak and trees and grounds, maybe Big and Little Miss will enjoy living in a city apartment, with nothing to break the silence but the shriek of brakes and the crash of colliding automobiles, and police car and fire wagon sirens, and the sounds of other tenants in the building who are not quite ready to lay down and hush at 1 or 2 a.m.

WILLIAM FAULKNER, to his sister

MAY 1

1852

We entered upon a mountainous region of wonderful beauty, and finally descended to *La Ciudad de los Angeles* (The city of the angels). About a mile north of the city we stopped with the family of Hernando's uncle named Jimnes. Here we remained two days to let our horses rest, and I was glad of the opportunity, being almost tired out with the long ride. Owing to fatigue some objects of interest were not visited; but at the Jimnes home the orchards, vineyards, and flowers, with the delightful climate, impressed one with the idea that here was the veritable Garden of Eden.

THE REV. JOHN STEELE

1926

Our publicity man has just left—he's been offered a better job with the Hal Roach studios and I'm going to miss him terribly. We were such good friends. He used to listen so patiently to all my little troubles and love affairs. He is a confirmed bachelor and seemed to get an awful kick hearing of my escapades with my bohemian artist friends. . . . the other art director—Anton Grot—is behaving himself but I have to keep my distance. Every time I pass his studio he beckons for me to come in and have a chat, but I pass by and tell him I'm too busy to talk. . . .

Saturday night Jones had a dinner party at his studio and I was invited with Muschi. Much to my embarrassment, my ex-boyfriend John was there. I didn't recognize him and treated him like a complete stranger. Most of the evening I stayed in the back room with Muschi and two other men and we were talking on socialism and art and music, etc. One of the men had read all the German philosophers such as Kant, Hegel, Nietzsche, as well as August Strindberg and Shaw, so we were talking for about 3 hours. . . .

About 2:30 in the morning we were all still sitting there in that back room arguing when we heard a knock at the front door. Muschi looked out and saw it was a policeman, so he made me put on my hat and coat and we left the house through the back door. I was terribly frightened. I thought surely the house was being raided and I'd land in jail and there'd be a lot of nasty publicity. . . .

. . . If one is proper at all times, one does miss so much. Sometimes you do get into interesting situations by acting on the impulse. Of course, on the other hand, sometimes you become involved in an unpleasant situation, however you have to take a chance at all things—otherwise one's existence becomes somewhat humdrum.

VALERIA BELLETTI

MAY 2

1847

For the last two days I have been more or less through the City of Angels or as it is in Spanish Ciudad de los Angeles, and must say they are the most degraded set of beings I ever was among, professing to be civilized and taught in the Roman Catholic religion. There are almost as many grog shops and gambling houses in this city as there are private houses. . . .

. . . The Spaniards in general own large farms in the country and keep from one to 20,000 head of cattle. Horses in abundance, mules, sheep, goats &c. Also the Indians do all the labor and the Mexicans are generally on horse back from morning till night. They are perhaps the greatest horsemen in the known world, and very expert with the lance and lasso. They are in general a very idle, profligate, drunken, swearing set of wretches, with but very few exceptions. The Spaniards conduct in the Grog shops with the squaws is really filthy and disgusting even in the day time. Gambling is carried to the highest pitch, men often losing 500 dollars in cash in one night, or a 1000 head of cattle.

HENRY STANDAGE

1928

After Bertha's dance program on Olive Hill we went to Laurvik's to a party, a perfect evening which was prolonged into the morning. . . . I have not been joyfully *borrachito* in many moons.

EDWARD WESTON

1942

The searchlights go on in the evening and shine all night. We have to turn off our lights at ten and shut our radio at eight. . . .

It's real cold in the night. I caught a cold the first night and I can't get rid of it. . . . We have to get up early to eat or else they tell you to come back tomorrow morning. Goodby!

SANDIE SAITO

1969

New restaurants open and are suddenly full of people; where did they eat last week? I often think of the Cinema Theater, of how it used to be three, or was it four years ago. The midnight movies, a line outside all the way down the block past the O Sole Mio pizza restaurant where the owner painted on the window, THIS RESTAURANT FEATURED ON TV. The long line outside the theater made up of friends, it was getting there, into the films, that was half the fun. We would stand there, or rush up and down saying hello, Garry Taylor, his arms full of the then-struggling eight-page *Free Press* wandering by, hey buy the *Free Press*. . . .

Inside the lobby, those who were friends of the manager, a smiling and enthusiastic supporter of the real underground movie makers, named Mike Getz, would welcome the regular crowd of freeloaders. We would sip the free lemonade from paper cups and chat about the week's events. There was Jack Hirshman and his wife Ruth in her Garboesque hat and matching face. . . .

Finally inside, the regular Saturday night show patrons gone, we wandered down the aisles, more hellos, sliding into our seats, eating the imported chocolate bars Mike sold from a little push-cart in the lobby. Then Mike's disembodied voice over the microphone explaining things haltingly but with care, about the films, or places we should remember to go, like peace marches and poetry readings, and then, finally the films themselves. . . . When it was over we would hang around some more, discussing what we had seen, planning to come again next week, seeing those friends we only saw on these occasions, but who were friends nevertheless.

It is all different now; Mike Getz is away in some woodsy retreat planning shows for a whole chain of theaters. . . . But I understand, it is more businesslike, and more efficiently run, no more free lemonade, no more freeloaders, and surely more profitable, and will survive and flourish without us.

LIZA WILLIAMS

MAY 3

1927

I am afflicted with one of those dreadfully ambiguous names, and I am always put to the necessity, as I am at present, of correcting very logical, but erroneous, impressions about it. I would have preferred a name such as "George" or "John" or "Henry"—something unspeakably common but undeniably masculine.

CAREY MCWILLIAMS, to Mary Austin

1960

So, in sum, I am more concerned than angry, more irritated than exhilarated, by what I see encroaching upon us everywhere today. Commercialism and quack intellectualism, the twin demons, the dual evils of our time as in every other time. To kick them both in the balls is my desire.

RAY BRADBURY, to Esther McCoy

1968

Last night, 1.00 a.m., while taking a walk around the block suddenly a car stops short beside me and two teen agers, evidently on dope, begin to bully me, me, curse me. I wasn't far from the house, so I just kept walking, they following. I thought at one point they would jump out and tackle me, but fortunately they didn't. And I who talk about violence, do you know what was in my mind then? To let them follow me right to the house, let them follow in after me, and then I'd go get my razor sharp machete, which I keep handy, and cut them to ribbons. This sort of slaughter, you see, I regard as "justifiable." Afterwards I began trembling. Not because of what they might have done to me, but what I might have done to them! Beware of the peace lovers, I always say. Beware of the just man! Do you know what it is to dance with rage? That's what I do inwardly again and again. Fortunately I always wear my Buddha-like mask.

Henry Miller, to his wife

MAY 4

1883

We have just got back from our tour through the Indian villages: (18 in all) my opinion of human nature has gone down 100 per ct. in the last 30 days. Such heart sickening fraud, violence, cruelty as we have on earth here—I did not believe could exist in civilized communities—and "In the Name of the Law."

If I were to write a story with that title,—all Indian—would you print it? I have never before felt that I could write an Indian story. I had not got the background, now I have, and sooner or later, I shall write the story. Has anybody used that title?—Is it not a good one? It seems to me so—If I could write a story that would do for the Indian the thousandth part what Uncle Tom's Cabin did for the Negro, I would be thankful for the rest of my life.

Helen Hunt Jackson

1939

Let me be Los Angeles

James Joyce, in *Finnegans Wake*

MAY 5

1942

The rushes. Ginger not brilliant in the last scene. She was trying to give an Academy Award performance of an old lady, not the straightforward performance of a girl in love, forced to hide as an old lady. Worked at RKO all day.

CHARLES BRACKETT

1942

My body is shivering and will not stop. I wonder if a nervous breakdown is like this. I cannot afford to become ill, but after moving to the hotel, having to pay even more attention to my surroundings makes it even more difficult to sleep, and I am troubled. . . .

This kind of evacuation seemed like a spur of the moment thing, and I felt I was being jerked around like a puppet. After five, six days, there probably won't be a single Japanese remaining in Los Angeles.

. . . We, who until war broke out, thought we would live in America for the rest of our lives, became labeled as the enemy.

AOKI HISA

MAY 6

1936

Someone is building a house next door and all day I hear the slap of falling boards, the ring of saw and tap of hammers. To some people these sounds would be an irritation but to me they are pleasing. They have many delightful associations. They suggest the building of new towns and more intimately my own share [in] the several houses I have built or repaired. I think of my father's house in Dakota, in 1881; of the additions I made to the house in West Salem; to my share in the enlargement of the Onteora homes. It all has definite meaning. I can tell by the stroke of the hammer whether the men are setting studding, laying floor or putting on roof boards. I can tell by the sound of the saw whether a plank or a beam is being cut. I enjoyed building. I do yet, and the smell of new lumber is still a joyous agent. It means homes, good wages, firesides.

HAMLIN GARLAND

1943

We live our by now deeply habituated waiting-room days among our palms and *lemon trees*, in social concourse with the Franks, Werfels, Dieterles, Neumanns—always the same faces, and if occasionally an American countenance appears, it is as a rule so strangely blank and amiably stereotyped that one has had enough for quite some time to come. . . .

I have made up my mind to give the war time for one more novel, so that when it's over Bermann can march in through the Brandenburg Gate with four unknown books of mine. The completion of the *Joseph* [*and His Brothers*] is already well in the past; it was finished in January. . . .

Now I have something very different [*Doktor Faustus*] in mind, something rather uncanny, tending in the theological and demonological direction . . . the novel of a pathological, unlawful inspiration.

Thomas Mann

MAY 7

1853

I am . . . satisfied that any treaty made with these Indians without their first feeling our power would be of no avail—How easy [it would be] for those interested to make up a party and pay them a visit and convince them that they can no longer steal with impunity.

Benjamin Davis "Don Benito" Wilson

1927

B. came, bringing me a dainty glass fish,—M., a rare visitor, arrived with gardenias, followed by K. with a passion flower. Another day of near complications!

Edward Weston

1929

This is the most horrible, unreal place in the world, on a dreary curve of the coast, I have rheumatism dreadfully here, and never felt so down-and-out anywhere. . . . I live at a hotel and taxi-cab out to see mother in the afternoon.

Oh, if only this dreadful thing had happened at home, in a human land, where mother would have had her lovely grandchildren to watch and work, where there were dear old friends, kind neighbors, memories, God. There is no God in California, no real life. Hollywood is the flower of all the flowers, the complete expression of it.

Willa Cather, to Dorothy Canfield Fisher

1992

And yet the neighborhood survives, mango vendors and *paleta* carts flourishing in the morning-after calm like the cheerful green shoots that sprout from a newly charred forest floor, noodle shops and dumpling houses, doughnut stands and *taquerias* that swept away the broken glass and were running again the morning after the troubled afternoon. A lone, well-lighted Salvadoran restaurant in a blocklong burned-out mall stands improbable sentinel, churning out *pupusas* and *carne asada* although surrounded on either side by ruined stores, smoking rubble and military patrols.

Jonathan Gold

MAY 8

1901

The President arrived at 2 and is staying at the hotel Van Nuys. Cloudy day.

Don Juan Bautista Bandini

1901

I am glad to be in this great state, whose population today is more than one-third of the entire population of the United States over which the first president presided during eight years;

and I cannot stand in this presence without recalling those splendid pioneers of American civilization. Kearney and Stockton and Fremont, who blazed the path of progress and of civilization and dedicated this mighty empire of the Pacific coast to liberty and union forever. You have now, residing in your beautiful city, that aged woman who shared with General Fremont in his early and later trials and triumphs. I am sure you will all join with me in reverent and affectionate regard. . . .

They say liberty does not thrive under a tropical sun. Did liberty ever thrive more grandly than in the state of California and throughout our southland? I congratulate you upon the condition of the country in its entire extent from the bottom of my heart, for myself and for my associates, for this glorious welcome to this city, which I visit now for the second time. Twenty years ago, when I was here, you had a population of a little more than eleven thousand. Today you have a population of more than a hundred thousand, and in the last decade you have made a larger gain than any city of the country of fifty thousand inhabitants, a percentage, I believe, of over one hundred per cent. I congratulate you upon your local prosperity, and wish for you all love and contentment in your homes and prosperity in all your occupations. I beg to bid you good afternoon.

President William McKinley

1903

TWO YEARS LATER

Stayed at home all day. Thought of going to Los Angeles to see the parade for the Fiesta de las Flores and the arrival of President Roosevelt—the actual president of the nation visiting these parts—and at the moment I was leaving the house with Margarita, whom I was taking with me, Harry Gorham arrived to say that his father had died last night and as he had been such a close friend of mine he wanted me to be a pallbearer at 2 p.m. tomorrow. I felt so badly I didn't go to Los Angeles.

DON JUAN BAUTISTA BANDINI

1903

I greet you and thank you for the enjoyment you have given me to-day. I cannot say how I have appreciated being here in your beautiful state and your beautiful city. I do not remember ever seeing quite the parallel to the procession I have just witnessed. . . .

When I come to speak of the preservation of the forests, of the preservation of the waters, of the use of the waters from the mountains and of the waters obtained by artesian wells, I only have to appeal to your own knowledge, to your experience. I have been passing through a veritable garden of the earth yesterday and to-day, here in the southern half of California, and it has been made by the honesty and wisdom of your people, and by the way in which you have preserved your waters and utilized them. I ask that you simply keep on as you have begun, and that you let the rest of the nation follow suit. We must preserve the forests to preserve the waters, which are themselves preserved by the forests, if we wish to make this country as a whole blossom as you have made this part of California blossom.

In saying goodbye to you I want to say that it has been the greatest pleasure to see you, and I am glad, my fellow Americans, to think that you and I are citizens of the same country.

PRESIDENT THEODORE ROOSEVELT

1919

We eat and sleep Tarzan. . . . The dog is named Tarzan, the place is Tarzana. . . .

. . . A guy bobbed up day before yesterday with the plan of a whole village he wished to plant in my front yard—school, city hall, banks, business houses, motion picture theater—and it was labelled City of Tarzana, which sounds like a steamboat.

EDGAR RICE BURROUGHS

MAY 9

1850

Declarations Taken in Relation to the Massacre of Dr. Lincoln and His Party on the Colorado River.—Deposition of William Carr.

On this ninth day of May, in the year of Our Lord, Eighteen Hundred and Fifty, before me, Abel Stearns, first Alcalde of the District of Los Angeles, and Judge of the first instance in the criminal law, personally appeared William Carr, who being duly sworn, deposeth. . . .

Deponent, since he has been in Los Angeles, has heard some reports in reference to Glanton, or others of said company, robbing or otherwise mistreating Americans and Sonoraians. He has been with said company from the beginning, and positively and unequivocally denies the truth of such reports. . . .

As to the Indians, they always professed great friendship for the company, were continually about the premises, ate habitually in the houses, and were always treated with kindness personally.

WILLIAM CARR, as deposed by Abel Stearns

1901

Went to Los Angeles to see the floral parade. It was very large and very pretty headed by the President and his Cabinet. There was an enormous crowd. I have never seen so many people in the city. In the afternoon came to the Soldiers Home as the President was due to come there. He arrived at 3 p.m. and after seeing the retired soldiers drill he went back to Los Angeles.

DON JUAN BAUTISTA BANDINI

MAY 10

1856

In California there is no justice, no equality, no liberty. We ask in the name of reason and common sense if it would not be better for us to emigrate to the only asylum that guarantees our liberty.

FRANCISCO P. RAMIREZ

1926

I think I'm run down and I'll just have to quit going out so much and look after myself a bit. Mr. Goldwyn has been very considerate during my indisposition, which came as rather a surprise because his former secretary had told me that unless a girl was well and fit, he could be annoyed with her.

VALERIA BELLETTI

MAY 11

1939

Out here we have a strong progressive movement and I devote a great deal of time to it. Yet, although this new novel is about

Hollywood, I found it impossible to include any of those activities in it. I made a desperate attempt before giving up. I tried to describe a meeting of the Anti-Nazi League, but it didn't fit and I had to substitute a whorehouse and a dirty film. The terrible sincere struggle of the League came out comic when I touched it and even libelous. Take the "mother" in Steinbeck's swell novel—I want to believe in her and yet inside of myself I honestly can't. When not writing a novel—say at a meeting we have out here to help the migratory worker—I do believe it and try to act on that belief. But at the typewriter by myself I can't.

Nathanael West, to a critic

1941

It's the world's most sophisticated boulevard but I've seen a barrel organist with peaked hat and dancing monkey steal the thunder from a world premiere. . . . Half a block from my office I watched a mockingbird nest and raise her brood and the fledgling birds get more attention than Clark Gable. . . .

Early last Christmas morning practically the whole boulevard belonged to a little wirehaired terrier. He was a dirty little waif of a dog but someone had tied a bright red Christmas bow around his tail. And conscious of the splendor, he carried himself with such solemn dignity that he had the whole street in fits of laughter. . . .

The most informal, easygoing street in the nation and everybody wears the clothes that suit him best—or attract the most attention. The most bizarre rigs, from sun suits to ermine capes, mingle on the boulevard without causing heads to turn or tongues to wag.

Hedda Hopper

1943

I have a private office in the MGM administration building with desk, typewriter, phone and two easy chairs and a view over a pretty flower garden and the foothills of the San Bernardino Mountains. I came West in grand style. I had a compartment as far as Chicago and from there on, a lower berth on the Super Chief. It was a lovely trip and I rested and enjoyed it.

Tennessee Williams, to his parents

MAY 12

1911

As I was coming here this evening and reflected upon the name of this association, my thoughts naturally went back to that great man whose name you have adopted. And I asked myself, what would Jefferson say. . . .

The great antiseptic in America is public information and public opinion. You can clarify and purify the worst things in life by simply letting the eyes of honest Americans have access to them. So that we are driven to the conclusion that ["the political machine"] design[s] to accomplish things which they do not care to have exposed to the public view. They want privileges which are exclusive—they want those things which they alone should enjoy—they want protections to which they are not justly entitled.

Look at the other thing that is giving us trouble—it is simply another side of the same picture. Look at the corporations.

We are not hostile to corporations if corporations will prove that they are as much interested in the general welfare and the general development as we are. . . . America is not jealous of wealth, but it is jealous of ill-gotten wealth. America is willing to give largess of infinite fortune to anybody who will serve her, but she is very chary, if she could have her own way, of giving fortunes to anybody who will impose upon her. . . . The alliance of these men with politics is the most demoralizing thing that could possibly descend upon any country. And it has descended upon us. Those are the things that need correction in our politics, and these are the things to which a man who acted in the Jeffersonian spirit would have to address himself.

Woodrow Wilson

1920

We stage an orgie—so delightful that it knocks me out. Copulation is beginning to effect [*sic*] my heart.

Theodore Dreiser

1943

I had lunch with Christopher [Isherwood] today. I invited him to lunch at the Brown Derby. I recognized him at once, just by instinct, and he does look just the way I imagine myself to look—it was funny.

I like him awfully, and I think he must have thought me rather school-girlish about his writing which I place with Chekhov's.

Tennessee Williams

2006

Pierre and I drove all the way out to UCLA last night, for a much-anticipated concierto de Richard Thompson. . . . Bueno, first off, nos tomó más de dos horas y media to get there. Según Mapquest, it should take fifty-two minutes. . . . We could *never* afford Westwood, ni siquiera any other of the even semi-close-to-UCLA barrios en un sueldo cacadémico, no matter how "good." . . .

For the privilegio de vivir en el über-hip Westside, tendríamos que cough up.

SUSANA CHÁVEZ-SILVERMAN

MAY 13

1848

I took a ride with my friend Doña Arcadia Stearns to day—It was a lovely afternoon and I have seldom spent so pleasant a time—I have many fears that were it not for that hateful incumbrance of a husband she has I should never leave California! He was along with [us] last evening kept close to her side but he need not have been jealous of me—I did not know when I went to ride with her that a large party were going—I have never attempted any puppyism with her and never will—

. . . I leave here in a few days for Santa Iago on a visit of pleasure in company with Capt Smith, 1st Drag and Lieut Davidson, same corps. They go to visit the battle ground of [San Pasqual] for the purpose of having the bodies of the officiers who fell there removed to a better place—

LIEUTENANT JOHN MCHENRY HOLLINGSWORTH

1943

Yesterday, I had lunch with Tennessee Williams, the writer. He's a strange boy, small, plump and muscular, with a slight cast in one eye; full of amused malice. He has a job with Metro. He wanted to buy an autoglide to ride to work on. I tried to dissuade him, but he insisted. We went to a dealer's, and he suggested a very old junky machine which is obviously going to give trouble.

Christopher Isherwood

2003

My name is Kevin Roderick. I am an author, a journalist, an Angeleno and wear assorted other labels. I suppose I'm also now a blogger. . . .

L.A. Observed is a logical step in my online evolution. . . . You can't be a serious consumer of L.A. news without registering at the LAT site, for instance. Submit bogus demographic data if it makes you feel better. I'm on the books as a 99-year-old woman with no income and an Alaska zip code at sites with the temerity to ask. . . .

I can't say yet how active this site will be. Let me know how you think it's going by email. If you don't want your email to show up on the page, say so. If you are rude and abusive I may use it anyway with suitable derision applied.

Kevin Roderick

MAY 14

1888

There is something in the crisp, rarified air of this pretty city that acts like a stimulant upon the human system. Take a walk down Spring street (the principal thoroughfare) any bright, sunny day, and you will be struck by the keen, tingling thrill of life. There are no loafers, no dawdlers, no gossipers, no obstructers of the public highway. Even the bootblacks are relegated to their apportioned recesses, and the transplanted bore forgets, in the pushing throng, to buttonhole his victim.

. . . Think of the amount of capital required to grade miles upon miles of streets, build reservoirs, bore artesian wells, plant flowers, lay out orange groves and construct city pavements; to build in such a place, without any surety of people! it is very much like putting the cart before the horse. There is no end to those newly-sprung places. They form a perfect net-work about Los Angeles.

It is the easiest thing in the world to be drawn into the land fever. Real estate offices are as plentiful as bees on an August day. You pass along and you see some such sign as the following: "Bargain! For one day, Tract of land, Utopia, $25 to $100 per lot." This looks interesting; to buy a lot of land for $25 and sell it, perhaps, in a week or two for $50, titillates the mercenary palate. You are like a dull fly in the toils of an affable spider, with this difference, that, nine times out of ten, you take your turn at being the spider and someone else becomes the fly.

Undoubtedly Southern California is the garden spot of America, and judging from its past prosperity and progress it must hold a magnificent future. No one, even the most prejudiced, can dispute its advantages. The most stolid and lymphatic native must be stung into an appreciation of his country's resources and dream that he has reached that Biblical land flowing with milk and honey.

Harriet Harper

1929

If I ever get away, I'll never come within a thousand miles of the place again. Everything is commonplace and nothing is real. Even the mountains round about look like papier mâché movie sets. . . .

The hotel clerk is a hero because he has a child that is "used" in the movies. A few blocks away a retired farmer from Iowa sits in a pseudo-Norman tower in his shirt sleeves eating pie with his knife; he saw the tower in one of DeMille's pictures, and liked it and copied it. Not far from him are three bungalows that look like Egyptian tombs; they were copied from Egyptian tombs in the movies. There are strange cults everywhere—fake oriental, etc.: hermits in the canyons. Well, you would think all this incongruity might be interesting; but it isn't. It is only dull. All the stupidities of all the world center here. Back of the stupidity is a cold, crooked-hearted commercialism—not merely in the movies, but in business generally—that is appalling. There is a veneer of free western heartiness over it. It is an outfit of skinners. They skinned the Indian; they skinned the Mexicans and Spaniards around the country formerly; they skinned the later settlers from the Middle West; they are here to skin tourists; they skin each other.

Don Marquis, to a friend

1935

This magnificent structure [the Griffith Observatory] will be of value not only to the scientists, but its greatest attraction will be to the masses of other citizens who will now have an opportunity to see how the universe is constructed.

Robert Millikan

1935

I finally offered my resignation. In typical Hollywood fashion it was rejected. I was fired two days later.

Eric Knight, to a friend

MAY 15

1945

A day largely involved with [*The Lost Weekend*] . . . tried to work out a substitute for "The early morning sunlight hitting the grey tin of the ashcans" lines. . . . I talked with Billy in New York about our proposed cuts and Billy purported to be suicidal about them. . . . I've got to talk to Rosza about the music, which must have an excitement it now lacks.

CHARLES BRACKETT

1950

It appears that any Monday I shall go to jail.

DALTON TRUMBO

MAY 16

1928

A big step forward in modern civilization was made last night here in Los Angeles (the last place you would expect civilization to advance). It was a dinner given at $100 a plate, with the distinct understanding there would be no speeches. The place was sold out and everybody tickled to death. The funds from the dinner were divided among those who wanted to make speeches but were not allowed. Everyone in the hall received $100.

WILL ROGERS

MAY 17

1887

The train killed a man last night—mangled him. He was a laborer and a stranger here. Grand Opera co began in Los Angeles there will be five performances.

Don Juan Bautista Bandini

1939

We had an hour to spare, and we spent it finding an apartment.

Christopher Isherwood

1982

Tonight we all met at the demonstration to protest CBS' cancellation of the *Lou Grant Show*. If people took every Monday night to walk 3 km, meet with their friends and talk, it would really change their lives. As it is, they only get out into the street once in a great while. For demonstrations. And how many trees have I seen them cut down since I've been here? The people I know are caught up in their individual lives or their jobs. . . .

I walked over to CBS from my place here on Orange Drive. The colors of the sunset were amplified by the smog particles in the air. The palm trees silhouetted à la Ruscha.

Aaron Paley

MAY 18

1847

Walked over to Don Luis, met a large party of ladies. Spent a pleasant time Had the band there, gave them some musick. Rode the Col's horse home. Saw a beautiful Spanish girl there, gave her a bouquet, & murdered Spanish at her at a great rate.

LIEUTENANT JOHN MCHENRY HOLLINGSWORTH

1918

Came home. Spent the rest of the afternoon on the throne of China. I was constipated.

AGNES DE MILLE

MAY 19

1961

New York is a real city—Los Angeles has no navel.

BRENDAN BEHAN, to his half brother

1968

My determination to eliminate RFK is becoming more and more of an unshakable obsession. RFK must die. RFK must be killed. Robert F. Kennedy must be assassinated. . . . Robert F. Kennedy must be assassinated before 5 June 68.

SIRHAN SIRHAN

2004

The baskets are 10 feet high, with giant and very forgiving backboards. A couple of kids from the neighborhood start playing with a kickball at another hoop, and we invite them to join us instead. They are young, fifth-graders, so we split them up: Carlos plays on Steve's team and Matthew joins me. We play two games of two-on-two and one game of H-O-R-S-E. Matthew's third-grade brother, Justin, who can't quite throw a ball up to the basket yet, watches from the sidelines.

Talking to Carlos, I learn that his father also works at City Hall. I realize that Carlos Jr. is the son of a janitor I know, Carlos Sr., who has told me before that he lives in the neighborhood. I have an extra basketball at home, so I give Carlos my ball and walk home to dinner.

MAYOR ERIC GARCETTI, then a city councilman

MAY 20

1927

A letter at last came from Consuela, who took six or eight prints of mine to New York. I wanted to have her arrange for an exhibit, and to show the work to several persons, among them Alfred Stieglitz.

She writes: "Stieglitz seemed disappointed. He thought your technique was very fine but felt the prints lacked life, fire, were more or less dead things not a part of today."

If I had sent my toilet, for instance, how then would he have reacted? And must I do nothing but toilets and smokestacks to please a Stieglitz! Is his concern with subject matter? Are not shells, bodies as much of today as machines?

EDWARD WESTON

1937

Through pristine San Clemente which I remember from Laguna days—all white bldgs. with red tile roofs—such an uncomfortable looking place—one rebel gas station has painted green bills on his windows and we bet the town council will soon see to him.

CHARIS WILSON

MAY 21

1846

All agree a separation from Mexico is absolutely necessary.

HENRY DALTON

1943

I think it is one of the funniest but most embarrassing things that ever happened to me, that I should be expected to produce a suitable vehicle for [Lana Turner]. . . . I feel like an obstetrician required to successfully deliver a mastodon from a beaver.

. . . I no longer feel any compunction whatsoever about the huge salary I am getting, as I shall certainly earn it.

Christopher Isherwood warns me that I must not take to drink, as most Hollywood writers do.

TENNESSEE WILLIAMS

MAY 22

1939

I walk along the sea on Sunday. It is a beautiful day—cool and sunny. The cottages that were closed are now being opened, those for rent occupied. Out of one cottage tumbles a family of Jews—mamma and three or four assorted children and papa himself stands in front of the door to his neighbor's cottage—planted in the very middle of the sidewalk, right in front of the door. Mamma is on the stairs of her cottage and talking to her chicks; one is going back into the house, another to the sea, still another up the street. . . .

The Gentile couple (a dark young man and a slender blonde girl) are trying their best not to see him, although he has placed himself, big belly, big smile and all, right in the middle of the sidewalk in front of the door. They enter the house, gazing intently at a dog in a neighbor's yard and when they reach their door they almost hop into the house and close the door quickly behind them.

Charles Reznikoff

MAY 23

1850

Twenty times in our presence they stated that they were at war with all Americans, and the chief himself told us we were the last party that should ever cross there, and that he intended to keep "muchos" Indians scattered along the road, to kill the Americans as they came along and take their animals.

Jeremiah Hill

1919

No one can imagine what this means to the young people of this part of the world nor what this institution will one day become.

UCLA Vice President Ernest Carroll Moore

1940

Do you want parking meters in front of your place of business?

Al Waxman

MAY 24

1880

As this is my last evening, I am going to the library to play chess.

I am here but I don't see any of the chess fiends. Ha! Here comes Mr. Gillmore. I don't like to play him much on my last night here as he is the best player that plays here. He is too hard a game for me to tackle. But I'll play him anyhow. He can't do more than beat me.

We have played the first game and I got beat. We are in the second game and I have the advantage so far. Ha! That was a bad move I made. That beats me. I did not see his castle. Colonel Morey says I had the game sure, but I made a mistake and am beaten again. This is the last game we can play. I must win this game or be disgraced. Mr. Gillmore has a good deal of confidence now. He thinks he will beat me easily this time. At the fifteenth move the game is about even. After the twenty-fifth move I think Mr. Gillmore has a little advantage, but I think I can lay a trap for him here. If he makes a certain move, he's gone.

He makes it and I mate him very prettily in three moves. Mr. Gillmore looks rather sad. He says he could have won the game but Colonel Morey says I had the best of it all the way through. Anyhow I have won the last game I have played in Los Angeles.

As it is ten o'clock, the library is closing. I just stopped in to Noel's on the way home. I stayed there fifteen minutes, then I went home with Johnny Bourjette. Just met Pa at the corner of Main and Third Street. He asked me to take a little walk. We went downtown. We went until the courthouse. Pa went into Jerry's Chop House to eat some oysters. I did not eat any as I don't like them.

MANNIE LOWENSTEIN

1935

Schoenberg teaches me counterpoint now. And I am very happy because my work seems to please him. Today he turned to the other two pupils and said: You see, I don't even have to look at it (my exercises), I know they're right. He is a teacher of great kindness and understanding and it is a rich comfort that he gives. . . .

And now—, Xenia. All I know is that she will be here early in June; that there was a formal announcement (her sister's idea) in order that "showers" might follow; and that I am, according to mother, as unprepared as if I were living on the streets (Xenia knows this and says she will accept even starvation with me "gracefully"). . . .

I ran into a lady who has a daughter. And she claims that although the injections are necessary that they alone will not do the thing, that diet is of supreme importance. She has taken the whole matter very scientifically. Vitamins . . . Yeast. A vegetable juicer.

JOHN CAGE, to Pauline Schindler

MAY 25

1888

Everyone is a Bohemian, a civilized nomad, and finds his meals wherever fate lands him. If he discovers the aching void while he is in the adobe town, he asks the handsome, dark-eyed señorita for hot tomales and chocolate. If he is in Chinatown he gets a cup of delicious tea and a bird's nest. If he feels flush he crosses the elegant threshold of "Koster's;" if poor he tries the "Silver Moon," where, for twenty-five cents, you get soup, several kinds of meat, all vegetables in the market, ice-cream, pie and coffee. You can live like a prince, or you can dine luxuriously as a pauper.

There is an old cathedral down in adobe town, the "Cathedral of the Queen of the Angels," where I rather like to find myself. It is built of adobe, and has no special architecture, being low and broad, with an ill-proportioned attempt at cruciform, and possessing an altogether familiar and undignified air, standing forth on Main Street like some rotund, worldly abbot, brushing his skirts against the sordid stream of human life. Passing through a graveled yard, with a great wooden paintless cross set in its center, you find the side entrance. The door is always open; you pass inside and see a wooden floor, worn into little shelving hollows by the friction of faithful feet. It is the oldest looking, darkest, dingiest sort of a church imaginable, though built in 1823, and comparatively in its prime. The straight-backed, wooden pews are cut and scarred, and boast neither cushions or stools. Against the low, white walls, the different stations of the cross are marked by crude lithographic representations. . . .

I often punctuate my walks by a quiet seat in this unlovely sanctuary, for its very mustiness is redolent of those old days when the sun lay in long lazy bars across the clustering adobes; when the Mexican with his broad sombrero, and the senorita with gleams of bright gold swinging from her ears, lived their dreamy, purposeless lives, and weened not of the great city that was to spring up and crush out their sunny solving of existence.

Harriet Harper

1938

Going to breakfast along one of the alleys of the studio, I find a row of actresses waiting on camp chairs and benches outside one of the stages. They are young girls, mostly, and as I look at the faces I see (unsurprised) that they are very good-looking—I think one of them would create a stir in a restaurant or a bus, but all strung out like that, with their heavy make-up on, they mean no more than a lot of slick magazine covers. They are every bit as good-looking.

Charles Reznikoff

1941

E., the kids and I went to a British War Relief party at C. Aubrey Smith's place on top of Coldwater Canyon. It was a large party filled with professional and non-professional character parts, and it was a grave troubled party—none of the British arrogance so irritating in times past, which would be so welcome now. I had a feeling that it was an odd and touching way to see an Empire shake, if not crumble, at a garden party in Hollywood.

Charles Brackett

MAY 26

1919

A few students were blowing horns about the campus & others were detonating anvils. Jubilation was in the air & I gave the word for an hour of it. They came from everywhere . . . with more shouting & cheering than they ever had in them before.

ERNEST CARROLL MOORE

MAY 27

1937

Edward [Weston] does century plants in the Krasnow backyard.

CHARIS WILSON

1960

We want all the leisure that man has given us (in printing, in moviemaking, even in the typewriter, the bicycle, the curtain wall), but we want the machine to stop in the other fellow's case and handicraft-ism to prevail—and places to walk returned to us—hedgerows, the benches in Pershing Square. What serves the age and does the least damage to the spirit?

ESTHER McCOY, to Ray Bradbury

MAY 28

1921

The freshness of the air. The sea wind. We drive onto the end of Beach Drive. Then back and park the car. Go to one of the best places and have sundaes, lemonades, etc. At 10:30 start back. Delightful air. How far flung L.A. seems. So plain that one could enjoy life here with the car. Back via Main, West 8th, West 7th, West 6th. Vermont, 3rd., Western and Sunset to Detroit. 11:30. We discuss the fun we had. To bed. Helen and I laugh at Myrtle & Grell. A fine, delicious round. To sleep.

THEODORE DREISER

1942

With lang, on the beach, thought about a hostage film (prompted by heydrich's execution in prague). there were two young people lying close together beside us under a big bath towel, the man on top of the woman at one point, with a child playing alongside. not far away stands a huge iron listening contraption with colossal wings which turns in an arc; a soldier sits behind it on a tractor seat, in shirtsleeves, but in front of one or two little buildings there is a sentry with a gun in full kit. huge petrol tankers glide silently down the asphalt coast road, and you can hear heavy gunfire beyond the bay.

BERTOLT BRECHT

MAY 29

1943

Do you know Christopher Isherwood or like his work? I visited him last night at his monastery. He is going into one in Hollywood, of all places. It is a miniature copy, architecturally, of the Taj Mahal and when I entered about eight girls and three men, including one Hindu, were seated on cushions in a semi-circle about the fire-place, all with an absolutely expressionless silence. . . . Isherwood suggested we go out for a walk. I cannot surmise his real attitude toward "the family"—he is English enough not to speak his mind very frankly—but I am wondering a little if he is not going to write a wonderful story of what is going on there.

TENNESSEE WILLIAMS, to his publisher

1965

If [Simon] Rodia [the creator of the Watts Towers] had set out to pick a place in which to build a huge work of art and avoid having it recognized, he could hardly have picked a better place than Los Angeles. In Los Angeles, a bizarre structure may not even be seen; for the city is, of course, a vast sprawl in which practically nobody walks anywhere and few people drive without having a particular objective in mind. Even if it is seen, it is likely to attract little attention; people in Southern California accept a profusion of lawn sculpture and miniature castles with moats as a natural product of a large retired population and a climate that permits outdoor hobbies.

CALVIN TRILLIN

MAY 30

1940

Now comes a retired United States army officer with a new war weapon which he says "is so effective it will blow up an entire community."

We wonder whether he deserved a medal for his discovery or whether he should be blown up by and with his new weapon.

AL WAXMAN

1944

After my nap went to Ginger [Rogers's] house, a hard one to find, and funny and unbelievable and elaborate and uncomfortable when one got there. Sat on one of two pale salmon-colored couches before a log fire and told her *To Each His Own* and, bless her, she loved it. Drank it in with exactly the reaction I had hoped, said she wanted to play it but needed a whale of a director. She said she'd been in enough mediocre pictures, this she thought could be superb. We embraced and I drove like a bat out of hell to Joan Crawford's to have a cocktail with Joan and Phil. A cocktail proved to be two singularly strong Daiquiris in a room with a log fire, on a pale satin couch—all much more knowing than Ginger's but of the same general sort. Two little blonde adopted children were put through their mannered paces.

CHARLES BRACKETT

2003

I am a man of simple pleasures, one of which is driving around Southern California with the windows down, searching for restaurants that throw off the right scent.

Several years ago, on Pico just east of Bundy in West L.A., I swerved to a stop after passing the Talpa. I may not know much, but I know how a proper Mexican restaurant is supposed to smell from the street, and this one had the right look, too. Very little money had been sunk into the exterior design.

Inside, the joint was just as unpretentious. Formica table tops, artificial plants, a mural of rural Mexico.

I headed for the bar and ordered a fat burrito and a cold beer from a man named Andres Martinez.

The Dodgers were on TV, a warm summer breeze was blowing in through the back alley, and I felt like a dog having its belly scratched.

I don't get to Talpa often enough. But in bits and pieces for several years, usually during Dodger games, Andres has been telling me a story. It began when I told him I had lived in Philadelphia.

"Oh," Andres said. "My daughter is in Philadelphia. She's in medical school."

He was obviously a proud papa, but his modesty kept him from gloating.

Over time, I picked up on the fact that he and his wife, Guillermina, were both working at Talpa to keep up with the cost of tuition.

On another visit, Andres, who has a sixth-grade education, told me his daughter was just about done with law school at Loyola.

"I thought she was going to be a doctor," I said.

"That's the other daughter," Andres told me. "This one's going to be a lawyer."

He and his wife, who didn't finish high school, were paying for that, too, on the proceeds from this little hole-in-the-wall restaurant. A doctor and a lawyer, I thought. That's a lot of tacos.

"At $1.95 a taco?" Andres said. "Yes, that's a lot of tacos."

. . . "What happened to my kids is a real big thing," he said. "When I went to Philadelphia for my first daughter's graduation, and they announced her name, I cried. I was just a little guy from a small town in Mexico, San Gaspar de Los Reyes, Jalisco."

Andres is 65 now, and with all the bills paid, I wondered if he and Guillermina would finally give themselves a break and sell the Talpa.

Maybe, he said, because although he loves his family of regular customers, 30 years is a long hustle.

But on the other hand, there's no rush to retire. Cynthia has a child now, Andres said, and he and Guillermina are expecting big things for little Lucia, who is 8 months old.

"We've started a college fund for her," he said.

Steve Lopez

MAY 31

1939

The tree outside is sad. It will die, I think.

MALCOLM LOWRY

1970

In the afternoon we went with David to Griffith Park, where there was a Gay-in. Only it wasn't very gay or very well attended. The police had been by, earlier, harassing them because they were distributing leaflets without a permit. Nobody got arrested but it scared a lot of people off. . . .

Lee introduced to me an elderly man named Morris Kight who was wearing a silk dressing gown and a funny hat and who appeared to be directing the proceedings. He married two pairs of girls, explaining that this wasn't a marriage but a "mateship." We had to join hands and chant something about love. Kight also introduced me publicly and called on me to speak, so I said, in my aw-shucks voice, "I just came here because I'm with you and wanted to show it."

CHRISTOPHER ISHERWOOD

JUNE 1

1910

I have been hidden down here in Los Angeles for a month or two and have managed to get off a little book to Houghton Mifflin, which they propose to bring out as soon as possible. It is entitled "My First Summer in the Sierra." I also have another book nearly ready, made up of a lot of animal stories for boys, drawn from my experiences as a boy in Scotland and in the wild oak openings of Wisconsin. I have also rewritten the autobiographical notes dictated at Harriman's Pelican Lodge on Klamath Lake two years ago, but that seems to be an endless job, and, if completed at all, will require many a year. Next month I mean to bring together a lot of Yosemite material into a hand-book for travelers, which ought to have been written long ago.

John Muir

JUNE 2

1930

The Zep[pelin] goes back home tonight, with Lady Drummond Hay, Karl von Wiegand—all the same passengers they always have. They ought to change the cast on that thing. People will get the idea that it can't haul anybody else.

Will Rogers

1979

Out into Hollywood Boulevard. There is nothing of the breathtaking beauty of New York about this city. Low, flat, sprawling and laid-back—like a patient on a psychiatrist's couch. . . . Two limousines arrive to take us to the Bruin Theatre in Westwood where *Brian* is to be "sneak previewed." At the theatre we find a full house and 1,000 people turned away. Meet the Warner's executives who are, understandably, grinning pleasurably.

It's a marvellous showing. Great laughs and applause on a scale we have not yet seen for *Brian.* At the end Eric leads the rush out—and gets into the wrong limousine—whilst Terry and I stand on the sidewalk and talk to one or two of the audience and those waiting—who are not of the tear-your-clothes-off fan type and want to talk quite unsensationally about the movie. . . . Later in the evening TJ gets woken in his room by a present from Harry in the shape of a Los Angeles naughty lady.

Michael Palin

JUNE 3

1907

At last, word this morning from Cousin Jennie Graves, announcing that Clifford was a little better. It is a bad case of typhoid, complicated by Bright's disease. He apparently died in a convulsion, on the 23rd, but his friend Dr. Moxon seized a knife and cut a blood-vessel. The blood was congealed and he cut a larger one—finally succeeded in drawing three pints—then injected a solution of salt. Life returned!

Olive Percival

1942

What do they think we are anyway? Oh well, I'm not going to school now. They're sure anxious to keep us dumb just like morons. Golly! All my plans of going to college and all that are all gone. All I could think of now is be a dumb ox and not ever graduate high school.

The food is getting better now (It's about time!) You know what happened? The other day district VI and VII all got diarrhea. 4:00 a.m.... Man, it looks as if the whole camp got sick with the food. They ran out of toilet paper too, right in the middle of the night. Boy! . . . Woo P.U.! Those guards thought there was going to be a revolution.

SANDIE SAITO

1966

At a lecture I am asked to pronounce my name three times. I try to be slow and emphatic, "Anaïs—Anaïs—Anaïs. You just say 'Anna' and then add 'ees,' with the accent on the 'ees.'"

ANAÏS NIN

JUNE 4

1926

HOTEL AMBASSADOR

Tell it not in Wardour Street, but I'm beginning to extract a certain sardonic amusement out of Hollywood. It takes itself so seriously, these days. And it's so self-centered that one sometimes wonders, as one sits in the Cocoanut Grove, whether there is such a place as New York, or Chicago, or indeed the United States.

So I've seen little of Los Angeles, which the unkind satirist claims to be so boastful a township that they had to christen the huge U.S. dirigible after it, because that was the only name they could give to the biggest gasbag in the world.

Gilbert Frankau

1938

Worked at Billy's all morning completing the script by about 1:00. Went to Universal and read the last forty pages. . . . Afterwards Hugh made a rather uncomfortable demand that Joe [Pasternak, the producer] say what the credits were to be. Joe said if our script were used as was, "Original Story by F. Hugh Herbert—Screenplay by Charles Brackett and Billy Wilder." . . . Hugh sulked.

Charles Brackett

JUNE 5

1912

It seems to me that we had more pleasure in those days than we do now. We were not driven from morning till night. We felt more at liberty to take a day off, to go into the woods picnicking, trout-fishing or hunting. Our pleasures were simpler than they are today. There was less artificiality, less style. In 1875, everybody in Los Angeles knew everybody else. There were no such class distinctions as we have today. The people here had grown up together. Some of them had gotten rich and others had remained poor, but the rich and the poor were still friends.

JACKSON ALPHEUS GRAVES

1939

The dinner Saturday night had Walter Conrad Arensberg (his poems are in the first edition of the Monroe anthology) among the guests. A curious man. Completely German in appearance. Al tells me he is busily engaged in proving Bacon wrote Shakespeare and employs five secretaries for the purpose. Has a three-story house full of modern paintings—a very large Rousseau, the original "Nude Descending the Stairs," Brancusi sculpture. Has a mild gleam in his blue eyes somewhat like a madman and sometimes spoke in a little voice, sentences that were uttered like maxims and which I did not understand, although I tried to appear intelligent.

. . . And Arensberg told the excellent story of the little girl who saw "sky writing" and rushed into her mother with the cry that "God is doing his home-work!"

CHARLES REZNIKOFF

JUNE 6

1925

I'm stuck in the office waiting for a phone call from Sid Grauman (owner of all the big theaters in Los Angeles, also the Egyptian Theater in Hollywood) and have nothing to do.

. . . Last night the motion picture industry gave an electrical pageant which was the most beautiful thing I have ever seen. Magnificent floats all lighted in stunning effects and all the stars in Hollywood were there. . . . My boss was in the first car with Mr. and Mrs. Harold Lloyd and Norma Talmadge. By the way I had to pull strings to get him there, but I succeeded so he was quite pleased with me.

. . . There were more than 100,000 people outside of the Coliseum who couldn't get in, and cars were parked for blocks and blocks around the place. I don't think I have ever seen so many cars in my life before.

. . . One day of the week it rained all day and the Shriners sure did razz the Californians. Most of the natives couldn't understand why it should rain at this time of year, as it is very unusual. . . . Others were standing on the policemen's boxes in the middle of the street in their bathing suits with fishing rods.

Valeria Belletti

1948

Up here in the breath-taking mountain spring, I can but feel a twinge of sympathy for all you money-grubbing bastards in Hollywood as you struggle against falling box office and recalcitrant studio treasuries. It's much simpler to borrow money and live graciously.

Dalton Trumbo, to his attorney

JUNE 7

1927

School. Made fire by friction.

GLENN T. SEABORG, co-discoverer of plutonium

1940

Here the term *fifth-column activities* is already so overworked as to be nauseating, and the air is full of spy scares and rumors of armed invasions. This noon we hear over the radio that the veterans of the last war are trying to raise a volunteer army of 100,000 men in Southern California to combat foreigners. It is sickening.

Two new air schools are to be started in the valley, it seems, to turn out a hundred pilots every ninety days. That seems a terribly short course to me, but I suppose it's not much harder to handle a plane than an automobile, and I'm pretty sure I could learn the mechanics of a car in less than ninety days.

The siding is almost up, and the house looks fine and solid, although much yellower than we'd thought. It will darken with time. I hope we're here to see it when it's chocolate black.

M.F.K. FISHER

1943

At 12th and Central I came upon a scene that will long live in my memory. Police were swinging clubs and servicemen were fighting with civilians. Wholesale arrests were being made by the officers.

Four boys came out of a pool hall. They were wearing the zoot-suits that have become the symbol of a fighting flag. Police ordered them into arrest cars. One refused. He asked: "Why am I being arrested?" The police officer answered with three swift blows of the night-stick across the boy's head and he went down. As he sprawled, he was kicked in the face. Police had difficulty loading his body into the vehicle because he was one-legged and wore a wooden limb. Maybe the officer didn't know he was attacking a cripple.

At the next corner, a Mexican mother cried out, "Don't take my boy, he did nothing. He's only fifteen years old. Don't take him." She was struck across the jaw with a night-stick and almost dropped the two and a half year old baby that was clinging in her arms. . . .

Rushing back to the east side to make sure that things were quiet here, I came upon a band of servicemen making a systematic tour of East First Street. They had just come out of a cocktail bar where four men were nursing bruises. Three autos loaded with Los Angeles policemen were on the scene but the soldiers were not molested. Farther down the street the men stopped a streetcar, forcing [the] motorman to open the door and proceeded to inspect the clothing of the male passengers. "We're looking for zoot-suits to burn," they shouted. Again the police did not interfere. . . . Half a block away . . . I pleaded with the men of the local police substation to put a stop to these activities. "It is a matter for the military police," they said.

AL WAXMAN

JUNE 8

1847

Got the blues very bad indeed in consequence of Isidora having jilted me She appears to have forgotten me entirely during my short absence.

LIEUTENANT JOHN MCHENRY HOLLINGSWORTH

1927

Last evening I had printed, and ready to show, all shell negatives: two "interested" girls. . . .

Of course, they were "interested,"—"thrilled"—but not to the point of spending money, yet they were wealthy girls. Do they think I show my work to be flattered?—That I am hungry for praise? Well I'm hungry for money and discouraged. . . .

I have to show my prints so often that I detest every one of them. I suppose this is all right if I am forced by my reactions to create new.

Edward Weston

1937

Chan and Edward to Griffith Park . . . and they almost get hoosgowed because you cant photo in the park without a permit.

Charis Wilson

1954

One moment of tenderness and a year of nerves and intelligence, one moment of actual fleshly tenderness. . . .

As of now I am 28, for the first time older than I dreamed of being. The beard a joke, my character with its childish core a tiring taste. . . . I am saddled with myself.

Allen Ginsberg

JUNE 9

1921

At meal Helen taken with a violent attack of gastritis. We try milk of magnesia. . . . Then I think of the electric vibrator and that relieves her. Very much relieved myself. Such fierce onslaughts make me very sad. To bed and I read for awhile in *Old College Towns.*

THEODORE DREISER

1968

The Ambassador, a venerable hotel miles away on Wilshire Boulevard, was the Kennedy headquarters and that was the place to be. . . .

It was about eighteen minutes after midnight, a few of us strolled over to the swinging doors that gave on to the pantry. They had no glass peepholes but we'd soon hear the pleasant bustle of him coming through as the waiters and the coloured chef in his high hat and a bus boy or two waited to see him.

There was suddenly a banging repetition of a sound that, I don't know how to describe, not at all like shots, like somebody dropping a rack of trays. Half a dozen of us were startled enough to charge through the door, and it had just happened. It was a narrow lane he had to come through, for there were two long steam tables and somebody had stacked up against them those trellis fences with artificial leaves stuck on them, that they used to fence up the dance band off from the floor.

The only light was the blue light of three fluorescent tubes, slotted in the ceiling. But it was a howling jungle of cries and obscenities and flying limbs and two enormous men, Roosevelt Grier the football player and Rafer Johnson, I guess, the Olympic champion, piling on to a pair of blue jeans. There was a head on the floor, streaming blood, and somebody put a Kennedy boater hat under it and the blood trickled down like chocolate sauce on an iced cake.

There were flashlights by now and the button-eyes image of Ethel Kennedy turned to cinders. She was slapping a young man and he was saying, "Listen lady, I am hurt too" and down on the greasy floor was a huddle of clothes and staring out of it the face of Bobby Kennedy. Like the stone face of a child, lying on a cathedral tomb. . . .

A dark woman nearby suddenly bounded to a table and beat it and howled like a wolf, "Stinking country, no no no no."

Alistair Cooke

JUNE 10

1847

I fear you are deceived in your good opinions of American rule. If they continue as they have commenced, it will be bad indeed for they acted till lately in a most scandalous manner. Their credit is now lower than the Mexicans in many points. They do not manifest honest principles.

Henry Dalton

1942

Thank you very much for your note. I am all right now, but so far, I've been ill for four days here. It's from the food, but the food is getting better.

Don't work too hard to end the semester! I really feel like a dope for not going to school. I miss it, believe it or not.

Sa-yo-nara is written: [Japanese characters]. Don't forget it now! Please write again.

TOMOKO IKEDA, to a school friend

JUNE 11

1847

Col. Mason now Governor of California. One of the orders was relating to the case of John Allen, alias—who belonged to Co E of the Mormon Battalion and who had been in the calaboose some several weeks for desertion of his post as a picket guard. He did not belong to the Church. . . . Joined the Battalion at Fort Leavenworth and never was a Mormon, manifesting a very ungovernable spirit throughout the whole of the journey. His sentence is to have half of his hair shaved and to be drummed out of town.

HENRY STANDAGE

1919

The players selected [for the first L.A. Philharmonic] number among the best instrumentalists to be found on the Pacific Coast. They are all salaried men, removed from any participation in cabaret work, parades or the fatiguing engagements of five or six shows a day.

EDWIN SCHALLERT, for the *Los Angeles Times*

1939

Rather horrible night with a picked up acquaintance Doug whose amorous advance made me sick at the stomach—Purity!—Oh God—It is dangerous to have ideals.

TENNESSEE WILLIAMS

1969

Hey! I have never criticized any Architects about their attitude toward California, ever. But I *do* criticize Eastern literary critics who, for the most part, neglected Chandler and Hammett when they were alive, and are now neglecting Macdonald.

As for myself, time and again, when I bump into New Yorkers they say, "How can you *live* there in L.A.?! How can you *Create*?" BULLSHIT! . . .

My own director and producer of *Illustrated Man,* New Yorkers both, have never BEEN to Disneyland. Pure snobbism.

RAY BRADBURY, to Esther McCoy

JUNE 12

1847

She is the most perfect coquette I ever saw. She was dressed in a rich pink and gold silk, with a shawl on worth $300! I never saw her look better. I was in full uniform and entered with her on my arm. She was the belle of the evening.

Went to take leave of Isidora She is going to the country. We parted good friends.

LIEUTENANT JOHN MCHENRY HOLLINGSWORTH

1921

How is it over there—with work? I still can't accept the idea of spending all my life here.

RUDOLF SCHINDLER, to Richard Neutra

1954

Pershing Sq.: Suddenly in the middle of downtown black ant traffic & little buildings, the little banana grove on the corner of Hill. There is this big block park on model of Mex town—except it has green flat rectangle of grass with benches all around in the sun—hardly any shape—and an outer perimeter for walking without benches, but you can sit on concrete steps—all the old types, something different from Bryant Park, because they all look respectable & there's no one young, all look clean & model with low palms all around & plantain leaves with bursts of tropic artichoke. Energy sprouting up on the sides—and a few high palms too.

ALLEN GINSBERG

JUNE 13

1847

Went to water my mare with only a halter on and a Spanish woman scared my mare purposely and caused me to be thrown. Thereby hurting me some . . .

[It] is the custom in this country to keep immense herds of all domestic animals which are reared with little or no expense as they require neither feeding nor housing and are always sufficiently fattened for the slaughter houses. . . .

Mr. Williams kills every summer a large number merely for the hides and tallow, leaving the meat to rot on the ground. Of late years Mr. Williams had made large quantities of soap by boiling the fattest of the beef so as to procure all the grease possible. He has a kettle 10 feet deep, the upper part of which is constructed of wood 10 feet also in diameter. This is filled with meat and left to simmer down when the grease is dipped into a box or bin 10 or 12 feet square and the meat thrown away. The grease is converted into soap using a kind of earth instead of ashes or lye. The Indians do this work.

HENRY STANDAGE

1927

Started to work—interrupted at the critical moment—that is my story of yesterday. . . . I had not met her for years, not since the night she spent here, and wanted to be seduced but wouldn't. I'm sure she is no longer virginal! Someone had more persistence or desire than I had. . . .

"Take off your clothes" I said. I felt not a flicker of response to her. Instead of figures I made a few heads. Her body was youthful, strong, brown from the sun, and sea winds,—yet I was repulsed.

. . . I'm so angry with myself for being easy.

EDWARD WESTON

1936

A brief walk to the Pacific Ocean will sharpen the dullest writer's grammar and improve the finest stylist's rhetoric. . . . anyone is privileged to appear in its presence without having to pay admission. . . . It is there, the Pacific, and a brisk walk each morning to it is one of the things a good writer must perform. . . . There are several other rules, but they are boring. The most important rule, according to everybody, is to run like hell after the money. It helps to prolong the manufacture of automobiles. . . .

The slickest rule of all, however, is: Don't write. I will gladly teach anyone the fundamentals of not writing. There is no cost, no obligation. You don't even have to clip a coupon. All you have to do is think it over carefully.

William Saroyan

JUNE 14

1847

Allen had half his head shaved and at retreat was drummed out of town, being marched between 4 sentinels in charge of a Corporal. Drummers and fifers in the rear. He was marched through town at the point of a bayonet and the musicians playing the Rogues March. Not allowed to return during the present war, and liable to be taken up and kept in irons till the close of the war.

Henry Standage

1936

I had no more chance of changing Hollywood or stabbing one decent idea into its head than I have of moving these mountains around me by whistling to them to come to heel!

Now I sit in a shack, eight feet by eight, in the middle of an alfalfa field, and am completely happy and never think of films all day long. In our wide valley the mountains reach up, always changing in the light, on three sides. I cut hay and build a house. I irrigate land and make a living alone.

Let me tell you about my place. At night the oil lamp burns and the great Pullman trains go swinging past with people in them looking out. I always used to sit in trains and see a light in a shack and wonder who the person was. And now I know. . . .

My dog learns quickly. She was a house dog. Now in a flash she becomes a country dog. . . .

Now I am an honest man again. When I get a house built, alone, without help, my penance is over for the months I took money and did nothing in Hollywood. . . .

Irrigation, water! Life here is water! Coming from four hundred miles away. Coming in concrete pipes. Flowing down ditches. . . . Water company scout-cars roaring round the valley, spying, reporting unlucky people who have allowed water to get away from them. . . .

I regain sanity through a simple thing. I like the land. Why not be on it? These Swedes and Mexicans are good people. I like them and get along with them. . . .

I shall become a sane individual again out in this valley. I almost begin to think what a picture it would make.

Eric Knight, to a friend

1939

I had the experience Sat. night which confused and upset me and left me with a feeling of spiritual nausea.

Tennessee Williams

JUNE 15

1937

I have to unfortunately report to you that at the Stendahl Gallery No. 445, the panel painting "Whitish" was cut from the frame with a razor blade; luckily I had a photograph which I had copied in order to send it to all art journals and newspapers, so that if it appears in the trade everyone knows about it. But of course I hope that the police, whom I will inform tomorrow, will find it first so as to use the opportunity to do a little publicity: that Kandinsky's pictures are so valuable that someone would steal them. The same thing happened to Klee and I got the picture back.

GALKA SCHEYER, to Wassily Kandinsky

1943

The snarls of our relationship have been miraculously ironed out in my mind by my personal perusal of my diaries. . . . The vicissitudes through which Wilder and I have been together struck me forcibly and made other things negligible.

CHARLES BRACKETT

JUNE 16

1891

It seems to be possible from my continued friendliness and perhaps tenderness in some past letters you may have misunderstood my position—have had some hope that I would someday be yours again. Do not deceive yourself dear. My life is too precious to me to waste anymore of it like those seven years we spent together.

Not wasted in some ways & I grant full of deep experience and that pain that means growth. But you will know how it unfitted me for any work and how since you left I have done good work and lots of it—— have made a reputation in one year. The difference is too great. Work I must, and when I live with you I can't. Therefore I shall never live with you again as a wife. I know it's hard for you but I can't help it. You must take the hard . . . truth and make the best of it.

Kate is well and happy and very glad to be at home after our trip. I'll write more soon, but this was on my mind to-day.

Sincerely,

Charlotte Perkins Gilman, to her husband

1979

Los Angeles had been coming to me all my life, but this was the first time I had come to it. Prejudices are useless. Call Los Angeles any dirty name you like—Six Suburbs in Search of a City, Paradise with a Lobotomy, anything—but the fact remains that you are already living in it before you get there.

Clive James

JUNE 17

1905

The accursed telephone has annoyed me so much—one can't do anything with these operators. Cloudy day.

Don Juan Bautista Bandini

1954

I ate & drank & stared until my shit was black & I vomited blood on Vine St. & wandered sick & lonely past Sunset to sit down in gold brick Pantages Theater and see the last comedy [*Utopia*] by wasted Laurel & Hardy still fat to watch them destroy the world before they die and came out in a prophetic rage against Hollywood and went to my aunt's house vomiting on the way to recover my heart.

ALLEN GINSBERG

1979

On my last night in LA I dined with Joan Didion and her husband John Gregory Dunne at their house in Pacific Palisades. His-and-hers twin Toyotas stood nose to nose in the driveway. Mexican food was served. Both writers unashamedly thrive in Los Angeles. Dunne's excellent long article about California ["Eureka"] in *New West* for January 1, 1979 is an unbroken paean, while even Didion's famously mordant title essay in *Slouching Towards Bethlehem* is written more from fascination than from fear.

Both writers make their money from writing movies and use the money to buy time in which to write their books—a system pioneered by William Faulkner. Both writers know in advance that scripting the remake of *A Star is Born* for Barbra Streisand must inevitably entail a certain literary contribution by Ms Streisand herself. They know exactly what the difference is between compromise and capitulation. If two people so intelligent can live in Los Angeles on their own terms, then the place has become civilised in spite of itself. I enjoyed their company very much and did my best not to let them know that I had swallowed a habanero. They probably thought my muffled sobs were due to homesickness.

At midnight Hector and Alphonse fetched me away up

through the hills to Mulholland Drive. From a look-out high on the ridge I could see all the way down the coast to Balboa and inland to the Sierra Madre. Turning around, I could see the whole of the San Fernando Valley. It was all one sea of light. This is where the first space voyagers will come from. When our children leave the Earth and sail away into relative time, they will have the confidence of naivety. They will have forgotten what it is like not to get anything you want just by reaching out. In a way the Angelenos have already quit America.

CLIVE JAMES

JUNE 18

1943

They are very patient with me here, extremely kind and friendly, almost embarrassingly so, and don't seem to mind when I go off on other material for a while, as I've been doing with the long short story "The Gentleman Caller."

TENNESSEE WILLIAMS

1946

I used your $5 to buy some magnificent yellow pyjamas with little coloured flowers, a thousand thanks.

THEODOR ADORNO, to his parents

JUNE 19

1907

Such a busy hodge-podge of a day yesterday—mixed business and society . . . hurried on to the California Club. . . . The Bosworths were there and were roaring along very pleasingly. She looked almost pretty, in her pink linen frock and leghorn hat, covered with red roses. . . . Didn't get home until late, just a few minutes before my guests arrived! After such unlovely haste, I always vow to retire to my pine-tree in the Sierras.

Beautiful, clear skies and cool breezes—then wonderful, half-misty moonlight effects! It is hard not to sit up at the window and wonder about it all.

OLIVE PERCIVAL

1920

We dine in the Chinese restaurant, overlooking the water. The blue black water and the stars. We stop to see the chimpanzees running little motor cars on the track. I laugh to see how they grab hold of each other's car and hold each other back. Then we ride on the merry-go-round. Then walk to Venice and ride on the giant racer. The big dips make Helen a little sick. Then we get on the car and come home—not before listening to the singers before the racer place. They are so very town-dandy-ish, so American wisenheim and patronizing and blase. Is amusing. The little bungalow looks fine and we crawl in with a sigh of content.

THEODORE DREISER

1964

Alan Swallow came to Los Angeles for the Publishing Conference. . . . He was the only panelist who did not talk about money. He talked about the writers he had loved and published because he had loved them. . . .

We gathered afterwards for an evening of talk to which he had invited the writers he publishes. . . . how I dislike the snobbish attitude of the East about a "little publisher out West."

Anaïs Nin

JUNE 20

1941

I've always thought that novels should only be written if there is something in them that *must* be said, and now here I plan to write one simply because it will be good for me. But maybe I'll have something to say that I don't know now. It will be hard, and I feel lazy yet gnawed, so I'd better get to work.

. . . There was a little bird in the house today, not very nervous. We took the screen from the closet window.

M.F.K. Fisher

2017

It's ridiculous but when I start against the Mets I'm very aware that Jerry Seinfeld's mood is in my hands.

Brandon McCarthy

JUNE 21

1937

We must to town, and the weather is nasty warm, the city stinky beyond the fondest nightmares.

Charis Wilson

1938

Worked at the studio all morning, getting no place. To the [Screen Writers Guild] office at noon to oversee a bulletin. Hardly had I returned to the studio before I had a call from Phil Dunne that an interview arranged between [screenwriters] Dudley [Nichols], Phil, myself and the great god [producer] Joseph Schenck was to be right away. All very unofficial and secret. Rushed over to Twentieth Century-Fox and was led with the others into the Presence. Schenck completely charming, said he had no animosity against the Screen Writers Guild. . . .

He practically guaranteed us recognition. We left jubilant. I returned to Paramount and read up on French shooting, in the desperate hope that we could [gin up] something for the part of *Midnight* on which we are stuck.

Charles Brackett

JUNE 22

1946

We landed at the airport of Los Angeles, breathing fresh air after the stifling atmosphere over the desert.

I felt happy. I believe, in every sensitive person born in the Northern climate, there lives a longing for the South where the human race originated. The prospect of living among palm trees like Robinson Crusoe in our children's books, among flowers which were in blossom all year around, in an even climate, just as near to the sea as to the mountains whose outlines reminded me of Greece—seemed fabulous.

One could browse among old books in bookshops of the street around the corner, some open late in the evening. A few blocks further I came to Pershing Square, shaded by palm trees, where every seat was taken on the long benches which criss-crossed it. In the center reformers and fanatics made speeches just as in Hyde Park and were surrounded by people who had a good time joking about what they heard. . . .

The reason why the streets appear so lifeless is that the small businessmen have been driven out of the expensive residential areas. I am accustomed to take walks in the evening and do not like to look at the forbidding façades of elegant homes but wish to see something going on in the streets. I like to look at shops where people are still busy or to pass through places where people are amusing themselves in the open. I decided, therefore, to settle near the [Los Angeles County Museum of Art in Exposition Park]. . . .

A part of the Spanish population still lived in the museum area. Since they take life easier, these people are being slowly driven out by hard-working Americans. In the afternoons and on holidays one could see them lying on the green lawns in front of the museum, enjoying the sunshine, in light dresses. They formed a considerable proportion of the visitors to the museum and were never in a hurry, for which reason art probably penetrated deeper into their minds than into that of the casual American visitor, who does not give the seed of his impressions time to grow.

William R. Valentiner

1971

I love seals and swim with them and play tag, sometimes close enough to reach out and touch, but I don't touch. Seals—I'm actually talking about sea lions here—have terribly powerful jaws, have to eat raw fish. But I've never heard of one attacking a human being in the water. In fact it appears, doesn't it, that most of the tales we hear of ravening beasts like wolves and mountain lions have been invented by us to excuse our own bloodthirstiness.

Ross Macdonald, to Eudora Welty

1976

I just lazed around today—played vacation in the suburbs.

I can't understand L.A.—It's totally given up its public spaces to the car. The only places left for meaningful interaction are private areas.

Aaron Paley

JUNE 23

1935

About 10:30 we hiked up the high trail, and after reaching the summit, we went along the firebreak to a higher summit. . . . Back by way of Kay Cañon. Big lunch—grilled steak—tamales—cherry tarts—good time.

Henry O'Melveny

1968

Dear Ms. Kael,

Ben Hecht didn't write *Roxie Hart.* I did. I take it as a compliment, of course, that you attribute it to Hecht, but if you had let me know you were going to be sloppy about it I could have named you a score of other pictures I've written that you would have been welcome to attribute to somebody else, anybody else, in fact.

This mistake shakes me. I was coming to take what you wrote as gospel. Now I don't know. It's like discovering that the Encyclopedia had blown one.

NUNNALLY JOHNSON, to Pauline Kael

JUNE 24

1847

For a Californian to ride 100 miles a day is quite common, nor does it appear to require any extraordinary effort. 100 miles a day are as frequently driven by them as fifty by the people in the United States, in truth with them it is but an ordinary day's ride, but which is generally performed by two or three horses. Their great exploits with the lasso in catching wild horses and cattle are astonishing. . . .

They will, when on full gallop stop and pick up a lasso from the ground, or even a piece of money, without either halting or dismounting. They never walk even the shortest distance. They are never on foot, only when entering a house, at which time they will take a lasso, made of hair, one end of which is fastened to the neck of the horse and the other end held by them. . . .

I saw a game played by these Spaniards. I saw a cock (or as the

Yankees say, a rooster) was buried in the sand save his head only. The Spaniards rode by in turns on a full gallop, trying at the same time to pick up the cock, several being successful and none falling from the horse. These horses are much better trained for the saddle than ours. They endure fatigue much more than the American horses.

Henry Standage

1940

The radio is off its top, even crazier than back east. One whirl of the dial and you want to jump out the window. All day every day they sell GOD here, and I mean sell him, along with used cars, soap and dainties for milady. Also Swing mixed with news of Disaster in Europe on the scale that you know. So I can't listen to the radio. I'm invited to the home of Mrs. William Wyler to a swimming party. Sounds ducky, isn't it? I'm going, mainly because Wyler is a nice intelligent sort of man and I'll play a little pool. But his house is full of refugees, most of whom, God help me, I hate. That is, most of them in Hollywood. . . .

I must find some way to live that does not involve this Paradise. I hope I will. I have some new ideas; we'll see. Be careful of money. For lack of it can ruin your life. Cagney, who is a millionaire, at least, says in an answer to every implied criticism of Hollywood in the industry;—"There's always Wednesday!"

Elia Kazan

JUNE 25

1931

I planted an acre of potatoes and, as none of them has come up, I am inclined to think that they were planted upside down and are probably making their way slowly to the Antipodes.

EDGAR RICE BURROUGHS

1976

In spite of a first degree smog alert and 90° heat, I took public transportation to Ventura Blvd to walk and shop—to be honest—it's depressing. Both the buses and the boulevard are mere phantoms of their Bay Area counterparts. Ventura Blvd. can't even lift a finger to Shattuck. If it was all condensed into one small stretch with people using their feet to get from store to store, perhaps it might be good . . .

The buses are depressing in the Valley—few and far between—everyone is driving—the expanses of concrete, driving areas, parking lots are incredibly discouraging for the pedestrian.

AARON PALEY

JUNE 26

1888

It is whispered that San Francisco is already growing jealous of this Southern city, and as for San Diego—that it goes off into a convulsive fit at the mere mention of the name. These are rumors, however, that I do not altogether credit, and merely give them for what they are worth. I know that Marion and I are quite happy to be back here again; that we greeted the mountains, and the orange groves, and the vineyards, and the brisk, busy streets with a smile of true affection, and we confided to each other in the midst of our twelve bundles, that there was no place like Los Angeles.

HARRIET HARPER

1930

The actual work is negligible. . . . So far I have had eight collaborators. The system is that A. gets the original idea, B. comes in to work with him on it, C. makes a scenario, D. does preliminary dialogue, and then they send for me to insert Class and whatnot. Then E. and F., scenario writers, alter the plot and off we go again.

I could have done all my part of it in a morning, but they took it for granted I should need six weeks. The latest news is that they are going to start shooting quite soon. In fact, there are ugly rumours that I am to be set to work soon on something else.

P. G. WODEHOUSE

1939

There is more social life out here than in a rabbit warren during the rutting season, and it is this which may drive me crazy first. We have seen all the best patios, the largest swimming pools. . . .

Jack Warner wanted to know yesterday if I was any relation to Edna Ferber—was I her husband? I spelled my name and then pronounced it. Zane Ferber? he said. Any relation to Zane Grey? Elliott Nugent patiently explained the whole thing and Warner nodded. On his way out of the party he stopped and shook hands. Good-bye, Ferber, he said. So long Baxter, I said. It's a great place.

JAMES THURBER

JUNE 27

1847

Relieved from guard at 8 a.m. Spent the day in my tent receiving instructions in the Spanish language. Our officers are becoming more and more like men, giving us as many privileges as they can conveniently. They have not been more than half as strict for a few days past. In fact they seem to realize that their power as military commanders will soon be gone and that their influence will go too.

HENRY STANDAGE

1921

Well—[Hollyhock House] stands. Your home.

It is yours for what it has cost you. It is mine for what it has cost me. . . .

Can we not pronounce benediction upon it, now, absolving the building at least from rancor and false witness?

Whatever its birth pangs it will take its place as your contribution and mine to the vexed life of our time. What future it will have?—who can say?

Faithfully yours,
maimed as it is—
FRANK LLOYD WRIGHT, to Aline Barnsdall

1973

The *Tonight Show* is an all-American institution. At one go, Python will be seen by the few aficionados in New York and San Francisco, and also by the Mormons in Salt Lake City, the tobacco farmers of Louisiana and the potato growers of Idaho. . . . To make things more nerve-wracking, it was to be recorded as a live show, with no stops or retakes, for the tape had to be ready an hour or so after recording to the various parts of the States for transmission the next evening.

A great air of unreality. Here was Python going out to its greatest audience ever, and to us it was no more than a hastily organized cabaret. We were totally unknown to the audience, and felt like new boys at school. At 6.00 the recording started. This week Joey Bishop, one of F Sinatra and D Martin's buddies, was hosting the show as regular host Johnny Carson was on holiday. Bishop was on good form, fluent and funny. When it came to our spot he produced our two latest LPs and tried, quite amusingly, to explain the crossed-out Beethoven cover. All good publicity.

Michael Palin

JUNE 28

1945

Everybody has a garden but they look pretty amateurish: corn too thick, etc., though tomatoes do better. Gardening people miss the Japanese, who used to do all that around private homes. They made a bad mistake in not watching their Japanese gardeners and learning something while they had the chance.

William Faulkner, to his wife

1993

First day of jury duty. I had heard they were calling panels for the Menendez brothers' trial, but I didn't necessarily believe it because I thought that case had been settled a long time ago. Even I knew that Lyle and Erik Menendez were the Beverly

Hills teenagers who had shotgunned their parents to death in their home because they were greedy for their inheritance. When Erik Menendez walked into the courtroom, my blood went cold.

HAZEL THORNTON

JUNE 29

1847

The Col. Addressed the Battalion on the necessity of keeping troops here till more could be transported from the U.S., endeavoring to persuade the Battalion or at least one company to enlist for another year. . . . Lieu. Canfield next rose and said it would be the best thing we could do to re-inlist as our means were small and likely to be expended in reaching our families. . . .

Cap. Hunter said it had been hinted that there was a prophet somewhere in the camp, he believed among the privates; if so, he wished he would come forth and give us the word of the Lord on the subject. . . . Meeting dispersed, 15 or 16 names being obtained for re-enlisting.

HENRY STANDAGE

1937

Bought a paper on the way out to Santa Monica. The bodies have been found. Bodies being those of three Inglewood girls, ages 7, 8, and 9, missing a couple of days. The police with some clews are now searching out what the paper describes as a "Mexican-looking, maniac degenerate."

Near Ventura, Cole driving about 42, a cop waves us to the road side. Asks to see Cole's license and looks piercingly at me.

Edward produces his press card. Cop says "Who's that in the back seat?" Edward: she's a member of our party.—another overhaul from the cop's gimlet eyes. "O.K." says he. And explains he's "working on this Inglewood thing" and couldn't get a good look at me as we drove by. Of course I was dressed in my usual faded blue shirt and pants, but the real trouble was I had just lit up my pipe for the first time in months, and he saw it clamped in my jaw as we went by. Pleasant day over the old familiar road, no excitement.

Charis Wilson

JUNE 30

1939

It was true! It was true! The weather was perfect. Under a monotonous bolt of blue, relieved by not even an amateur cloud, I walked. Every day was like the day before and there was no hope that there would ever be bad weather. . . .

But When It Rains—

Rain is the great catastrophe. A pall hangs over the whole city and the incomplete write-up and photographs for eastern papers all entitled "Sunny California" don't help a bit. . . . But once the rain sets in and really becomes a downpour the "native sons" treat it as a great adventure. What children they are when it rains! First they lose face and sulk. Then they laugh and exclaim over it and pretend it is as great a novelty as snow in Africa would be. They hold out their hands to it. They lift their faces to it.

Willard F. Motley

1939

I am grateful rather than angry at the nice deep mud-lined rut in which I find myself at the moment. The world outside doesn't make it possible to even hope to earn a living, while here the pay is large (it isn't as large as people think, however) enough for me to have at least three or four months off every year.

Nathanael West, to Edmund Wilson

1942

I am working on various shifts of the 4th Interceptor Command and find it is very important work and keeps me on my toes. I don't suppose the censor will let me tell you all about it but it is connected with aeroplane work and wonderfully carried out. They treat us well too, give us a meal and transportation. I am quite proud of the work and am glad I am strong enough to do the work. . . .

Bless you sweetheart—I wish I could answer a letter from you! Love from your Mother.

Ruth Wolffe Merritt

1943

Lunched and Word-Gamed at the table, amused at the fact that Billy knew from my expression before he read my words in the Word Games that I was trying to get away with murder. Wonder if he has read all my recent thoughts about him as easily.

Charles Brackett

JULY 1

1927

I start the new month with a new love! I am not surprised. F. and I were forecast to have this experience—at least once.

She came to be photographed again. From the last time I have one extraordinary negative. She bent over forward until her body was flat against her legs. I made a back view of her swelling buttocks which tapered to the ankles like an inverted vase, her arms forming handles at the base. Of course it is a thing I can never show to a mixed crowd. I would be considered indecent. How sad when my only thought was the exquisite form. But most persons will only see an ass!—and guffaw as they do over my toilet. . . .

We drove to Pasadena. We drank. We kissed. She was an artist with those lips————

EDWARD WESTON

1993

The judge called us into the courtroom one by one and asked us about the first questionnaire. . . . I admitted to having heard they were making a movie about this case.

HAZEL THORNTON

JULY 2

1907

The tableaux vivants, the last day of the Friday Morning Club, were unusually splendid. . . . I posed as a Chinese singing-girl. They said it was "pretty," whereas my intent was to be "funny!" . . .

My birthday yesterday was almost as dreary as possible. An extra hard grind and an extra high temperature, 94 degrees. I would like a holiday and a merry making sometime on my "fete-day." . . . Now next year, when I am 40, I hope to have a notable party.

Am trying to write pot-boilers, these hot evenings—but do not get on at all, my old head is so tired and I would so much oh! So very much rather do nothing. Really my mental condition is semi-comatose. How stupid I must seem to the world! Certainly, I bore myself!

Olive Percival

1927

One reason I'm keeping this diary, as Mother insists on calling it, is because I *have* grown, in so many ways besides inches and vocabulary. I'd like to see if I have the mentality to write what I *want* to write—what I think. I doubt it. Damn it—what's my idea in forever playing to an invisible audience? Or not an audience so much as an observer? Sometimes, in those rare moments of companionship that flicker between people I meet and me, I almost say what I want to, and then as I say the words in my mind, something utterly different comes out of my mouth and is twisted into a meaning I don't recognize—hate—sneer at. Well, I shall see—maybe—and this book will be amusing, even if it doesn't say what it's supposed to—maybe.

M.F.K. Fisher

JULY 3

1928

Monday I dropped in at DeMille's and was put to work immediately. One of the writers needed a girl and I was sent to him.

VALERIA BELLETTI

1965

David Selznick died on June 22. . . . The funeral was on the 25th at Forest Lawn. It was a sad grey day with drizzle. George Cukor gave us directions; he was having a great time, and talked so loud that someone came to shush him. He told Sam Goldwyn, "Now Sam, you're going to go in front of the coffin, with Bill Paley. . . . The rabbi will go first, of course." "Why should the rabbi go first?" Goldwyn asked. This may just possibly have been a deadpan joke, but he certainly seemed a little gaga, vaguely smiling and telling everyone, "You look good." He said to me, referring to David, "He was very fond of you," and then added, "We're all very fond of you." So I had to forgive him. If I'm not careful, I soon won't have any mortal enemies left. . . .

Katharine Hepburn read Kipling's "If." When she got to the last line, she turned to the coffin and said, "You'll be a Man, my son!" I later heard that George Cukor thought this a supreme touch of artistry. I thought it farcical. One expected David to put his head out of the coffin and exclaim, "*Now* she tells me!"

CHRISTOPHER ISHERWOOD

1976

Spent the day at the beach. Again, the water was so warm although the air was much cooler. . . .

I picked up Susie and we got some bbq'ed chicken and went

to see 2 of 4 seasons by Vivaldi and some Brandenburg Concertos by Bach played by the L.A. Philharmonic at the Hollywood Bowl. It was really an ideal setting. The night air was warm, not a cloud in the sky, overhead the 2 searchlights formed a perpetual cross.

There wasn't any visible structure in the mountains. We seemed alone in the mountains. It's at places like this when L.A. is at its best. People mix together easily from all parts (like they do at the beach) and the weather and the setting make it.

AARON PALEY

JULY 4

1847

Independence. This day was celebrated by the troops at Pueblo de Los Angeles. . . . A short address by Col. Stevenson and the name of Fort Moore given to the fort at Ciudad de Los Angeles. . . . An offer made to the Spaniards to have the Declaration &c. read in their own language, if desired; not read.

HENRY STANDAGE

1891

No. I will not live with you again—not even in the same house. I know too well what that would amount to. Not as your wife in any case. How can you ask me again when you KNOW! Nor will I come to Providence on any terms. You have to live there? Well, I don't. And I will not go abroad with you. As you know I have been planning and hoping these years to have you go—alone. I will not accompany you on any terms. And for my work—that is my life and I shall pursue it as long as I live, whether you consent or not, approve or not. I had my work to do before I ever knew you, you know.

I am sorry very sorry to have to put these things so plainly, but you would have it. I hope you will not ever need to ask again. We two must part—and then . . . an end to it.

All goes well here and you need to be under no concern about my health, it is fast becoming established. Regretfully but sincerely,

CHARLOTTE PERKINS GILMAN

1933

So at last I landed in Hollywood! [Impresario José] Rodriguez met me at the station—he looks exactly like Zangara the would-be assassin of Roosevelt. He is native of Guatemala, and one can even discover some sing-song element in his dashing English. He was with his wife (second, I suspect, for in the course of conversation he mentioned his 11-year-old son). His wife had a dog in her arms. They drove me to this hotel which is situated on the Hollywood Boulevard, corner of Highland St. Half-a-mile up Highland St. is the Hollywood Bowl. I walked up after Rodriguez went and came upon this imitation-antique amphitheatre. The moon and Jupiter shone down on this auditorium around which so many petty passions raged. . . .

He is very brilliant, very self-assertive and, it seems to me, without nerves. I am seeing him tomorrow morning—we'll rearrange the programs—he is enthusiastic over the fanfare idea, he is writing the program notes, and I am delighted with this. . . .

My room is fine, but it has a superfluous bed. Three dollars a day, no weekly rate. Rodriguez said to the manager that the Hollywood Bowl Association will take care of the bill. I don't bank on it, however.

NICHOLAS SLONIMSKY, on José Rodríguez

1991

Independence Day. Altman party in Malibu. Dress code; red, white and blue. Buy US Flag stickers and plaster my clothes, hair and face with them, and trek up the coast looking like a stamped parcel for just about the best party I have ever been to. Why? Well, I will try. . . .

EASE. In every sense. Their condo is on the Pacific Ocean. I don't mean NEAR, but ON the beach. The living room is dominated by the sound and sight of the pounding surf immediately beyond the wall-to-wall windows. Katherine is the coolest, keenest hostess I know, makes everyone feel hugely welcome, every detailed arrangement seem effortless, unfussed.

She has been married to Bob for thirty years, and they kind of "top 'n' tail" one another with an outward show of EASE. Like hand-hewn spoons. . . . Please, God, when my turn swifts up, do NOT let me fit a rug to my balding cranium or wrench some designer jeans around my saggy "cheeks." Remember this wisdom. EASE. . . .

Then there are fireworks over the Ocean, from Malibu Patriots. Food, candles, dancing, singing and I know no matter how I try to write this it will be a mere cornball to what it was like to be there. Apart from the absence of wife and baba, THIS is a night of perfect happiness. Unalloyed. PURE. Enough to make me cry, knowing it now, in the moment rather than reconstituted in memory.

RICHARD E. GRANT

JULY 5

1941

I spent 3 hours wandering round L.A. It is the most awful city, isn't it? The only good thing in it was a marvelous Rare Book shop, wherein I browsed contentedly.

PETER PEARS

1941

The war of [Los Angeles and San Francisco] is a thing of the past. It never was much more than a publicity gag, and now the world has more important wars to worry about.

L. M. GIANNINI

1943

Dear brother,

I hope to God that you are well.

As for us we are all well thanks to God's grace.

Without anything from you that I could refer to, I'll send you this.

The 25th of last month marked three months since we've received a letter from you. We know that there is a lot of work for you here.

That must be why you haven't been able to write. But we hope to God that soon you'll write to us, or that you'll return home soon. We know that they're bringing those that were in Europe over here so that they can go home. So, God willing, we'll see each other again soon. . . .

The 14th of last month I sent 15 pesos to my Uncle Fernando, I sent him 5 personally but it's just that I haven't written to him yet to tell him. Mom and I have a lot of work to do, me with the kid and Mom with her chickens she has 40 chicks 3 hens and 1 rooster and in her garden that she waters every morning and evening. . . . I think that this is all for now, greetings from the whole family and from my mother and the kid. Your sister that doesn't forget you, and that hopes to God that you return soon.

Benedicta M. Magaña

JULY 6

1847

The glorious 4th is over! We had a splendid ball at night. The room was crowded. Isidora was there Great attention paid her by all but me I did not even speak to her. I had taken a very active part in the ball and worked hard, but I felt mortified and disappointed that I could not dance!

Lieutenant John McHenry Hollingsworth

1928

Dr. Moland went over to me. I said: "It's got away from us, hasn't it—and gone much farther than you expected." He said: "Yes, it has—and I can't quite understand it."

Anyhow, it's in damned bad shape.

Miss Christie applied the radium and I went to sleep on it for an hour and a half.

Charles Lummis

JULY 7

1870

Blakely broke down the dam, placing a log across the side ditch: I with my walking stick removed the log to let the ditch free. When he attempted to stop me, I told him I would break the hand that touched it. He did it and I struck his hand as hard as I could. He then pushed me into the Zanja and drew his pistol to fire on me: Marcos came up and ordered him to put up his pistol or he would fire on him. . . . he finally put up his pistol and after some words withdrew. I ordered the men to replace the dam and continue watering.

HENRY DALTON

1902

Signed a petition or protest against putting "mezcla" on the edge of the sidewalk in place of the wood that is there now. It is too expensive and there is no need for such expense at the present time.

DON JUAN BAUTISTA BANDINI

1918

After more or less delay, I decided to go out to my uncle's dairy for the summer, and there I am now—and have been for almost a week. Something tells me I shan't read or write much this summer, although I did compose one . . . on the milk route. My day's schedule runs something as follows: 3:30 a.m. get up; 4:00 a.m., milk; 5:00 a.m., bottle milk; 6:00 a.m., deliver milk; 8:00 a.m., eat breakfast; 8:30 a.m., wash bottles; 10:00 a.m., clean milking shed; 10:30 a.m., clean cow yard; 12:00, eat dinner; 12:00 to 3:00 p.m., do miscellaneous jobs and sleep; 3:00 p.m., milk; 4:30, bottle milk;

5:15, deliver milk; 7:30, eat supper; 8:30, go to bed. Now I know why Burns was a poor farmer. The only way I can keep from becoming utterly bovine is to recite poetry and compose . . . while I am working. I am getting some great material for the latter. I am also collecting material for a sonnet-sequence on hog raising.

YVOR WINTERS

1950

What matters is that I should work, constantly, every instant. There is so endlessly much to do. For instance:

The novel. Get on with it—never mind how, as long as I make a draft.

This reviewing for *Tomorrow.* Chose a book [he chose Ray Bradbury's first novel, *The Martian Chronicles*]. Start thinking what you'll say about it.

CHRISTOPHER ISHERWOOD

JULY 8

1940

We have moved into a rather magnificent roomy house in a hilly landscape strikingly similar to Tuscany. I have what I wanted—the light; the always refreshing dry warmth; the spaciousness compared with Princeton; the holm oak, eucalyptus, cedar, and palm vegetation; the walks by the ocean which we can reach by car in a few minutes. There are some good friends here, first of all the Walters and Franks, besides our two eldest children, and life might be enjoyable were it not that our spirits are too oppressed for pleasure—and for work also, as I discovered after some initial attempts.

THOMAS MANN

1942

Incidentally, I'm going out with [Japanese characters] now. He's a swell fellow. We go to these dances that they give every Thursdays and Saturdays. I heard that you're not getting along too bad in L.A. either. Come, come, Molly, out with it! Who is it this time?

. . . I'll be saying "goodbye" now, til we meet again.

SANDIE SAITO

1974

"California dreaming is becoming a reality," is a line from a Mamas and the Papas song of a few years ago, but what a dreadful surreal reality it is: foglike and dangerous, with the subtle and terrible manifestations of evil rising up like rocks in the gloom. I wish I was somewhere else. Disneyland, maybe? The last sane place here? Forever to take Mr. Toad's Wild Ride and never get off?

PHILIP K. DICK

2007

It's official; in a year of lasts I declare this to be my very last 4th of July in *la ciudad de* South Gate. My first was in 1948 so I guess it is about time. . . . In fact, the "new" Latin Gate looks quite a bit like the old "Anglo" Gate. The Mexi-Gaters take pride in ownership and my dear Annetta Avenue is be-lawned and nicely painted. So, on those rare occasions when I "inte-Gate" I don't feel too foreign or on guard. . . .

In 1960 I personally threw about fifty cherry bombs into the Pacific Ocean when the family rented a beach cottage at Surfside. Mostly, we celebrated by standing on the Whitneys' front lawn as the impressive pyrotechnic show took place at the South Gate Park or guzzled precious beer from Gracie's liquor and smoked up Tareytons in the Knowltons' back yard as a Red Devil "lawn party" was torched up using neighborhood safety techniques comprised of a galvanized trash can lid and a garden hose. . . .

Now in 2007 as I approach a terrible birthday with a zero on the end I crave only peace and quiet tempered by sips of red wine and Dodger heroics crooned over by the great Vinny. Such is not possible in my home surrounded by three separate construction projects (worked on all day on the 4th) and the local miscreants who amuse themselves in the wee hours by disrupting the neighborhood with M-180 blasts in one of the nearby concrete ravines. . . .

This is the new Los Angeles and the Raider nation mentality for which it stands. As for me, I have had enough and will begin my search for that remote lighthouse with a garden in the coming months.

Glen Creason

JULY 9

1847

This evening I took a walk through the Gardens and Vineyards of Pueblo. Pueblo de Los Angeles or City of the Angels is situated near latitude 33 degrees N. a few miles from the Coast. It contains a population of about 5000—chiefly Mexicans and Indians. There are but few foreigners at this place. It contains about 1000 buildings, which are small and otherwise inferior, the walls of which are generally constructed of adobes (sun dried brick).

HENRY STANDAGE

1939

Took Billy to a Dr's to deliver a package of excrement.

CHARLES BRACKETT

1976

When I think about last night (note—Mitch and I drove up to the observatory and got stoned to experience the Laserium), I am just so impressed. I really feel I experienced more than just a light show. It was so in tune with the images I felt they carried me to new extremes. It's funny how things can change so quickly. . . . For the most part, I've given up the idea of renouncing the automobile while I'm in L.A. The entire lifestyle is centered around its use and in order to enjoy L.A. it's necessary to utilize the medium of the city. Namely, the car.

AARON PALEY

JULY 10

1847

Today the Spaniards commenced a bull fight. Last night we lay on our arms, cannons loaded &c. on account of some rumours afloat. The Col. and others were invited to a ball at this festival and it was rumored that the Spaniards had taken this as the best opportunity to retake Pueblo. . . .

In the public square they had erected or made a large corral (or vast arena) in the form of an amphitheater, which is circumscribed by a post and rail fence around the exterior of which are successive circular seats rising above one another, to the height of twenty or thirty feet and of sufficient extent to accommodate many people. Timely notice having been given by preparing during the past week has caused a universal attendance at this scene of cruelty savoring so strongly of barbarity, cruelty and indolence. General Peko the late commander in this war, and all the principal officers in the Spanish service are here, together with the Priests, mingled with these semi-barbarians. The gen himself going in on horseback several times and fighting the bull with a short spear. Several bulls fought during the day; one horse gored by the bulls.

HENRY STANDAGE

1933

Spent all afternoon with [José] Rodriguez, first at the station KFI and then for light supper at his place. There is a possibility of a national hook-up for the Saturday night broadcast. Watch the Sat. papers carefully. I will be asked to talk for four minutes! The only trouble [is] that it will come in after midnight Boston time. Buy the *N.Y. Times* on Sat. and look up whether their stations carry this broadcast.

NICOLAS SLONIMSKY

1951

A writer discloses himself on a single page, sometimes in a single paragraph.

RAYMOND CHANDLER

1976

I picked up Gisele at her house in Woodland Hills at the end of the world.

AARON PALEY

JULY 11

1847

Bull fighting again commenced today in good earnest. Quite dangerous to be in town. Some horses gored by the bulls in the combat. 2 men considerably hurt and Cap. Davis' little boy thrown about 20 feet by a bull although not much hurt. The bull broke out of the enclosures and fight continued till late in the evening. Gen Peko took quite an active part today. He was very richly attired as was also many others.

HENRY STANDAGE

1852

There was a "grand" celebration here on the Fourth, on Sunday. Mr. Hayes did not join in it. He heard the speeches, but did not go out to the dinner. There was a speech in English, and one in Spanish. They were to have had a procession through the town, but this turned out to be a few men on horseback, racing through the streets, nearly all drunk. The dinner was at a vineyard about a mile from town; I heard it was a very good dinner, but they were there only a short time, returning to town in the same style they left it, and spending the afternoon in firing cannon, drinking, and riding around on horseback.

EMILY HAYES

1961

I have too long put off sending you a message about *Newsday.* As a newspaper, it is beautifully affirmative about life. It is sweet, keen, strong and quiveringly alive. It is in terrific contrast to the *Los Angeles Times.* Sometimes when I ask myself, "What in the hell is wrong with this paper?," I find myself answering, "Somehow it seems to try to love people and life and can't quite make it."

CARL SANDBURG

JULY 12

1938

This finds me like stout Cortez, gazing on the Pacific and about, in all human probability (which is not by any means certainty, since the picture industry is strictly sub-human), to prepare the life of Madame Curie for the screen. Which should be rather an interesting job, if only the sub-humans will leave one reasonably in peace—a most unlikely contingency, alas.

ALDOUS HUXLEY, to T. S. Eliot

1956

I just can't afford to live here. There's nothing for me to write about. To write about a place you have to love it or hate it or do both by turns, which is usually the way you love a woman. But a sense of vacuity and boredom—that is fatal.

I send you large amounts of love and I know damn well I sound like a bitter and disappointed man. I guess I am at that. I was the first writer to write about Southern California at all realistically, as the UCLA librarian [Lawrence Clark Powell] admitted when asking [successfully] for my original manuscripts for the Special Collections of their library. Now half the writers in the country piddle around in the smog. With lots and lots of love,

Raymond Chandler, to a friend

2005

Oh, why did I leave? And was it right to come back here, a Califas, to come home? *Is* this home?

Susana Chávez-Silverman

JULY 13

1922

You know how I crave sunshine. And it does not seem to enervate me. I think I felt better here than in most places,—certainly than I felt in New York. And when I left there in 1919 I was rather run down. Out here I picked up not a little. As for being through at 50,—well, words won't help to counteract that save words in book form.

Theodore Dreiser

1937

The film was to be shown at the Los Angeles Philharmonic Auditorium [just across Fifth Street from] Pershing Square, gardens where the bums clustered in the twilight under subtropical boscage. . . . Outside the hall neon lights shone: HEMINGWAY AUTHOR—SPANISH EARTH.

Anthony Powell

1937

Last night I went to see the Joris Ivens film,—*Spanish Earth,* at the Philharmonic. Some of it is . . . very vivid. The music was annoying,—it kept drowning out the soundtrack. An immense crowd. Ernest Hemingway spoke,—or rather read a paper. Very large fellow,—lame. Stood before the stand with his feet spread far apart. He got them together, once, but then he turned . . . so they spread apart again. After finishing the paper he turned abruptly and walked off stage. Curious how many faces you come to recognize at these meetings,—gets to be a family affair almost.

CAREY MCWILLIAMS

JULY 14

1935

it's never cold so it's never hot so it's full with a great and little emptiness—the emptiness of sick people . . . BUT 1 miraculous ocean!!!

E. E. CUMMINGS, to Ezra Pound

1949

There is no auditing at the UCLA summer session—I went four days until I was ejected—The classes (with one exception: Meyerhoff's Philosophy 21) promised to be mediocre, anyway—

I now have a social security card and a job as a file clerk at Republic Indemnity Co. of America—Bob's office—at $125 a month, five days a week, beginning Monday—

I am reading *The Decline of the West.*

SUSAN SONTAG

JULY 15

1926

Do you know that boy I raved to you about, Gary Cooper? Well I raved so much about him to Mr. Goldwyn, Mrs. Goldwyn, Frances Marion and our casting agent—and in fact to anyone who would listen to me—that Mr. Goldwyn finally wired to camp and asked our manager to sign him up under a five year contract. I was happy that he did this. Of course, this only makes the rift between us wider because he wouldn't have a thought for me since he is now on the road to bigger things, but I am happy anyway and I shall always cherish the thought that I helped him.

VALERIA BELLETTI

1940

I finished the book three days ago and am started on the typing. It is a pleasant book, in a quiet, unimportant way, and I do hope we at least get some advance royalties on it, as we need the money.

It is steadily hot now, with delightful nights. We eat in the patio quite a lot.

The country, or our hills rather, are turning a soft coppery brown, very beautiful. In the valley the apricot pickers are living in tents under the trees.

M.F.K. FISHER

JULY 16

1847

At 3 p.m. Cap Smith . . . mustered us out of service. . . . 3 cheers were given, and many left with the animals they had purchased for a camping ground 3 miles up the San Pedro River.

HENRY STANDAGE

1891

Conversed concerning the appropriation of water in the San Gabriel Canyon for purposes of power.

HENRY O'MELVENY

1938

At the studio this morning, getting only about three pages before Billy tore off to the races.

CHARLES BRACKETT

JULY 17

1958

Forgive the haste of this meager note, but I am dictating this as I run down Ventura Boulevard with my secretary right behind me.

She is the Olympic champion in the two-mile cross-country event, and so is in better form than I. In fact, I expect her to overtake me within the next half mile, at which point she will be dictating to me.

NORMAN CORWIN, to the lyricist E. Y. "Yip" Harburg

1960

It's like living on another planet down here. TV is the principal pursuit. You glue yourself to it. If you want to take a walk you get in your car. To go to the grocery or the liquor store you must have a car, though you could walk it in 20 minutes. Must confess one thing about the American—he's awfully kind and courteous behind the counter. Amazing what you can ask them and have them do for you with a genuine smile. (Even to cashing a check.) "The client is always right." Every house for miles around is a good one, costing from 20,000–100,000 dollars each. Nothing lacks, not even the garbage disposal in the sink, which makes a noise like giants being strangled under a hood. Frightening—but efficient. . . .

. . . Watching TV I caught up on the ball games. Takes about 2 ½ for a game to unroll.

. . . If Kennedy dies in office will have Johnson from Texas, about the narrowest-minded group of people in America, Texans. He's rich too, and proud of having been a school teacher. Can you beat that?

Three strikes and out! The Dodgers are in the lead.

HENRY MILLER, to Lawrence Durrell

1961

Last Saturday night went for the first time in my life to the Hollywood Bowl, the guest of Mr. and Mrs. Andre Kostelanitz [*sic*], taking with me as fellow guests Lilla Perry and Betty Peterman. It was a kind of a Grand Canyon of an audience, every seat taken, twenty thousand people, to hear an all-Gershwin program. A master of ceremonies named Cassidy at the intermission, before reporting coming events, suddenly was saying, "We have present with us this evening a man who has become a legend in his own time, Carl Sandburg." On the instant a spotlight played on me and I stood up and stretched my right arm to this announcer and then to the twenty thousand innocent people assembled. So there we are, "A legend in our own time." And what you and I have to say is, "Jesus, it could be worse!"

CARL SANDBURG, to his wife

1970

Today I wanted something to happen, something that would say—it has all been for this, leading to this, this is it, THIS IS WHAT IT IS ALL ABOUT.

Outside the smog glides by and the day passes from light to shade and the TV news is sodden and Sunday-minded and my stomach hurts in anticipation of my scheduled discharge and the electricity continues to work because we have paid the bill, paid all our bills, but there must be something else.

LIZA WILLIAMS

JULY 18

1939

Cooler!

Am resting a bit—in my very busy fashion. Rest for me is largely changing occupations. Transplanted a lot more herbs this morning, completing a big circle under one of the loquat trees.

. . . C. told me of the recent domestic strain. Her father has gone (great relief to her mother) to live his own separate, selfish life as before. She is to use his little house in the garden for his studio, much needed.

OLIVE PERCIVAL

1939

As I was dressing this morning, I had a disheartening concept of what my aging body requires. It is not only a poor, fumbling, tremulous machine; it is a decaying mass of flesh and bone. It needs constant care to prevent its being a nuisance to others. It stinks. It sheds its hair. It itches, aches and burns. It constantly sloughs its skin. It sweats, wrinkles and cracks. It was a poor contrivance at the beginning—it is now a burden. I must continue to wash it, dress it, endure its out-thrusting hair and fingernails and keep its internal cogworks from clogging. The best I can do for it is to cover it up with cloth of pleasing texture and color, for it is certain to become more unsightly as the months march on.

HAMLIN GARLAND

JULY 19

1870

Hauled dung all day to smoke out the grasshoppers.

HENRY DALTON

1964

I am beset by a kind of fantasy. I see men, healthy, well-fed, hefty, riding small creatures up a steep and rutted path. From the distance I cannot tell whether the beasts are lions or burros. . . .

The creatures emit weak and halting sounds, difficult to comprehend; the riders make orations, wise, eloquent and powerful. Certainly, their remarks make more sense than the cries of the beasts.

When I come out of this fantasy and try to make sense of it, I realize that the novel has been captured and tamed, its makers seduced or intimidated by the critics. . . . The novelists, lions grown mangy and toothless, have been brought in for display by the menageries of English departments. The position is undeniably attractive, secure with tenure, protected from the risk of the jungle of ordinary readers, given the meat of love and acceptance on classroom and lecture-hall schedule.

And even if the post is not made official, there is feeding in fellowships, grants and subsidies, administered by the critics and scholars who must be impressed.

ROBERT KIRSCH

JULY 20

1870

A DAY LATER

Hauled dung all day to smoke out the grasshoppers.

HENRY DALTON

1946

The other day a man came to my house representing a group of prominent Beverly Hills citizens who were circulating a petition which would place restrictive covenants barring all but Caucasians from the block in which I live. I read this list of sponsors very carefully, and found there the name of an actor who, like a good many people in motion pictures, has risen to affluence from the nickels and dimes paid into the box office by working people, including, I daresay, Negroes. It struck me so oddly that I began to laugh, and this man they had hired to pass the petition around said, "What are you laughing about?"

So I said, "You go and tell this actor that I am laughing about him sending this kind of a petition around." Because, I said, it wasn't so long ago that actors couldn't buy property in nice neighborhoods either. . . .

You go and tell that actor, I said to the man, that I'm getting up a petition too. And if he'll sign mine, I'll sign his.

DALTON TRUMBO

1961

Can I help it if my hair is short? Damn everyone who makes cracks at it. . . . I feel like hell.

WANDA COLEMAN

JULY 21

1933

This morning every Jewish Job's comforter of the orchestra came up to me and tried to dissuade me from playing Schoenberg. The argument is always the same—it drives away the crowd, Goossens played modern works and was never engaged again, there is no personal feeling against me, but it's in my own interests etc. etc., in the same monotonous scale. . . .

The radio people gave a talk about me this morning (I didn't hear it) saying my concerts created a sensation. The fact is that when a resident conductor played Tuesday night, a program of "good" music, the attendance hit a low for the two weeks. They cannot reason that away—for my concert drew a larger crowd on an afternoon, and without a celebrated soloist. Well, this Sunday ought to be a cinch. . . .

Capablanca called again and brought his book on chess. He is awfully nice and friendly.

NICOLAS SLONIMSKY

1934

We have a lovely home but almost no recreation. Zulime feels this more than I do. She is hungry for some sort of diversion but I hate the moving pictures with such bitterness that to go to them with her is to destroy all her pleasure in them. They all seem bent on showing the sexual organs of women. Somehow in every picture there is a disrobing scene or a dance which displays not merely legs and thighs but the female crotch. Seemingly no other object can be depended upon to interest our public.

HAMLIN GARLAND

JULY 22

1887

We went to Malibu in the morning with the intention of staying some days. . . . We took a Chinese cook and a driver. Reached Malibu in the afternoon very tired and the carreta we came in was broken. Warm clear day.

DON JUAN BAUTISTA BANDINI

1907

Many people daily gather to watch the Hawaiians in the surf at Venice.

Santa Monica Daily Outlook

JULY 23

1847

This morning the 3rd. Fifty made a start for home. . . . Travelled 20 miles to a ranch belonging to Gen Peko and encamp'd. This Rancho or farm seems to be the remains of an old Mission, several houses here covered with the old-fashioned English tile. Here are 2 large gardens and vineyards. One of these, I should think contained 200 acres. No grain raised in these enclosures but plenty of fruit such as grapes, figs, pears, apricots, cherries, plums, peaches, apples, and likewise black pepper, olive, date, palm tree and various others too numerous to mention.

HENRY STANDAGE

1887

Yesterday Mother through her new attorneys notified me she would not stand by her contract. This of course will lead to a very unpleasant law suit.

WILLIAM BANNING

1943

New York makes you hard and grubby, California relaxes you too much. Reading back through my journal to the summer I was here before, Laguna Beach in 1939, just before the war broke out in Europe—those far-away days. . . .

During that summer I was care-taker on a chicken-ranch while the owners were away. For days I would forget to feed the chickens, life was so dreamy, then I would make up for it by feeding them too much. About half of them died, fell on their backs with their feet sticking rigidly up, and I left the ranch in disgrace for New Mexico.

TENNESSEE WILLIAMS, to his publisher

JULY 24

1855

The idea of liberty in the United States is truly curious. . . . Certain people have no liberty at all. It is denied by the courts to every person of color. . . . But there is the great liberty of any white man to buy a human being in order to arbitrarily hang him or burn him alive. This happens in states where slavery is tolerated and the vilest despotism runs wild. This, in the center of the nation that calls itself a "model republic."

FRANCISCO P. RAMIREZ

1949

We spent this afternoon driving around the hills & the beach. L.A. is a weird town. For its size (much larger in area than New

York) it's got a very small central section. The rest is residential—poor like Coney [Island], middle-class like Flatbush, tony like Westchester—but the surroundings—high hills, almost mountains—are quite terrific. And the beach is beautiful—in places like the Riviera—other places like Asbury Park.

NORMAN MAILER

JULY 25

1933

There is a funny situation out here now. The sound men are on strike, and the other unions, camera men etc. are evidently going out with them. We "Writers" (a funny thing out here—when anyone asks you what you are you say "Writer") have a new union and a very radical one, organized by such old "movement" men as Howard, Lawson, Ornitz, Weitzenkorn, Caesar, and practically every editor of The Call since Abraham Cahan's day. But there's no chance of our ever striking—behind the barricades we'll go willingly enough, but organized labor action never. I went to a union meeting where there was some big talk, but at the slightest bit of Producer opposition we'll fold like the tents of the Arabs. The strange thing is that almost all the members of the union admit it themselves. Today when I came to work there were pickets in front of the studio, and it felt queer to walk through them. A Writer, one of them shouted, and lip-farted.

NATHANAEL WEST, to Edmund Wilson

1950

I don't want to conclude this letter without mentioning the great danger which the American nationalism might provoke. Will it not finally degenerate into anti-Semitism? We have seen such things.

Arnold Schoenberg, to Aaron Copland

JULY 26

1943

Don't know why all my vitality is gone. Maybe this climate, maybe lack of creative interest. "The Caller" doesn't excite me and nothing else does. . . .

I don't have the strength to move my literary pawns around the stage anymore. They are too heavy to push and they used to spring so lightly. And they have fallen into a sullen dumbness, after all their excited speech. Poor dummies! They sit and stare at me resentfully from the Shadowy Stage of my heart, and I can't help them today.

Some day I will again.

Tennessee Williams

1945

I've been here since June 7. In that time I have written one complete screen play, 145 pages. Two. Spent two weeks working at night and on weekends fixing up a picture for Ginger Rogers. Three. Spent two other weekends writing a 50-page story which we hope to sell to Howard Hawks. I'm doing all this to try to make enough money to get the hell out of this place and come back home and fix Missy's room and paint the house and do the other things we need. Along with this I attend to matters at the farm by correspondence with James, giving him directions and solving his problems.

William Faulkner, to his wife

2004

And even more than my—these days near obsessional—devouring of words, la salvación está en esto: my feverish *scratch scratch scratching* of rust-colored, fat, felt-tip pen. ¡He aquí! Con este acto puedo—*tengo* que—expiar, extirpar la angustia. Mitigar. Paliar. What else to do?

Susana Chávez-Silverman

JULY 27

1890

When my awful story, "The Yellow Wallpaper," comes out, you must try & read it. Walter says he has read it FOUR times and thinks it the most ghastly tale he ever read. Says it beats Poe, and Doré! But that's only a husband's opinion.

I read the thing to three women here however, and I never saw such squirms! Daylight too. It's a simple tale, but highly unpleasant.

I don't know yet where it will be. If none of the big things will take it I need to try the *New York Ledger.* Have you that in its new form? Kipling and Stevenson etc. etc. write for that now, so I guess I can.

Charlotte Perkins Gilman

1933

This place is not at all what I expected. It isn't very fantastic, just a desert got up to look like Asbury Park. And so far I've bumped into none of the things I expected and was prepared for by reports and plays like *Once in a Life Time.* The studio I am working Columbia is a highly organized and very practical business place. Five minutes after I arrived I was given an assignment a picture called BLIND DATE and I have been working nine hours a day on it since then with a full day on Saturday.

Nathanael West

1955

Nobody's spoken to me in less than a shout and I've been riding in nothing but Cadillacs and Thunderbirds. Fortunately, I am a level-headed, thoughtful sort of chap, and capable of being swayed by this sort of gaudy nonsense. Marilyn Monroe and I are just going to go ahead with our plans and get married, then settle down on her 12,000-acre citrus ranch, and make our own little world.

Elia Kazan

JULY 28

1939

Mrs. C. says now she is devoted to Genealogy—makes charts, etc. She comes of the best intellectual stock of old New England.

Olive Percival

1941

Most Hollywoodites are nice, but they have had to adopt a jungle attitude to exist. . . .

. . . A man who makes five thousand a week considers a man who earns five hundred per week a pauper not good enough to associate with. . . .

. . . Knowing the right people is more important in Hollywood than any place else. But being a relative of a big shot is even better. . . .

. . . Publicity is the life blood of the industry and they will do anything for it—even behave like human beings. . . .

. . . No matter how sappy the person, if he is a click he is worshipped. But a fine human being who is a flop is avoided like a disease. . . .

. . . All the highest paid brains haven't done as much for the celluloids as a sweater and a pair of sheer stockings and the right gals to fill them. . . .

. . . Hollywood is an amazing little fair land full of devils. An ermine-lined Hell. It is as colossal as it says it is; and it is as petty as its detractors claim. It's a star-spangled ride to Paradise.

WALTER WINCHELL

1972

Last night we went to Henry Miller's home. He limps and he is in pain, but he hesitates to undergo surgery. His mood was good. . . . Of course we both carry in our minds images from the past. I always see him dynamic, walking forever all through Paris, joyous. He always sees me as I was, lively, a dancer. . . .

Henry's Japanese ex-wife was there. She never loved him; for this I dislike her. . . . On one wall the shelves are filled with the translations of his books in fifteen or twenty languages.

ANAÏS NIN

JULY 29

1929

Books the Los Angeles Public Library believe might contaminate the morals or literary tastes of their readers should not be tolerated in Tarzana, and when we consider the fact that some hundred million [*Tarzan*] readers all over the world have already been contaminated, we should exert every effort to keep Los Angeles the one bright spot in the literary firmament.

EDGAR RICE BURROUGHS

1939

Big money did not immediately soften Burroughs' hatred of modern life. His great aim was to escape from civilization, and, as soon as he had money, he went to Southern California.

ALVA JOHNSTON

1941

We've just re-discovered the poetry of George Crabbe (all about Suffolk!) & are very excited—maybe an opera one day—

BENJAMIN BRITTEN

JULY 30

1769

We proceeded for four hours on a good road, with the exception of two very steep hills. We halted in a very large valley where there was much pasture and water. Here we had to construct a bridge to cross the gully. I consider this a good place for a mission.

GASPAR DE PORTOLÁ

1769

We left Los Ojitos, where there was another earthquake of no great violence, at half-past six in the morning. We crossed the plain in a northerly direction, steadily approaching the mountains. We ascended some hills which were quite rugged and high, afterwards we descended to a very extensive and pleasant valley where there was an abundance of water, part of it running in deep ditches, part of it standing so as to form marshes. This valley must be nearly three leagues in width and very much more in length. We pitched our camp near a ditch of running water, its banks covered with watercress and cumin. We gave this place the name of Valle de San Miguel. It is, perhaps, about four leagues from Los Ojitos. In the afternoon we felt another earthquake.

MIGUEL COSTANSÓ

1928

Flew into a Los Angeles airport this morning to wait till the fog raised to get over to another one at Santa Monica, when all at once a plane dropped down through fog that was thicker than smoke in a Presidential nominating room. And who crawled out of the thing but the kid himself, Lindbergh! . . . Fog don't stop that lad. I asked him where he was going and he told me, "Confidentially, East."

WILL ROGERS

JULY 31

1876

Earthquakes occur fairly frequently, usually in August.

LUDWIG SALVATOR

1937

I've been kept busy every minute. The first thing to settle was the Memorial Concert. There were two groups working against each other, one—the ASCAP which wanted to run one at the Shrine Auditorium—the proceeds to go to a scholarship fund—the other group was the Hollywood Bowl organization which wanted the proceeds of their concert to go to themselves as there is usually a deficit at the end of the season. . . .

I packed a trunk with suits, shoes, etc. and will send it by freight Monday.

IRA GERSHWIN, to his mother

AUGUST 1

1935

Sat through a very uninteresting performance of the Tschaikowsky *Sixth Symphony* in order to hear *Beethoven's Violin Concerto,* Heifetz playing superbly. And these continual complaints that we, if I may include myself among musicians, are making, I was forced to make again. After hearing the Tschaikowsky once, which I believe everyone who has entered a symphony hall has, I see no necessity for hearing it again, since, by virtue of sequence upon sequence and repetition upon repetition, one is forced hearing it once to hearing it scores of times. . . . And the programs here at the Bowl are generally bad. . . .

My study with Schoenberg is progressing steadily. We have reached four-part counterpoint, second species. He is very good to us, and takes great pains teaching us. His English has become very good. He is even able to be witty with the use of words, which represents a certain level of mastery. He is moving, I believe into another house. And I understand that he has been engaged by the University here for another year. They promise to present many of his works. . . .

Xenia is an angel. We have been married now almost two months. It is always very beautiful. . . .

August 3rd we have a meeting of your composers, modern, of Los Angeles. I don't know exactly what will happen. Wm. Grant Still will be there, and some other negro composers. They have asked me to play something.

JOHN CAGE

1942

This is a strange and curious place.

William Faulkner, to his agent

AUGUST 2

1769

We halted not very far from the river, which we named Porciúncula. Here we felt three consecutive earthquakes in the afternoon and night. We must have traveled about three leagues today. This plain where the river runs is very extensive. It has good land for planting all kinds of grain and seeds, and is the most suitable site of all that we have seen for a mission, for it has all the requisites for a large settlement. As soon as we arrived about eight heathen from a good village came to visit us; they live in this delightful place among the trees on the river. They presented us with some baskets of pinole made from seeds of sage and other grasses. Their chief brought some strings of beads made of shells, and they threw us three handfuls of them. Some of the old men were smoking pipes well made of baked clay and they puffed at us three mouthfuls of smoke. We gave them a little tobacco and glass beads, and they went away well pleased.

Fray Juan Crespi

1856

Almost all the newspapers from the north are continually filled with reports of lynchings in the mines. And, oh fatality! only Mexicans are the victims of the people's insane fury! Mexicans alone have been sacrificed on gallows raised to launch their poor souls into eternity. Is this the liberty and equality of the country we have adopted?

FRANCISCO P. RAMIREZ

1933

I gave the watercolor to Diego R[ivera]. He was very pleased. He too was just in a very annoying and difficult situation, because he was stopped from completing his wall murals in the Rockefeller Center. He still is answering correspondence from three years ago and is the subject of much contention in America just now. I am trying to get him some connections here. For now he is still busy in New York with the murals, but wants to do film and is dying to do so.

GALKA SCHEYER, to Wassily Kandinsky

1941

"Why do we go wrong in our relations with other human beings? Because of a basic inattention." [Josiah Royce]. . . .

Try to avoid negative emotion. Most newspaper reading, especially in wartime, is crying over spilt milk. . . .

Begin to lead the rationed life: no more toys, only tools. There isn't any such thing as human nature; we can rise to anything because we can sink to anything. . . .

Our ideal should be to accept unlimited liability for all the acts of our fellow human beings. We are all members with one another.

CHRISTOPHER ISHERWOOD

1943

As for "The Gentleman Caller," I have devised a new ending for it, considerably lighter, almost happy, and I'm having to re-write the earlier scenes to jive with it.

As for Metro, by the time my six months are up here, I hope that I will have been gripped by some really big theme for a long play, one deserving entire devotion—In which case, I would retire to Mexico and live on those savings until it is finished.

Let's face it!—I can only write for love. Even then, not yet well-enough to set the world on fire. But all this effort, all this longing to create something of value—it will be thrown away, gone up the spout, nothing finally gained—If I don't adhere very strictly to the most honest writing.

TENNESSEE WILLIAMS

1959

Aunt Frieda had a wonderful cold chicken lunch, string beans, potato salad, tomato and lettuce salad, hot rolls, fresh pineapple, coffee cake and tea ready for us yesterday when we came. Both she and Uncle Walter are handsome, fun, and so young in spirit. They have a little green Eden of a house, surrounded by pink and red and white oleander bushes, with two avocado trees loaded down with (alas) not-yet-ripe fruit, a peach tree, a guava tree, a persimmon tree, a fig tree and others.

Aunt Frieda has had some wonderful adventures and is a great storyteller. Ted gets on magnificently with Walter; we simply love them both. It is amazing how Frieda resembles daddy.

SYLVIA PLATH

1966

This is the story of the United Space Ship Enterprise. Assigned a five-year patrol of our galaxy, the giant starship visits Earth colonies, regulates commerce, and explores strange new worlds and civilizations. These are its voyages . . . and its adventures.

GENE RODDENBERRY

AUGUST 3

1769

On our way we met the entire population of an Indian village engaged in harvesting seeds on the plain. In the afternoon there were other earthquakes; the frequency of them amazed us.

MIGUEL COSTANSÓ

1769

At half-past six we left the camp and forded the Porciúncula River, which runs down from the valley, flowing through it from the mountains into the plain. After crossing the river we entered a large vineyard of wild grapes and an infinity of rosebushes in full bloom. All the soil is black and loamy, and is capable of producing every kind of grain and fruit which may be planted. We went west, continually over good land well covered with grass. After traveling about half a league we came to the village of this region, the people of which, on seeing us, came out into the road. As they drew near us they began to howl like wolves; they greeted us and wished to give us seeds, but as we had nothing at hand in which to carry them we did not accept them. Seeing this, they threw some handfuls of them on the ground and the rest in the air. . . .

We judge that in the mountains that run to the west in front of us there are some volcanoes, for there are many signs on the road which stretches between the Porciúncula River and the Spring of the Alders, for the explorers saw some large marshes of a certain substance like pitch; they were boiling and bubbling.

FRAY JUAN CRESPI

1967

[Executive producer] Mort Abrahams drove out for an inconclusive discussion on what I should say in the final speech, looking at the ruined Statue of Liberty. Fox wants to shoot three versions, giving them all possible choices. I obviously prefer to shoot only the speech I wrote, since this is my only chance to put muscle behind that choice. Besides, it's the best. I can't believe the Code still forbids the use of "God damn you!" It's surely acceptable in the context of this speech; Taylor is literally calling on God to damn the destroyers of civilization.

CHARLTON HESTON

AUGUST 4

1769

We made camp near the springs, where we found a good village of very friendly and docile Indians, who, as soon as we arrived, came to visit us, bringing their present of baskets of sage and other seeds, small, round nuts with a hard shell, and large and very sweet acorns. They made me a present of some strings of beads of white and red shells which resemble coral, though not very fine; we reciprocated with glass beads. I understood that they were asking us if we were going to stay, and I said "No," that we were going farther on. I called this place San Gregorio, but to the soldiers the spot is known as the Springs of El Berrendo, because they caught a deer alive there, it having had a leg broken the preceding afternoon by a shot fired by one of the volunteer soldiers, who could not overtake it. The water is in a hollow surrounded by low hills not far from the sea.

FRAY JUAN CRESPI

1847

Lieut Stoneman 1st Drags quarters were broken open and his trunk robbed of seven hundred dollars—I had just left his quarters with him and on our return we were informed by Mrs Flores that two men had broken in the house—she saw them from her door which was next—We made great exertions last night to discover the thieves but as yet have not been successful—I am truly sorry for poor Stoneman—It is hard to lose money so far from home

LIEUTENANT JOHN MCHENRY HOLLINGSWORTH

1920

The reason I stay here is because this summer climate is without exception the finest I have ever known. Sky, mountains, the sea, light, temperature and a sensuous wind combine to make it perfect. 88 to go at noon. Cool winds 23¢, a blanket at night—and every night. No flies, no mosquitoes, no gnats, ants, cockroaches or bugs of any kind. Name me a better summer world with—of course—the exception of Baltimore.

JOHN FANTE, to H. L. Mencken

1957

The Almighty has withdrawn his hitherto effusive regard for me and struck me down. . . . On Monday I lay in the sun and bathed in the pool, and in the evening, just as I was dressing to go out and dine quietly with Leonard Spigelgass, I bent down to get some socks out of a drawer and was seized with a blazing pain across the small of my back. At first I thought I had slipped something but I suspected, and I was right, that it was my old friend "lumbago."

From then on the whole week became a highly coloured nightmare. Clifton sent me to an ass of a chiropractor, who was most sympathetic and kindly and tortured me more thoroughly than the Gestapo.

Noël Coward

AUGUST 5

1769

The scouts who had set out to examine the coast and the road along the beach returned shortly afterwards with the news of having reached a high, steep cliff, terminating in the sea where the mountains end. . . .

At the end of the canyon, however, the hills were somewhat more accessible and permitted us to take the slope and, with much labor, to ascend to the summit, whence we discerned a very large and pleasant valley. We descended to it and halted near the watering-place, which consisted of a very large pool. Near this there was a populous Indian village, and the inhabitants were very good natured and peaceful. They offered us their seeds in trays or baskets of rushes, and came to the camp in such numbers that, had they been armed, they might have caused us apprehension.

Miguel Costansó

1935

Here, at night, the people gather on the beach and light fires. Down the beach road it is like a decoration of fire-beads round the curve of the bay. And Japanese and Hawaiians and Americans sit and make love and get drunk, and the drunker most people become the louder they are, and the drunker the Hawaiians become the better they sing and play guitars and dance strange dances in the firelight, until they are so homesick they can only drink more and sing more. You watch and find yourself shut out because you are white.

There are still mountains here and palm trees and oranges and strange blossoms, but they do not touch me any more, either to delight or offend me. They are, just as I am.

Eric Knight, to a friend

1949

In this fourth year of drought everything is horribly parched, the stream is dry, the oaks losing their leaves, even the pine trees unhappy. A few more seasons of this kind of thing, and the whole of southern California will have gone back to the coyotes. Which might be quite a good thing, perhaps.

Aldous Huxley, to Anita Loos

2012

A crowd of about thirty people was gathered in a corner of Canter's Deli close to 11 p.m. on Friday night. It was a fairly grungy group, dominated by young people, but well seasoned with middle-aged duffers like myself. Graphic t-shirts were the uniform of choice, dreadlocks and face studs the predictable accessories of those who had shown up to be accessories to municipal misdemeanors. We were drinking coffee and milkshakes, laughing and kibitzing a few steps away from the Kibitz Room, where the evening's band could be heard warming up.

At the center of the group was Robbie Conal, a jolly, urban gnome in a chicken t-shirt. He was holding up his latest street poster, a Mitt Romney visage rendered in the classic Conal hand: over lined and jittery, a graphic manifestation of Conal's genius. . . .

We were Robbie's guerrilla postering crew. After two decades of watching his iconic posters crop up mysteriously on street corners around Los Angeles, I felt privileged to finally be there, at the center of the Los Angeles political art hub. . . .

"Ma'am, is one of these kids yours?" the larger of the two officers asked me. I parked, got out and identified Bunnyhead as my personal perp. . . .

These two officers immediately saw they had nabbed some newbies. They checked student ID's and asked about their SAT scores. They even went so far as to admire the poster and tell the kids they thought their political activism was admirable, but private property had to be protected. The crew nodded in perfect understanding. Because everyone was so cool, they gave the kids a break on the vandalism charge, and let them go with a curfew infraction. The guilty parties scraped the poster off the door, parents were notified, citations were issued and everyone went home. We await our court date and anticipate a small fine.

The evening was fun until it suddenly wasn't fun. Watching my daughter being questioned and fingerprinted by the police was not a peak parenting experience, and I must tell you, I questioned my own judgement. But this is where the rubber of progressive parenting meets the road of authoritarianism. Our family believes in free speech and political activism. Afterward we talked about how it would have been different if she had been out randomly tagging with malicious intent. It's a fine line between vandalism and street art, and I wanted her to be clear about where it lay. I also made it clear that I would have felt very differently if she had gone and done this without my permission or protection. Call me a hypocrite, but I encourage my children to question all authority except my own.

Erika Schickel

AUGUST 6

1769

This day we both said Mass, which was attended by everybody, and then we rested, receiving innumerable visits from heathen who came to see us from different parts. They had heard of the sailing of the packets to the coast and channel of Santa Barbara; they drew on the ground the shape of the channel with its islands, marking the route of the ships. They told us also that in other times bearded people, clothed and armed as they saw the soldiers, had come into their country, motioning that they had come from the east. One of them said he had been to their countries and had seen their towns formed of large houses, and that each family occupied its own. He added, besides, that in a few days' march, about seven or eight leagues to the north, we would come to a great river which ran between rough mountains and could not be forded, and that farther on we would see the ocean, which would prevent us from going on in this direction. The information gave us anxiety, but we put it off to be settled by our own eyes.

Fray Juan Crespi

1837

Perfecto Hugo Reid, native of Great Britain, Roman Catholic, resident of the City of Our Lady of the Angels, appears before your Lordship in the best legal manner to state: that during the term of three years he has lived in the above-mentioned city, engaged in business, et cetera, has benefited society in every way possible, and finding himself ready to enter into the state of matrimony with a native daughter of this country, respectfully requests and entreats your permission to contract this marriage.

Hugo Reid

1847

I relieved Captn Smith 1st Drag and went on as officier of the day—I have a guard of about twenty—volunteers and ten dragoons on the heights with two pieces of artillery and ready for a fight at any time the Calafornians want it—

Lieutenant John McHenry Hollingsworth

1952

The town is a horror of ugliness, flat as your hand and crawling with cars. Nobody dreams of walking anywhere and shops and houses are miles apart.

The sudden change is a bit bewildering, and I shall be glad to get over the first few days. One feels a little like the new boy at school but it is all amusingly new, though exactly like one had expected really. I think I have already persuaded them that a beard for Cassius is not a good plan.

John Gielgud, to his mother

AUGUST 7

1769

A little before three in the afternoon we set out to the north and crossed the plain, which is about three leagues wide, and went to camp at the foot of the mountains in a very green valley grown with large live oaks and alders. The water was sufficient for the animals though not over abundant.

Fray Juan Crespi

1932

Got a good rub down in morning and had steak. Went to stadium, warmed up, another hot rub. Ran second in the relay. We got 1st place and broke Olympic and World Record.

EVELYN OJEDA, née Furtsch

AUGUST 8

1769

We ascended by a sharp ridge to a high pass, the ascent and descent of which was painful, the descent being made on foot because of the steepness. Once down we entered a small valley in which there was a village of heathen, who had already sent messengers to us at the valley of Santa Catalina de Bononia to guide us and show us the best road and pass through the mountains. These poor Indians had many provisions ready to receive us. Seeing that it was our intention to go on in order not to lose the march, they urgently insisted that we should go to their village, which was some distance off the road; and we were obliged to consent in order not to displease them. We enjoyed their good will and their presents. . . .

It is a very suitable site for a mission, with much good land, many palisades, two very large arroyos of water, and five large villages close together.

FRAY JUAN CRESPI

1932

You folks all over the United States that thought these Olympic Games was just some real estate racket of Los Angeles and didn't come, you have been badly fooled. You have missed the greatest show from every angle that was ever held in America.... Regardless of hard times, there has been from 70,000 to 105,000 people every day. Regardless of this old town's boosting blowing, they certainly come through beautiful.... And say don't worry about the Japanese flying over here in case of war, those birds will swim over.

WILL ROGERS

1949

I've got a funny story to tell you about Ayn Rand. . . . It seems that a character by the name of Lenny Spigelgass, whom you may know, was working once at Warners in a writer's office across from hers. He didn't know who she was until one day, being the kind of blank-a-week who doesn't rate a telephone, he crossed the hall to use hers. She of course knows that all Jews are communists, and with the instinct of such people can pick a Jew at 50 yards in any kind of crowd you want to name. Poor Lennie knocked on her door, walked in, said may I use your telephone, and begin to reach for it. Whereupon Miss Rand reared back and spit at him. So help me.

NORMAN MAILER, to Lillian Hellman

AUGUST 9

1877

We reached the city of "Our Lady" at high noon of an August day....

You read Spanish, French, German and English newspapers,

all printed in Los Angeles. It is many-tongued as a Mediterranean sea-port, and hospitable as a grandee.

Yesterday and to-day are strangely blended. . . .

We went through a side door into the poor, neglected city of the silent. It has survived grief and friends. It is too old. Gray, wooden crosses lean this way and that, over graves that are nameless. Sealed tombs are crumbling. It lies there under the church wall in the glare of the sun, the autograph of death and desolation scrawled upon the dusty, thirsty and insatiate earth. It is consecrated ground, but dishonored by neglect. What would we have?

. . . The Mission Garden is not as old as the Garden of Eden, but it was a cultivated spot, for all that, when there was not a State between Pennsylvania and the Pacific Ocean but the state of Nature, and when saddles, bateaux, dug-outs and moccasins were the only means of conveyance. We came to a high wall and a low adobe, and halted in the shade of a great palm seventy feet high planted by a Franciscan two generations ago. It was my first acquaintance with the tree where it seemed to be at home. Its trunk was curiously fluted, and it spread its great palms as if it felt and enjoyed the sunshine. Our knocks at the gate brought the reply of a couple of dogs, and if I can judge of the canine gamut, I should say those dogs were hungry, and barked in the key of C sharp. They leaped, and looked through the cracks of the wall, and snuffed like a camel that smells water, barking their way up and down those cracks as boy runs his mouth along the holes of a harmonica and blows. . . .

. . . It is not a bit more like Irving's Alhambra than a Scotch kale patch is like the Queen's gardens at Kew.

Benjamin Franklin Taylor

1939

Your very kind and flattering letter of July 27th, in which you asked me to leave my footprints in cement at the World's Fair, reached me the morning I left New York for Hollywood. I am terribly sorry that I missed my big opportunity and only hope that you will ask me again the next time I come to New York.

I think the Sands of Time is a brilliant idea, and should have enjoyed seeing it myself.

Anita Loos

1952

Brando is a funny, intense, egocentric boy of 27, with a flat nose and bullet head, huge arms and shoulders, and yet giving the effect of a lean Greenwich Village college boy. He is very nervous indeed and mutters his lines and rehearses by himself all day long. Very deferential to me, and dragged me off to record two speeches of Antony on his machine. . . . He tells me he owns a cattle ranch, and after two more years filming, will be financially secure altogether!!

The parties are grand, but clumsy—awful food, too much drink, rather noisy and the weirdest mixture of clothes, women in beach clothes or full evening dress and the men in every crazy variety of sports clothes. But it is not difficult to pick out the people one wants to talk to, and the rest of the guests don't seem to trouble one or expect one to trouble about them.

John Gielgud, to his mother

AUGUST 10

1904

This morning at about 10 Petra came from Josefa's house to tell me that Alejandro was sick. Patricio went while I got ready to go and he told me that Alejandro was dead. I went at once and found him in his bed. He had shot himself in the mouth and had been dead for some time. Spent the rest of the day with the undertaker—arranging everything. Put Valenzuela to clean the room where the misfortune occurred. The undertaker took the body to his office on 3rd st. Sent Patricio to the rancho to lock all the doors and to see how everything was. Chata and Carolina Winston came and left at 8. Clear day.

Don Juan Bautista Bandini

1907

I waited by Echo Lake this morning for my car. The water was green as the trees; the dandified blackbirds strutted on the grass, so beautifully shaded by the big willows. Then three white swans sailed processionally around the little island. . . . A pretty summer picture.

Olive Percival

1910

I was very sad today, dearest, things seemed so very intricate, so hopelessly complicated—oh—sweetheart, if we work and hope and be good children! Is it possible—can happiness wait us? . . .

Goodnight,—all my heart is yours to keep—

Una Kuster, to her future husband, Robinson Jeffers

1939

YOU AND YOUR FRIENDS
ARE INVITED TO THE
PREMIERE
WEST COAST SHOWING
OF
PICASSO'S
MASTERPIECE
GUERNICA
AND 63 RELATED PAINTINGS
AND DRAWINGS . . .
DAILY FROM 10 A.M. TO 10 P.M.
AT THE
STENDAHL ART GALLERIES
3006 WILSHIRE BOULEVARD
LOS ANGELES CALIFORNIA

ENTRANCE FOR PREMIERE
TWO-FIFTY
(plus tax)
General Admission—
Aug. 11th to 21st, 100.
Students 25 c (plus tax)
BENEFIT SPANISH ORPHANS

Under Auspices of
MOTION PICTURE ARTISTS' COMMITTEE
Hillside 7361 for Reservations

EARL STENDAHL

1949

Lunch at the Farmers' Market with the [Stravinskys], Christopher Isherwood, and the Huxleys, the latter cooing to each other today like newlyweds, or oldlyweds making up after a spat. Owing to its extensive variety of salads, seeds (Aldous eats quantities of sunflower seeds, for his eyes), nuts, health foods, exotic fruit (Milton: "The savory pulp they chew, and in the rind"), the restaurant is a Huxleyan haunt. Most of the other tables are held down by drugstore cowboys, movie stars, Central European refugees, and—to judge by the awed glances in our direction—Aldine and Igorian disciples. All are vegetarians, for the nonce, and all nibble at their greens like pasturing cows. . . .

ROBERT CRAFT

1966

Space, the final frontier. These are the voyages of the Starship Enterprise. Its five-year mission: to explore strange new worlds; to seek out new life and new civilizations; to boldly go where no man has gone before.

GENE RODDENBERRY

AUGUST 11

1926

And Los Angeles is America. A jungle. Los Angeles grew up suddenly, *planlessly,* under the stimuli of the adventurous spirit of millions of people and the profit motive. It is still growing. Here everything has a chance to thrive—for a while—as a rule only a brief while. Inferior as well as superior plants and trees flourish for a time, then both succumb to chaos and decay. They must give way to new plants pushing up from below, and so on. This is freedom under democracy. Jungle democracy!

LOUIS ADAMIC

1962

Don and Aldous and I went down by helicopter from the National Aeronautics and Space Administration office in Santa Monica to the North American plant in Downey, to be told about the moon rocket which they are building there. Don and I chiefly accepted the invitation for the sake of the helicopter ride, and it was even more exciting than I had expected. The ease and abruptness of the ascent is like flying in dreams. It is as if you merely make an extra effort of the will—symbolized by the roar of the engine—and suddenly the ground tilts away from you and you are soaring. I was also reminded of Rembrandt's drawing of the angel leaving Manoah. Several people who happened to be passing watched our ascent into heaven with expressions of pleased amazement.

The city was shocking in its uniformity; all those roofs and little yards and bug-autos and occasional glittering green pools, so much of it, stretching away and away, you never saw the end of it. Only, in the background, the big mountains appearing behind smears of yellow smog.

The eager-beaver executives at North American were intimidated by Huxley's ghost-pale introspective intensity. He was like a ghost they had raised to speak to them of the future. And they didn't much like what they heard. Aldous held forth with his usual relish on the probability that the astronauts would bring back some disease which would wipe out the human race. And then he described the coming overpopulation of the earth. You felt that these people had bad consciences. They were making a fortune for their firm because the government will aid and abet them in playing gadgetry. So they keep reminding all who will listen that *if* they can go faster than the speed of light, and *if* they can reach an inhabited planet, and *if* the inhabitants of that planet are ahead of us in technics, and *if* they are willing and able to communicate to us what they know—why, then we shall be able to make great strides ahead.

Christopher Isherwood

AUGUST 12

1877

Pico House

Everything about here pleases me and I felt sorely tempted to take Dr. Congar's advice and invest in an orange patch myself. I feel sure you will be happy here with the Doctor and Allie among so rich a luxuriance of sunny vegetation. How you will dig and dibble in that mellow loam! I cannot think of you standing erect for a single moment, unless it be in looking away out into the dreamy West.

I made a fine shaggy little five days' excursion back in the heart of the San Gabriel Mountains, and then a week of real pleasure with Congar. . . . He has a fine little farm, fine little family, and fine cozy home. I felt at home with Congar and at once took possession of his premises and all that is in them. We drove down through the settlements eastward and saw the best orange groves and vineyards, but the mountains I, as usual, met alone. Although so gray and silent and unpromising they are full of wild gardens and ferneries. Lilyries!—some specimens ten feet high with twenty lilies, big enough for bonnets!

John Muir

1913

Los Angeles is wonderful. Nowhere in the United States is the Negro so well and beautifully housed, nor the average efficiency and intelligence in the colored population so high. . . . Out here in this matchless Southern California there would seem to be no limit to your opportunities, your possibilities. . . .

Los Angeles is no paradise. The color line is there and simply drawn. Women have had difficulty in having gloves and shoes fitted at stores, the hotels do not welcome colored people, the restaurants are not for all that hunger.

W.E.B. Du Bois

AUGUST 13

1993

[M.] is the tennis coach who was hired to coach Erik exclusively after his parents' deaths. He said he helped Erik get settled in an apartment in the Marina del Rey Towers and managed all his waking moments.

Hazel Thornton

2014

This landscape is volatile, the gods are throwing lightning bolts at swimmers in the sea, opening up the ground to swallow our chariots, rattling the earth with their stomach growls. That sense of Los Angeles should be in the book. Though I don't remember any earthquakes as a child, just the biting smog, the smog that bit my face and eyes and made me plead not to go downtown.

Dental work in Burbank, removing old silver filling, a worry about mercury. Dentist needed to scrape around near the nerve. Shots deep in the jaw. Anxiety. I asked for nitrous oxide and they'd procured it for me. Out of pocket and worth it. $50 a tank, the nurse said cheerfully. She sat by me while the Novocain took effect. Inhale inhale, that's the way to check out. Zooming out, I screen the entire film of Anatole Litvak's *Mayerling* in my head, the tragic romance, the doomed prince, the plot against the throne—thinking why my mother would have loved it so much. Danielle Darrieux' face is perfect for 19th century angst.

When the dentist asks if I'm doing ok, I tell him I'm working on my next book. I'm thinking of people I love—my brother Larry. I don't see him enough. I'm waiting for the words, "We're done now." I'm gripping the armrest and trying to relax. I'm remembering to breathe and wanting it to be over. According to the dentist, I kept murmuring "Nitrous in Gaza, Nitrous in Gaza." I solved world peace.

From my nitrous oxide dental experience, I hurtle downtown via the 110 Arroyo Freeway to a mandatory session at Central Library with our "disaster expert" who explains how to evacuate the building in the case of a) an earthquake b) a fire c) a gas leak and d) a sarin attack. "Remember," he says, "when the planes flew into the WTC, the whole building was twisted. So don't count on using those doors to exit."

I felt queasy. Slept 5 hours. Awoke to read about explorer Percy Fawcett in the living hell of the fecund Amazon, lianas choking trees, the competition for light, poison darts, children roasting on a spit, maggots in the flesh, mosquitos in the eyeballs.

LOUISE STEINMAN

AUGUST 14

1907

Am reading modern Japanese fiction. There are several Japanese book-stores in town, each an extremely interesting place. . . . All these revelations of the Japanese mind and heart convince me anew of the childishness there is in forgetting that all races of men are brothers—that we all know the same struggles, the same hardships, the same loves and hates. O! that "the civilized world" would but believe this utterly and stop the unspeakable sin of War!

Olive Percival

1925

Dear Andrew:

. . . Sunday there was a quite gay party that began about the middle of the afternoon and progressed until deep into the night. It was one mess of novelists, poets, critics, et cetera, successful, good, bad great and small. I went to see one of the said novelists, Gordon Young, Tuesday afternoon in order to gratify his avid desire to exhibit his library, which is said to be the best of the kind on the coast.

It is really a marvellous collection of old and rare books—first folios of Shakespeare, Spenser, Chaucer, and hundreds of lesser men, but the real prize perhaps is a copy of Holinshed's Chronicles imputed to be Shakespeare's.

Robert Penn Warren

1955

Lunch with Gore. I guess he's still wondering what I think of *Messiah,* his novel. Well, I don't. I'm bored and stuck fast. He asks quite often about my journal and talks apprehensively about the famous one Anais Nin is keeping—seventy volumes already!—in which he believes he figures most unfavorably. I believe he really thinks about "posterity" and its "verdict"—just like a nineteenth-century writer! And I don't know whether to admire this, or feel touched by it, or just regard him as a conceited idiot.

Christopher Isherwood

1962

Sports

I like tennis
But never had no one to play tennis with me.

Octavia M. Butler

1965

Every time a car with whites in it entered the area the word spread like lightning down the street:

"Here comes Whitey—Get him!" . . .

I believe the mobs would have moved into white neighborhoods, but it was getting late and many of them had to go to work Friday morning.

Robert Richardson

AUGUST 15

1850

When the city has no work in which to employ the chain gang, the Recorder shall, by means of notices conspicuously posted, notify the public that such a number of prisoners will be auctioned off to the highest bidder for private service.

City Council Minutes

1934

Here I sit, laughing and laughing. I have a secretary and a great big office and a lot of people bow when I pass, all of them hating my Dago guts—

I not only made these folks swallow that bilge-water but I did it to the tune of $1500, plus $250 a week for an indefinite period. Whoops! I never had so much money in the offing in my life; moreover, if my luck holds good I shall certainly bed Del Rio inside of four weeks. Even as a tiny tot behind the coal shed that woman was my objective, and once I sent her twenty-five cents for her picture. Ah, what an American idyll. . . .

Here's a good one on Erskine Caldwell. He is out here coining money hand over fist at Metro-Goldwyn-Mayer. The producers assigned him to the task of writing an original North Woods story. Caldwell is from the South, as you know. He was stumped. But he went to work and delivered a long script. He had no idea of what a "North Woods" story was about, so, on the last page of his script, the last line, he wrote in parenthesis, "(All of the above action takes place in the North Woods.)"

John Fante, to H. L. Mencken

1961

Some of the things that are going on made me sick. . . . who is going to help the people?

Cesar Chavez, to his mentor

AUGUST 16

1935

Jesus, I just this instant heard that Will Rogers was killed; I was doing an original script which I hoped to sell to Fox for him—

Don Marquis, to a friend

1945

I don't like this damn place any better than I ever did. That is one Comfort: at least I cant be any sicker tomorrow for Mississippi than I was yesterday.

WILLIAM FAULKNER, to a friend

1952

One begins to scent the jealousies and disappointments and ambitions much as in the theatre, only rather more concentrated out here, like actors crossed with Anglo-Indian civil servants who have a perpetual chip on their shoulders!

JOHN GIELGUD, to his mother

AUGUST 17

1846

To the People of California . . .

The Territory of California now belongs to the United States, and will be governed, as soon as circumstances permit, by officers and laws similar to those by which other Territories of the United States are regulated and protected.

But, until the governor, the secretary, and council are appointed, and the various departments of the government are arranged . . . persons who, without special permission, are found with arms outside of their own houses, will be considered as enemies and will be shipped out of the country.

ROBERT F. STOCKTON

1938

Corinne phoned good-bye. Feel quite a gap. Don't know what to think yet.

MARSHALL MCLUHAN

1946

If Howard Hughes intends to continue producing pictures like *The Outlaw,* his studio had better do something about research.

At any moment now I am expecting to walk into a theater to see Ulysses S. Grant attacking the Maginot Line, or Lydia Pinkham doing the Salome dance with the head of Senator Bilbo.

To anyone with the slightest knowledge of Western history, this most recent display of Western lore is painful, to say the least.

If I were a relative of either Pat Garrett or Doc Holliday, I'd sure sue somebody.

LOUIS L'AMOUR

AUGUST 18

1935

The papers this morning are filled with news and letters concerning Rogers. No one, not even a president, could command such space by dying, for Rogers has no enemy and politics does not bar anyone from speaking well of him. He is on the way to become a mythical character, but to me he was a homely character, a rancher with the mind of a wit and a philosopher. I think of him sitting obscurely on the ground with the grooms while a polo game was going on. Even when playing he avoided notice as much as possible. He came usually in ranch clothing, a soft hat drawn low over his face. On a horse he was transformed. He rode lightly, gracefully, in cowboy style, and he played a superb game. He wore a red over shirt which showed his white sleeves to the elbow and my dim eyes were able to follow him. He was everywhere on the field, his voice ringing out in command. When his boys played with him, they were a host!

HAMLIN GARLAND

1936

Worked with Billy Wilder, who paces constantly, has over-extravagant ideas, but is stimulating. He has the blasé quality I have missed sadly in dear Frank Partos. He has humor—a kind of humor that sparks with mine.

CHARLES BRACKETT, on meeting his partner

1962

I like the Giants but I think the Dodgers best and I want to see the Yankees beaten. It don't much matter who does the job.

LANGSTON HUGHES

AUGUST 19

1942

Life is going on much the same as usual here with occasional excursions into Hollywood—to concerts that [John] Barbirolli conducts at the Bowl, and to see odd people that are, have been, or may be useful to any of us. It is an extraordinary place—

absolutely mad, and really horrible. I can't really attempt to describe it, because it has no relation to any other place on earth. It actually isn't a place by itself but a suburb of Los Angeles, which is the ugliest and most sprawling city on earth. The chief features of Hollywood are that the things that one worries about so much don't matter a damn—money, time, distance, behaviour, clothes (especially for men). It is completely unreal. . . .

One house we stayed in was built like a boat, with a moat round it,—in the middle of all the other houses—which anyhow are any and every style from a native-mud-hut to an Indian temple—via Pagoda & Spanish villas. . . .

The driving is mad—I saw a wonderful little argument between 2 cars the one on the right wanting to go left, across the other which wouldn't give way. After blowing its horn madly for about 1 minute (they were both travelling about 45 down a main Boulevard), it started to swerve madly about—like this [diagram] until finally it just barged into the side of the other, & there was an awful crash—just because neither would give way!

BENJAMIN BRITTEN, to his sister

1948

How I long to surrender! How easy it would be to convince myself of the plausibility of my parents' life!

SUSAN SONTAG

AUGUST 20

1886

At 8 o'clock we await the train for Santa Monica, one of the finest resorts of the Pacific coast. The train is long and filled with passengers going to the coast to spend the day. We ride through continual orange groves and fruit orchards loaded with fruits of all kinds, oranges, figs, lemon, plums, olives, peaches and grapes, until we reach the little town of 1,000 inhabitants which lies upon the sandy bluffs around the horseshoe curve of the Pacific coast.

Here we find a happy place to spend a summer day. Along the coast is a village of tents which are homes for the hundreds that are spending the summer here. A long canopy built of boards extends along the shore, where, protected from the sun, we may sit and watch the many as they go in and out of the water. . . .

Back of this awning are extensive bathing houses, where all kinds of baths can be secured. Hot, cold, salt, fresh, plunge, steam, or private. We secure our valuables, and avail ourselves of an ocean bath. The sea is rough, and as we are unused to jumping the waves, we hold to the rope while they carry us under, much to the amusement of those who are accustomed to the waters. Conscious of the fact that too much bathing is not well for those unused to the water, we secure dry clothes and sit upon the walk to watch the royal fun of the tent dwellers who swim in the splashing waves. It is now noon so we secure lunch, sold by the pound, and sit in the sand along the shore and gather the lengthy sea-weeds as they come drifting in, from which we secure the snarly roots for ornaments in our home, press a few of the long, jelly-like leaves for our collection. . . . After supper we continue our wandering through the electric lighted streets, taking in all that is of interest in this city home of the invalid.

Sue A. Sanders

1935

Hope he's as good at that [portraiture] as he is at seaweed-ploughed fields sand erosions & cypressroots!

E. E. Cummings on Edward Weston

AUGUST 21

1936

As I was dressing this morning, I realized as never before that this old body of mine must soon be delivered up to the flames. In the natural course of events, I shall cease to animate it. It has served me well for seventy-six years, but it is wearing out. To dwell on this side of life does no good but it would be foolish to ignore the inevitable. I would rather think of committing my body to the flame of a furnace than of surrendering it to the earth. We all know this change must come but we do not act upon this knowledge. We go on from hour to hour and day to day, as we should do, till the inevitable demand must be met. After all, the living—even the aged—are concerned with life, not death. To most of us life is worth living even at seventy-five.

HAMLIN GARLAND

2008

Un coyote, te lo juro, about three feet from me. Not running, not walking. Un poco como yo iba, ese southwestern ícono. . . .

de cuando en cuando, their howls cut through, rise above the muffled roar de la 210E freeway extension. I can hear them after dark, when the winds change pero la rush hour traffic hasn't died down del todo. Los high-pitched howls drift in, a mournful, choral overlay to the *whoosh whoosh* de la 210, por la ventanita de la master bathroom.

SUSANA CHÁVEZ-SILVERMAN

AUGUST 22

1859

San Pedro. The point—the beach—the hill!

RICHARD HENRY DANA

1934

It's not very funny around here—but it is certainly worth seeing—I must be softening up through affection and easy living and the luxuries of the imperial bed chamber—because I find myself feeling about [Josef von Sternberg] and the Paramount lot like a small boy who's just been sent to boarding school—still I've almost ticked off a week already—I've spilt the milk and now I've got to lap it up—so that's that. But I don't think I'll be found in these parts soon again. . . .

I'm in bed reading Chekhov's letters and meditating on the ideas for a movie of Mr. Von S. I'm fed by phony Russian waiters who bring up phoney Russian food from the restaurant downstairs.

JOHN DOS PASSOS

AUGUST 23

1965

I really miss him as a person now—do you know what I mean, he's not so much "The Baby" or "my baby" any more, he's a real living part of me now, you know he's Julian and everything and I can't wait to see him, I miss him more than I've ever done before—I think it's been a slow process my feeling like a real father! I hope all this is clear and understandable. I spend hours in dressing rooms and things thinking about the times I've wasted not being with him—and playing with him—you know I keep thinking of those stupid bastard times when I keep reading bloody newspapers and other shit whilst he's in the room with me and I've decided it's ALL WRONG! . . .

I'll go now 'cause I'm bringing myself down thinking about what a thoughtless bastard I seem to be—and it's only sort of three o'clock in the afternoon, and it seems the wrong time of day to feel so emotional—I really feel like crying—its stupid—and I'm choking up now as I'm writing—I don't know what's the matter with me—it's not the tour that's so different from other tours—I mean having lots of laughs (you know the type hee! hee!) but in between the laughs there is such a drop.

JOHN LENNON, to his wife Cynthia

AUGUST 24

1907

I feel rather blue tonight because a boy that I have known since he was a baby 20 years ago is dead; and because an old man that I like still more killed him. Procopio got a war-path rage on him yesterday and ran amuck after Amate . . . Poor old Amate did just right. The boy meant to kill him and was perfectly competent to kill 3 or 4 like him—even barring the boulder he had in his hands.

Procopio did beautifully for 36 hours—all day yesterday and all night last night (at least till 6:15 when I quit him this morning) and all day to-day; but at 5 to-night with his tossing around and getting up (the disadvantages of the neurotic type) he broke something and collapsed almost like the flickering out of a candle in the wind. I have a hole in me within an inch of the same place and with the same caliber of a ball, which made me grunt for a few days, but has stayed quiet for 25 years and doesn't bother me at all. But the boy was even less patient than I am; and his troubles are over.

I took poor old Amate in to-night to surrender himself to the police; and the dead wagon has just gone away with what is left with Procopio. . . .

I have seen a good many killings of various sorts and have been mixed up in some of them and have the autographs of several; but I don't think any has saddened me as much as this. Nobody else could get along very well with this boy, who had a beautiful poetic face and would do anything for me but had constant wheels in his head—one of the most neurotic types I ever saw. And the little old man who had to kill him to keep from being killed, is this old troubadour who has delighted so many hundred of our friends.

I think there is really no way to arrange these things right until all such disputes are put in the hands of the Czar—I of course being Czar.

Charles Lummis

1934

What I did on arriving at this remarkable burg via Ford trimotor somewhat gone with vomit, was to take one look at Mr. von S[ternberg] . . . and dive into bed with an attack of rheumatic fever.

I've been so thoroughly in bed that I've seen nothing of Red raids or the Epic campaign. The odds are 2 to 1 in favor of Upton Sinclair getting the Democratic primaries, but everybody thinks the conservatives will gang up on him and elect Haight in November. However one should point out that three months ago the same everybody was poohpooing the Epic business. . . .

. . . This is my last emergence into the big money.

John Dos Passos, to Edmund Wilson

1935

At the Writers' Club Robert Cromie of Vancouver delivered a lecture using a huge map of the world. After the lecture Will [Rogers], fascinated by the map, went up and began to point out the spots where he had been. They included about everything this side of the Arctic Circle. Apparently that was the one place he hadn't seen.

Rob Wagner

1969

I forgot to mention how, when we left Acres of Books and were on our way home, we noticed one of the two very impressive bridges—much more impressive than Sydney Bridge, *I* think, and outrageous looking too, like roller coasters—between Long Beach, Terminal Island and San Pedro. I had never seen them before. Neither had the boys. So of course we had to drive over them. All around was this almost comically ghastly junk-landscape, reeking of oil.

Christopher Isherwood

AUGUST 25

1929

Met Bobby Jones and had a chat with him about Peachtree Street. I know nothing about the game, but he strikes me as being a man that would be mighty discouraging to play against. There was 6,000 watching him play golf. Shows you the advancement that game has made. Why, six years ago there wasn't fifty pair of misfit knee breeches in this whole State, and ten years ago there wasn't 6,000 folks in Los Angeles that would lie to you about anything but real estate.

The Zep lands here tomorrow. We was the only town that would go out and get a hitch rack to tie the thing to.

Will Rogers

1993

She managed Erik [Menendez]'s money for him and says he had no interest in it. The things he did spend money on (apartment, furniture, Jeep) were in keeping with his parents' lifestyle.

Hazel Thornton

AUGUST 26

2013

Chilling at Melissa's house after spending all day tending to business. While watching Congress on C-SPAN tonight, I had a revelation. (I don't normally watch C-SPAN but my remote froze while I was changing channels trying to find Animal Horror Stories and Pets Who Kill.) The revelation is this: When a member of Congress refers to another member as "my distinguished colleague," what he means is "that dim-witted asshole," and when he says "with all due respect," he means "fuck you and the lobbyist you rode in on." I love America.

JOAN RIVERS

AUGUST 27

2012

Today it is official, I guess, that I am old. . . .

I saw Sandy Koufax pitch from the dugout boxes, saw that rising fastball and the 12 to 6 curve ball that was impossible to hit. I personally remember my team winning five gonfalons and was curbside at every Laker parade since 1980. I sold programs at the Memorial Coliseum as a kid and saw every Ram home game for over thirty years. I went to UCLA when the village was all Mediterranean pink and Coach John Wooden made me think the Bruins would always win every game. I drove an Impala when it was new and tasted a chubby champ handed to me by a car hop at Harvey's broiler when boys put Butch wax in their pompadours to make them stiff. I was at Disneyland when it opened and remember running on the spongy asphalt down Main Street and once rode the Matterhorn behind Walt Disney. I parked cars in the 60's and had my hands on all the grand muscle cars when they had that new car smell. Oh man.

. . . When transistor radios were introduced it seemed this was the greatest technological advance ever, especially when I heard Vin Scully announce a game like the greatest poet who ever lived. Last week, I listened to him on my iPhone. . . .

Above all else, in my adult life I owe the Los Angeles Public

Library almost everything. When I started to work as a librarian I was able to compare dirty old Central to being a janitor, a salesman, a ticket broker, a newspaper drudge and a parking lot attendant and I felt like a King. When I started I sat at a reference desk with rotary phones that were connected to a switchboard operator, put periodical requests into Lampson tubes, searched a card catalog and met the most interesting people in my life, including the mother of my daughter. From that desk I have seen the world turn and things happen that I could never have dreamed. . . .

From that humble perch in the heart of Los Angeles I met movie stars, a presidential candidate, famous writers, and hundreds of really incredible librarians who taught me everything I know. By a set of incredible strokes of good fortune I actually wrote a book that is in the Library of Congress. Thank You so much LAPL.

While I might groan when I stand and get up too many times in the night to whiz and can't see fine print too well or need a pinch runner in softball I am still filled with hope for tomorrow, for a new adventure that might surprise me almost as much as falling in love in the Autumn of my years, which already happened once. So, today I am old but I still don't need no rocking chair.

Glen Creason

AUGUST 28

1929

The Zep, in taking off here in Los Angeles, just missed spoiling a great trip and killing everybody by missing a high tension line surrounding the field. Towns bury their dead but they never bury their electric lines. . . . There is one sure fire recipe for a pilot in a strange town, that don't know where the field is located. Locate a high tension line, follow it till it crosses another higher tension one. There is almost sure to be a field there. If not, follow it till it comes to an intersection of three or more lines and there will be located the city's municipal field. It's as sure as the sure fire method of locating a speakeasy by following the town's leading citizens.

WILL ROGERS

1937

I have prepared what I call an Outline of Eccentricity. . . .

Hawthorne always washed his hands before reading a letter from his wife.

George Moore owned a pet python.

James Fenimore Cooper could not write unless he was chewing gum.

IRVING WALLACE

AUGUST 29

1907

E. L. Doheny's $150-a-plate banquet to [meet the] Mexican Ambassador to U.S.; at the Alexandria. I sit next to E.T. Earl—the hated owner of "the Express." Bad month for me with angina.

CHARLES LUMMIS

1936

American Fascism will get nowhere without a dictator. Somewhere he exists; somewhere in the murky valleys of politics lurks the American Hitler. Soon or late, he will appear. Let us pray that when he comes, he will have the mark of the beast set on his brow, so we shall know him.

PHILIP DUNNE

1969

I had gone into this dress shop and inside it was freaky everywhere. Mirrors and silver shining areas and sales people with long hair and the clothes were all "groovy," fancy with gimmicks in imitation of our spontaneous fantasy of dress. The place was loud with earblast rock and I stood there feeling paranoid watching the rich kids from Brentwood and Beverly Hills buy "our" clothes for $40 a dress. I got out of there fast.

LIZA WILLIAMS

1970

Ruben Salazar, the prominent "Mexican-American" columnist for the Los Angeles *Times* and news director for bilingual KMEX-TV, walked into the place and sat down on a stool near the doorway to order a beer he would never drink. Because just about the time the barmaid was sliding his beer across the bar a Los Angeles County sheriff's deputy named Tom Wilson fired a tear gas bomb through the front door and blew half of Ruben Salazar's head off. All the other customers escaped out the back exit to the alley, but Salazar never emerged.

HUNTER S. THOMPSON

AUGUST 30

1910

From 8 a.m. to 4 p.m. in a carriage going up Mt. Wilson. Several dangerous turns in the road, at one of which we all had to get out. Road so narrow that there is no chance for teams to pass. Outer wheels within a foot of the edge (and death) for a large part of the way.

EDWARD CHARLES PICKERING

1942

Lubitsch is a very good mind, and the first man who seems to feel as I do about Hollywood—commenting that he felt it disgraceful that people put on glaring expensive clothes to attend special openings and dinner dances for sweet charity, while gaping crowds stand round for hours to see them pass into a place, and while the poor gink who married Norma Shearer has to stand there and hear the public speaker call: "Miss Shearer's car, please—Miss Shearer's car!"

No one else thinks this is bad, and to mention it is to be a vicious attacker of a noble industry that is giving its all—or at least ten per cent of its all—for the patriotic effort. Patriotic efforts are phooey, and designed for people who have no patriotism. For if a man has patriotism he is giving everything he has and can't go anywhere to give another ten per cent.

But it was nice. Lubitsch is to do the Germany (Enemy Series) film for us, but his outlined opening starting with Wagner and the Schiller theory just is going to get wiped out when the organization gets going on it. It'll never go, boys.

ERIC KNIGHT, to his wife

AUGUST 31

1937

Sat around again and filmed the ending of *Juliet,* where I had to execute sixteen *coquettes* six times from different angles—that makes ninety-six *fouettés.* Afterward my knees felt like macaroni.

VERA ZORINA

1959

The day before yesterday we moved here—to 145 Adelaide Drive. We are both still in the first delight of being here. Principally, it's the view—being able to see the sky and the hills and the ocean. We can see the hills from our bed. Don is so delighted, it warms my heart. But this is a real house, a long in-and-out place of many rooms and half-rooms, passageways and alcoves. And, in spite of the power pole and power lines and TV aerials, there really is a hillside privacy and snugness—something that suggests a run-down villa above Positano.

CHRISTOPHER ISHERWOOD

1967

EIGHT YEARS LATER

I am out on the deck. It isn't too hot yet and it may not be so hot today because there are a lot of high clouds. There are bees in the grape ivy and too many helicopters in the sky; they make more noise than the jets, with their motorbike clatter.

I wish I could describe how I feel. . . . I have such a sense of increasing pressure, the expanding population pushing us into the sea. Then why stay here? Not all places are like Southern

California; indeed, if you object to population-pressure you could hardly choose a worse one. I don't know why we should stay, except that we both love this house. We'll probably remain in it until circumstances pitch us out. (On T.V. last night there was a documentary about earthquakes, in which it is stated that southern California must expect a major quake any time!)

Christopher Isherwood

SEPTEMBER 1

1939

At the studio almost completely kept from working by Billy's feeling that Poland has been betrayed by England—which announced itself as waiting for a reply to an ultimatum. . . . As we came home, we learned that the reply to the ultimatum was due at 2 a.m. our time—evidently no reply from Germany has been received.

CHARLES BRACKETT

1948

Wasted the evening with Nat. He gave me a driving lesson and then I accompanied him and pretended to enjoy a Technicolor blood-and-thunder movie.

SUSAN SONTAG

1956

Girls are what boys want, young men get, and old men think about. I have long intended to counsel with you on this matter as a father should, and will delay it no longer. . . .

Let us assume you are at a dancing party, and a girl strikes your fancy . . . at some moment during the dance when the music is soft and languorous, draw your lips close to her left ear and whisper—distinctly but not so loudly that others can overhear—a sequence of lewd and obscene words. Do not weave them into a sentence, and if inadvertently you do, in no circumstances allow the sentence to conclude with a question mark. Far better the short, simple, sturdy words in artful arrangement, and nothing more. . . .

If she turns away from you and runs across the floor to her mother's arms, chattering away and pointing at you, put her down for a prude, and turn your eyes otherwise. . . . The number who turn away from you may be considerable, but in them you have lost nothing. If, however, among all that company of girls, just one continues to dance with you—oh my boy, my boy!

Your mother and I send our blessings. Cherish us in your heart and honor us by your conduct.

DALTON TRUMBO, to his son

SEPTEMBER 2

1856

We have the best physician in Los Angeles, Dr. John S. Griffin, yet he relies entirely on cod liver oil. A sort of influenza is prevailing in the city, so common on this coast and so severe often at Los Angeles. . . .

Quail-shooting is a favorite sport here, the ground simply alive with them in some parts of the county. Wiley killed 7 deer yesterday.

JUDGE BENJAMIN HAYES

1942

Sometimes here I begin to doubt myself. [Director Anatole] Litvak says, as I spoke of films: "Did it ever occur to you that you're all wrong and we in Hollywood are all right?" And, you know, that almost gets you. For a fatal moment I believed him. And then, of course, I believed what only any man can believe—his own reason. I cannot believe that this town, its manifestations, its puny films, can be right.

Eric Knight, to his wife

SEPTEMBER 3

1932

Today, on any Atlantic or Pacific Beach . . . our problem confronts us—a comely, up-to-the-minute young miss, wearing one of these new streamline, backless, almost frontless, part-time strapless, 1932 bathing suits. It stands to reason that now and then the pinkish young party of the first part is a-going to get a coupla splashes too far out, and somebody's got to bring her in. . . .

At my swimming pool in Beverly, where once in a while I have to fish a young woman out, I'm having a net made, just like the ones the boys use for seining minnows—only bigger. I'm fitting it out with a bamboo pole and am just going to snag 'em out.

Tom Mix

1941

The old adolescent days (or nights) of lying alone looking at moonlight on the eucalyptus leaves are gone. Now when I turn off the switch, I twitch. Now I am afraid of quiet and the dark, and my mind, riddled like an old oak chest with four thousand loathsome wormholes, creaks and crunches at itself and makes insufferable such earlier pleasures.

M.F.K. Fisher

1962

Visit with Henry Miller in Los Angeles . . . He looked more than ever like a Buddhist monk, with the same jolliness. He had a picture of a Buddha on his wall as if this were his model. He was the same Henry with the scrutinizing eyes and mellow voice.

He talked about his children. He loved them more than anyone (as Eve wrote me). He had not slept the night before because Val, his sixteen-year-old daughter, still had not come home at four a.m. . . . His son had broken his ankle surf-boarding. They both came in. They looked like a million other teen-agers. I could not have said: these are Henry's children.

"Success, oh Anaïs, success does not mean anything. The only thing which means anything are the few special letters one gets a year, a personal response."

He was unchanged, modest, unaffected, naïve, no ego showing. The Henry who wants to be thought a saint . . .

He said he was not done with writing, but that the world did not give him time now. He was on his way to a writers' conference.

Anaïs Nin

SEPTEMBER 4

(the city's traditionally observed birthday though no firsthand observers thought to record it)

1954

Those people treat writers like bootblacks. Worse.

Nunnally Johnson, to Fred Allen

1981

Not a big day. Met with Al Haig—the world is still exploding. The French ambassador to Beirut was gunned down by terrorists doing the Syrians' work.

Met with Jim Watt. He's taking a lot of abuse from environmental extremists but he's absolutely right. People are ecology too and they can't forage for food and live in caves.

Saw a film on Begin, a kind of character study. He'll be here Wed.

Had a pleasant evening with a stack of horse and western magazines.

RONALD REAGAN

SEPTEMBER 5

1876

On arriving at the point of junction at Lang Station the entire working force of the road—some 4,000 strong—was seen drawn up in battle array. Swarms of Chinese and scores of teams and drivers formed a working display such as is seldom seen. The secret of rapid railroad building was apparent at a glance. The spot selected for the ceremony was on a broad and beautiful plain surrounded by undulating hills on the one side and the rugged peaks and deep gorges of the San Fernando mountains on the other. The scene was one worthy of the painter's pencil, but by some strange oversight, no photographer was present and the picture presented will live only in the memories of those whose good fortune it was to be present. . . .

After the cheering had subsided and the crowd had been induced to stand back a short distance, Gov. Downey introduced

L. W. Thatcher to Col. Crocker as the public spirited jeweler who had manufactured the gold spike and silver hammer to be used in the ceremonies. Col. Crocker thanked him for his appropriate gift, and said the company would treasure them in its archives as souvenirs of the great event.

The spike is of solid San Gabriel gold, the same in size as ordinary railroad spikes; the hammer is of solid silver with a handle of orange wood. Taking the hammer in one hand and the spike in the other, Col. Crocker said, "Gentlemen of Los Angeles and San Francisco, it has been deemed best on this occasion that the last spike to be driven should be of gold, that most precious of metals, as indicative of the great wealth which will flow into the coffers of San Francisco and Los Angeles when this connection is made, and is no mean token of the importance of this grand artery of commerce which we are about to unite with this last spike. This wedding of Los Angeles with San Francisco is not a ceremony consecrated by the hands of wedlock, but by the bands of steel. The speaker hopes to live to see the time when these beautiful valleys through which we passed today will be filled with a happy and prosperous people, enjoying every facility for comfort, happiness and education. Gentlemen, I am no public speaker, but I can drive a spike!"

Los Angeles Star

1929

"El Pueblo" came of age between dawn and dusk on the 5th day of September, in the year of our Lord, 1876, and of the Independence of the United States of America, exactly the one-hundredth. At two o'clock in the afternoon, more or less, at a tiny settlement then and since known as Lang's Station, sequestered in the depths of Soledad Cañon, Charles F. Crocker drove the golden spike that completed the Southern Pacific Railroad and gave to Los Angeles its first all-rail contact with the Atlantic Seaboard.

Phil Townsend Hanna

1939

It is 104 here today but the papers in this godawful hellhole proclaim "Angelenos Suffer No Discomfort." That would be too bad. I hope the sons of bitches burn up.

James Thurber, to the *New Yorker* office manager

SEPTEMBER 6

1847

I went on a gunning expedition to day and was galloping along with the rest of the officiers when my horse tripped and fell with me roling on and bruising me very much, breaking also a very handsome gun I had with me—One duck was the contents of my game bag when I got back to barracks—where I found letters from home—I laid myself down on the bed and though suffering much from pain caused by my fall read my letters with much pleasure

Lieutenant John McHenry Hollingsworth

1927

A rather eventful day—Father went to a luncheon of the cast of Gentlemen Prefer Blondes and sat with Charlotte Treadway, the leading lady. She wrote a message to me on his menu—Mary Frances, Just oceans of health, happiness, and success—Charlotte Treadway. Aha! She almost sent word that she'd be glad to hear from me. We're all going to the last night of the play, as a last windup, and I may meet her. . . .

Bob Ridgeway called tonight and, after talking for what seemed hours, asked me to go to the show tomorrow night. He's a pathetic person. I think I like him—and I'm afraid he's a little off about me. It won't hurt him—but I hate to have him spend his hard-earned salary on a person who cares so little for him.

M.F.K. Fisher

1961

Last night, a mysteriously happy dream. Just wandering about in a landscape. How seldom my dreams are absolutely free, as this one was, from anxiety!

America to resume underground atom tests, after third Russian explosion.

Bye now.

Christopher Isherwood

SEPTEMBER 7

1940

The young writer here seldom understands his own nature. It is like some magic cow that chews and chews whatever is in sight. It drinks water, absorbs sun and air—it is a female organism. And then it gives milk, or milk is taken from it. The cow does not understand what made the milk; the artist seldom understands what made the artwork. But a certain passivity is germane to creation (call it creative repose, perhaps)....

Really, how much more important to me is this journal than the completion of a play or even two!

Clifford Odets

1956

In the press office of the NBC television studios, three busy gentlemen dropped their concerns with George Gobel and Queen for a Day and Wally Cox to come over and chatter animatedly about Iowa. "Tell me about Muscatine," pleaded one balding executive who had cut short a conversation with Eddie Fisher when he learned there was somebody from Iowa on the premises.

"I know a guy who came from Davenport," was the contribution of the former editor of the *Los Angeles Mirror,* "did you ever run into Dale Carroll?"

It's funny. Everybody you meet tells you how marvelous it is to be in Los Angeles, but wants to hear all about the place he left to come here. . . .

You don't talk about smog in Los Angeles, unless you want to be put down as a boor and an undiplomatic agitator. The natives defend the weather as an act of faith, and woe unto the unwary who dares make a critical remark.

Even the newspaper weather reports sidestep the naughty word. A forecast will say, for instance, "Light eye irritation in central, foothill and San Gabriel Valley sections. But morning trash burning will be permitted." This, translated, means that there will be a little smog, but not enough to prevent citizens from putting a match to the week's accumulation of waste-paper.

Sylvia Strum Bremer

SEPTEMBER 8

1905

Don Juan died on Friday the 8th of September at 2:40 p.m. and was buried on Monday the 11th of September at Calvary cemetery in Los Angeles in the family vault.

Don Juan Bautista Bandini's son, in his father's diary

1934

We as a family were turned down for the Bel Air Bay Club because we were connected with the movies. . . . The Fred Astaires were excluded at the same time, to Fred's bitter shame, I understand.

Charles Brackett

SEPTEMBER 9

1847

I received letters a few days ago from home informing me, that Edward had enlisted in Walker's company on the 9 of February It was on the 17 April that I dreamed of his death I now fear very much that it is true.

Lieutenant John McHenry Hollingsworth

1956

I sat down in a motel in Pasadena with the dog, cat and one child, while Cleo and the two girls moved in with my sister. I had kept my electric typewriter, and by the second day of residence, I was operating it as fast as the Lord gave me the strength to do.

DALTON TRUMBO, to two friends

SEPTEMBER 10

1935

I am deep in a short, swift novel of California that really has the stuff [*You Play the Black and the Red Comes Up,* which Knight published under the pseudonym Richard Hallas]. Every character in it is mad, miserably and futilely mad . . . insane. It truly reflects the country. . . .

I believe I've mended, and I know nothing and no place and no studio and no man and no set of conditions could ever hurt me again in the place that the studio experience kicked me.

Meanwhile, I always have this typewriter, who looks at me open-faced each morning and loves me like my dog does.

ERIC KNIGHT, to a friend

1939

Signs of age increase. I lose my glasses. I forget names and dates. I get tired early. I lack initiative. Decisions are difficult. Interests weaken and grow fewer. Each day is just another twenty-four hours. Shaving, bathing, changing my shoes are burdens. My main concerns now are correspondence with my narrowing circle of friends. I still enjoy an hour or two at the polo game, and a few biographic films make me forget my perplexities and the Old World War.

HAMLIN GARLAND

2001

As I neared the top of the stairs on that last lap, a deceptively fresh-looking Bambi-type wearing designer-brand workout leggings and swinging a cornsilk ponytail in rhythm with the stride of her thighs caught sight of me just as I was about to pass her on the left. Not to be out-staired by someone so fashionably profane—admittedly, I'd left my Jean-Paul Gaultier leg warmers at home, natch—she increased her speed and began racing me. We reached the top of the stairs at precisely the same moment: I on the left, she on the right. Without so much as a dollop of hesitation, Kicking Screaming Gucci Little Piggy violated Etiquette Rule #7 and plowed into me on her way back down. Annoyed but preoccupied, I headed away from the stairs to walk off the workout. Piggy, however, annoyed and apparently off her meds, decided she wanted an apology:

"Excuse you!" she screamed in front of the twenty people standing at the top of the staircase . . . "That was rude!"

I immediately spit back in a mocking squeal-like voice, "That was woode!"

She looked quite cute in her Cynthia Rowley cashmere sweater, even as she yelped, "You should be sorry!"

Fighting every urge to walk over and nudge her Gucci ass slightly off balance and watch her tumble down 150 stairs, I point out, "You should stop eating twinkies!"

I didn't know I could be so cruel. Please Lord forgive me.

HEATHER B. ARMSTRONG

SEPTEMBER 11

1952

We are now at the killing of Caesar, a very messy proceeding—the daggers spout mock blood which splashes over clothes and faces, and then they want to photograph the scene again from another angle and everyone has to wash and change and make up all over again, making endless delays on to the already tedious procedure.

The nicest Hollywood gag I have heard so far happened the other day, when the live pigeons were sitting patiently all day on the plinths and columns of the Forum. They are apparently clipped so that they can't fly about, but one daring bird was bold enough to flutter to the pavement, where he was strutting about. The cowboy character who looks after the animals noticed him and went over and was heard to remark severely "Now get back up there. Go on, didn't you hear me? Don't you want to work tomorrow?"

John Gielgud, to his mother

SEPTEMBER 12

1904

Most of yesterday's steamer party went to Pasadena to-day, stopping off at South Pasadena to see the Cawson Ostrich Farm. There, after examining the stock in the store of plumes, eggs and stuffed birds, and purchasing some as souvenirs of the visit, they entered the farm proper. The entrance is surrounded by palm trees, cactus gardens, roses in abundance, and well laid out walks, the whole combination making a beautiful garden. The tour of the farm itself was most interesting. There are about 250 of the dilapidated looking birds in the different corrals, and they seemed glad to have visitors call upon them, as they rushed to the fences and grinned pleasantly at their callers. It was necessary for the guides to warn the visitors all the time not to get too close, as the big fellows make a practice of grabbing at anything that glistens in the sun, and would as soon swallow a diamond stud or gold badge as a bite of apple or orange.

One of the guides supplied the party with oranges, and the way a whole orange would slide down that long neck excited the admiration of all. They could be watched going down the whole length until they finally disappeared. "Such a neck for cocktails or high balls!" was the general exclamation of envy from the male visitors.

Unnamed pilgrim, Knights Templar of Pennsylvania

1943

Sat. night a moon nearly full.

The unprecedented sex activity continues. The night that I don't desecrate the little god all over again is exceptional. . . .

I keep draining creative energies that don't seem to build up again, been back on the gentleman caller lately, and it has turned into a comedy bordering on fantasy—And is probably an abortion. No urge too deep to create it. but all I desire in the world is to create something big and vital. If only I could make myself—find some groove that would permit it—Stop for a while and get fresh for a major work on Some strong theme. The blue devils eased off—only nip at my heels now and then.

Tennessee Williams

1993

Last week I was screaming at the top of my lungs, louder than I ever have, "I USED TO PLAY HANDBALL! I WAS IN THE FUCKING SCHOOL CHORUS!" It was so painful to remember who I used to be.

AMY ASBURY

2001

The day after the attacks, I was driving near my house when another driver abruptly pulled out of his driveway directly in front of me. I did not respond as I normally do, with cursing and exasperated hand gesturing. I simply braked, sighed and let him take the lead. At the next intersection, we pulled up to the stop sign abreast of each other. He was turning right, and I was continuing straight ahead.

We turned toward each other. "I'm sorry," he mouthed, offering a penitent look. I nodded, mouthed "OK," and drove off, wondering about the origins of the alien that suddenly inhabited my body.

ELLEN ALPERSTEIN

SEPTEMBER 13

1939

On to Hollywood, to see "Mutiny on the Bounty!" Again disappointed. Evening only. Advertisements said "Any Time." . . .

Very tired—very melancholy—My life looks to me a long series of stupid failures—I'm too old now to expect Success—or Happiness or Comfort!

OLIVE PERCIVAL

1940

I've spent so much time doing work that I didn't particularly want to do that what does one more year matter. They've let a certain writer here direct his own pictures and he has made such a go of it that there may be a different feeling about that soon. If I had that chance I would obtain my real goal in coming here in the first place.

F. Scott Fitzgerald, to Zelda

1962

Oliver Evans came to teach at San Fernando State College. Because the house is hard to find, we met at the supermarket. Strange meeting. He has no friends here so I set about introducing him. . . .

. . . He had difficulty fusing academic people with his writer friends. . . . the professors all sat on one couch in a row, and the writers on another couch (Christopher Isherwood, Don Bachardy, Gavin Lambert, etc.). There was a comical barrier, almost visible.

Anaïs Nin

SEPTEMBER 14

1910

I didn't mean to cry today—I meant to show you how brave I could be,—but not to see your dear eyes—not to feel your lips against my throat—the intolerable pain I am to feel through endless months, came over me like a flood.

Una Kuster, to her future husband, Robinson Jeffers

1933

The dinner at the University Club was counted a great success and I think it was. The great dining room was filled with a handsomely dressed entirely urban throng and the speaking was interesting and not too long. . . .

In a sense it was a welcoming dinner to a newly arrived citizen, for not many knew that I had built a home here. Some of the messages and letters spoke of regret of my leaving the East and I felt a pang of the same regret, but, after all, what would a few more years in New York avail? I had done my active work, my committee work, and am in a better situation to write here than there, and my chances for an added year or two are stronger. . . .

Altogether it indicated that my Middle Border books and *Main-Travelled Roads* had taken place in the minds as history and that they had a fair chance of surviving all changes in literary styles. But (as Rogers shrewdly remarked) I suspect that the speakers had not read my other books. However, I cannot complain of any neglect.

HAMLIN GARLAND

1934

I sit here. I have nothing to do. I have had nothing to do for days. I have had nothing to do since I came here. No one opens my office door. No one hints what might be expected of me to earn my handsome salary. No one knows I'm here, or gives a good Goddamn. . . .

I would go home as a final gesture except that I won't be licked by damned idiocy. I shall now stay here and rot in my beautiful office. My cadaver shall begin to smell. They will think it is just the normal smell of a completed film somewhere. Then, years later, another writer shall be given my office. He'll find my skeleton here, sitting amid a welter of pay checks I shall never cash. . . .

You wouldn't believe that a place could be like this. The sham and the indescribable beauty.

That's the real hell of it. It should be the most marvellous place in the world. You can't picture it, because California has never told the truth to the world even about California. . . .

When you arrive here, you don't come to the Los Angeles station. They drive out and meet the train at Pasadena. You are whisked into a gorgeous Cadillac. That's showmanship! After that you can rot in your office unknown and unsung. . . .

I know that out of all this hodge-podge there must come something. There are men here who know and who long and who desire. They are slowly beginning to outnumber the pants-pressers. Some day they will break through—the total pressure will be too great for the soft surface. And then watch the films. Just as the sun-dried soil of this parched land springs miraculously to bounteous return the moment water touches it, so from the manure and dirt that are these now-reigning moguls will burst marvellous film-growth. The soil is arid and barren now. It needs only the water that courageous men can bring.

Eric Knight, to a friend

1946

When speech first came into the movies, I felt it was a mistake, as it not only created the barrier of language, thus making Hollywood pictures understood only by the English-speaking peoples, but it also slowed down the telling of stories which had heretofore been projected through emotion and action. I thought motion pictures would benefit more by marrying with music rather than speech.

Not until I saw Dudley Nichols' *The Informer* did I realize how effective, though not as universally understood, the combination of the three—music, pantomime and speech—could be.

Lillian Gish

SEPTEMBER 15

1908

Sing with the moon. Lots of fish in my trap. Jorgenson building new boat. . . . we catch 2, 5-ft., sharks from our wharf. . . . my great stunt of dictating on the car, going and coming, Brownie got so she could take dictation almost as if at the table.

CHARLES LUMMIS

1938

It is a dark evening, it looks as if we should have rain, but the Japanese gardener is outside the house watering away just as if the sun were burning things up. Mummy is sitting on the sofa reading the evening paper, and I am at the card table writing a letter. Can you guess who I am writing the letter to?

The Good Humor man has gone tinkling by; I think he must be a little surprised that nobody asked him to stop at our house any more; I expect a man who sells ice cream at the Owl Drug Store misses you, too.

OGDEN NASH, to his children

SEPTEMBER 16

1932

Finally had the conference with Mr. Selznick, Adela Rogers St. Johns, Cukor. . . . My ideas for lightening the picture fell absolutely flat. . . . The conference brought on a violent attack of the

Hollywood blues. . . . how dangerous to smother one's talent in cream.

Charles Brackett

1940

I started to work this morning . . . got all my notes in order for the book on eating. I don't want to write it particularly, but I want to write. It is like having the itch. Now that I have started to work again, I am easier, as if I have put ointment on my mind.

M.F.K. Fisher

SEPTEMBER 17

1857

I went necessarily into the City to-day, and chanced to meet but four or five acquaintances, two of them among the French. One managed to get in a word of sympathy; others expressed much even by their manner, as they bowed to me. At different times several of my Jewish friends have addressed me. "It is the lot of all," they uniformly say, but in a soft tone that makes the words fall gratefully upon the ear.

Judge Benjamin Hayes, about Emily Hayes

1940

In the evening Fay [Wray] and I went to the house of Dolores del Rio in Bel Air. We were to have dinner with her and Orson Welles, her light of love. She is a typically Mexican woman, charming, feminine, chatting lightly, and feeling about anything that catches her eyes. We drove to a restaurant where Welles joined us later, tired with work [on *Citizen Kane*]. He was very gracious and articulate, as usual, in fact articulate enough to be very glib. I did not mind this. In fact he is a sort of biological sport, stemming out of Lord Byron through Oscar Wilde, I should say. But he has a peculiarly American audacity. Of other people he said just what he thought of them, with scorn and derision; with us he was deferential, once referring to me as "in the foremost ranks of the talents of the world."

I liked best when he suddenly said of himself, "I have a touch of rhinestones in my blood," meaning he is part-charlatan.

This dinner, as I later told Fay, depressed me because I want to do and be all the things he is being and doing. A prime trouble with me is wanting to be all men; wanting, too, as Welles is trying to do, to beat the game. I want to be a poor poet and a powerful businessman, a sensational young man and a modest artist with a secret life. I understand every impulse in the American man because I naturally have the impulses myself.

I found that I disagreed with everything Welles said and I like him in spite of that. He is a very octopus of evil, but for all that there is a good side to him, a sense, for instance, of humble people. A communion of intelligence is possible with him; finally, too, he also is in opposition to the values around him, even though they may finally swallow him up.

CLIFFORD ODETS

1991

Keanu came over and hugged me warmly as if I were a favorite aunt, then he loped back to a place by the table. Maybe it was only a hug for the boss's wife, but I treasured it. The color of his skin and hair, his height, the width of his shoulders, the casual easy way he wears his wrinkled T-shirt and scruffy blue jeans reminds me so much of Gio. Today is Gio's birthday. Suddenly I could see the last moments we were together on Mother's Day 1986, standing on the sidewalk in front of the apartment in Washington, D.C. I could feel our last hug, my right hand touching the thick, dark wavy hair at the back of his neck, my left arm wrapped across his T-shirt against the thin taut muscles in his thin young man's back.

I realized that while I was thinking about Gio I had unconsciously moved to a chair alone by the costume racks. I thought I was being very calm just reviewing thoughts from the past in my mind when a wave of grief welled up and spread across my chest into my throat and a low animal cry escaped from my lips. My face contorted as I stifled a moan and quickly concealed myself behind a row of hanging overcoats. Finally I regained my composure. I wiped my face on the striped sleeve of a man's shirt and slipped between women's dresses to exit by a side door. Outside, Tom Fox, the video technician, was laying cable and waved a cheery "Hello!" I could feel tears choking my voice and hurried across the street and up into the little office apartment where I could be alone. As I stood weeping by the window, watching the school children in the play yard below, deep wracking sobs rose out of my chest. As my body began to unclench I happened to look at my watch. It was just after 11 a.m., the time of Gio's birth twenty-eight years ago.

Eleanor Coppola

SEPTEMBER 18

1912

Thank you indeed for the invitation to contribute to the new magazine. I am indeed eager to make good with such a group, and three times interested in such an Illinois enterprise.

I'm emphatically a citizen of Springfield, Illinois, and Sangamon County, and shall return in a year to stay forever more. If I may be confidential I have been horribly homesick for a month—and fear that (spiritually speaking) I shall hobble through the rest of my expedition.

I should probably send you something to be considered for publication in a month or so.

Vachel Lindsay, to Harriet Monroe

1978

The Santa Ana winds cleaned the city tonight. Washing the sky with her eastern tails. The moon, two days waning now, still bright and clear. I could see Catalina this morning from Dad's office. . . .

The Santa Ana keeps blowing—a soft wind from the East—warm, gentle and harsh all at once.

I seem—or feel to be at an enormous crossroads. I've so many paths available to me—but no real commitments to any yet. I can do anything—but still again—I know that I must make a choice about which skill—trade (whatever) I shall concentrate on—do for a couple of years. Going away is only postponement. . . . I need to get started. I really do. And waiting in L.A. is just too much for me. Too much pain. Strange emotions. Too much—

Aaron Paley

SEPTEMBER 19

1934

Now I am in our house. We have lived in it ten days and nights, and we are very happy in it. It is a good peaceful little house. We grew tired before we finished painting. . . .

At night we eat a simple but rather large dinner slowly by candlelight. The dining room is white and cool, with the silly yellow organdy curtains with big white polka dots on them moving across the sill silently in the air. Then Al goes to his study and I read or write or bathe. Then we read—now Crime and Punishment—and go to bed.

M.F.K. Fisher

1939

The job at Goldwyn's lasted *one week.* Goldwyn and [director Sam] Wood had a fight on the set, and Wood said he'd quit if he had to rehearse the characters in new dialogue. Eddie Knopf told [agent H. N.] Swanson my stuff was grand and that he'll get me back some way.

Very encouraging. Almost as much fun as the war. . . . And so it goes. I can't possibly pay Scottie's Vassar tuition of $615.00. I'm working today on an Esquire story to get her back here.

F. Scott Fitzgerald, to his agent

1965

Eureka!

Octavia E. Butler

SEPTEMBER 20

1925

Well, it's Sunday again and I'm at the studio. I was here until 8 last night and before I left, Mr. King asked me if I wouldn't be so kind as to come in again today and naturally, I couldn't refuse him. Miss Marion, Mr. King and a special title writer are retitling Stella Dallas so that it will be ready to be previewed tomorrow night at Pasadena. We had one preview of it at San Bernardino last week. . . . However, this doesn't mean much because most of the people of San Bernardino are ranchers and their opinions count for naught. . . .

The weather here is glorious, but awfully dry. We haven't had a bit of rain since about the 10th of June. One day is just like the other, hence you can never start a conversation with "Isn't this awful weather we're having?" which you must admit is quite a drawback in making new friends, especially with the opposite sex. When I meet a new fellow, all I can say is "Aren't the stars bright tonight!" or some other such dumb remark—and that ends it. You just have to talk about other things or appear stupid.

VALERIA BELLETTI, to a childhood friend

1945

Actually mailed two copies of the mss. on Southern California book today.

CAREY MCWILLIAMS

1945

I'll write to Hemingway. Poor bloke, to have to marry three times to find out that marriage is a failure, and the only way to get any peace out of it is (if you were fool enough to marry at all) keep the first one and stay as far away from her as much as you can, with the hope of someday outliving her. At least you will be safe then from any other one marrying you—which is bound to happen if you ever divorce her. Apparently man can be cured of drugs, drinking, gambling, biting his nails and picking his nose, but not marrying.

WILLIAM FAULKNER, to Malcolm Cowley

SEPTEMBER 21

1938

CARMEL HOTEL, SANTA MONICA

To begin with trifles, the grand party on Sunday was all right. Cukor and Helen Westley and even Nazimova were amusing. Millie served champagne to begin with. I had none because I had had some sherry and was a little afraid of getting sick inopportunely. They told some funny stories: of Tallulah Bankhead who insisted that cocaine was not habit-forming and who said she knew because she had been taking it for seventeen years.

CHARLES REZNIKOFF

1946

The famed climate has one flaw—you can't eat it.

DICKSON HARTWELL

SEPTEMBER 22

1847

We have been engaged for some days in the trial of private John Smith 1st Drags for robbing Lieut Stonemans quarters which I have before mentioned—He was brought into the court room this morning looking very much immaciated—a mere shadow of what he once was—he has not recovered yet from his wound and I think from the hacking cough he has is fast approaching the grave—he plead guilty to all the charges brought against him—

LIEUTENANT JOHN MCHENRY HOLLINGSWORTH

1916

At the Summit of the Cajon Pass our troubles ended.

EDGAR RICE BURROUGHS

SEPTEMBER 23

1846

Captain Gillespie, you are hereby ordered to surrender the fort within twenty-four hours, or you and your men will all be killed. Signed,

GEN. JOSÉ MARÍA FLORES,
to Captain Archibald H. Gillespie of the California Battalion

1923

Los Angeles is silly—much motoring, me rather tired and vague with it. California is a queer place—in a way, it has turned its back on the world and looks into the void Pacific. It is absolutely selfish, very empty, but not false and at least, not full of false effort. I don't want to live here, but a stay here rather amuses me. It's a sort of crazy-sensible.

D. H. Lawrence

SEPTEMBER 24

1846

Believe the bearer [Juan Flaco, who rode from Los Angeles to San Francisco in fifty-two hours]

Captain Archibald H. Gillespie,
to Commodore Robert F. Stockton

1923

I am setting off tomorrow with Gotzsche down the west coast, by train, to Mexico again. I am glad to go. America drys up the natural springs of one's soul. But I've had quite a nice time here—people are very nice to me.—It's a very selfish place, Southern California, in a rather simple way. People care about *nothing* but just the moment. But also that can be pleasant.

D. H. Lawrence

1934

A young man, whose name I believe is Nertz, was writing the real screen play behind the scenes. I'm darn sorry I wasn't able to stagger round the studios some more. It was interesting there though the horrid stalking of intangibles makes it more nerve-wracking, I imagine, than the average industrial plant. . . .

Having been for a few weeks in the big money makes us feel strangely broke and parsimonious. Also we are faced with paying our debts—I don't think the big money is what it's cracked up to be.

John Dos Passos, to Edmund Wilson

SEPTEMBER 25

1886

Rita de Celis, Cayita and Robert Bettner went to San Vicente with me this afternoon. We brought pears from the trees and ate figs. Mr. Baker and Arcadia came. He says that a vein of gold has been found in the San Vicente hills. Put 2 cans or 10 gals in the gas machine. Cloudy in the morning—clear for the rest.

Don Juan Bautista Bandini

1926

At 2:00 p.m. we arrived at Los Angeles. Immediately a whole bunch of delegates led by the mayor entered the carriage. Every delegate wore a ribbon with an inscription in gold: "Welcome Danchenko." They brought all of us to the platform where a boys' band played a comical reception on mouth organs and some girls in Egyptian costumes gave out oranges from huge baskets. Then they delivered a speech and presented Vladimir Ivanovich with a golden (cardboard) key to the city. The delegates, among whom were the representatives of the city administration, the press, cinema, theaters, and clubs, all wanted to shake hands with us, to give us flowers and fruit. An enormous crowd of people was standing on the platform; the boys' band was playing some kind of march. Innumerable shots for newspapers and the cinema were taken. But the most comical thing was that in the heat of the celebration, the United Artists representative took me aside and divulged, "We know that Mr. Danchenko is a great celebrity, and we've been given an order to arrange a proper reception for him, but we do not know who in fact he is."

SERGEI BERTENSSON

1991

I think that people who keep notebooks and jot down their thoughts are jerk-offs. I am only doing this because somebody suggested I do it, so you see, I'm not even an original jerk-off. But this somehow makes it easier. I just let it roll. Like a hot turd down a hill.

I don't know what to do about the racetrack. I think it's burning out for me. I was standing around at Hollywood Park today, inter-track betting, 13 races from Fairplex Park. After the 7th race I am $72 ahead. So? Will it take some of those white hairs out of my eyebrows? Will it make an opera singer out of me?

CHARLES BUKOWSKI

SEPTEMBER 26

1925

Do you remember when Thomas Ince suddenly died on a yacht party? Well, Marion Davies, Hearst, Charlie Chaplin and a number of others were on that party and according to the wild rumors around the lots, it is said that Hearst became very much incensed over the attention Charlie was paying Marion—after a few drinks, they got quarreling about it and Hearst either shot at or threw something at Charlie. Charlie ducked and Ince got the blow and died a few hours after.

I don't know how true this tale is—but I've heard it from a number of people and they all seem to believe it. I can't really say that I believe it because I know how ready people are to talk and I usually give anyone the benefit of the doubt until I'm positive. . . .

Am going to a beach party tonight—we are going to build a big fire on the beach and have supper there. This seems to be quite a popular diversion for the "younger set" in Hollywood. I've never been to one before so I'm looking forward to having a good time.

Sunday morning Nancy and I are going on a hike with the Sierra Hiking Club. We leave at six in the morning and there will be about 100 in the party and we will ride in busses to the mountains and then hike.

VALERIA BELLETTI, to a childhood friend

1943

Very comfortably propped upon an arrangement of pillows, I lie on my bed after the usual effort to write has ended with the revision of 1 page. A shuddering glance at the play had convinced me not to touch that today.

The room is full of California's gay sunlight and noise of voice on the walks and traffic.

I am about to smoke and read Jung.

Tomorrow if I get my check I will take a trip somewhere. . . .

I have accepted sex as a way of life and found it empty, empty, knuckles on a hollow drum.

TENNESSEE WILLIAMS

SEPTEMBER 27

1927

San Diego can rightfully claim a great credit in the flight. But you can't beat Los Angeles. They had to get in on it somehow. They claim they raised the pigs that the ham sandwiches were made from that Lindy took to Paris. The pig was raised on Hellman's ranch. . . .

P.S.—In five years this town will have grown till it reaches Tijuana, Mexico. Then it can rightfully be known as the best city in America.

EDMUND WILSON

2007

Las montañas San Gabriel. A la izquierda, chaparral still slightly charred from the wildfires hace ya cuatro años.

SUSANA CHÁVEZ-SILVERMAN

SEPTEMBER 28

1938

On Sunday Mummy and I went sailing—to Catalina Island on an enormous boat. The masts were much taller than our house, and when the sailor was putting the sails up he climbed the highest mast like a monkey—but coming down he didn't bother with the mast at all; he just slid down the rope.

When we got far out on the ocean the captain got out a fishing line with a big hook on the end. He tied the other end to the rail, and we all waited to see what would happen. Nothing did happen for so long that we forgot all about it. Suddenly the line gave a jerk and we all ran to pull it in. There was something very heavy at the other end. We pulled and pulled, and pretty soon we saw an enormous fish. He was so heavy that we could hardly pull him into the boat. It was three feet long and weighed about thirty pounds, and had big goggle eyes. A sailor cut him up and gave us a piece to take home, which José cooked for our dinner the next night; it was delicious. The name of that fish was an albacore.

We anchored off Catalina, and after supper we flashed a light on the water, and hundreds of flying fish began to fly. They really did, and they were beautiful. They were about eighteen inches long, and you see them swimming like all the other fish. But they have two fins just like a bird's wings, and when they get excited, or when some big hungry fish is chasing them, they spread them out and rise out of the water and skim through the air very fast. Mr. Mankiewicz, who owns the boat, gave me a long stick with three barbed points on the end and asked me to try to spear one. I did try, and I did spear one, much to everyone's surprise. But I was sorry after I had done it, because flying fish are not good to eat, and I don't like to kill anything uselessly.

Ogden Nash, to his children

1960

I have a large, elegant, two room office, first time in my life I've had my name in brass letters on a door and where a good gal who was secretary to Norman Corwin, Francesca Price Solo, answers the phone in a soft voice, "Carl Sandburg's office": it's worth a nickel to hear.

Carl Sandburg, to his wife

2016

Walking down Bunker Hill steps at night. Sound of a conch? Echoing out of the parking garage. A strange figure: a young Japanese man in baggy white pants, sandals, backpack carrying an enormous horn of some animal, five feet long. Not a shofar, not a ram's horn, he says when I ask, but the horn of an antelope from Yemen. He wants to talk to me about the Second Coming, about the man that "you call Jesus." He tells me how "we are distracted by the things of this world," and I concur, nodding gravely, "Yes, we are," and bid him good night.

Drive home down Beaudry Street. There's my one-legged friend, the ghost with no language, no teeth, no clothes, no home, no bed, no friends. He is there day after day.

He curls himself up on the bus bench despite the struts designed to prevent homeless people from lying down; he's so slight, so diminished, that he fits under the curve of the cold metal. His blanket is blackened with dirt.

I pull over, get out to talk to him. He babbles. I don't know the language. Maybe Vietnamese? Friendly/angry? I have no idea. I hold up water he nods yes, I point to my mouth, does he need food. He shakes his head. For weeks after the first encounter, I stop en route home to leave a bottle of water beside him, as if he is some roadside shrine. He is usually under the blanket, asleep. I fear he'll die out there in the sun, half-naked, staring into the void. What does he eat? I call County Homeless services and miraculously, a human answers. They'll send a team.

LOUISE STEINMAN

SEPTEMBER 29

1858

Before sunrise of the 29th he was lying in the bushes at San Francisco, in front of the Congress frigate, waiting for the early market boat to come on shore, and he delivered my dispatches to Commodore Stockton before 7 o'clock.

ARCHIBALD GILLESPIE,
on courier Juan Flaco's fifty-two-hour
Los Angeles–to–San Francisco ride

1929

We are travelling across the Californian desert in Mr. Schwab's [railway] car, & we have stopped for 2 hours at this oasis. We have left the train for a bath in the hotel, & as it is so nice & cool I will write you a few of the things it is wiser not to dictate.

Hearst was most interesting to meet, & I got to like him—a grave simple child, with no doubt a nasty temper—playing with the most costly toys. A vast income always overspent: Ceaseless building and collecting & not vy discriminatingly works of art: two magnificent establishments, two charming wives; complete indifference to public opinion, a strong liberal & democratic outlook, a 15 million daily circulation, oriental hospitalities, extreme personal courtesy (to us at any rate). . . .

At Los Angeles (hard g) we passed into the domain of Marion Davies; & all were charmed by her. She is not strikingly beautiful nor impressive in any way. But her personality is most attractive; naïve childlike, bon enfant. She works all day at her films & retires to her palace on the ocean to bathe & entertain in the evenings. She asked us to use her house as if it was our own. But we tasted its comforts & luxuries only sparingly, spending two nights there after enormous dinner parties in our honour. We lunched frequently at her bungalow in the film works—a little Italian chapel sort of building vy elegant where Hearst spends the day directing his newspapers on the telephone, & wrestling with his private [Chancellor of the Exchequer]—a harassed functionary who is constantly compelled to find money & threatens resignation daily.

We made gt friends with Charlie Chaplin. You cd not help liking him. The boys were fascinated by him. He is a marvelous comedian—bolshy in politics—delightful in conversation. He acted his new film for us in a wonderful way. It is to be his gt attempt to prove that the silent drama or pantomime is superior to the new talkies. Certainly if pathos & wit still count for anything it ought to win an easy victory. . . .

We went on Sunday in a yacht to Catalina Island 25 miles away. We had only one hour there. People go there for weeks and months without catching a swordfish—so they all said it was quite useless my going out in the fishing boat wh had been provided. However I went out & of course I caught a monster in 20 minutes!

WINSTON CHURCHILL

1932

I have just been listening to Cesar Franck's Symphony in D Minor.

I turned out all the lights and danced to it—then to Saint-Saens' bacchanal in *Samson and Delilah,* until everything whirred.

I had some terrific experiences in the wilderness since I wrote you last—overpowering, overwhelming. But then I am always being overwhelmed. I require it to sustain life.

. . . I feel I must return sometime to the Grand Canyon.

But I turned my back to the solitudes and one chill, foggy dawn, I arrived in Los Angeles, where I discarded my sombrero and boots for city garb. For a week I worked intensively in black and white. Also I've been reading, and now, of course, I'm attending UCLA. I got in by rather a fluke. My chemistry grades were low, as you remember, but, in transferring credits from Indiana a D in advanced algebra was magically changed to an A, which balanced the chemistry deficit. . . .

Haven't you met Mr. Weston? If not, do it by all means or you are making a mistake. I think he is by far the most interesting and genuine person in Carmel. Tell him that you are a friend of mine.

If you plan to come back, I think you are foolish to pay bus fare. Send your bulky belongings by freight or parcel post, forget your timidity, and rely on the public. There are always exceptions to the general inhospitable type, if you have the fortitude to wait for them. . . .

EVERETT RUESS, to a friend

SEPTEMBER 30

1912

The old town don't look the same. By the old town we mean Los Angeles. But not looking the same is a habit with this little pueblo. . . . It's got so that a person can't reasonably spend a two weeks vacation and come back here without the aid of guide book.

GEORGE HERRIMAN

1935

O the juse the juse/ they don't amews.

E. E. CUMMINGS, to a friend

1974

I drove to U.C.L.A. today in my carpool. . . . I was showing off and I wouldn't listen to Jeff's advice. On Beverly Glen I was just hauling ass. Jeff said they used radar but I didn't believe him. But lo and behold I was pulled over by a police car. With radar I was clocked at 50 in a 25 mph zone. They radio to a car waiting at a side street and then I was nailed. I was nervous, then that passed, then came a feeling of frustration. Why didn't I listen? Did I have to be such a show off? I was upset. I knew that this would be just another stupid expense to add to Dad's financial situation. I have definitely learned my lesson (I hope). I am going to make a determined effort to stop speeding. I don't need to prove anything to anyone or myself. I'm really in no hurry. Patience—mellow out.

Aaron Paley

OCTOBER 1

1926

We watched the new Douglas Fairbanks film *The Black Pirate.* The whole film is made up of Fairbanks' favorite tricks and has nothing in it with regard to content.

The scenes, taking place on a big sailing ship, are staged quite well. The ship itself, the sea—all those look very beautiful and real. You can imagine my surprise when in the yard of the studio I saw that very ship and its real size standing in a very large pool without water? It turned out that the pool would be filled with water, and it would replace the sea.

SERGEI BERTENSSON

1961

From the steep mountains on the east side of the lake, one could look west at endless rows of purple mountains around the Griffith Park Observatory. One behind another. They looked like a Japanese screen. . . . Every color shone like a jewel for a moment and then dissolved; and even the gray clouds, the smoky scarves, were iridescent. For a few instants, all the sunsets of the world, Nordic, tropical, exotic, condensed over Silver Lake, displaying their sumptuous spectacle.

There was a house being built on the side of a mountain facing the sunset and the lake. . . . There was a desert rose terrace, a garden being planted, a place carved in the garden for a pool overlooking the lake. There was a magnificent fireplace like that of a castle.

I discovered the architect was Eric Wright, the son of Lloyd Wright and grandson of Frank Lloyd Wright.

Anaïs Nin

OCTOBER 2

1934

I'm trying to like California. I wish I could put on paper what it's like. The countryside, dusty pepper trees, rolling hills, serrated mountains, is all curiously divided into planes. I couldn't see why at first, but I suddenly solved it the other night. It's the lack of rains. It's so dry here all is dust. The dust lies at the end of the day hovering over the land. The light hits the dust clouds, and gives that curious hazy separation to the planes of distance. . . .

I try to rationalize this whole country, and excuse it. If the people are nuts, it is because after the flat middle lands this is Heaven to them. If they strew the place with the ostentatious vulgarity of palm trees, it's because they still can't believe in the miracle of landing in a land where palms will grow. If their houses are cheap-jack, it is because they're afraid of earthquakes which crumble brick and stone buildings. If they dress like fools, it's because this is the tropics in a way, and anyhow our own sane clothes are about as foolish as could be conceived for such living conditions. So the women wear pants and shorts, and everyone lives in a sort of cheap-jack fugitiveness as if all this would vanish suddenly and they'd have to live back on earth again. A temporary feeling everywhere—waiting for what? Earthquakes, some sectarian Domesday, the collapse of the motion picture industry, the millennium? I don't know. I only know that I believe in film, and must stick to that as long as I can.

Eric Knight, to a friend

1934

The carcase is almost what the medical books call ambulant, and I've said good bye to Paramount, so I feel very much better. It's not exactly anything to be unhappy about (except when you find all the money going to pay back debts) but it's nothing to feel very good about either—it's like endorsing absorbine junior or Beauty Rest mattresses—Working in the movies as part of the technical staff would be more interesting but it's a life. I've been in bed ever since I got here talking to the studios over the phone and listening to Epic, Angelus Temple and the Christian Hebrew Synagogue on the air—California's a great place right now. You can look out the window and watch the profit system crumble.

John Dos Passos, to a critic

OCTOBER 3

1933

Today was very hot. It reminded me a little of the days off Guatemala last year, when my bones felt gone from the flesh, leaving a limp yawning emptiness. But today I felt sleepy, and all afternoon fought against drowsing by changing my position often and violently as I lay on the chaise longue. . . .

Upstairs I can hear Dave taking a shower. He is growing used to football practice again. For two weeks or so after it started, he was so tired that he was far from civil—and he still expresses disapproval or grouchiness by a discarding of all politeness. He is a fine boy and a charming one, but when he is sullen there are few humans more unattractive.

M.F.K. Fisher

1939

PLEASE ANSWER ABOUT TUITION MONEY STOP YOU HAVE NO IDEA HOW MUCH A HUNDRED DOLLARS MEANS NOW

F. Scott Fitzgerald, to his agent

OCTOBER 4

1860

At about seven a.m. we anchored opposite to San Pedro, four hundred and twenty miles from San Francisco, and the end of our voyage. Here we leave the steamer, which goes on to San Diego. At the edge of the water is a high bank, and from this the plain extends far as we can see. There are three adobe houses on the bank, and everything looks just as it did when Dana described it in his "Two Years before the Mast," more than twenty years ago. We landed in the steamer's boats, and after an unsavory breakfast at one of the houses, a wagon was produced, to which four half-broken California horses were harnessed. The men hung on to their heads, swayed about, and at times raised themselves off their feet as the animals struggled, till the signal for starting was given, when they sprang off, simultaneously, and the released animals dashed away at full speed. The driver occasionally looked in to ask us, on which side we wished to fall when we upset. This seemed to be his standing joke, and one which I thought it not improbable might become a serious question with us.

The plains were covered with thousands of cattle and horses, quite reminding us of the descriptions of old California times. In the twenty-five miles of our journey, there were but two or three shanties, erected by squatters who were raising cattle, and not a fence or enclosure, except the corrals about them. We reached Los Angeles in about two hours and a half, having changed horses once on the way.

As we approached the town there was a marked change from the treeless sterility of the plains. We found ourselves winding through the midst of vineyards and gardens, and on all sides saw workmen engaged in the manufacture of wine.

William Ingraham Kip

1946

A day on the dubbing stage. When I met Billy in the office I knew he was in one of his moods, and his mood proved to be the persecuted one. The Rebel discriminated against. This comes on him now and then—he craves occasional persecution as animals crave salt. With the passing of years, however, and his great success, it's getting goddamned hard to find any persecution. The best he could do today was that John Farrow is allowed to drive his car on the lot and that whereas Bing Crosby is given $25,000 for saying one syllable on the screen, he and I were asked to speak two lines in *Variety Girl* for nothing. At first he said he would do so for an automobile, then only if $125,000 was given to the Jewish Blind. I may add that I've never known the Jewish Blind to haunt his conscience before.

Charles Brackett

OCTOBER 5

1928

I came near being bumped off today—but aside from a lame back where they bumped me, I am all right. And it was worth while, everything considered.

. . . I quite detected cars coming from in front and about to turn—, but, a big car the other side came whizzing around, and though the man jacked her down mighty fast hit me in the small of the back pretty hard. Two feet more headway would have broken my back. He cussed me out.

Charles Lummis

1945

Bad news at Warner Brothers Studio this morning in the strike. I drove out . . . around noon, but the pickets had vanished and all was quiet.

Carey McWilliams

1961

It was very thoughtful of you to send me a book explaining James Joyce's "Ulysses." All I need now is another book explaining this study by Stuart Gilbert who, if memory serves, painted the celebrated picture of George Washington which hangs in the Metropolitan Museum. I realize that there is some two hundred years' difference in their ages, but any man who can explain Joyce must be very old and very wise.

You disappeared rather mysteriously the other night, but I attribute this to your life of crime in the movies.

Groucho Marx, to Peter Lorre

OCTOBER 6

1956

Cecil Blount DeMille's *The Ten Commandments* was previewed this week for a company of two hundred and sixty-three archangels in a temple of strawberry meringue especially built for the occasion on the Paramount back lot. Y. Frank Freeman led vespers with a reading from the letter of "a Protestant church leader" to the effect that "The first century had its Apostle Paul, the thirteenth century had St. Francis, the sixteenth had Martin Luther and the twentieth has Cecil B. DeMille."

After heaping portions of the Sacred Host had been served up in a rich sauce with seconds for everybody, de Mille himself, clad in the rosette of the Order of the Holy Sepulcher, appeared among them on a Technicolor screen to explain his affection for the Almighty. The picture was then revealed.

DALTON TRUMBO, to a friend

1964

Every day I receive a letter from a librarian asking if I would not give the originals of the diary and letters to their library. They are not aware that because they did so little to contribute to my reputation as a writer, because they were passive spectators to my difficulties, the diaries are my only capital.

ANAÏS NIN

OCTOBER 7

1933

Now, the effigies of these beautiful young persons, with their fadeless smiles of satisfaction and delight, adorning pages of our leading periodicals or emblazoning the fences of our daily walks, and all revealing their lustrous and impeccable teeth, back to the ultimate molar,—must inevitably convince the present generation, even in periods of depression, that the declaration of Browning's "Pippa" ["God's in his Heaven / All's right with the world!"] understates the truth.

JULIAN HAWTHORNE

1941

I never really enjoyed strapping good health, but also scarcely ever have a serious illness; the organism is in good order, and basically I think that my constitution, by its whole tempo and character, tends to patience, endurance, a long pull; to carrying things to their end—not to say to perfection. It is this instinct that explains the urge toward a new establishment, toward building. . . .

. . . The house is making slow progress; the steel window and door casings were very long in arriving, and sometimes labor is short too. At best we shall be able to move in by the middle of December, but the architect advises us not to count on that. Oh well, patience is my strong point.

THOMAS MANN, to a friend

OCTOBER 8

1542

Came to the mainland in a large Bay . . . named it "Bahía de los Fumos" [Bay of Smokes] on account of the many dark billows seen there . . . engaged in intercourse with some Indians captured in a canoe. . . . The bay is 35 degrees latitude; it is an excellent harbor and the country is good with many plains and groves of trees.

Juan Rodríguez Cabrillo

2016

Warm evening, after swimming at the Y. Sitting above Central Library, on a bench on the "Spanish Steps"—a replica of a historic place that is really this place, my perch above the library, half-moon rising, a sense of urban bustle: the security guard from the corporate tower, the pulsing beat from the new tourist attraction, the long glass slide to oblivion. *Blade Runner*–esque LED high-stepping video dancers now replace the Russian émigrés' soulful portrait of Our Lady of Porciuncula, painted by hand in Renaissance hues. Santa Anas warm and dry on the skin. Water burbling from the fountain, below Robert Graham's high-breasted bronze woman-child, austere in her perfection.

My city. I am drawn to this perch at a particular moment late in the day, when there's a shaft of sunlight straight below me extending through the axis of Central Library, entering through Fifth Street, exiting out the Hope Street doors onto the street where I was born. Hope Street.

I sit still and let all the stories wash through me from Gordon Davidson's funeral that morning at Leo Baeck Temple. Rabbi Beerman's spirit was there too, waiting to take Gordon to a production of "Angels in America" in Heaven. Gordon just walks into the play. He already has a role, everyone knows who he is, the Moses of L.A. theater. Moses with a grin, Moses with a last view from his hospital bed of the marquee of the Kirk Douglas Theater.

My throat is still sore from the drip drip drip. A week where the city has exhausted me. Each lurch on the road, each discourtesy, sense of body confinement a distress. Note to self—always have an audio book in the car.

In the shadow of the tallest building, U.S. Bank Tower, the "other" target of 9/11. The cause of all the bomb threats called into the library in the months and years after 9/11. All of us having to trundle out of the building, sometimes the only place you'd meet and mingle with someone who works on Lower Level 4, the History Dept stacks, everyone jovial. And the night when we hosted a Chilean novelist and the alarm sounded. We all had to move out of the post-lecture reception in the courtyard out onto 5th Street in the dark, leaving our keys and wallets behind. We were out there a half hour until the library security officer walked over to me and, motioning to our guest—could he speak with him? He asked the young novelist, "Do you have any known enemies? Anyone who would want to hurt you?" Alberto rolled his eyes and confessed, "Yes," he said, "Gabriel Garcia Marquez hates my novels." The security officer carefully wrote it down on his notepad.

We were all looking for evidence in those days.

LOUISE STEINMAN

OCTOBER 9

1947

Billy has formed a habit when there are others about of saying with a sigh that it was I who kept him from enlisting at the outbreak of the war. . . . When however a chance at a commission came and he did consider going to make moving pictures in a uniform, I advised him that I thought it would be just as well for him to make them in the studio—he was just getting his first chance as a director, he hadn't enough authority to impress himself on the Army—and I thought it was time for him to press ahead, making pictures which because of their pleasure giving powers would do more good, because they expressed him more fully than any Army made picture could.

CHARLES BRACKETT

1962

When I last saw swami, on the 4th, he asked about my meditation. I said I was finding it helpful to keep reminding myself how near my death may be. Swami then told me that Vivekananda had said: If you are trying to know God, you must imagine that death is already gripping you by the hair; but if you are trying to win power and fame, you must imagine that you will live for ever.

CHRISTOPHER ISHERWOOD

OCTOBER 10

1940

Mr. Hitler is a skyrocket whose fuse has already been lighted. He is a one-chance rocket. Soon he must fall and come to earth, fulfilling the nature of the rocket by spluttering to death in the dark. This does not mean he will not do great damage before he dies, probably by his own hand.

CLIFFORD ODETS

OCTOBER 11

1927

We went to see how a big mass scene on the square before Notre Dame de Paris was shot at the Universal studio. This involved about 600 people. There was much noise, animation, banal gesticulation, and swinging of hands. Barrymore himself, in the comic makeup mask of "the king of fools," sitting on the head of a statue of a horse, played with full nerve, was brave, vivid, and graceful like a statue.

SERGEI BERTENSSON

1943

Southern California is a retreat for all failures.

SINCLAIR LEWIS

OCTOBER 12

1939

Some day East Siders will wake up to the fact that we are entitled to representation in conjunction with our taxation. If the East Side is to be taxed equally with taxpayers in other sections in the city it seems to us that the East Side is due for an equal amount of representation in the various branches of government.

Al Waxman

1956

I now go to football games to watch my son down there risking his very stern for good old Franklin High. We are the smallest school in the league, yet consider that we have already beaten Glendale and San Pedro, and you can see how good we are. I stand while the school song is sung at the conclusion of each game, and watch Chris out there on the turf with the team, standing reverently facing the stands, helmet off for the hymn, and bless my old soul if I don't for a moment think that there are things one can believe in with all one's heart. Although, when the hymn is over and I've returned to the house and sit with my first drink, I can't for the life of me think what they may be.

Dalton Trumbo, to a fellow blacklistee

1969

I was stunned as one is when one reaches the fulfillment of a wish and finds it suddenly granted beyond one's imagination. Of all the things which have been said, written about the Diaries, you wrote what has the deepest meaning for me—you answered as only someone who *is* a writer *and* a critic and a *human* being could.

Anaïs Nin, to Robert Kirsch

OCTOBER 13

1913

I have made a contract under which Bosworth, Inc., has the rights to make moving pictures of all my works. Bosworth, Inc., has made a fine seven-reel picture of *The Sea Wolf,* authenticated over my signature with twenty-five feet of moving pictures of myself writing at my desk. All other films made by Bosworth, Inc., will be similarly authenticated.

Jack London

1924

Tonight is so beautiful. The moon is so big and yellow and looks like a picture through the trees in front of my window. I'm beginning to get romantic again in this warm climate.

The two girls in my room are out—one with a boy friend and the other has to work nights as she is a telegraph operator.

I didn't mind staying here by myself today because there is an auditorium right next to my window and the opera singers here in Los Angeles are practicing for 2 weeks. They tell me that they practice here every day during their stay so that I expect to be entertained for nothing for the rest of the week.

Valeria Belletti, to a childhood friend

OCTOBER 14

1849

Traveled 7 miles and came to San Graviell Mission, the most beautiful location that I have seen in this country, the garden filled with oranges and olives and other fruit trees. We then traveled 3 miles and camped.

HENRY W. BIGLER

1932

Went to the house David Lewis and James Whale have taken, for dinner. . . . It is very Spanish, with a red ruled living room whose long windows look out on magnificent views on three sides. . . . Dorothy Arzner, the only woman director, came in later. A fine, sad, abstract-minded spinster. She drove me home, stopping en route to show me her house, a Greek house immensely appropriate to the Vestal of the Cinema.

CHARLES BRACKETT

OCTOBER 15

1973

Re:

Your November issue, "On the Scene" section on Mr. Hunter S. Thompson as the creator of Gonzo Journalism, which you say he both created and named. . . . Well, sir, I beg to take issue with you. And with anyone else who says that. In point of fact, Doctor

Duke and I—the world famous Doctor Gonzo—together we both, hand in hand, sought out the teachings and curative powers of the world famous Savage [Robert] Henry, the Scag Baron of Las Vegas, and in point of fact the term *and* methodology of reporting crucial events under fire and drugs, which are of course essential to any good writing in this age of confusion—all this I say came from out of the mouth of our teacher who is also known by the name of Owl.

OSCAR ZETA ACOSTA, to Hugh Hefner

2002

So Jon and I are parking the car, and the parking structure is monstrous, one of those structures that goes five floors underground, and the only empty spaces are on the fifth floor in a remote cavernous corner.

And we don't necessarily mind, because we're going to see one of those arty movies that's only playing at like three screens in the entire country, and parking doesn't really matter when you get to see a movie that people in Oklahoma really want to see, but won't get to see for a very long time because they don't live in LA or New York. When you think about it, they live in Okla-fucking-homa, and I know that the wind sweeps down the plain and that everything is O-fucking-K, but they really should be living in LA. We've got arty movies here.

Anyway, we make our way to the elevator, and because we're on the bottom floor of the monstrous parking structure, we have to wait a few minutes for the next ride. And Jon and I are looking at the three other people waiting with us, three complete strangers, and we're all silent, and we're all letting each other know through like telepathy or something that, yes, we're all here for the arty movie. People like us, people like those who are waiting with us, we don't have to talk about how cool we are. All you have to do is look at our arty vintage shoes.

So the elevator finally arrives and we all clamber in, all five of us, and the doors close and we go up only one floor. And the doors open to let in those waiting on the fourth floor and there's this couple standing there totally making out, groping and fondling and everything, his back to the door, she's facing the elevator.

And as the doors open she realizes that five people are watching this detailed reproductive display, so she stops kissing the guy and tells him to stop, stop, cut it out, stop, the elevator is here. But he really doesn't care, he's trying to get his game on, so he continues to grope and he's very earnest about the groping.

And she's getting annoyed, so she finally forces his hands off her body and stops him with one final "cut it out!" So he reluctantly gives up the groping and turns to enter the elevator and as he turns around all five of us in the elevator realize that this gallant groper is none other than Giovanni Ribisi.

And he realizes, shit, there are five people standing there watching this and he knows that we all know who he is, and so he gives us this pleading, furrowed brow that says, please, for the love of god, don't ask me about the *Mod Squad,* I don't know what I was thinking, can I please just have my dignity?

And all five of us are cool enough that we know better than to call attention to a celebrity. You just don't do that here.

HEATHER B. ARMSTRONG

OCTOBER 16

1937

Preparations for my next picture *Shanghai Deadline* have not quite reached what I might call the "Hell—Let's Shoot It" stage and consequently there are numerous story conferences, at which tremendous attention to the minutest detail of dialogue and characterization is paid by all concerned, and advance scripts marked "Revised Temporary Final" are issued to the principals. It never pays, however, to *read* these scripts as the entire story is invariably rewritten on the set, the dialogue improvised by the players, and the characterization moulded by the Director in accordance with his day-to-day moods, whims and fancies.

GEORGE SANDERS, to his father

1965

Why Dick,

. . . At the moment I am in LA, or possibly only think I am, and who knows for how long . . .

later,

Pyn~chon~

THOMAS PYNCHON

OCTOBER 17

1925

It is a hard job, this cross-country driving. We got into the traffic at Hollywood last night and it is frightful. There and here the traffic policeman keeps hurrying the cars to drive faster.

LAURA INGALLS WILDER, to Almanzo Wilder

1951

An old acquaintance of mine, James Agee, many years the movie reviewer on *Time* and latterly engaged in doing a script for John Huston on *The African Queen,* is also on the beach and occupying a room in Dotty's house (no romantic connection; he spends his time drooling over some unseen dame Dotty calls The Pink Worm). Parker says Agee consumed three bottles of scotch unaided last Friday. I didn't get Agee's closing quotations on Parker's consumption. They both exist in a fog of crapulous laundry, stale cigarette smoke, and dirty dishes, sans furniture or cleanliness; one suspects they wet their beds. All this, added to an absolutely manic pitch of fear out here on everyone's part that he's about to get about to be jugged by the FBI—and people *are* being [thus] jugged and blacklisted—makes for a Hollywood that is nothing like any I ever knew, a combination of boom town gone bust and Germany in 1935. By Monday I was in such a dreary frame of mind I was strongly tempted to cry frig to my various assignments and jump the eastbound plane.

S. J. PERELMAN

1962

I want you to know this is a literary family. Tony came home from school the other day with a composition entitled "Why I

Must Not Talk in Class," for me to read and sign. His father, on the other hand, is sending you *his* compositions for you to read, sign, and return. Find, enclosed, unless some crook with excellent taste has rifled the envelope looking for first edition material that he can sell as hot goods to the Huntington Library.

The pieces are from a book to be called *Overkill and Megalove* which World Publishing has scheduled for spring publication, always allowing that there will be any paper or people by then. Tell me frankly what you think and why you believe they are great. . . .

Fuck the New York Yankees.

Norman Corwin, to E. Y. "Yip" Harburg

1969

Somewhere out in an undesignated space my friend Turtle is watching the stars. He sent me a message of greetings last week and an invitation to "come and see us"—the us being a commune in the hillsides, full of sweet smiles and good vibes. But I can't because tomorrow comes and I come with it fully charged with the pursuit of career and achievement and excitement that is doing something in the city.

Liza Williams

OCTOBER 18

1919

The neighbor's dog (a very gentle, affectionate doggie—white with yellow spots) was killed yesterday by a motor car, at top of the hill. We are very lonely, as he came to us to be fed regularly—his owner feeding him nothing but vile-smelling chicken-food.

Olive Percival

1930

There is no Los Angeles face. Almost any other great city will have an imaginable characteristic physiognomy. . . . The Los Angeles picture, nevertheless, would be a very remarkable thing—namely, the truest conceivable representation of the whole American face, urban, big town, little town, all together.

Garet Garrett

1973

I visited Henry Miller after serious surgery, fourteen hours and eight hours on separate days. He was so weak and frail. He is blind in his right eye from being too long on the operating table. He does not hear well. When he asked to have the pillows removed so he could slide into bed and rest, I felt almost as if he was going to curl up and sleep forever. . . .

I don't want to live as Miller has, limping, in pain, not able to travel and now for the second time undergoing major surgery. Henry once so healthy, joyous, lively. Tireless walker, hearty eater.

But let the sun shine on a beautiful autumn day, let me have a morning free of engagements when I can work on Volume Six and I am light again. Stay alive, Anaïs.

Anaïs Nin

OCTOBER 19

1941

Picked out the suit Sam Goldwyn is giving me (one also for Billy) for the script.

CHARLES BRACKETT

1991

I drove to the studio this morning to visit the set. Inside a huge stage at Columbia Studios a grand Victorian mansion had been built. I loved seeing the furnishings, all the rich silks and brocades in a perfect harmony of muted color. Francis took my hand and said, "Come see this." He led me to the bedroom to look at the large round headboard for Lucy's bed with its carved bat designs and thick tassels.

The room opened onto a terrace overlooking the garden. We walked down two flights of wide stone steps to a fountain and a pond with water lilies blooming. Beyond, I could see the entrance to the crypt and a hill with family gravestones. There was a rose arbor and a maze of high hedges. Francis said, "All this garden is built in the pit of the stage where Esther Williams' swimming pool once was."

ELEANOR COPPOLA

OCTOBER 20

1927

We've been to Catalina for two days, San Diego and Tia Juana for four days. I went to the races but lost $2.50. Played roulette and lost—played the money machines and lost—in fact luck is just against me it seems, but I'm not worried. I feel ever so much better than in N.Y. and that's something to be thankful for. The weather is simply marvelous—so warm and sunshiny. We've only had one cloudy day since I've been here. . . .

Tomorrow I am going to really make an earnest effort to get a job and if I can't get a job at the studios I'll go downtown [to] Los Angeles in some law office temporarily.

VALERIA BELLETTI, to a childhood friend

1945

I think I have had all about all of Hollywood I can stand. I feel bad, depressed, dreadful sense of wasting time, I imagine most of the symptoms of some kind of blow-up or collapse. I may be able to come back later, but I think I will finish this present job and return home. Feeling as I do, I am actually afraid to stay here much longer. . . .

My books have never sold, or [are] out of print; the labor (the creation of my apocryphal county) of my life, even if I have a few things yet to add to it, will never make a living for me. I don't have enough sure judgment about trash to be able to write it with 50% success.

WILLIAM FAULKNER, to his agent

OCTOBER 21

1906

6 hours at the carpenter's bench which resulted in my putting the grille in Bertha's door and hanging it on its hinges. Poor Amate had his fingers eaten up with the sulfuric acid in the cement and sat around and lent me his moral support while I toiled; and Keith lent me his immoral support and asked me 17,000 questions by count (he counted) in a voice that I used instead of a bit when I had to bore any holes in hard wood.

CHARLES LUMMIS

1940

Had dinner upstairs with Luther and Sylvia [Sidney], after this going for a walk down Hollywood Boulevard. They told me of a scene that happened in Ciro's nightclub here the other night. [Anatole] Litvak, director, and [Paulette] Goddard, actress, were drunk there together. They have been sleeping together, in public, for weeks. Drunk at Ciro's, sitting at a ringside table, he took out her breasts and kissed them passionately. They were stopped by the help but later continued the same thing on the dance floor. For this the management banished them to the outer sanctum of the bar. There A. Litvak suddenly disappeared, finally was discovered under the bouffant skirt of Miss Goddard on his knees, kissing the "eagerly sought triangular spot" with the blissful unawareness of a baby at a bottle.

For my part, I told Sylvia, I would rather be like Litvak than lead a life of wooden caution.

A warm feeling came to me when I began to think about the trio play this evening. I hope to come to it again with real excitement. Part of the theme of this play is about how the men of our country irresponsibly wait for the voice and strong arm of authority to bring them to life, etc. So comes fascism to a whole race of people. Danger ahead—I see it all over, even in myself. Nothing stands for authority and I wait for its voice! There is something in men in the world over today that welcomes dictatorship; the children are seeking for the father to arrange their lives for them!

CLIFFORD ODETS

OCTOBER 22

1962

I don't know why I'm starting a new volume at this point. The day isn't auspicious—nothing memorable but the death of Cezanne. And today is foggy. Rather snug, as foggy days are in the Canyon. . . .

A whole week of no work, except preparations for the reading I gave last night at the Garden Grove High School auditorium. (This was looked on by the organizers as a historic event, because it was the first lectures given under the auspices of the future Irvine branch of the U.C., UCI, which has at present no buildings, no students, almost no faculty except the chancellor and some other administrators, nothing but one thousand acres of land.) I have got to get on with Ramakrishna. And I must keep at the novel, just for the sake of provoking a breakthrough.

CHRISTOPHER ISHERWOOD

2003

It's hard to convey the tranquility and normalcy of these neighborhoods—the skateboarding kids, the Pizza Huts, the garage sales—while still presenting a truthful picture of their crime problems.

In fact, what many people in Los Angeles think of as this city's "bad neighborhoods" are in many ways indistinguishable from those with milder reputations. They brim with aspiration and middle-class comfort, even as they distill every kind of despair. I pass blocks of graffiti on Slauson Avenue in the morning before stopping in at the bright new Western Avenue Starbucks, inevitably full of well-dressed commuters listening to cutting-edge blues. This is just northwest of where the 1992 riots broke out, and the area is now booming, construction everywhere: a new Gigante grocery store, a new Subway sandwich shop.

But just across the street is the permanent swap meet where a shootout broke out recently amid a crowd in daylight.

JILL LEOVY

OCTOBER 23

1848

Here I got the first news of the discovery of gold—obtained it from a negro—It seems incredible—They say that men in some instances have made as high as $50. a day—It seems incredible! But, they insist here it is true.

ORVILLE C. PRATT

1940

2000 words today and all good.

F. Scott Fitzgerald

OCTOBER 24

1871

There has been a Chinese massacre . . . a most disgraceful affair, the like of which is fortunately not on American records. Some members of different Chinese secret societies fought over the possession of a woman. . . .

A few Celestials were taken to jail in consequence. The disturbance was thought to have ended and the jailbirds were taken the next day before the police court for preliminary hearing. . . .

No sooner had the court set the day for trial than the Mongolians repaired to their own quarters, where a new fight ensued, which soon attracted a multitude of Mexicans and Americans from that vicinity. . . .

The heathens fought desperately and an officer, Robert Thompson, who attempted to quell the riot, was killed and his deputy, Bilderain, was wounded, which naturally roused the boundless anger of the white mob. . . .

One of the heathens ventured into the street and was at once caught by his pursuers, taken about four squares and hanged to the doorway of a corral amid the abjurations of the enraged spectators. Having tasted the blood of the almond-eyed stranger, the combined mob of Americans and Spaniards now largely reinforced, began the real massacre. As the beleaguered heathen had barricaded doors and windows, a crowd of hoodlums in desperate frenzy climbed upon the roofs, broke holes through and shot the inmates, males, females, young and old. . . .

It may seem amazing that so-called civilized communities should have to witness the frenzied destruction of nearly a score of human lives, even though the provocation was very great. When quiet was restored, there were eighteen bodies found dangling in mid air, some from window casings, some from lamp posts, while one or two had actually been tied to the seat of farm wagons and others to awnings, among these the body of a child!

FRANK LECOUVREUR

OCTOBER 25

1908

I anxiously await Saturdays so that I can see your little letters, my love. All week I've been waiting to see if you show up, from my cell through the window on the alley, which is the third window. . . .

When you all pass by the third window on the alley, stop if only for a half minute so that I can see you well. My dear: I feel that you are feeling a bit of pain. Would some of my kisses where you hurt make it well? I would give them so tenderly that you would feel no discomfort. I know, my life, I understand that you miss me as much as I miss you. But what can be done? More than the tyrants, it is our friends who are keeping us in jail, because their laziness, their indolence, their lack of initiative has tied them up, and they do nothing. I believe that they love us and have us in their hearts; but this isn't enough to rescue us. What's needed is that they work in an effective manner for our liberation, and they're not doing that. Everyone comes forth in manifesting their sympathy for us and deploring our situation. We are devoting ourselves to putting an end to the tyrant in Mexico and nobody will lift an arm to stop the tyrant's henchmen. There is much that could be done in our favor, but little or nothing is being done, and nothing, of course, is being gained. There should be a commission that is constantly after the press so that something could appear favorable to the prisoners, as much in the local press as that outside of California. . . .

Goodbye my love, look closely and you'll see that it is our friends who are keeping us prisoner through their apathy. Receive my immense love and adoration, you, the only woman who makes my heart beat. What I've told you isn't a reproach for you, my angel. You're doing everything you can, and I thank you from my soul. If you don't win in this struggle against despotism and do not rescue your Ricardo who loves and adores you, it won't have been for lack of effort on your part. With all my soul, your Ricardo kisses you tenderly.

RICARDO FLORES MAGON, to his beloved

1919

Convincingly proving his ability to weld into shape a new organization and his capacity for realizing both the musical and artistic content of his programme, Walter Henry Rothwell, as conductor of the Philharmonic Orchestra, yesterday startled Los Angeles out of her symphonic slumbers and introduced what might be termed a new epoch in local musical history. The concert was [the] first afternoon event of the series to be given at Trinity Auditorium. The audience was not especially notable as to size, the glamour of a premiere was not broadly apparent, but the people who were there represented musical taste, and their appreciation, particularly after they were fully convinced that the result was real, brilliantly testified the triumph achieved by the musicians under the scholarly, and at the same time, unconventional leadership of the new conductor.

It was evident as soon as the orchestra members had assumed

their places on the stage that the backers of the enterprise have spared nothing money can buy in their effort to give a new importance to music in this city. No doubt, the chief credit for this belongs to W. A. Clark, Jr., who officially and unofficially is the sponsor of the enterprise. And don't worry about Mr. Clark not taking an active interest in his prodigy, because he has been watching its growth ever since the first rehearsal, and he was there yesterday and as proud as any sponsor should be over a prodigy's debut.

. . . In his interpretations Rothwell seemed at his best in the movements affording the opportunities for broader contrasts. His renditions of the symphonic poem, "Les Preludes" and Chabrier's "Espana," are the most distinct triumphs and were greeted with bravos. His effects were equally brilliant in the rapid movements of the Dvorak "New World Symphony."

. . . You could realize at times that he was not getting the finer effects he desired, but that will be only a matter of rehearsals now, for everything indicated yesterday the certainty of a triumphal first season for the Philharmonic Orchestra.

EDWIN SCHALLERT, for the *Los Angeles Times*

1920

Work on *An American Tragedy* & letters. Helen collects $35.00 from Metro & gives it to me. Wonderful session in evening—after dinner at Petitfils. Helen has a streak of perversion in her. Makes me promise never to teach any other girl to osculate my penus as she does!

THEODORE DREISER

OCTOBER 26

1929

Last night I went to the Carthay Circle Theatre to see Will Rogers in his first talking picture, *They Had to See Paris.* Marvelous! I was astonished at Will Rogers's work. To call him a comedian is unjust to his art—the word is too small. He is one of the greatest HUMORISTS I have ever seen, but he is also a great ACTOR! His characterization is not of one small-town garage-store owner in Oklahoma, but of every small-town garage-store owner in America.

ERNST LUBITSCH

1951

The Audrey Hepburn test you made is a fine piece of work, and I just wanted to tell you how much we liked it here at the studio. You gave us a good look at the girl's personality and charm, as well as her talent. As a result of the test, a number of producers at Paramount have expressed interest in casting her.

I can't say at the moment whether or not we will use Miss Hepburn in Roman Holiday, but if we don't you may be sure it will not be because of anything in the test—which is as good as any I've seen in a long time.

WILLIAM WYLER, to a fellow director

1963

My friend, the forest ranger, decided I had been working too hard and needed diversion. "I'm going to take you to visit the oldest things on the planet." As we drove north from Los Angeles, I assumed we were going to the redwoods. . . .

. . . It seemed as though we had landed in a spaceship on another planet, the planet Mars. Out of great expanses of bare, white, bone-colored rock grew a few scattered trees, nothing else. The trees were short, stunted, twisted and gnarled, only a few green needles, a symbol of strength and defiance. The forester said they were bristlecone pines, the oldest known living things. Methuselah, the eldest, is 4,600 years old. Many were growing here when the Egyptians were building the Pyramids. He explained these trees are the only plants that can survive here, exposed to high winds, growing on very poor rocky soil with very little rainfall. They have been able to survive by allowing most of the tree to die so that a small part may live on in equilibrium with the harsh environment. They grow incredibly slowly, in one hundred years only one inch. Their twisted roots have been almost completely exposed by four hundred years of erosion. Many of the pines had been sculptured into objects of powerful beauty by wind-blown sand, by ice and by fire.

Anaïs Nin

OCTOBER 27

1925

Last night on the way home from dinner, Ruth and I walked down our street and were remarking how beautiful it was. The sky was a deep blue and the stars were so twinkly—the street is a broad one and lined on both sides with huge palm trees. The houses are all set back with lovely lawns in front (everything is quite a new green now since the rain we've had) and the pale moon shining through the palms threw weird shadows on the lawns. It looked so enchanting. Ruth and I just stopped and drank in the beauty.

Valeria Belletti

1934

I still have my fine office, I still have my emptiness: but I think it fairly well established by now that I am "not quite the man for the job." For it is all a process of wearing down. It seems they expect you to come here with the ember of revolt glowing somewhere. They smile and wait for it to get dampened in the application of non-resistance blankets. They seem to say: "We will let this fellow make his protestations for his soul's sake, and then, having made them, he can get to work." But if you won't let revolt die, then you're not the "man for the job." If desire goes on burning fiercely, you are an outcast.

ERIC KNIGHT, to a friend

1943

Done delightfully in the Palisades when I went out on my bicycle just now. Have gone to bed with cigarettes and a book, A life of Rimbaud.

Feel good. Ruin is still in abeyance. Good night. En avant, wherever you are!

TENNESSEE WILLIAMS

OCTOBER 28

1890

September was a blur of bodily and mental suffering. I am coming back, surely, to strength and nerve. I can walk—not yet alone for I need Lily's arm, dear good child—a quarter of a mile. And daily I take an hour or two hours sometimes on the cable cars—they glide so smoothly they tire me less than a carriage. And then I am not obliged to speak, or say thank you as I must even to Mrs. Severance who is the only one I have seen. I get home tired, but wholesomely tired now. At first it was depressing. But there are unexplored depths in us that only solitude of heart can find—a weary exploration but leading nearer to Divine strength.

JESSIE BENTON FRÉMONT, to her nephew

1941

At the studio all day but too nervous about our *Ball of Fire* preview to do any effective work. . . . motored to the Academy Theatre in Inglewood for the preview. It went well, slow at first, then getting into its full stride for a grand old-fashioned movie, with yells of laughter from the audience. . . . Find myself feeling the pleasure of a complete amateur let in on momentous doing.

CHARLES BRACKETT

OCTOBER 29

1939

As you probably know, the punch line of *Gone With the Wind,* the one bit of dialogue which forever establishes the future relationship between Scarlett and Rhett, is, "Frankly, my dear, I don't give a damn."

Naturally, I am most desirous of keeping this line and, to judge from the reactions of two preview audiences, this line is remembered, loved, and looked forward to by millions who have read this new American classic. . . .

As you know from my previous work with such pictures as *David Copperfield, Little Lord Fauntleroy, A Tale of Two Cities,* etc., I have always attempted to live up to the spirit as well as the exact letter of the producers' code. Therefore, my asking you to review the case, to look at the strip of film in which this forbidden word is contained, is not motivated by a whim. A great deal of the force and drama of *Gone With the Wind,* a project to which we have given three years of hard work and hard thought, is dependent on that word. . . .

I do not feel that your giving me permission to use "damn" in this one sentence will open up the floodgates and allow every gangster picture to be peppered with "damns" from end to end. I do believe, however, that if you were to permit our using this dramatic word in its rightfully dramatic place, in a line that is known and remembered by millions of readers, it would establish a helpful precedent.

David O. Selznick, to a censor

2001

Yesterday morning at approximately 9:30 a.m. PST, a smallish rumbling earthquake hit Los Angeles and woke me from a drooling slumber. It was the first earthquake I've ever been awake or sober enough to experience, and like any other natural disaster frightened me into rabid cable news channel surfing and knuckle gnawing for the rest of the afternoon.

Rounding out the list of phobias that render me a paralyzed, shivering goose bump—fear of heights, rodents, spiders, and hairy toes to name just a few—is a mammoth anxiety over potential natural disasters, thoroughly aggravated in my youth by my older brother's daily tortuous threat: "Do what I say or the tornado will come and get you."

Tornado season in Tennessee starts in mid-March and continues through July, sometimes hiccupping into the latter part of September. When thunderstorms aren't uprooting forests or rearranging acres of farmland, the South often suffers hailstorms, flashfloods and torrentially ghoulish winds during this season. Rarely is there a week not littered with severe thunderstorm warnings blinking in red Helvetica across the bottom of "Days of Our Lives." . . .

18 years later and over 1000 miles from any weather conducive to tornado formation, I've got earthquakes to worry about and no siren-ific warnings or radar screens to issue me into the tub and into safety. I wonder how long I can stand under a doorframe before passing out.

HEATHER B. ARMSTRONG

2007

As I head down the Thompson Creek trail esta mañana, iPod-less, tuning in, instead, to a chirpy sky just beginning to clear of post-fire smoke and ash—por apocalíptico que parezca, just the "typical" Califas fall conflagration—I *do* know one thing for sure. Si el Bruce was born to run, yo nací para escribir.

SUSANA CHÁVEZ-SILVERMAN

OCTOBER 30

1916

You ask when we expect to return. Have rented this house until June 4 and shall probably stay the limit. To my surprise I like it here very much. I do not know when I have been more contented. We have a very pretty little place with many flowers and trees, and a good lawn. . . . The children are playing out in front now with no wraps, and wearing sox. . . .

There are oodles of writers here, too. . . . If I could establish a colony of human beings, it would be a nice place to live permanently.

EDGAR RICE BURROUGHS, to his editor

1926

This place is fit only for Christians. Its first gift to me was a nasty bronchitis. Every visitor, I hear, gets it, on account of the dry, idiotic climate.

H. L. MENCKEN, to his wife

OCTOBER 31

1927

Five people killed in plane yesterday and it is headlined today in every paper. Saturday in Los Angeles at one grade crossing seven were killed and six wounded and the papers didn't even publish the names.

It looks like the only way you can get any publicity on your death is to be killed in a plane. It's no novelty to be killed in an auto any more.

WILL ROGERS

1956

Dear Robert: Passed through LA with Gregory, alone, preceding Orlovsky brothers, to give reading for Anais Nin, [Stuart] Perkoff, silly Lawrence Lipton and 70 other assorted strangers from Coastlines magazine and friends of Lip and Nin. Someone heckled Gregory so I drunkenly screamed take off your clothes and be naked, which then realizing what I was saying I went and did myself, to my great surprise. They made me put them back on before reading Howl, which I read with great wildness and lovely abandon so the night turned out fine.

ALLEN GINSBERG, to a fellow poet

1956

. . . what are we to say, then, of a man
who takes off his clothes in someone else's living room?
are we to applaud?
what is his nakedness to us?
what we care about his poems?
do you realize that he is in the lite? how can i
be expected to read?
he makes too much noise!
he says dirty words!
he needs a bath!
he is certainly
drunk!
i hope he soon realizes that this is, after all, now
& we have many wonderful things to amuse us
we want to see clowns
we go to the circus
is he gone yet? can i come out now?

STUART PERKOFF

NOVEMBER 1

1885

On the first of November of the said year two deputy sheriffs, one a Spaniard named Martin Aguirre, notified me that they had orders to deprive me of the place, and I answered them to do as the law commanded them. The officers were provided with a cart, which they loaded with furniture, seeds and a set of tools belonging to my trade, and at the distance of two miles, more or less, in the public road, threw these things out; in this way they made two or three trips. My wife and three other women followed the cart on foot. I remained in my house watching the saddest event of my life. The officers then asked me whether I would not leave the place. I answered to act according to their duty; then four persons took hold of me, put me in the wagon, and placed me with my family and goods.

In that sad situation we remained eight days and nights, not knowing what to do, for we had not the means of moving and did not know where to go; for all that vast country for many miles belonged to the man who had despoiled me of my property. I came to Los Angeles, and the Bishop promised to harbor me in one of the ruins of the mission while I considered what I should do. I could not move then because it began to rain, and the rain lasted four days. That rain weakened our bodies, as we had not the slightest shelter nor way in which to cook anything; for the little flour, sugar and other things the rain had spoiled.

The women were rendered helpless; my wife fell ill, and died in consequence of this. When the rain ceased, I moved to the mission with the little I had left, which was nothing.

My property on the land consisted of two adobe houses (made

of sun-baked bricks), two of wood, about forty chickens, a blacksmith's forge, with all my iron and utensils by which means I supported myself; everything disappeared and the most cherished of my life, my dear companion.

ROGERIO ROCH

1919

Enroute from Salt Lake to Los Angeles. Awaken at dawn in berth with Helen. I insist on rutting here. She protests but kisses me & lets me. . . .

The Orange Groves. Helen & I on the back platform. Her joy and beauty. We reach Los Ange. 7 p.m. Helen's efficiency. Phones. The incident of the boys. We get off at the wrong corner. Finally reach the Stillwell at length & Grand Ave. Room 523. The nice service. We dress & go to a restaurant in Spring Street. Not much. Then back to hotel & spend a delicious night together. I am crazy about her.

THEODORE DREISER

NOVEMBER 2

1942

lang's secretary called to say that shooting was starting and I was *"invited, more than invited."* The first scene lang shot was one wexley and I had cut; the heroine is arguing with her aunt about her wedding dress—she wants a deeper décolleté. The heroine is cast with a fifth-rate English actress, a smooth doll with no character. The lord of the lens is sitting beside his camera, unapproachable, while beside me a german refugee doctor waits to give him his vitamin injections. Lang, of course, gives me an unconvincing wave and says half-audibly, "hi, brecht! You'll be getting a script tomorrow!"

Bertolt Brecht

1978

Armistead [Maupin], on second acquaintance, impresses me greatly. He seems to be absorbing impressions constantly, which means that he is tremendously "responsive" in Kathleen's use of the word, and kind of mediumistic in the way he has psychic feelers out, testing the atmosphere. . . .

Today we had William Burroughs over to be drawn (brilliantly) by Don. Was not charmed when the gate buzzer buzzed and I opened to admit *five* people. . . . Does Burroughs always go around in mobs?

We had, however, known that Paul Getty was coming. . . . Indeed, Don and I had a joke. Don wanted me to ask about his kidnapping. "Say to him, if you'll tell me about it, I'll lend an ear." Paul proved to be not only fairly pretty, though spotty and looking much older than twenty-two (his claimed age), but also really charming and genuinely interested in our collection of pictures. A mop of curly reddish hair concealed his ear-lack.

Christopher Isherwood

NOVEMBER 3

1888

Oh! who can describe the real estate agent of Southern California! And what would California be without him? Notice him as he leans at his office door, with a flower in his button hole, while over his suave and seductive countenance ripple ravishing dreams of carloads of Eastern tourists wishing to buy lots.

Harriet Harper

1929

Out here somewhere prowling around is the Assistant Secretary of the Navy for Aviation. He was a naval ace of our late war. Just think of appointing a man that knew something about the business he was appointed to. I think that should call for a Senatorial investigation, knocking good politicians out of a job like that.

Will Rogers

1942

I have now to go and vote. I hope Governor Olsen and Will Rogers will be elected.

Galka Scheyer

1978

The plane ride stretches on until the hour seems to last an eternity and we'll never come down. At this point, I always want to keep going. . . .

Los Angeles appears. Its unsure beginnings creeping northward—not knowing when to stop and where to begin. We begin the descent—so soon?

So quickly.

Must we come down just yet?

She's yellow now. She's skating so low on the horizon that there's no place left to go but up. Yet down, down and down we continue. Shaking and bumping like a four wheel drive jeep across the desert. . . .

Remember the rugs—positive and negative spaces, borders interlock. If L.A. was a carpet, I wouldn't buy it. It's missing all the essential geometric properties. All of them. It just spreads monotonously. But beautifully from this altitude. I'll be fair as I put the pen away.

Aaron Paley

NOVEMBER 4

1892

I cut down a eucalyptus tree sixty feet high and made a pole and began laboriously to worm its point down through the bottom of the shaft. The process would have discouraged anyone not possessing the sublime faith that we possessed that a few inches or a few more feet at the most would tap for us incalculable wealth.

Suddenly gas spewed out and oil flooded the shaft to a depth of ten or fifteen feet in a few moments.

E. L. Doheny

1956

One of Ginsberg's poems was called *Howl.* It was a great, long, desperate wail, a struggle to make poetry out of all the objects, surroundings and people he had known. At times, it reached a kind of American surrealism, a bitter irony; it had a savage power. At moments, it did seem like the howling of animals. It reminded me of Artaud's mad conference at the Sorbonne.

Then a man in the audience challenged Ginsberg in a stupid way. "Why must you write about the slums? Isn't it enough that we have them?"

Ginsberg was in a frenzy of anger. He proceeded to take off all his clothes, throwing each piece to the audience. My friend Ingrid received the soiled jockey shorts. He provoked and challenged the man to come and expose his feelings and his real self as nakedly as he had. "Come and stand here, stand naked before the people. I dare you! The poet always stands naked before the world."

The man in the packed audience tried to leave. Ginsberg said: "Now let someone dare to insult a man who offers what he feels nakedly before everyone. . . ." The way he did it was so violent and direct, it had so much meaning in terms of all our fears of unveiling ourselves. The man in the audience was booed and hissed until he left. People began to throw his clothes back to Ginsberg. But he sat at ease on the couch and showed no signs of dressing again. . . . The two poets went on reading for hours. I left, thinking it was like a new surrealism born of the Brooklyn gutter and supermarkets.

Anaïs Nin

NOVEMBER 5

1906

Good day! My bullfrogs have come—and are now sitting in my bath tub waiting till I can make a good cage for them in the fountain, so that they can increase and multiply, and also so that they can't eat up the minnows and the goldfish. . . . 4 fine brutes. They are somewhat impressed by their journey in a tight box all the way from Chicago. . . . But the bawmy air of California will doubtless put them in singing trim very soon. Really, I do feel mighty good at getting them. There is nothing in the world that I like better to hear than these old basso-profundos at night. I am going to get some tenor frogs from the cañons and believe I will have Amate teach them all parts so we can have an octet. . . .

The usual kaleidoscope in town . . . trips to architects, and picture framers, and bookshops.

CHARLES LUMMIS

1912

I have an Ayrdale pup, who looks as much like Bernard Shaw as it is possible for a dog.

ROBINSON JEFFERS, to Una Kuster

1926

AMBASSADOR HOTEL

This place is a genuine horror. If I described it literally I'd be set down as the damnedest liar ever heard of. Architecturally it is inconceivable, and the people all seem to be imbeciles. The movie folk, by comparison, are enlightened and civilized.

H. L. MENCKEN, to his wife

1934

I went back on the booze pretty heavily until Saturday night—neglecting studio, dignity, and so on. And was I sick Sunday and today! This morning I showed up at M.G.M. for the first time since last Tuesday and squared myself, but didn't get much work done, since the publicity department took up most of my time, what with photographs, interviews and the like.

I'm still surprised at the fuss the *Thin Man* made out here. People bring the Joan Crawfords and Gables over to meet me instead of the usual vice versa! Hot-cha!

. . . I love you something awful and days are years till I see you again! And I'm not five feet nine and I'm not going to be an actor and don't pay any attention to the publicity the studio is sending out on me: I gave 'em a free hand and they've gone pretty nutty.

I suppose you'll see the Johnsons on their Eastern jaunt—they said they were going to look you up. I love you and miss you and love you and miss you and not much else.

DASHIELL HAMMETT, to Lillian Hellman

1940

SLEEPING LATE STOP STUFF ON DINING ROOM TABLE HOORAY FOR ROOSEVELT AFFECTION SCOTT

F. SCOTT FITZGERALD, to his amanuensis

NOVEMBER 6

1946

Helen telephoned to say that there was quite a crowd of strikers outside Paramount and that they'd shouted insults at her and she'd already telephoned Billy, who said he couldn't bear to look at my face today anyway.

CHARLES BRACKETT

2002

So the landlord came by last week and suddenly realized that the secure building we're all paying to live in isn't necessarily a traditionally "secure" building. In fact, the secure building we're all paying to live in happens to be the same secure building several homeless people are using as a home base of sorts, stashing mismatched Reebok tennis shoes, foam pads and over-sized panties in the corners of the secure roof space.

Why she suddenly realized just now that this secure building isn't really a secure building is gobstopping, because I know of at least four tenants who have complained to her specifically that the secure building we're all paying to live in lacks a certain sense of, I don't know, security.

Heather B. Armstrong

NOVEMBER 7

1849

Seeing a few ducks alight at a little lake, almost like a running stream, I went after them, and found some hundreds of gadwalls, and bald-pates, and in half an hour had sufficient for all our company, which I need not tell you we enjoyed, though not cooked at Baltimore "à la Canvasback."

Hundreds of California marmots are seen daily, at a distance looking like a common squirrel, so much so that the men all call them squirrels; their color varies very much, being every shade of grey and reddish brown.

As we stood looking at all this, from a hill higher than the one on which we were, swooped a California vulture, coming towards us until, at about fifty yards, having satisfied his curiosity, though not mine, he rose in majestic circles high above us, and with a sudden dash took a straight line, somewhat inclining downwards, towards the mountains across the valley and was lost to sight.

John W. Audubon

1919

Her interest in all things seductive. Licks my P & A—cant let my Roger alone. Always getting it out & feeling it. Comes off with me now very quickly. Didn't at first. We dress. I start keeping these notes.

Theodore Dreiser

NOVEMBER 8

1937

Since mid-September we have been in California—very agreeable and amusing and fantastic and interesting. The place of virtualities, where absolutely anything might happen. Meanwhile almost everything is happening—movies, astronomy, sweated labour in the fields, philanthropy, scholarship, phony religions, real religions, all stirred together in a vast chaos in the midst of the most astonishing scenery, ranging from giant sequoias and rock peaks to date palms and red hot deserts.

Aldous Huxley

1950

I went to one of the film lots, and while there I paid a visit to the studio where Humphrey Bogart and Fredric March were rehearsing. As we stood there, one of the big light bulbs burst. No one was badly hurt. Mr. Bogart had a slight scratch on his forehead from which blood trickled down. But I saw no other casualty and was not even startled by the explosion which, though a little louder than that from an ordinary bulb, was not very unusual.

Little did I realize that the newspapers would seize on this mild excitement to give us some very hectic hours answering the telephone because of the reports that there had been some real danger present. This was all nonsense, but just showed me again how easy it is to create an excitement out of nothing.

ELEANOR ROOSEVELT

NOVEMBER 9

1849

We have passed many fine old Missions, at least six or seven, but though in the midst of beautiful land, with hundreds of horses and cattle, and many herds of sheep and goats, the indolence of the people has left all decaying, and they live in dirt and ignorance, and merely vegetate away this life in listlessness, except for the occasional excitement of a trade in horses, or a game of monte. We have had many melons, late in the season as we are; they are pulled and put up as the French do pears, and keep fresh for many weeks.

All the people here ride well, and fast, many without saddles; these latter tie a rope, or if they have it, a surcingle, buckle that around the body of the horse, and stick both knees under it, so that it is a great assistance to them. The gallop is the usual gait at which they travel. The continual absence of wood gives an appearance to all the hills, of old fields, but many of the valleys are truly beautiful; fine sycamores, oaks and cottonwoods along the water making everything look refreshing to a degree that none can realize but those who have been for weeks exposed to sun and rain, keen winds and cold nights, without woods for shelter or fire; in cooking we have often had to keep up a fire with weeds, some men attending to this, while the others fried our meat, made coffee, and what we *called* bread.

Los Angeles. This "city of the angels" is anything else, unless the angels are fallen ones. An antiquated, dilapidated air pervades all, but Americans are pouring in, and in a few years will make a beautiful place of it. It is well watered by a pretty little river, led off in irrigating ditches like those at San Antonio de Bexar. The whole town is surrounded to the south with very luxuriant vines, and the grapes are quite delightful; we parted from them with great regret, as fruit is such a luxury to us. Many of the men took bushels, and only paid small sums for them.

The hills to the north command the whole town, and will be the place for the garrison.

San Pedro, twenty-seven miles south-west, is the port, and is *said* to have a good harbor. All the country round is rolling, and in many places almost mountainous. Before you get to the Coast Range the soil is most of it very good, and the cattle are fine; wild mustard grows everywhere, to the height of five feet or more; in the richest soil attaining seven and eight feet, and we have twice cooked our meal with no fuel but the stalks of this weed.

John W. Audubon

1927

Well, I have my Ticket and Destination—but not Train-time as yet. . . . town at 2:25 and up to Dr. Tholen. He had received his analysis from the Clinical Laboratory with the verdict "malignant." . . . He is a real nice man and a good workman, and I came away with much respect for him, and in entire resignation, as I always have for anything that can't be helped. . . . Came down to 6th and Spring, and trotted around four blocks to get some sweetpeas for my home folks.

Charles Lummis

1991

Tom Waits stepped out from one of the chambers in his costume. His hair had been shaved up the back in odd little ridges. The front, left long, was sprayed gray and stuck out from his head. His teeth had been stained black and brown and he wore filthy long underwear and a torn, dirty Victorian coat. He had pointed period shoes, unbuttoned, flapping open on his dirty bare feet. Each of his hands was covered with a bizarre cagelike glove made of dark stained leather around his wrist and then thin bent metal rods over his fingers with leather caps at the tips. He held a battered tin plate with his asylum food, a moldy crust of bread covered with a squirming mass of maggots, strange orange worms, dead flies, a large potato bug and a selection of beetles. Tom was gently pushing them around the plate saying, "Hey, you, move over."

The bug wrangler was standing nearby. He had several additional tins of maggots and beetles. He occasionally prodded the contents of Tom's plate to make sure they were all moving. He had an assistant with several boxes of candy beetles that were added to the plate so that when Tom picked up something to eat in a scene he could select the candy. Tom was having difficulty picking up anything with his caged fingers. Eiko and the propman were called in. They tried putting honey on Tom's leather fingertips so the candy insects would stick. It didn't work. They tried double-faced sticky tape and then spray adhesive. Tom was very patient as he tried hard to pick up worms from the wriggling mass. Finally the shot setup was complete and they had to shoot. They decided to frame over Tom's shoulder and let the second unit get shots of him actually eating from the plate.

ELEANOR COPPOLA

NOVEMBER 10

1869

Take it altogether, it is a unique old town, full of oddities and whimsicalities. Half the population is Mexican, the other half American, English, Scotch, Irish, German, and the Lord knows what; yet there is a goodly number of intelligent, refined and accomplished people, who reside here and give tone to society. . . . It contains a population, they say, of about twenty thousand. . . . If not the first, it is the second edition of the true Garden of Eden. . . .

We remained nearly a week at the ranch, known as the San Joaquin. . . . The ranch is amply watered by springs, and a chain of small lagoons, extending through it, centrally, supposed to be a subterranean river, from the connection there is in the hidden currents that pass from one lagoon to another. . . .

These lagoons terminate in a small bay, which extends from the ocean into the ranch about two miles. On the shore of this bay I saw a camp of Mexican fishermen, who were engaged in manufacturing oil from the carcasses of sharks, which they catch in abundance along the sea coast. They go out to sea in small boats, and catch the sharks by harpooning or shooting them, as they rise to the surface in their eagerness to swallow the bait flung to them. When caught, they are towed into the bay, and so great is the number of their skeletons lying about the camp, that the atmosphere, throughout the entire vicinity for miles, is rendered impure and even offensive. Nothing of this kind, I believe, can offend the olfactories of a Mexican.

The largest cheese ever made in the world, was made on one of these dairy ranches. It was made during the late war, and weighed four thousand pounds. It was sold in San Francisco at fifty cents a pound, for the benefit of the "Sanitary Fund." The butter, as well as the cheese, is manufactured by steam power. In this business, fortunes may be made or lost in a single year. Little things cannot be done in California; it must be great things or nothing.

HARVEY RICE

1939

The desert sun shines bright in Los Angeles early in the morning so that people cannot sleep on. Therefore, the Babbitts bound brightly from their beds in a mood to beam upon their fellowmen, and in this spirit gather once a week to breakfast jovially on ham and eggs. . . .

Mr. Willis Allen, a real estate salesman and go-getter who had been a cheer leader in college, now promised the poor $30 every Thursday. . . .

WESTBROOK PEGLER

1954

I attended the Episcopal Church of the Advent. It is a sweet little church which had almost faded out of existence but has been brought back by the determined efforts of the new young rector, Rev. Dr. Pratt. He now has 800 parishioners enrolled where there were only five at the time he took it over.

They have a nice custom here. At the end of the service everyone goes into the parish house and coffee and doughnuts are on hand. Strangers are welcomed and this gives them a chance to meet people which, in a city where 5,500 new people come in every week, must be very helpful.

ELEANOR ROOSEVELT

NOVEMBER 11

1919

Armistice Day. Holiday commemorating the armistice with the Germans—Nov. 11—1919. I was with Bo last year & walked down through Central Park—watching the wild joy of the people. Today baby & I wake in our room at 338 Alvarado. Every day sunshine here. I had a dream last night that I got off the train & that it started without me but I ran after it & with difficulty made it. Helen & I indulge in a delightful round, as usual. She has the most teasing methods. Talks all the time & tortures me into an orgasm by her sweet brutalities & descriptions. Up at 9:30 & go to the little restaurant in 7th St near Alvarado. . . .

Later baby & I get to playing in bed. Her beauty just knocks me. It is unbelievable—a dream of fair women. She looks like an angel or a classic figure & yet is sensuality to the core. We indulge in a long suck & then I put her on her knees. A wild finish. Return to my work. The poems & flowers here seem in no wise affected by the sharp coolness which begins at about five. A wonderful climate. We go downtown at 6:30 to the B. & M. cafeteria—a very large affair. A very fair diner for 90 cents each but no atmosphere. Afterwards we try to find a theatre but cant. Go to Grunwalds Movie. . . .

Has the full forward, lavender lids & bluish white eye lids of the sex extremist. Uses the most coaxing & grossly enervating words of any girl I know. (Theo & Helen are between the sheets & no one sees what they are doing. No one, No one. Oh—oh—no one. Theo is between Helen's thighs—Helen's soft white thighs. Theo is fucking Helens cunt. Yes—he is—yes—yes—oh. Theo is fucking her and Helen is taking it—giving herself to him—her belly—her tittys—her thighs—oh—oh). So on to orgasm.

THEODORE DREISER

1949

Billy asked me to look at a new arrangement of the ending. I did so and disapproved. Had to argue the point with Billy. He had tacked the explanatory speech about Norma's madness at the very last. It was put in to avoid a bad laugh as she started down the stairs . . . but destroyed the drama of the last shot by calling on the audience to use its brains. . . .

. . . Doran came with discouraging talk about the casting of pictures that would be necessary now the exhibitors were to control product.

CHARLES BRACKETT

NOVEMBER 12

1851

This night I was alone in the office, where I slept. . . . I had been closely examining and digesting the voluminous evidence on trial; at length finished, and was thinking of going to bed. I stepped outside the door; the moon was well up over the houses; a pleasant, beautiful night. It was between ten and eleven o'clock. The streets were unusually quiet.

I noticed some horsemen slowly riding out of the plaza. . . . I noticed them merely; thought nothing of it, and went back into the office, leaving my door nearly closed. I sat down again at the table.

I was there but a moment or two, before I heard the sound of a horse approaching the office. It occurred to me, "Here comes one of my Californian friends, to see me," which they were in the habit of doing, at any hour. This idea it was, probably, that made me go to the door; perhaps, fatigued with writing, I would have been glad to see anybody. Fortunate that I did go to the door, instead of remaining seated, because the assailant might have been truer in his shot....

Upon examination, it was found that the ball had passed through my white hat, then through the door, and lodged in the adobe wall opposite.

JUDGE BENJAMIN HAYES

1854

A person lives a whole life time in a very short period in this country of wonders and of extraordinary and exciting events— Thus while I have been here in Los Angeles only two weeks, there have been it is said eleven deaths, and only one of them a natural death—all the rest by violence—some killed in quarrels—some in being taken for crimes—some assassinated. Many of these are of the low drunken mexican or indian class. Last week a mexican called up an Irish woman who kept a drinking establishment and as she was opening the door he shot her in the breast he then rode around to the Bella Union and snapt his pistol at a man who immediately pursued him on horseback to took him prisoner, but refusing to surrender the man shot him in the groin and took him. He died the next day in the jail yard, the woman whom he had shot died also the next day.

I saw the poor fellow lying in the jail yard writhing in his wounds. I thought surely the way of the transgresser is hard.

THE REV. JAMES WOODS

1927

Bertha invited me to the second symphony directed by [Georg Schnéevoigt]: Stravinsky's *The Fire Bird* was given.

I had only heard it on the phonograph,—which I now realize is entirely inadequate. What amazing music! It held me thrilled: my hair stood on end!

We should have left at the finish of *The Fire Bird,* for the following Mendelssohn violin concerto was like drinking milk after tequila. And even Beethoven's *Eroica,* the last number,—I heard as in a daze. Indeed I slept through parts,—reacting from the tremendous stimulation of Stravinsky.

Edward Weston

1934

One thing Hollywood has done. It has made me so sick of made-up stories, that I never want to have anything to do with another, even characters I make up myself.

Eric Knight, to a friend

2016

There are people at risk, people in danger. Mr. Kim poured out his heart to me in his dry cleaning shop yesterday; he has never done that before. Told me how he came from Korea, from a dictatorship, from 20 years of curfew and banned protest, how free he felt when he got here to America, to Los Angeles. How fearful he is now. I tell him I am afraid too. "But you're a white woman," he counters, suggesting I have nothing to worry about. "But I'm a Jew," I tell him. "But they don't know," he says. "They can't tell." I listen to his shpiel even though I'm late to get to the studio to meet Charlotte, who is in a dark mood indeed. How can we dance the way we feel? How can we move at all? We try moving to Leonard Cohen's voice, his new album. Did he know the results before he passed from this world? He died on Monday, a day before the election; he couldn't have known. Maybe he didn't want to know. Maybe he didn't need to know. He knew the sparks of the divine were in everyone, even if they can't always see them.

Louise Steinman

NOVEMBER 13

1985

Lunch at noon at Universal with my friend H., a studio official responsible for a little item called *Miami Vice.* Two years ago, my friend H. was a wreck, a frustrated novelist writing the same first forty pages of a novel about a black baseball player and a white heiress over and over again. Now he is on the studio payroll at two hundred bills per year, sitting atop the hottest show on TV.

"I'm not gonna lie about this," H. said. "My wife's father's best friend is really a hot agent. He got me in the door. That's the way Hollywood works."

We ate and watched Lew Wasserman eat. It looked to me as if we basically did it the same.

"So I was in Miami, and Don Johnson wants to direct the next episode of the show, and the producer says, 'Sorry, Don, but we already hired this guy, Fred Finortner or something, to do the next episode. He's really hot in episodic television.' And Don just looks at the producer says, '*He's* hot?' They got the point. Don's doing the episode."

"So, what's next for you?" I asked my friend.

"I'd like to direct, maybe a few episodes and then a feature," H. said. "I think features are where it's at."

"You have any of that money you owe me?"

"As soon as I do my first feature," H. said, and then I left.

BEN STEIN

2016

Super moon tonight rising from the east as I watch from the west side of dry Silver Lake . . . listening to Leonard Cohen's prophetic mysterious words and feel tears on my cheeks for a darkness we sense is coming.

Trump announced he is making immediate plans to deport people. That he intends to fill the Supreme Court seat with a justice who will overturn Roe v. Wade. Get ready to go out into the street. Here we go.

A wave of appreciation for Los Angeles, for California washes over me as I round the street on my moonlit walk, sensing the great San Gabriels looming to the east and the gentle tilt of the LA basin . . . some comfort just knowing that California supports human rights, that our state legislature is against racism and homophobia and misogyny. Big marches planned for inauguration weekend, stay tuned.

As I head down Earl Street for my walk tonight, Charlie—as usual—out washing his pick-up truck, listening to the police scanner. "Overdose on Broadway," the voice says loud and clear as I walk by. The Stars and Stripes ripples from the metal pole implanted in concrete at the foot of his driveway. Charlie, gay man, Republican, flag-waving Vietnam veteran. Go figure . . .

LOUISE STEINMAN

NOVEMBER 14

1937

Up the valley to hollywood, and a few crazy drivers that almost annihilate us make it certain we have entered the los angeles city limits.

CHARIS WILSON

1967

Finally, a criminal eight weeks late, [Igor Stravinsky] is given an arterial injection of radioactive phosphorus, by a doctor in a rubber suit and what might be a welder's helmet. Three nurses, like the three queens accompanying Arthur to Avalon, wheel the patient to a lead-lined room in the basement. . . .

He asks to come to the restaurant with us. He will be able to do that very soon, I tell him. But after considering this for a moment he replies, heartbreakingly, "Oh, I realize I am not able to eat with you, but I could watch." He also begs to be taken for a "promenade" in the car.

ROBERT CRAFT

1969

Spent last Sunday in that small grass thing called a park next to the County Museum. That's a park, I suppose, because it has grass, and it has the La Brea tar pits, carefully enclosed in wire mesh so we can't become fossils, and cement statues of sabermouth tigers and their babies, and a place guarded by police dogs where what look to be students sift through mud looking for more fossils. The museum is having a Van Gogh exhibition. The waiting line to get in stretches about two blocks long. I asked the guard if that was usual, such a long line. "He had a very tragic life, you know," the guard said, "and he painted all those pictures in so few years . . ."

LIZA WILLIAMS

NOVEMBER 15

1929

Believe it or not—and being a constitutional skeptic, probably you won't—but I've got to kind of liking this place. I was sick all the time before; now I feel pretty well; also, the kid is picking up somewhat. These things change the point of view. . . .

For a quarter of a century I've thought myself possessed of a deep wisdom somewhat tinged with a cosmic melancholy; now I discover that it was merely chronic constipation. A great many philosophies of life would go down the sewer in this fashion if the bowels functioned properly—but it must be a natural evacuation not induced by artificial means. One should spring from his couch, singing, and place oneself in the proper position in the toilet—(*le cabinet,* I shall say to you, for you, too, have traveled)—carolling all the time. The agreeable tenor of one's voice is punctuated by the deep, glad bass of the bowel.

. . . Even in my remote childhood there could've been few of these idyllic strains from the ringing gut, or I should remember them. . . . There was no toilet paper in the villages of northern Illinois in my infancy, nor in my strenuous youth. One either rasped one's anus with a corncob, or poisoned it with printers ink from a leaf of Montgomery Ward's catalog.

. . . I may do some work for the movies; I may not! I think, perhaps, such work might tend to increase and confirm the rediscovered peristaltic action which I enjoy. On the other hand, it might make it run into a flux. The art of life is to find and hold the proper tension.

Don Marquis, to his oldest friend

1943

Now I play my Hawaiian records and smoke my second pack of cigs for the day. . . .

Today for the first time in a month or so I wrote pretty nicely. On the last scene of "Gentleman Caller." I have returned to the original version of it. It won't be a total loss after all. But it is very, very sentimental. Ah, well, I am not Dostoevsky nor even Strindberg. I must work within my limits.

Tomorrow I will take a bike trip through Hollywood to Pasadena. I have bought a new pair of glasses.

Hungry! And happy?

I will ride over to the "Quick and Dirty" for a midnight meal. Heigh Ho!

TENNESSEE WILLIAMS

1970

November 15 (Sunday). I began OMEGA MAN today. We started with a small crew (no sound) and me in the Sunday-silent downtown streets.

CHARLTON HESTON

NOVEMBER 16

1849

Leaving Los Angeles at one o'clock, with forty-six mules and ten men, I making the eleventh, and two of the number being my true friends Browning and Simson, we passed eastward of the town, and followed the little river of the same name, and camped on the best grass we had had, and with so good a beginning, expected to have the same for our poor animals for the rest of our journey, and in some degree recruit them and heal their sore backs.

Leaving this rancho we camped five miles further on our way, up an arroyo, in tall, rush-like grass, where we had only bad water, being so charged with sulphur and various salts as to be undrinkable. The hills are of a friable, whitish clay and sandstone, and after a very steep ascent, we gradually descended into a beautiful valley to the rancho San Francisco, and encamped in sight of it with good water, and plenty of wood. In the morning Rhoades killed the first black-tailed deer that any of the party has secured. We found it very good meat, and quite enjoyed it.

John W. Audubon

1906

Hunt sent me over a wonderfully handsome color elevation of the Southwest Museum to-day. If we build it on these very lines it would be the handsomest Museum in the world. . . .

Kroeber [Anthropologist Alfred, father of Ursula K[roeber] LeGuin] rather won my heart this morning . . . he is so frank and young a lad that one can't get as disgusted with him as one does with the 60-year-old incompetency that can't fall out of the back end of a wagon. His lecture is to-morrow night and I hope we can get an audience for him.

Charles Lummis

1969

I am going crazy and can't stand the post office job any longer. I have one of two choices—stay in the post office and go crazy (I have been there eleven years) or stay out here and play at writer and starve. I've decided to starve.

Charles Bukowski, to an editor

NOVEMBER 17

1940

Just now T. and I went out from the warm lighted study and the whuddering firelight of the living room to the porch and watched a half rainbow grow and die against the hills. . . .

It's long since I wrote here. There are days when I want to, but I am too content—and other days my spirit is too black. Today, after a weekend of company and, just now, a highball, I am verbose but uninspired—and today I choose to write. My mind is full of my own despair, muted fortunately. It is best to write of things like weather and furniture.

The weather toys with rain: to rain—not to rain. I long for rain, to help the plants and more especially the springs—which are still strong, thank God. There is an occasional spate of warm gray drops against the patio windows, and the fire feels good. I brought in several logs, just as the weather changed. . . .

The springs are flowing sweetly. The tank springs leaks, and we go up now and then and whittle a plug or two of soft pine and fill the holes. In a year or two we'll have to build a reservoir, preferably of stone. The land around the house is much as we found it. I've cleared it off near the buildings, because of fire, and behind the house have cleared and nourished a little rocky knoll planted with tamaracks, which may someday be beautiful. It must have been planted there among the rocks by old Captain Hoffman. The little dwarfed trees respond almost pathetically to encouragement. . . .

My heart is heavy, thinking of my friends in France and of England so hard pressed. I can hardly bear to think of anything at all these days, and dwell resolutely on the growth of a kitten or an acacia tree and the progression of clouds in a winter sky.

M.F.K. Fisher

1949

I think the movie code would make a first-rate story for you. As much as it's discussed, I can't remember a really thorough examination of its operations. There is constant argument that it should be revised, after something like twenty years, and rewritten in the light of whatever progress we've made during this passage of time, but if there is any actual move in that direction I haven't heard about it. It was particularly awkward during the war, when millions of people were killing each other without being arrested and tried for it, a clear violation of the code.

NUNNALLY JOHNSON, to his editor

NOVEMBER 18

1952

Southern California talks of itself as the Southland, and is hardly even a part of the Union—when you mail letters to the rest of the country you drop them into a post-office-slot marked *The States.*

RANDALL JARRELL, to John Crowe Ransom

2013

On this oddball anniversary I will just give twenty things I learned. . . .

6. When you least expect it something great will happen but pretty girls/boys don't want you, they want the reference book.

7. No matter what people say when they leave, you will never hear from them again.

8. There is nothing on this job that is more important than

your kids or significant other. Go home if they need you. Also text them or make calls within reason. Yes, that is against the rules . . .

9. Call in sick at random and go to Disneyland or the race track or lay in bed half the day. No one will really notice or suffer that you were not there that day.

10. Be nice to all library staff and especially branch librarians because someday they might be your boss or the person that hires your kid.

11. Try like hell to be kind to patrons, it is not their fault they are really clueless about a lot of simple stuff.

12. Participate. While you might feel silly wearing a Cat in the Hat hat you will thank yourself later. . . .

16. If your supervisor takes [himself] too seriously, go somewhere else, they are not going to change.

17. Tell co-workers they are good, especially if they are good.

18. Speak to groups, eventually it gets easy and fun.

19. As horrible as it sounds, go to Guild meetings occasionally.

20. Say something ridiculous to a patron or co-worker every shift.

GLEN CREASON

NOVEMBER 19

1862

I shall deliver at Acapulco or at a place indicated by the government, all the rifles I am able to acquire.

HENRY DALTON, to Benito Juárez

1941

Welcomed charmingly, accommodated superbly in the "motel" in which they lived for a long time—Max had already bought us a car, and Gretel drove us back home from Max's house, Max leading the way in his car. In the afternoon they took us on a big driving tour along the coast. Landscape of incomparable beauty, reminiscent of the French Riviera. We are happy and hope you will come soon.

Hugs from your child Teddie

THEODOR ADORNO, to his parents

NOVEMBER 20

1854

I have to-day pronounced sentence of death upon David Brown, accused of the murder of Pinckney Clifford. Despite the forming of a threatening mob, he has been duly tried and convicted.

. . . To Brown, on overruling the motion for a new trial, I made no remarks directly but incorporated them in my observations on the motion, (intending, however, to Soften his feelings, if possible, and I believe he was somewhat affected). To Luciano Tapia, one of the murderers of Barton, I made an address, to explain the nature of his offense as an *accessory;* I do not think that he comprehended me at all, and am not certain if, at the very last, he recognized the justice of his punishment.

JUDGE BENJAMIN HAYES

1944

Got a wire from Charles Jackson to call him in New Hampshire, lunched at Lucey's . . . the first day Lucey's functioned under its new management. When the call from Jackson came through it was to say the United Liquor interests were trying to make him [insist on doing], or consent to do, a prologue for [the adaptation of his novel] *Lost Weekend.* Then a long list of criticisms of stuff in the picture he had thought too articulate. It included all of the more effective speeches. I offended him deeply when he used the term "articulate" by saying "Oh, you prefer the 'Well, I mean' sort of tradition?" We will change none of them.

CHARLES BRACKETT

NOVEMBER 21

1969

I had to go out to Pitzer College in Claremont to give a reading. I read some of my columns to the somber stare of the students. . . . "But what about your political commitments?" they asked. I had been reading columns about feeling, about finding one's own way of seeing things, about relating to other people with intensity and spontaneity, about what seem to me to be basic things that have to be self-achieved before you can do much about convincing other people . . . they had me flummoxed. They seemed to want me to write "up against the wall" instead of anything lyrical in celebration of humanity and its capacities.

"What do you do?" I asked in return. They had a problem, it seems. Everything was too good, they complained. If they wanted to change something at Pitzer, they had only to go to the administration and the administration changed it. . . . What they wanted was something to fight, all the other campuses were in turmoil, protesting, fighting, trying to make changes, and there at Pitzer it didn't take a fight or a boycott, it was all negotiable. Well, tough shit, too bloody bad, there they were in an optimum situation, able to get the kind of education they wanted and they were frustrated by not having a fashionable enemy. . . .

As I was leaving, the student who was walking with me to the car said, "You know, I think the faculty here is more hip than the students."

LIZA WILLIAMS

2002

The movers will be here in about an hour, and the only things left to pack are the computers, the cds and everything in the storage unit downstairs, which just so happens to be the same storage unit to which we can't find the key, which at first seemed like a total disaster, because in a situation like this, when you need to get into that storage unit more than any other time you've needed to get into that storage unit, it could be a total disaster. But when you think about the larger scheme of life, like getting to drive up the coast to Seattle to spend Thanksgiving with your brother and his 5-yr old daughter who likes to take Mr. Potato Head and put the body parts into all the wrong places because "that's what Picasso would do," and then drive to Utah, arriving triumphantly with liquor cabinet in tow and the funniest dog in the world who will unsuspectingly get to experience cold weather for the first time, who cares about the damn key to the storage unit.

HEATHER B. ARMSTRONG

NOVEMBER 22

1938

It is hereby earnestly proposed that the U.S.A. would be better off if that big, sprawling, incoherent, shapeless, slobbering civic idiot in the family of American communities, the city of Los Angeles, could be declared incompetent and placed in charge of a guardian like an individual mental defective. It is only wistful thought. . . .

Los Angeles is the source and home of more political, economic and religious idiocy than all the rest of the country together and a concentration point of shiftless and inefficient culls who, being too lazy or lacking the ability to make good in their native regions, drift in expecting to be fed from heaven or the public pantry. . . .

Los Angeles is a region, not a city. . . . But neither the size of the place nor the incoherence of its government accounts for the lunacy of the place and for which it is known above every other characteristic.

Westbrook Pegler

1963

What good is the dawn that grows into day
The sunset at night, or living this way
For I have the warmth of the sun within me at night
The love of my life, she left me one day
I cried when she said, I don't feel the same way
Still I have the warmth of the sun within me tonight
I dream of her arms and though they're not real
Just like she's still there is the way that I feel
My love's like the warmth of the sun, it won't ever die

Mike Love and Brian Wilson

NOVEMBER 23

1919

Los Angeles. Helen sets clock for 7:30—but at 6:30 wake & in the dawn indulge in one of the loveliest rounds ever—she lying on her side one arm up. We laugh & dress and at 8 leave for Pacific Station En route to Santa Catalina. Down town on West 1st street. Breakfast in a Cafeteria Quick Lunch—a new proposition to me—Get our own steak & waffles. Then to Station & take 3 car trolley to San Pedro. The mountains in the distance—small towns—Cattle, oil wells etc. Arrive at San Pedro at 10 a.m. & take boat for Santa Catalina. Helen looks too sweet in her light grey gorgette & grey hat. Seats on side of boat. . . .

The gulls on the upper deck. We whisper love stuff all the time. Arrive at 12:30. Walk along Maine Street. Lunch in a cheap restaurant. Santa Catalina doesn't impress us much. The glass bottomed boat. . . .

See perch & sea goldfish in their native haunts. The diver after Abalone Shells. Back to dock. Aeroplane takes passengers at 100 per minute for a 10-minute flight. Then onto boat again. The blue sea. Rainbow. A whale. . . .

We come home and go straight to bed. Very tired but before long we pull a heavy screw, finally getting down on the floor on pillows to avoid the squeaking of the bed. . . .

Wants her beauty eaten by a big rough brute.

THEODORE DREISER

1941

The journey from Los Angeles station to our motel (a group of cabins for automobile drivers, each consisting of two very nicely furnished rooms and bathroom, kitchen and garage) takes a good hour by car. Los Angeles is 30 miles or so more from the sea, while the places around where we are now living still extend past Hollywood—to Santa Monica, Brentwood Heights, Pacific Palisades—in hollows that approach the sea and line the coast itself. The beauty of the region is so incomparable that even such a hardboiled European as myself can only surrender to it.

. . . Best of all are the incredibly intense, in no way reproducible colors; a drive along the ocean around sunset is one of the most extraordinary impressions that my—by no means highly responsive—eyes have ever had. All the red, blue and violet activity found there would appear laughable on any illustration, but it is overwhelming if one sees the real thing. As well as this, the more southern style of architecture, a certain reduction of advertising and one or two other factors combine to form something that is almost like a cultural landscape: one actually has the feeling that this part of the world is inhabited by humanoid beings, not only by gasoline stations and hot dogs. The entire wider vicinity here is somewhere between city and country.

THEODOR ADORNO, to his parents

NOVEMBER 24

1602

We continued our voyage, skirting along the coast until the 24th of the month, which was the eve of the feast of the glorious Santa Catalina, when we discovered three large islands. We approached them with difficulty because of the head-wind, and arrived at the middle one, which is more than 25 leagues around.

FATHER ANTONIO DE LA ASCENSIÓN

1793

The coast took a direction S. 67 E., sixteen miles to the north point of a deep bay, off which lie two or three small rocks; this point, which I called Point Dume, bore N. 59 W.; the south point of the same bay, being the easternmost point of the main land in sight S. 67 E.; this being a very conspicuous promontory, I named after Father Vincente [Dumetz]. . . .

The north-west side of this bay was observed to be composed chiefly of steep barren cliffs; the north and eastern shores terminated in low sandy beaches, rising with a gradual ascent until they reached the base of a mountainous country. . . .

According to the Spanish charts, I at first supposed this bay to be that which is there called the bay of St. Pedro but I was afterwards informed that this conjecture was ill founded. I had also been given to understand that a very advantageous settlement is established on a fertile spot somewhere in this neighbourhood within sight of the ocean, though at the distance of some miles from the coast, called Pueblo de los Angelos, "the country town of the angels," formed in the year 1781. This establishment was looked for in all directions, but nothing was perceived that indicated either habitations or inhabitants.

George Vancouver

1847

I was on guard some days ago and was obliged to put private Van Beck under arrest. He has a wife here and she was furious on hearing of it. She had always done my washing, and we were on the best of terms. As soon as she heard of the arrest, she started for the guard house with a pot of hot coffee determined to throw it in my face, but meeting Lieut Bonnycastle, she told him what she was going to do. He begged her not to do it, for said he, "Madame, Lieut H is a very diffident young man, and you will frighten him to death."

She then went to the Col and told him, of her resolution. He advised her not and told her to take care what she did. She said Col. I thought you were more of a gentleman than to permit Lieut H. to put my husband under arrest. She then came to the Guard house and commenced abusing me at a high rate asked me if I thought she had nothing to do but to bring her husbands breakfast up there and said she had left all my clothes hanging on the line and that she prayed to God that they might all be stolen.

I was all smiles and bows, told her that I regretted very much my having given her the smallest trouble that I was sorry that I had been obliged to punish her better half and begged her not to let any one steal my clothes. She did not throw the Coffee in my face but gave it to her husband to drink It was well she did so for had she done other wise I should have put her in one of the dark cells of the guard house! It created a great laugh at the mess table, at my expense.

LIEUTENANT JOHN MCHENRY HOLLINGSWORTH

1925

Among the many things we have done to arouse the hostility and antagonism of Mexicans has been our treatment of them in our fiction, where they are nearly always portrayed as heartless scoundrels. I believe that a policy of consideration and fairness toward our sister republic in our literature would do much to lessen this hostility.

EDGAR RICE BURROUGHS

NOVEMBER 25

1925

A very peculiar change is being wrought in me these days, especially since this "affair" with D.H.... All the obscure, half hearted promptings of my emotional nature that I thought were centered around my artistic work, for the past few months have dried up.... this central, emotional, imaginative part of me is not interested in law, and always is seeking a way out—books, booze, or women.

CAREY McWILLIAMS

1940

Los Angeles denies the existence of slums. But go across the river to South Gless Street. You'll find a woman and her nine children living in a four-room house, every room of which leaks when it rains. Rain drips down into the faces of the children as they sleep. It lays all day long in puddles on the floor. Because of defective plumbing, the family uses a gallon tin can for sanitary purposes, disposing of the contents in the back yard.

Across the street sewer gas leaks into the kitchen where eleven people eat three meals a day and three children sleep at night.

Over on Pecan Street is a two-room shack owned by a loan association which has fought low cost housing for Los Angeles. There is no inside plumbing; there are holes in the roof through which you can see the sky; old car license plates are employed to stop holes in the walls. I called the loan company and asked the rent. Have you ever tried to rent a slum, Mr. Robinson? Expect Spanish inquisition methods. The more children you tell the prospective landlord you have, the more highhanded he becomes. The agent for the loan company opened the conversation with, "You on relief?"

I said no, and inquired what difference that might make. With the most callous candor the agent informed me that a relief investigator would not approve the dwelling. He asked where I worked, and when I named a fictitious firm, he inquired as to wages and the date of payment, and then asked the number of children. You see, it is always taken for granted that the people who must live in these stink holes are what we are pleased to call "encumbered." (Encumbered with children who are expected to grow up into patriotic citizens to defend their country.) Finally he asked about my health. Was it possible that sickness would cause me to be laid off, thus stopping my income and the wherewithal to pay the rent, making it necessary for the loan company to have me evicted? Knowing the low resistance to disease of slum dwellers, he might well ask that.

THEODORE DREISER, to Edward G. Robinson

NOVEMBER 26

1906

I just had a letter to-night from the Summit where the Santa Fe drops over the divide into [Cajon] Pass, from Mrs. Davis, wife of the Station Agent, but herself pretty smart and a good deal of a poet and an artist. She says there are three feet of snow up there. I was thinking of going up and take a shot gun to defend myself against the quail, which are said to be very dangerous.

CHARLES LUMMIS

1949

We showed an enormously improved picture to an audience which responded beautifully, giving lots of spontaneous applause at the end. I sat next to Bill Holden, who wore glasses and kept his head down, and still was recognized. . . .

I thought with amusement what a surprise it would have been to Mr. and Mrs. Brackett of 605 N. Broadway, Saratoga Springs, New York, could they have been told that 57 years after the arrival of their matutinal son he would be celebrating on the other side of the continent a pleasant event in a medium of which they'd never heard.

Charles Brackett

NOVEMBER 27

1602

On the 27th of the month, and before casting anchor in a very good cove which was found, a multitude of Indians came out in canoes of cedar and pine, made of planks very well joined and caulked, each one with eight oars and with fourteen or fifteen Indians, who looked like galley-slaves. They came along side without the least fear and came on board our ships, mooring their own. They showed great pleasure at seeing us, telling us by signs that we must land, and guided us like pilots to the anchorage. . . . Many Indians were on the beach, and the women treated us to roasted sardines and a small fruit like sweet potatoes.

Father Antonio de la Ascensión

1826

Cattle skulls in rows on each side of the road conveying the Idea that we were approaching an immense slaughter yard.

Jedediah Smith

1826

We got ready as early as possible and started a W. course, and traveled 14 m. and enc. for the day, we passed innumerable herds of cattle, horses and some hundred of sheep; we passed 4 or 5 Ind. lodges, that their Inds. acts as herdsmen. There came an old Ind. to us that speaks good Spanish, and took us with him to his mansion, which consisted of 2 rows of large and lengthy buildings, after the Spanish mode, they remind me of the British barracks. So soon as we enc. there was plenty prepared to eat, a fine young cow killed, and a plenty of corn meal given us; pretty soon after the 2 commandants of the missionary establishment come to us and had the appearance of gentlemen. Mr. S. went with them to the mansion and I stay with the company, there was great feasting among the men as they were pretty hungry not having any good meat for some time.

Harrison Rogers, encamped with Jedediah Smith

NOVEMBER 28

1826

November 28th 1826. My party arrived and I had my things put into the room which I occupied. The Corporal who was called Commandant came to me and after a few preparatory compliments observed that the best thing I could do with my guns would be to put them in his charge where they would be safe for said the strangers visiting you will be constantly handling them they being a kind with which they are unacquainted. I thanked him for his kindness and gave him the arms though I knew he was influenced by a motive very different from the one assigned.

Jedediah Smith

1826

28TH. Mr. S. wrote me a note in the morning, stating that he was received as a gentleman and treated as such, and that he wished me to go back and look for a pistol that was lost, and send the company on to the missionary establishment. I complyed with his request, went back, and found the pistol, and arrived late in the evening, was received very politely, and showed into a room and my arms taken from me. About 10 o'clock at night supper was served, and Mr. S. and myself sent for. I was introduced to the 2 priests over a glass of good old whiskey and found them to be very jovial friendly gentlemen, the supper consisted of a number of different dishes, served different from any table I ever was at. Plenty of good wine during supper, before the cloth was removed sigars was introduced.

HARRISON ROGERS

1949

The mass yesterday with [conductor Harold] Byrnes was very good and attracted a good public. What a terrible hall that Wilshire Ebell Theatre! . . . All the voices sounded like behind the curtain.

IGOR STRAVINSKY

NOVEMBER 29

1826

At 11 O Clock the Father came and invited us to dinner. We accompanied him to the office adjoining the dining room and after taking a glass of Gin and some bread and cheese we seated ourselves at the table which was furnished with Mutton Beef Chickens Potatoes Beans and Peas cooked in different ways. Wine in abundance made our reverend fathers appear to me quite merry. An express had been forwarded by the Commandant to the Governor at San Diego. (My two indian guides were put in prison immediately on my arrival charged with being runaways from the Mission. They were about 16 years of age and from what I saw of them I thought them fine honest and well disposed boys.)

JEDEDIAH SMITH

1935

BANANA CENTER, CENTRAL PARK, EL-LAY

This became Pershing Square in the war-mad days, but it is still Central Park to me and still "Cannibal Island" to the skidway.

"May I speak to you?"

"Surely."

"Have you been saved?"

"I'm sorry, but your subject doesn't interest me."

The young man bows and walks away, and I mentally collapse from astonishment. Such passivity before pagan resistance is unlike evangelical votaries.

Endless, endless movement.

Loitering figures—lingering, lurking.

Some have been heard to say that no respectable person would allow himself to be seen in the park after dark. Huh! I walk about under the thousand shadows of the bamboo and banana trees with utter unconcern.

HARRY PARTCH

NOVEMBER 30

1826

There was a wedding in this place today, and [the explorer Jedediah Smith] and myself invited; the bell was rang a little before sun rise, and the morning service performed; then the musick commenced serranading, the soldiers firing, etc., about 7 o'clock tea and bread served, and about 11, dinner and musick. The ceremony and dinner was held at the priests; they had an elegant dinner, consisting of a number of dishes, boiled and roast meat and fowl, wine and brandy or ogadent, grapes brought as a dessert after dinner. Mr. S. and myself acted quite independent, knot understanding there language, nor they ours; we endeavored to appoligise, being very dirty and not in a situation to shift our clothing, but no excuse would be taken, we must be present, as we have been served at their table ever since we arrived at this place; they treat [us] as gentlemen in every sense of the word. . . .

Our 2 Ind. guides were imprisoned in the guard house the 2nd. day after we arrived at the missionary establishment and remain confined as yet.

Harrison Rogers

1943

I am being sued by the motor scooter company as I refuse to pay them for the scooter after it proved a Jonah. I had signed an unread contract that held me responsible for the entire sum even with scooter returned. The sheriff has been sieging my Santa Monica apt. trying to serve papers on me but I have successfully evaded him so far. He hasn't tracked me to Pasadena yet. I intend to return at midnight, pack up and be out before daybreak. I understand that if he doesn't touch me with the papers I can escape the suit.

TENNESSEE WILLIAMS

2007

Native-to-the-southwest plantas: la salvia. Always my homecoming scent. The soft dryness of mimosa-powdery dust bajo los eucaliptos y pinos.

SUSANA CHÁVEZ-SILVERMAN

DECEMBER 1

1924

I look around and hardly believe it can be me in this beautiful place. We pay $50 a month for it which includes gas, electricity and private phone. We have real silverware and all aluminum pots and pans. . . .

We live near the big Fox studios and you run into some funny characters on the street. They come off the lot in their make up and outfits so that you see cowboys, old gents with long hair, looking like the 49'ers; men in society clothes and in fact all kinds of rig-outs. This sure is a queer burg, but I like it better than Los Angeles. It's nearer the mountains and is higher so that the air seems better than in L.A. It takes me about 40 minutes to get into Los Angeles and the fare is only 5 cents.

Valeria Belletti, to a childhood friend

1967

The taste of milk can be cut with larger swigs of Scotch. This news raises [Igor Stravinsky] out of the apathy—black melancholy, rather—into which he had fallen the day after his homecoming, when he had apparently expected to be able to skip rope. After dinner we listen to Opus 131 and the *Dichterliebe,* the first music heard in the house since he entered the hospital. And with the music he comes to life, grunting agreement with Beethoven at numerous moments in the quartet and beating time with his left hand, which is protected by an outsize mitten, like the claw of a fiddler crab.

Robert Craft

DECEMBER 2

1920

We would, all of us, like to be somebody in this great, indifferent, cruel swirl. And only see what in the main happens to us.

THEODORE DREISER

1949

All musical enterprises here are in an ultraprecarious situation at the moment. Only large and long-established organizations, with their committees, patrons and subscriptions, can survive. And, unfortunately, these societies offer only the most popular repertory.

IGOR STRAVINSKY, to a friend

DECEMBER 3

1946

A long talk with a Dr. Hortense Powdermaker, who is working on a study of Hollywood from a purely anthropological point of view. At 4:30 Zoltan Korda and Aldous Huxley arrived, without the copy of the script they'd promised. . . .

I've met Huxley before, but let me restate him again: tall, elegant, in an utterly careless way, quite beautiful of feature despite the one silvered eye and utterly beyond my power to like. Helplessly aloof from one. . . . Frankly, I detest this writer, whose work I worship. . . . Jokingly I say, "I expect the best thing since

Euripides from you." He smirks, and I realize that this goes into his experience as a comic saying of a Hollywood producer.

CHARLES BRACKETT

1950

I'll be staying out till middle or late January, working on a script with John Huston, *The African Queen,* from [the] novel by C. S. Forester. If everything works out right, it could be a wonderful movie. . . . The work is a great deal of fun: treating it fundamentally as high comedy with deeply ribald overtones, and trying to blend extraordinary things—poetry, mysticism, realism, romance, tragedy, with the comedy. . . .

I haven't read a book, heard any music to speak of, or seen a movie or but one play, since I have been out here. For the present, I don't miss them either. I see a lot of people and like most of them. Compared with most of the intellectual literary acquaintances I avoid in New York (who are—wrongly—my image of New York) they are mostly very warmhearted, outgoing, kind, happy, and unpretentious—the nicest kind of company I can imagine.

JAMES AGEE, to an old teacher and friend

DECEMBER 4

1847

Everything is quiet though I think that the country is in a very unsettled state, things will not be so long there must be a change.

LIEUTENANT JOHN MCHENRY HOLLINGSWORTH

1860

We had been invited to a ranch and vineyard about nine miles east, and went with a friend on Tuesday evening. It lies near San Gabriel Mission, on a most beautiful spot, I think even finer than this. Mr. Wilson, our host, uneducated, but a man of great force of character, is now worth a hundred or more thousand dollars and lives like a prince, only with less luxury. His wife is finely educated and refined, and his home to the visitor a little paradise. We were received with the greatest cordiality and were entertained with the greatest hospitality. A touch of the country and times was indicated by our rig—I was dressed in colored woolen shirt, with heavy navy revolver (loaded) and huge eight-inch bowie knife at my belt; my friend the same; and the clergyman who took us out in his carriage carried along his rifle, he said for game, yet owned that it was "best to have arms after dark."

Here let me digress. This southern California is still unsettled. We all continually wear arms—each wears both bowie knife and pistol (navy revolver), while we have always for game or otherwise, a Sharp's rifle, Sharp's carbine, and two double-barrel shotguns. Fifty to sixty murders per year have been common here in Los Angeles, and some think it odd that there has been no violent death during the two weeks that we have been here. Yet with our care there is no considerable danger, for as I write this there are at least six heavy loaded revolvers in the tent, besides bowie knives and other arms, so we anticipate no danger. I have been practicing with my revolver and am becoming expert. . . .

Even here the San Fernando Valley looks fertile, yet you could take a patch in the middle of a hundred or a hundred and fifty thousand acres, where it does not touch the hills, where there would be no water for over half of the year. Hence the land is owned in large ranches, and those only in the more favored places. On these ranches, as there are no fences, the cattle are half wild, and require many horses to keep them and tend them. A ranch with a thousand head of cattle will have a hundred horses. The natives here are lazy enough, but are slowly giving way before the Americans, with whom they do not assimilate.

WILLIAM H. BREWER

1939

Coming back to the hotel from lunch in the only Hebe delicatessen in town with Laura, I just saw a lady of sixty strolling down the boulevard wearing a pair of shiny black silky teen pajamas with a lace collar and a brooch at the throat. She obviously wanted to tell me how much money her son was making, but I beat her to a stop light and hid behind a bougainvillea.

The temperature is about ninety-eight and everybody says we are in for another hot spell. The only thing Laura and I have accomplished thus far is to decide that this is *really* our last trip here, forever. If we can get the dough to make those changes in our house and repair that buckled bank balance, we hope to blow taps over a glorious career in this branch of the entertainment world. If our estimates are right and we have only one life to lead, it isn't going to be led here.

S. J. PERELMAN

1952

Patsy and I and friends of hers went to Disneyland yesterday. It was simply divine and I *longed* for you to have been there. You get into a little launch on Jungle River and glide away past, crocodiles, gorillas, giant butterflies etc., and the divine young man at the helm (in very tight white ducks and jersey and a peaked cap) does a commentary of wonderful camp—now steady here, folks, it's dangerous here—over the rapids, shooting off a pistol at intervals as a huge hippo rears its head into the boat, and rubber arrows go flying past, mad life-size clockwork (I suppose) animals and natives. I can't tell you what fun. Then we went on two *mad* rides—the Snow White one with shrieking witches and sound effects, pitch dark passages, sailing through walls that open and close behind you, figures leaping out as you pass—and another Peter Pan, in which you go up a slope in a small boat through opening windows and appear to fly over London, model Big Ben and all, and descend at a hair-raising angle passing Hook and Smee and the Pirate Ship all posed and shaking their fists from the deck below—and a ridiculous mining train with the driver and guards in ten gallon hats (and jeans) puffing through caves and deserts and descending to a brilliant cavern of jewels and waterfalls. It really was a hilarious afternoon. And it is 85 degrees here in the daytime!, hotter than the South of France. So it is all rather fun but a bit exhausting too. The *pace,* and the cars and the mad ladies and sexy looking boys on every corner. If I ever do a picture here again you *must* come out. You would simply adore it.

John Gielgud, to his partner

1960

The hygienic boys go on merrily producing buildings of the most amazing inconvenience and inefficiency. I have bumped my head and then roasted in Niemayer's Brazilian hotels—low ceilings plus glass walls in a tropical climate. What idiocy. And from India I hear bitter complaints (from the Indian ambassador most recently) of Corbusier's entirely non-functional buildings in the new Punjabi capital. And see a recent Scientific American article in which the author contrasts the wonderful "performance" of primitive architects using mud and sticks and leaves with the folly of the skyscraper builders of New York, whose glass walls leak and impose (because of the greenhouse effect) unbearable strains on the cooling systems—not to mention the people.

Aldous Huxley, to the architecture critic Esther McCoy

DECEMBER 5

1932

Selznick is the big noise; he is young, massive, well-educated, and with tremendous vitality. The others, whom I can't remember for the moment, were equally pleasant. . . .

I was then picked up by a man named Perry Lieber, an awfully nice fellow who is at the head of the publicity department, and he took me into the block where the executive writers are kept chained up, and I was given a room, the key thereof, and the telephone book, which helps me to get into touch with everybody in the block. . . .

Afterwards I saw Selznick in his office with Cooper, another member of the executive. He was the man who did "Chang" and "Four Feathers." They want me to do a horror picture [*King Kong*] for them. . . .

I find it so dry that my lips have to have some kind of treatment. I think the thing to get is colourless lipstick. . . .

I was photographed this morning twice at the desk, once with my feet up, telephoning, and once the conventional intense picture, writing.

The publicity man said: "I've never had anybody like you, Mr. Wallace, to deal with. You take three-quarters of my work off my shoulders." I explained to him carefully that I was not a seeker of publicity, but that when it came I thought it ought to be done properly!

He told me that I had no idea of the trouble stars gave when they arrive by train and are snapped on the platform. Which is remarkable, remembering that these film stars owe a terrific lot to this kind of publicity.

The Beverly-Wilshire is famous in Los Angeles newspaperland for the jealous care they show about protecting their guests from the Press, and you cannot get past unless the person to be interviewed is absolutely willing.

EDGAR WALLACE

1934

Life is a pit into which we are dropping and we shall be not-knowing before we reach bottom, so why try to scratch the sides of the walls as we go down? . . .

I am now an authority on torture. I have been railroaded into this magnificent office now more than three months. I have undergone the humiliation of not even being considered or given anything to do. . . .

Why, why, why, did they do this? Why have they brought me here to pay me fat money for sitting here? . . .

Last night the bankers came out here. The studio threw a big luncheon. Stepin Fetchit and Bill Robinson (Negroes both) tap-danced for the bankers.

ERIC KNIGHT, to a friend

1937

Today edward makes a sitting of a poetess, helene mullins, who is deaf and eyes bad and large scar from recent auto accident—she was run into—which fractured her skull.

CHARIS WILSON

DECEMBER 6

1942

I watched a friend last night who had invited me to his home for supper, stop at seven grocery stores to find butter and found none. The street lamps are hooded from above here, wardens patrol the streets for cracks in window shades, etc. There are barrage balloons along the coast, and searchlights (and of course, A.A. [anti-aircraft], hidden) in all sorts of unexpected places throughout the city: in all the canyons, and now and then on the playgrounds of schools. They expect a bombing here. But nobody is afraid of it. . . .

There is something here for an anthropologist's notebook. This is one of the richest towns in the country. As it exists today, its economy and geography was fixed and invented by the automobile. Therefore, the automobile invented it. The automobile (for a time, anyway) is as dead as the mastodon. Therefore the town which the automobile created, is dying. I think that a detached and impartial spectator could watch here what some superman in a superheated diving-bell could have watched at the beginning of the ice age, say: a doomed way of life and its seething inhabitants all saying: Why, Jack Frost simply cant do this to us. It's not so. That's not ice we see; that's not cold we feel. We've got to be warm. We cant live otherwise.

William Faulkner, to his stepson

1967

It is a marvelous day, brilliantly sunny and warm although the San Bernardino Mountains glitter like Kilimanjaro with new snow. But my leave-taking is the hardest I have ever had to go through. It will only be a few days, I tell [Stravinsky].

Robert Craft

DECEMBER 7

1860

In Camp at Los Angeles, December 7.

Well, we are in camp. It is a cold rainy night, but I can hardly realize the fact that you at home are blowing your fingers in the cold, and possibly sleighing, while I am sitting here in a tent, without fire, and sleeping on the ground in blankets, in this month. We are camped on a hill near the town, perhaps a mile distance, a pretty place. . . .

The houses are but one story, mostly built of adobe or sunburnt brick, with very thick walls and flat roofs. They are so low because of earthquakes, and the style is Mexican. The inhabitants are a mixture of old Spanish, Indian, American, and German Jews; the last two have come in lately. The language of the natives is Spanish, and I have commenced learning it. The only thing they appear to excel in is riding, and certainly I have never seen such riders.

Here is a great plain, or rather a gentle slope, from the Pacific to the mountains. We are on this plain about twenty miles from the sea and fifteen from the mountains, a most lovely locality; all that is wanted naturally to make it a paradise is water, more water. Apples, pears, plums, figs, olives, lemons, oranges, and "the finest grapes in the world," so the books say, pears of two and a half pounds each, and such things in proportion. The weather is soft and balmy—no winter, but a perpetual spring and summer. Such is Los Angeles, a place where "every prospect pleases and only man is vile."

As we stand on a hill over the town, which lies at our feet, one of the loveliest views I ever saw is spread out. Over the level plain to the southwest lies the Pacific, blue in the distance; to the north are the mountains of the Sierra Santa Monica; to the south, beneath us, lies the picturesque town with its flat roofs, the fertile plain and vineyards stretching away to a great distance; to the east, in the distance, are some mountains without name, their sides abrupt and broken, while still above them stand the snow covered peaks of San Bernardino. The effect of the pepper, fig, olive, and palm trees in the foreground, with the snow in the distance, is very unusual.

William H. Brewer

1941

(Japan Time: December 8, Sixteenth Year of Showa)

A bolt out of the blue sky, like water in one's sleeping ear, unimaginably fearful, cruel this reality—indescribably waves of strong shock and fear over my entire body; if I try to stop it, it becomes even stronger and overcomes me!

"At present, Japanese airplanes are bombing Hawaii's Pearl Harbor!"

I heard those words from a young waiter at the Chinese restaurant, Sankohro, in Los Angeles. Unimaginable that it was winter; it was a warm Sunday, around eleven o'clock. . . .

My chest is pounding! The waves from the stone of uncertainty that had been thrown into my chest, while half believing, get bigger. Ordinarily delicious dishes of food are all bitter and tasteless. I taste strange saliva in my mouth.

My two daughters, Yoko, age twelve, and Sachiko, age ten, ate so fast it was difficult to see where they swallowed it and hurriedly went out to buy a special edition of newspapers being announced on sale in the street.

Looking at the newspaper they brought back, in large bold letters that appeared two inches square, "WAR . . . ," I involuntarily gasped! I had been completely mentally unprepared and felt as though I had been hit with a sledge hammer. Blood rushed to my face, and breathing became difficult, and in inverse proportion, my feet inside my shoes, starting from the toes, started to get cold as ice. I looked down, covering both cheeks, and tried to organize my confused mind. My husband, with a sunken voice, said, "This is something we cannot do anything about, so let us all remain calm and do our best."

Mrs. Michinoue said, "Tomorrow tomorrow's wind will blow. Let us go with whatever happens." . . .

On the way home, Japanese we met all had worried faces drained of blood. What should we do? Dragged around by upsetting emotions, the afternoon hours passed. . . .

Cold sweat broke out on my face; in front of my eyes, I saw endless ash-colored waves.

Aoki Hisa

1955

I have started shooting the picture and all is confusion. The actors now want to know what the lines mean. At that rate we'll never finish.

Nunnally Johnson, to two friends

DECEMBER 8

1847

I was at Mrs Stearns a few nights ago and had a little quarrel with my sweetheart. She asked me to sit down in a chair by her, but I told her that I was afraid of Capt Smith, who I made out to be very jealous of as he had been paying some attention to her she seemed much hurt at my refuseing to sit down along side of her and told me if I was afraid to take the seat, that I ought to have my shoulder straps cut off and my mustaches. I then took the seat and told her it was an insult to an officer to tell him his straps should be cut off. She said not as great an insult as to plague me about a married man. I made up with her before I left that evening. We have been friends ever since. She has been very sick. Dr Griffin has been trying to cure her eyes that a quack has nearly put out. I went to see her last evening and was sitting at the window when her mother came in. She did not seem to like my being their talking to her daughter poor girl.

LIEUTENANT JOHN MCHENRY HOLLINGSWORTH

1887

Last night there was a celebration with [cannons] because of the news that the Government had chosen San Vicente as the place to establish the Veterans home. Clear day.

DON JUAN BAUTISTA BANDINI

1935

Los ANGELES is more than a city; it is a major controversy . . . An irate Hearst editor who departed the town in high indignation because we were unable to get excited over a little lost child, said in poison farewell from the back platform of the train: "This isn't a city; it's a goddamn conspiracy." . . .

What these literary hat-check boys—giggling over the discovery of cat's fur masquerading as sable—have not realized is that they are missing a great drama . . . Los Angeles was a milepost of destiny. It happened because it could not help itself . . . *Mañana es la flor de sus ayeres*—tomorrow is the flower of its yesterdays.

HARRY CARR

DECEMBER 9

1847

I went to bed and was awakened from a sound sleep by a loud explosion I was soon dressed and then heard the drum beating the alarm—I slept in the same house with Captn S—Lieut M and one Soldier—

We heard horses moving around the house and the first impression was that we were surrounded but as we were well armed we passed out at the back door into the yard and I opened the gate supposing we should have to fight our way through them but no enemy was in sight and we hurried to the barracks—There we learnt that a musket had been fired at the out posts and the guard had run in—the magazine had been opened to man the battery when a spark from a post fire fell in it and the explosion took place A number of men were hurt and some killed—some lost their eyes—The officier of the guard had a narrow escape, he was knocked down but soon recovered—But a small portion of the guard house was left standing—The Californians are much delighted at our misfortune—We buried our poor fellows a few days ago—

LIEUTENANT JOHN MCHENRY HOLLINGSWORTH

1873

I believe I promised, before leaving Tennessee, that I would occasionally write a letter for your readers. . . .

. . . In the Middle States, at this season, winter holds all nature in its icy thrall. The winds shriek their sad dirges through leafless boughs; the fallen leaves whirl in eddies before the blast; the cattle, shivering with cold, hug closely the southern side of the barn, and the people, with closed doors, talk of their supply of coal or wood, and speculate as to the probable length of the winter. This is a faint picture of winter, even in Tennessee. . . .

Here is a glimpse of our winter in Los Angeles: The winter rains have begun. Sitting at my window, two beautiful pictures are spread out before my sight. In an open yard before me, fuchsias swing their graceful pendants in the air, geraniums and heliotropes, roses and verbenas, and hundreds of other delicate flowers, mingle their perfumes. . . .

As I raise my eyes from this tropical picture, and gaze toward the north, how the brow of the Sierra Madre glimmers and glitters in its robe of snow! The mountain sides, up to a certain height, are clothed with green grass, and the robe of snow, now sparkling in the sunlight, seems like the bridal veil which winter has hung on the blushing brow of this soft, sunny land. Here summer and winter stand face to face. . . .

The country for miles around this city will, in a few years, be a tropical orchard . . . vegetables of all kinds grow to almost fabulous sizes. I saw a sweet potato, a few days ago, which weighed ten pounds, and an onion weighing two and three fourths pounds.

The future wealth of this country will be its tropical fruits. An orange, lemon, lime, or walnut orchard, is better than a gold mine.

John Shirley Ward

DECEMBER 10

1826

There was five Inds. brought to the mission by two other Inds, who act as constables, or overseers, and sentenced to be whiped for not going to work when ordered.

Each received from 12 to 14 lashes on their bare posteriors; they were all old men, say from 50 to 60 years of age, the commandant standing by with his sword to see that the Ind. who flogged them done his duty. Things in other respects similar to the last sabbath.

HARRISON ROGERS

1941

Max [Horkheimer] has been appointed an air warden!

THEODOR ADORNO, to his parents

DECEMBER 11

1906

A queer little rather interesting woman from Whittier came in—looks like a school girl on stilts, and a country school girl at that but has good ideas and is having a fight for them single handed against a lot of women of wealthier breeding and circumstances but less feeling—her mission being to preserve the old Gov. Pico residence near Whittier. I had no fight with her except to pull the purse strings of the Landmarks Club a little tight and tell her that we would help what we could but that the community must chase itself and do the major part of the main money raising, while we would be perfectly willing to tell them exactly how they must do the work and perhaps give them an overseer to see that they did it right....

I put my new invention into effect this morning and the two Library Guides went to work. They stand by the elevator and pick up the lost patrons that come in and don't know what they want nor where to find it and tell them both things.

CHARLES LUMMIS

1930

We climbed up to John Barrymore's eyrie today—nearly a thousand feet above Beverly Hills. He has two separate houses on this hilltop, one a curious little bungalow with a grass-grown tiled courtyard, and a handsome type of Spanish two-story house just beyond with a pool and fountain between. From the moment we entered the gate we were surrounded by "trophies" and "treasures." Both of the houses are museums with old furniture, old books, primitive weapons, paintings, drawings, prints, models of ships and all kinds of other queerities of no value to anyone else.

Below, on the hillside, he has an aviary with some sixty varieties of rare birds fluttering and chirping there. In another lower room were crocodiles—stuffed—trophies of his shooting. He told us with pride that his wife killed one of them, and also caught a fish nearly ten feet long. She, a blonde young girl, took us about carrying her baby on her arm. She did not seem at all the moving picture actress as she did this. She was very maternal and spoke with charm and intelligence. I do not wonder that my daughters like her.

After we had seen the house under her care, she took us up to see John who was convalescing from a tropical fever. He was not far from my concept of him but appeared more interested in art and literature than I had anticipated. There is something exotic in him, however, something not quite real. I think he felt in me and in [Garland's sister-in-law] Lorado something equally alien. . . .

He has a handsome head and good profile and speaks well but not noticeably well. He was respectful in tone.

Hamlin Garland

DECEMBER 12

1903

Spent the day at home. Elisa, a maid took the children to Los Angeles to see the toys adorning the shops for Christmas. Today the Examiner appeared for the first time property of W. R. Hearst owner of various other Democratic papers.

Don Juan Bautista Bandini

1938

Saturday night I was greatly exhilarated by the Fire Sequence. It was one of the biggest thrills I have had out of making pictures—first, because of the scene itself, and second, because of the frightening but exciting knowledge that *Gone With the Wind* was finally in work. Myron rolled in just exactly too late, arriving about a minute and a half after the last building had fallen and burned and after the shots were completed. With him were Larry Olivier and Vivien Leigh. Shhhhh: she's the Scarlett dark horse, and looks damned good. (Not for anybody's ears but your own: it's narrowed down to Paulette, Jean Arthur, Joan Bennett, and Vivien Leigh. We're making final tests this week, and I do frantically hope that you'll be home in time to sit in on the final decision. . . . At least when I am lynched I want you to be able to shout sincerely that I did the best I could.)

David O. Selznick, to his wife

1939

Capra (whom I could get you in touch with, if you like, through Ronald Colman, who is a very decent fellow) is very well meaning, but a bit stupid outside his specialty. His "Mr. Smith" struck me as very pathetic—all the more so as it was one of the few "idealistic" efforts made by the movies. All it amounted to was the sentiment that, if everybody were nice, how nice everybody would be! No smallest effort to explain why everybody was nice, nor how they could be persuaded to be a bit nicer. . . .

Meanwhile I hope you realize what distances in this town are. Disney, for example, is about 20 miles from here; Pasadena about 30 odd; Warner about 17; Universal about 20. You will probably be about six hours of each day in a car.

Aldous Huxley, to his brother

1969

And so perhaps this marks the end of an era. The gravestone—a face straight from central casting, long hair, wild hypnotically staring eyes, the king of "love" called Jesus and Satan and God. And what can we say, we look at that picture, we read the pathetic details of the murder, the senseless, useless, misdirected antagonism toward a world that they know, somehow, has cheated them of reason. Or My Lai, and *Life* magazine with pictures of the dead and the about to die, the eyes again, terror, despair, I want to cry. . . .

I am sick, made sick, sickened, nauseated, helpless, and almost without hope. Yesterday while shopping for a gift I glanced at the bare arm of the saleslady who was wrapping it for me. On her arm was a tattooed number. I am sick, we are all sick.

Liza Williams

DECEMBER 13

1847

We experienced a severe shock from an earth quake here last night at eight oclock and another this morning at day light—It shook me in my bed and made us all a little nervous—it was so soon after our gunpowder explosion—How much I miss poor Sargent Travers—he was a fine soldier and the only man I ever could get to feel the responsibility of his situation when on guard—poor fellow he has mounted his last—

LIEUTENANT JOHN MCHENRY HOLLINGSWORTH

1931

My first night in the new home was a very comfortable one. I slept very well. Everything is so dainty, and the sheets and linen generally are of such excellent quality. Robert brought me up my tea at a quarter to seven. I don't think he went to bed very much, he was so thrilled with his new opportunity.

This morning, however, there was nearly a tragedy. We ran out of milk! We telephoned frantically to our friend and saviour, Guy Bolton, who turned up in a golf suit with a bottle of milk under each arm, having motored round from North Camden. It is about six blocks away.

I went out in the garden and had a look at it. There are two big orange trees, if not three, in full fruit. There is even a pomegranate tree, a lemon tree, but I could not find the avocado pears or apples or whatever they are. There are quite a number of flowers growing, including a brilliant six-starred flower the blooms of which are about nine inches across.

Having only got meat for one meal, the new cook decided to give us salad and a strange omelette for lunch. It was quite good.

The new cook is about thirty-five, stoutish, coloured, and her name is Marie. She has large ivory earrings and a pleasant smile.

It was a most gorgeous sunrise, but it clouded up in the morning. Bob says it was a glorious sunset, but I was asleep. I have been working to-day at the new film, and have done twenty-seven pages of it. I hope to get the back of it broken to-night.

Edgar Wallace

1963

Aldous died quietly, without any pain in the end. He was absolutely clear, mentally. The day before he died, he finished dictating an article about Shakespeare. He wasn't told of Kennedy's shooting, which happened just a few hours earlier.

Personally, I was very pro-Kennedy; but I was still amazed at how much I minded. And, in this quite largely anti-Kennedy town, which has so little to unite it, it was amazing how much everybody minded. People just sat listening to the radio in their cars and sobbing. We were all in love with him, without knowing it.

Christopher Isherwood

DECEMBER 14

1929

Well, here I am! We got in last night & today I have eaten an orange, walked under palm trees, gone out to the studio, met dozens of people whose names I will never remember, been photographed with Mr. Griffith, dictated a lot of hooey to a stenographer, seen & heard screen-test of various Lincolns and Ann

Rutledges etc. The sun is actually out, the roses & poinsettias in bloom in the lush hotel garden. . . .

It is all quite mad. And everything is going well so far. And I'm lonelier than I can think about and miss you more than any words can say. *Gee!* Only—at the worst 83 days more. And by the time this gets to you it will be less. I don't mean to crab and I'll try not to. I like [D. W.] Griffith—he's a human being—and he certainly has been extremely decent to me. He is capable—which I didn't expect—and really laid himself out to be pleasant. We worked all the way out in the train and cut the thing about a third. Of course I imagine the final version—if there ever is one—will be entirely different. That seems to be the method. At present I'm giving my celebrated imitation of a piece of furniture. I don't know why anything happens and I don't try to find out. Tomorrow I am to be given an office—why? I don't know. And I'm also apparently going down with Griffith for the weekend to visit some millionaires named [Spreckels]. I don't know why I am doing that, either. Apparently, at the moment, Griffith likes to have me around as a sort of mascot. Things happen without sequence or consequence and I take them as they come. Tell Phil [Philip Barry] he really must see it. But not alone.

. . . We're going to get a nice house out of this—concentrate on the house—I am. Kiss the children for me. I miss them. Love to Mother, Laura & Bill. My darling, my darling, I love you more than anything that ever was!

STEPHEN VINCENT BENÉT, to his wife

1931

Perhaps in my radio contract I shall insist upon the reservation to me of the interplanetary rights. Why not? Radio rights and sound and dialog rights would have seemed as preposterous twenty years ago; and with my intimate knowledge of conditions on Mars and Venus, I, of all men, should anticipate the value of broadcasting Tarzan to the eager multitudes that swarm our sister planets.

Edgar Rice Burroughs

DECEMBER 15

1847

Lieut Davidson and Kit Carson returned from a scouting expedition to meet a body of mexicans that were coming into the Country to sell their goods,—they had but few arms and were friends to our cause—

Lieutenant John McHenry Hollingsworth

1939

We went down in the afternoon and that evening saw *Grapes* at Twentieth-Century. Zanuck has more than kept his word. He has a hard, straight picture in which the actors are submerged so completely that it looks and feels like a documentary film and certainly it has a hard, truthful ring. No punches were pulled—in fact, with descriptive matter removed, it is a harsher thing than the book, by far. It seems unbelievable but it is true. The next afternoon we went to see *Mice* and it is a beautiful job. Here Milestone has done a curious lyrical thing. It hangs together and is underplayed. You will like it. It opens the 22nd of December in Hollywood. As for *Grapes,* it opens sometime in January. There is so much hell being raised in this state that Zanuck will not release it simultaneously. He'll open in N.Y. and move gradually west, letting the publicity precede it. He even, to find out, issued a statement that it would never be shown in California and got a ton of mail, literally, in protest the next day. He has hired attorneys to fight any local censorship and is trying to get Thomas Benton for the posters. All this is far beyond our hopes. . . .

I can't tell you what all this means to me, in happiness and energy. I was washed up and now I'm alive again, with work to be done and worth doing.

John Steinbeck, to his agent

1940

I am still in bed—this time the result of 25 years of cigarettes. You have got two beautiful bad examples of parents. Just do everything we didn't do and you will be perfectly safe. But be sweet to your mother. . . . the insane are always mere guests on earth, total strangers carrying around broken decalogues that they cannot read.

F. Scott Fitzgerald, to his daughter

1957

I am fifty-two years old, and I have three children who shall soon require expensive education. I have perhaps ten years of peak work capacity remaining to me. During these ten years, in addition to educating the children, I must somehow accumulate enough reserve capital to provide for Cleo and me in old age. Otherwise I shall become a public charge. I am absolutely alone in the world. All of my relatives, instead of giving me money or willing me money, have cost me money. There is no one to provide for me except me, and there never has been. About six months ago I decided to face up to these facts and to set myself a schedule of work which would absolutely guarantee me the freedom I need to do that work which I hope and think will solve my final problem. . . .

In order to keep this madhouse going, I awaken each morning

between 3 and 5 a.m., although rarely as late as five. I work steadily until about one. Then I take a half-hour nap. Work steadily until 7 or 7:30 p.m. After that I take three stiff belts of whiskey to uncoil on, eat dinner, and go to bed. This schedule is absolutely unfailing, Saturdays and Sundays included. I was never a social person, but I am much less so now than formerly. I dread going out because it means drinking and lowered vitality for tomorrow. We do, however, go out perhaps once a month. Certain people are angry with me for turning down simple dinner invitations on the plea of work. It is getting to be assumed that either I am (a) getting snobbish, or (b) crazed for money. I cannot help these impressions, and I don't give a damn about them. I am doing not what is pleasing to me to do, but what I must and am determined to do.

DALTON TRUMBO, to a fellow blacklistee

1989

Breakfasted by the pool. The Sunset Marquis is small, low and laid-back. Many Brit guests and quite an assortment of rock musicians persevering with '70s hairstyles. One band were from Canada and awestruck to meet me. "Your tapes, man. . . . We play 'em all the time . . . they keep us going in the tour bus." Shades of '69/'70 all over again. Python and the rock world's strange compatibility.

MICHAEL PALIN

DECEMBER 16

1937

Certain writers have become very lax in the hours they keep at the Studio, coming in late in the morning and leaving early in the afternoon. This is not true of all the writers, but it unfortunately makes it necessary for me to send out a general note of this nature.

It is not asking too much for a writer to be at his desk sometime between 9:00 a.m. and 9:45 a.m.; even the elite in any other business come to work earlier than that. Therefore, I must insist that more regular hours be kept in the future by those of you who have been coming in late and leaving early.

JACK WARNER, to his stable

1953

If you take up the subject of puns again, you might consider the Circumstantial Pun, which calls for a very special and often highly complex set of circumstances for its use.

For example, our Mr. Kaufman once had one in mind which he confessed he doubted he would ever be able to use. The locale would have to be somewhere in the Orient during a war with the Japanese. The season should be late autumn, and on a particular morning our forces would have hanged a small Japanese spy. If such were the case and Mr. Kaufman were there, he felt that he could not unreasonably remark, "There's a little Nip in the air this morning."

NUNNALLY JOHNSON, to Clifton Fadiman

DECEMBER 17

1927

Today on the beach a mile below here, at Venice, I found myself talking literature, Spengler, Kant, Descartes and Aquinas . . . to a Bostonian of French descent . . . He turned out to be one of the best scholars I've ever met.

HART CRANE, to a friend

1940

Not dead. Nor down with flu—as is half Los Angeles. But merely entangled in that unprofitable thing known as the show business—going out to Hollywood or Beverly Hills or Hollywood every morning and not getting back to the hotel until 12 or 1 or 2 o'clock at night—since those remote districts are from where I live just about like going from Harlem to Philadelphia—and in this charming democracy of ours there seems to be no place for Negroes to live in Hollywood even if they do work out there occasionally. . . .

I do not enjoy this collective way of writing very much as I feel that when too many people are involved in the preparation of scripts, the material loses whatever individual flavor and distinction it might otherwise possess. That is probably what was the matter with ZERO HOUR. After everybody got their paragraph in, it was simply a depersonalized un-human editorial, well-meant but with none of the blood of life or the passion of mankind in it. I do not think plays, or even skits can be written by eight or ten people with various ways of feeling and looking at things.

LANGSTON HUGHES, to his agent

1981

Coming over the hill, the yellow haze was unexpected after the clean skies of the Valley. Off in the distance, the towers of downtown made their silhouettes known through the smog. A few new buildings had been added. The profile was a bit wider, but the same height, so it was beginning to look like one large rectangular mass. . . .

I drove to Beverly Hills to drop off a letter for P. The isolation of that ghetto of wealth sets the whole thing off even more than the way it is in Paris or N.Y.

This could be Teheran or Athens—or any of those types of metropolises. I feel how it is with all of the poverty concentrated in the bidonville and all of the wealth in but a few sectors.

Los Angeles is a funny town. If New York escapes off the American map towards the mid-Atlantic, L.A. has a tendency to drift south and east—as if it was a clean recuperated 3rd world city . . . Cairo.

Aaron Paley

DECEMBER 18

1858

And you, imbecile Californians! You are responsible for the lamentable acts we are witnessing. We are tired of saying: "Open your eyes, now is the time to assert your rights and interests." It is shameful, but necessary to admit that you are the sarcasm of humanity. When the time comes to vote, the first of your rights, you go about the streets in the carriages of [Democratic] candidates, and you will not cast your votes unless you are paid for them. . . . You are cowardly and stupid, inspiring nothing but disdain. . . . You might as well renounce once and for all noble sentiments and prepare to cast upon yourselves the yoke of slavery.

Francisco P. Ramirez

1929

This is Wednesday. Let me recount a little more about this madhouse. In the first place Hollywood—Los Angeles, Glendale, Pasadena etc. etc.—is one loud, struggling Main-Street, low-roofed, mainly unskyscrapered town that struggles along for 25 miles or so, full of stop & go lights, automobiles, palm-trees, Spanishy—& God knows what all houses—orange-drink stands with real orange juice—studios—movie-theaters—everything but bookstores. I am the only person in the entire 25 miles who walks more than four blocks, except along Hollywood Boulevard in the evening. There are some swell hotels—up in the hills or between L.A. & Hollywood—& a few night-clubs.

But in general, everything is dead, deserted at 11.30 p.m. There is the continual sunlight—the advertised palms—coolness the minute the sun sets—and plenty of people with colds. The boys go around without hats. They look like prize ears of corn. The girls, ditto. . . .

Last Monday, however, was D. W. Griffith night at the Roosevelt. I sat at the stag table with Griffith & a lot of the men who have at one time worked with him—and was included by the worried announcer in the list of those discovered by DWG, but nobody cared. But I stood up with the rest, had a spotlight played on me, and felt silly. . . .

The place was packed & everybody talked about when they wanted to fire Mary Pickford from Biograph because she wasn't pretty enough & when Chaplin got $5 a week—until I felt I had been there too. . . .

Saturday I may go over to spend the weekend with the McClures. And then—Lord—it will be Christmas. I shall go out & look sad-eyedly at all the Christmas trees on Hollywood Boulevard. My Lord, how I miss you. Oh Eastern wind, when wilt thou blow?

STEPHEN VINCENT BENÉT, to his wife

DECEMBER 19

1939

They're quarreling (out here in the movie world) as to which of 84 directors are entitled to the honor of filming that world's masterpiece—*Gone With the Wind.* T.S. Stribling's Trilogy—the source of most of it [—] is never mentioned.

THEODORE DREISER, to H. L. Mencken

1948

There are so many books and plays and stories I have to read—Here are just a few:

. . . Diary of a Writer—Dostoyevsky
Against the Grain—Huysmans
The Disciple—Paul Bourget
Sanin—Mikhail Artsybashev
Johnny Got His Gun—Dalton Trumbo

SUSAN SONTAG

DECEMBER 20

1993

All we have to do is decide whether we have a reasonable doubt or not—it's up to the prosecution to prove there was a plan to kill.

HAZEL THORNTON

2004

I come swinging in from Phoenix, riding shotgun on the bus with 'Lish for the last two hours of a 15,750-mile journey. We float down the I-10, cross over to the 134, past the sign for Occidental College (Terry Gilliam's alma mater), coming on home from Pasadena. It all begins to feel familiar. Odd that this should now feel like home, but it does.

It is a wonderful sight to see my tour bus outside my own front gate at last.

Tania and Wee (our Thai wonder woman) come to the door bleary-eyed.

The Greedy Bastard is home.

ERIC IDLE

DECEMBER 21

1864

And now comes the curse of God on the land—two years no rain falls, and famine with her grim reality compels the surrender of lands rendered tenantless of hoofs & horns already. The old spell is broken & Southern California will now be regenerated. The few stout hopeful hearts who have found courage to stand out for years hoping for a change will be rewarded. The great and splendid Estates will be broken up into small farms & thrifty industrious farmers and associations of them will take the place of the brigands who have made Santa Barbara, Los Angeles and San Bernardino Counties infamous.

BENJAMIN SILLIMAN

1942

There was an enormous blaze at Los Angeles station a week ago that probably claimed incredible numbers of Christmas packages, and we spent a few days worrying about what had become of the delicious fluid you had intended for us. But then, after we had already given up hope, the gigantic crate arrived—how much love went into the packaging, to say nothing of its contents—in good shape, and we were all the more glad for it. Accept our heartiest thanks. Last night we sampled the creme de cacao and found it quite excellent, worthy of the greatest tradition. Its consumption takes place in silence.

THEODOR ADORNO, to his parents

DECEMBER 22

1939

There are not many real Spaniards here, but large numbers of Mexicans. I have one Spaniard in my seminar—his father is a wine merchant, and Franco stole 1,000,000 bottles of sherry from him, so he has correct sentiments on Spain. . . .

I have a great deal of work here, most of it too elementary to be interesting. [His wife] Peter has so much to do that she is worn out—arranging for John and Kate, driving the car (everything here is 20 miles off), and spending hours a day on our permits to stay in this country, to get which we have to go to Mexico. The red tape has driven us both to the edge of insanity.

They assure us that it will rain soon—hitherto we have had endless sunny days—2 days ago the temperature was 84. One gets to long for wet and cold. . . .

Conrad is the joy of our lives—partly by his merits, partly because he doesn't know there is a war. He is very intelligent—he knows endless poems and stories by heart, and has a vast vocabulary. We love him and he loves the cat and the cat loves her dinner. Love is not the reward of services rendered.

BERTRAND RUSSELL, to a friend

1949

Christopher Isherwood wrote me a superb letter about *Sunset* [*Boulevard*], with which I plan to combat Billy's childlike resistance to retaking the questioning scene. Christopher points out, in highly literate English, why it's wrong—that the detectives seem to have read the end of the script.

CHARLES BRACKETT

DECEMBER 23

1895

It has been a very sad day. Rather cloudy and cold. Nothing in particular.

DON JUAN BAUTISTA BANDINI

1931

I took the scenario down to the studio, where I was interviewed by the "Variety" correspondent, a decent fellow called Fred Stanley, and, having handed the story over to [Merian C.] Cooper, I met him an hour later at lunch in the restaurant. There was a little bit about a missionary which he didn't think might get past the Will Hays office, but Cooper said it was the most powerful story of mine he had read.

I then went down to the animating room, where they are working on models of a prehistoric story [*King Kong*], the script of which I am going to write.

EDGAR WALLACE

DECEMBER 24

1932

Señor [Blasco] Ibañez [author of *The Four Horsemen of the Apocalypse*] arrived in Los Angeles. We became his host. Of course he would wish to visit the studios? Not at all, but the Missions, ah, yes, the Missions! But whom in this Land of Celebrities did he wish to meet? Only two persons—"Carlos" (Charlie Chaplin) and Upton Sinclair! It is the same with all distinguished authors. Sometimes they may omit the name Chaplin, but never Sinclair.

ROB WAGNER

1993

Christmas Eve. Went to Pacific Bell in the morning to say hello and have breakfast with my co-workers.

HAZEL THORNTON

DECEMBER 25

1884

I have been here a month—the last week rainy—but it is a soft warm summery sort of drizzle, which is delicious to drive in, after you have been dried up in Colorado, for months.—As for roses—& the rest—well you can't image it:—the people say there are "very few flowers just now" & then they proceed to idly snip off for you, your two hands full!—Los Angeles is just as rubbishy, barbaric, huddled, gay colored, as ever—the most un-American place in America—

—I am never tired, walking my horses up & down the streets, and gazing at the people.—I suppose they will begin to think I have something to sell presently!—or worse!

HELEN HUNT JACKSON, to Charles Dudley Warner

1941

A special edition of the Japanese-language newspaper came out saying Issei (first-generation Japanese) will turn in all shortwave radios and cameras to the police by 11:00 p.m., Monday. It was in last night's English newspaper. The one at our house is a radio with both shortwave and normal listening, so we called the radio shop and had the shortwave portion removed. . . .

Sewing instructor Mrs. M dropped by. She said, "For twelve years, I sewed only American things, but in the end, Americans are Americans, and we are Japanese. Since the war started, Americans ask me if everything is okay, but not one said Merry Christmas to me."

AOKI HISA

DECEMBER 26

1929

This Saturday will finish up the 3rd official week here—plus 2 days—for Uncle Tom. We get paid the following Wednesday—and that's a bright spot. It will be $3000 in the bank next week. Every now and then I look at that bank book—and at my return ticket.

STEPHEN VINCENT BENÉT, to his wife

1937

Don't think that I am a "convert" or "revolutionist." I am not a CP member. I have worked fairly closely with them locally because they seemed to be the only people doing any work. . . . I have never joined the Party because I have known that I could not work satisfactorily within its requirements.

CAREY MCWILLIAMS, to Louis Adamic

DECEMBER 27

1967

Lack of preparation, direction and cooperation from the very beginning have made this album the most unreasonable project with which we have ever involved ourselves. . . .

It all adds up to a lack of professionalism. The Grateful Dead is not one of the top acts in the business as yet. Their attitudes and their inability to take care of business when it's time to do so would lead us to believe that they never will be truly important.

JOSEPH B. SMITH, to their manager

1998

For the first time since he was diagnosed, Frankie was acutely, excitedly and happily aware of Christmas. Like any normal child, he chatted incessantly about Santa, Rudolph, the Grinch and other seasonal characters. He sang carols and other holiday songs and eagerly helped decorate our Christmas tree. . . .

I was pleasantly surprised when Uncle Joe said Aunt Hope was in fine spirits. She had even found the strength to go shopping for a Christmas tree. Without realizing it, I rejoiced that Aunt Hope would be with us for another Christmas. . . .

The very next morning, in predawn darkness, Uncle Joe called to tell me Aunt Hope had suffered a diabetic seizure and cardiac arrest during the night. . . .

. . . Frankie was the biggest surprise. . . . He was curious, as any small child is when first facing the reality of death. He was full of questions, like where heaven is and whether Aunt Hope would ever return from living there with Jesus. But he was also caring.

. . . Even amid the sadness of family tragedy, I became more confident than ever that Frankie will continue to overcome his autism. Not just because he has family, therapists, teachers and classmates who support him, but because he has a special new angel watching over him—an angel named, so very aptly, Hope.

FRANK DEL OLMO

DECEMBER 28

1847

Lieut Davidson gave a party last night—I had been there but a few moments when I was ordered to the command of the guard by Com S—I went to the guard house and found that the officier of the guard had been placed under arrest for getting drunk and raising the devil generally—I had been there but a few moments when I heard a great noise in the street and was informed that Lieut V—was drunk and trying to break into a store I then received orders from the officier of the day to arrest him—

I proceeded to do so, found him full of fight, knocked him down and had a general row with him—The Com came up in the midst of it and ordered me to take him to the guard house at the same time ordering him to be quiet—He behaved very badly and tried hard to throw the Sargent of the guard down—when he got half way to the guard house—he said if we would let him go he would walk—He then walked to the guard house very quietly but gave much trouble during the night being very noisy—He was sent to his quarters in the morning by the officier of the day but did not remain in them as he broke his arrest and got drunk again and was sent again to the guard house this morning and is there at present—

LIEUTENANT JOHN MCHENRY HOLLINGSWORTH

1930

The audience now is unlimited and eclectic. Radio brings to us one moment the swooning harmonies of Cesar Franck, and the next moment the frisky vulgarities of true jazz. Radio knows no boundary lines of taste. All music is "good music" in radio. . . .

Thus the function of the broadcaster is to be completely and unreservedly open and ready for every musical expression—

from the austerities of modal counterpoint to the whinings of boop-boop-a-doop. The broadcaster must regard each as equally important, because, sociologically and philosophically, they *are* equally important.

José Rodriguez

DECEMBER 29

1925

These last few weeks I seem to have gotten in with a regular "Greenwich Village" set of people and needless to say I have been having a wonderful time. Perhaps you wouldn't approve of some of these people—you know how funny they dress—and how unconventional they are—but dog gone it—they are interesting and you talk about things that the ordinary run of men do not find interesting. . . . you have to more or less overlook their moral characters. Most of these people are not married—just live together and they seem really happy.

Valeria Belletti, to a friend

1941

During the morning hours, it rained on and off, and even the clear part of the sky was fairly dark. Husband went to clear up the school association office. Our house radio was inspected by the police and passed; the camera was put in police storage. . . . Today I had a reason to visit Mr K.'s home, but in the streetcar and on the street, I was subjected to continuous unfriendly looks.

Aoki Hisa

1949

Finished rereading the Joyce, *Portrait*—
Oh, the ecstasy of aloneness!—

SUSAN SONTAG

1986

I requested two songs from KROQ tonight: "Changes" by Bowie, "Ever Fallen in Love" by the Fine Young Cannibals. The first because I haven't heard it in a while, and the second because they'll probably play it anyway. I'm still waiting. . . . I wish KROQ would play something I requested. It would give me a reason to go to bed. It's after midnight. . . . I feel as if I should put down a little more of what's happening to my life. I've dropped out of school. Spiritually, I guess, it's a big move. Possibly the first decision I've made entirely on my own.

CAROLYN KELLOGG

DECEMBER 30

1938

Signs of decay multiply. One eye is now useless. My teeth are growing thinner and hearing is impaired, and my feet are so tender that walking is a painful "process of falling," as Dr. Holmes called it. But [what] can a man of seventy-eight expect but growing disability? The worst of it is I have no one to help me now, no one to share the daily burden of maintaining this house and garden. My daughters have leaned so long on Daddy that they regard me as an everlasting prop. I have tried to arrange matters so that they can carry on if I meet with an accident, but it is very hard to bring myself to it. Sorting papers and the use of my eyes in reading letters is now a wearisome business, and I do not feel able to have it done. Looking ahead is a dismal business now.

Hamlin Garland

1941

This job here at the studio is not the end of things for me. It is a means.

Zora Neale Hurston, to a friend

1968

If I hadn't been ill I would have been there to pay my last affectionate respects to John [Steinbeck]. In addition to all the other reasons for my devotion to him, even when we didn't see each other for long stretches of time, he played an important role in my life, both personal and professional. For one thing, he provided me with the opportunity for an accomplishment that heightened my reputation forever after [the screenplay for *The Grapes of Wrath*]. For another, in this same accomplishment he brought me nearer to Dorris [Bowdon, who played Rosasharn and became Johnson's wife]. I can't think of anybody else who did anywhere near as much for my life.

Nunnally Johnson, to Steinbeck's widow

DECEMBER 31

1889

Dolly me la cielo. [Questionable Spanish for "Dolly lifts me to heaven."]

CHARLES LUMMIS

1933

It is 11:30. . . .

The radio grows louder and more maudlin. Here the fire burns bright. A. and I have just taken showers, and our hair is damp around the edges. Noni in a burning-colored dress looks cool. She is reading, and I see that her face is flushed. She and Dave were excited by the snatch of flood news. He sits by the radio. I think he is rather sleepy. He has black paint on his fingers from a drawing he made and burned, of a tree blowing and a little shepherd sitting under it in the falling leaves.

Now I will make the eggnog. I can't find a recipe. I'll heat milk, beat the eggs and sugar, add them, and stir in port and a little brandy. It may turn out—a kind of thin zabaglione, I suppose. I hope we'll sleep untormented into 1934.

M.F.K. FISHER

1949

Today: Two Wright Houses (Aztec Period) And *The Messiah* afterwards at the Rhapsody.

A new year! But no crap on this occasion.

SUSAN SONTAG

1975

This is just to round off the year—a very poor diary year and a hard but slow work year. . . .

Am now reading the fourth volume of Byron's letters. I really cannot say why I keep on at them. I hardly remember anything I have read—any phrase or fact—but I somehow like to breathe in his ambiance. Particularly while I am shitting. . . .

At the end of last year, I wrote about my great happiness with Don and my consistently poor standard of meditation. Both of these have continued throughout 1975. I ought to be more concerned about the meditation, I suppose; and yet I do keep at it and I ask Mother every day for more devotion and at least some sense of her presence. I do feel, I think, quite sincerely that she is my "refuge." And I suppose this is good, since it is balanced by the quite other sort of "refuge" I find in Don. What I am trying to say is that it is doubtless easier to feel that God is the only refuge when you don't have any human being to love and be loved by. But I do.

Christopher Isherwood

About the Contributors

Acosta, Oscar Zeta Chicano lawyer, activist, memoirist, novelist. Author of *Autobiography of a Brown Buffalo* and the un-squashable *Revolt of the Cockroach People.* Inspiration for the Samoan lawyer Dr. Gonzo in Hunter S. Thompson's *Fear and Loathing in Las Vegas.* Also immortalized in Thompson's *Rolling Stone* article about the Chicano movement, "Strange Rumblings in Aztlan." Like Ambrose Bierce before him, disappeared into Mexico. Quoted from *Oscar "Zeta" Acosta: The Uncollected Works,* edited by Ilan Stavans (Houston: Arte Publico, 1996).

Adamic, Louis Pioneering immigrant author of *Dynamite: The Story of Class Violence in America* and *Laughing in the Jungle.* Lived for a time in a pilothouse at the mouth of San Pedro Bay. Quoted from *Laughing in the Jungle: The Autobiography of an Immigrant in America* (New York: Harper & Brothers, 1932).

Adorno, Theodor Refugee philosopher. Wrote *The Psychological Technique of* [L.A.-based preacher] *Martin Luther Thomas' Radio Addresses* and most of *Minima Moralia* while exiled on the Westside. Quoted from *Letters to His Parents: 1939–1951* (Hoboken, N.J.: Wiley, 2006).

Agee, James Film and book critic, author of *A Death in the Family* and *Let Us Now Praise Famous Men.* Screenwriter of *The African Queen* and *The Night of the Hunter.* Visited Los Angeles periodically in the forties and fifties to interview filmmakers for *Time* and to work on screenplays, both produced and un-. These included one for Chaplin about the Little Tramp after a nuclear apocalypse, and *African Queen* for John Huston, whose demands for revisions and tennis games helped give Agee a heart attack. Quoted from *Letters of James Agee to Father Flye* (New York: Melville House, 2014).

AINSWORTH, ED *Los Angeles Times* columnist. Also ghostwriter of *The California I Love,* the autobiography of Leo Carrillo, who played the Cisco Kid on television and may well be the first person born in Los Angeles ever to become nationally famous. Quoted from the *Los Angeles Times.*

ALPERSTEIN, ELLEN Los Angeles journalist, blogger, and longtime contributor to laobserved.com, where this entry first appeared. By gracious permission of the author.

ANZA, JUAN BAUTISTA DE Basque explorer and governor of New Mexico under Spain. Quoted from *Anza's California Expeditions* (Berkeley: University of California Press, 1930).

ARMSTRONG, HEATHER B. Blogger known as Dooce; one of the first to make a living at it. Posts from dooce.com appear here by gracious permission of the author.

ASBURY, AMY Memoirist. Published in *The Sunset Strip Diaries* (Los Angeles: Estep & Fitzgerald Books, 2010).

AUDUBON, JOHN W. Son of the naturalist, writer, and painter John James Audubon, author of *Birds of America.* Quoted from *Audubon's Western Journal: 1849–1850* (Cleveland: The Arthur H. Clark Company, 1906).

BANCROFT, HUBERT HOWE The first great historian of California. Ran a virtual historiographic sweatshop, employing a phalanx of freelancers to help research and write his multivolume account of the state. Much reviled since, but patently unignorable. Quoted from *History of California* (San Francisco: The History Company, 1884–1890).

BANDINI, DON JUAN BAUTISTA Long-lived diarist, descendant of Californios. As with Don Pio Pico, the world he was born into bore little resemblance to the one he departed. Diary of Juan Bautista Bandini, Huntington Library, San Marino, Calif.

BANNING, WILLIAM Son of the entrepreneur Phineas Banning, who was known as the Father of the Port of Los Angeles for his indefatigable early efforts to move people and freight inland at a tidy profit. Banning Brothers Letters Collection, Huntington Library, San Marino, Calif.

BEALE, E. F. American soldier stationed at Fort Tejon, and commander of America's first Camel Corps.

BEHAN, BRENDAN Playwright, author of *Borstal Boy.* The letter quoted is viewable on a wall in the Dublin Writers Museum.

BELLETTI, VALERIA Secretary to Samuel Goldwyn and other studio heads, lovingly delivered from obscurity by film historian Cari Beauchamp. Quotations from *Adventures of a Hollywood Secretary: Her Private Letters from Inside the Studios of the 1920s,* used by kind permission of the editors, Cari Beauchamp and Margery Baragona (Berkeley: University of California Press, 2006).

BENÉT, STEPHEN VINCENT Yale-educated author of *The Devil and Daniel Webster* and *Western Star,* a long narrative poem about Manifest Destiny that won the Pulitzer Prize before Benét could finish it. He never did. Quotations from *Selected Letters of Stephen Vincent Benét,* edited by Charles A. Fenton (New Haven, Conn.: Yale University Press, 1960).

BENNETT, ALAN Screenwriter, novelist, and playwright of, among other works, *Talking Heads, An Englishman Abroad, The Madness of King George,* and *The History Boys.* Bennett first came to prominence writing sketches and acting alongside Peter Cook, Jonathan Miller, and Dudley Moore in *Beyond the Fringe,* a hastily mounted late-night revue at the Edinburgh Fringe Festival. They were the only four men in England brilliant enough to claim convincingly that they found one another boring. Bennett was the shy one and easily the most formidable dramatic writer of the three. In his fine script for *Prick Up Your Ears,* a hapless mortician tries to mingle the cremated remains of the British playwright Joe Orton and his partner, who has killed them both. The undertaker empties one urn into the other, then sprinkles some of those ashes back into the first. He looks about to make a project of it when Vanessa Redgrave, playing Orton's agent and executrix, deadpans: "It's a gesture, not a recipe." Bennett has also kept a diary for most of his life. He chanced through Hollywood for at least one film premiere and left unbesotted. Quoted from *Writing Home* (New York: Random House, 1995).

BERTENSSON, SERGEI Filmmaking factotum. Quoted from *My First Time in Hollywood,* edited by Cari Beauchamp (Los Angeles: Asahina & Wallace, 2015).

BIGLER, HENRY W. Pioneer, present the year before at the discovery of gold at Coloma on the American River. Quoted from *Journals of Forty-niners: Salt Lake to Los Angeles: with Diaries and Contemporary Records of Sheldon Young, James S. Brown, Jacob Y. Stover, Charles C. Rich, Addison Pratt, Howard Egan, Henry W. Bigler, and Others* (Glendale, Calif.: Arthur H. Clark, 1954).

BIXBY, AUGUSTUS SIMON Farmer from the famed Bixby dynasty, to whom the idyllic Rancho Los Cerritos once belonged. Diary of Augustus Simon Bixby, Huntington Library, San Marino, Calif.

BOUTON, JIM Baseball player, author of *Ball Four* and its cruelly forgotten sequel, *I'm Glad You Didn't Take It Personally.* Visited southern California in 1969 to play the Angels. Whether *Ball Four* robbed America of its heroes or, as many think, actually helped humanize the players in fans' eyes, these funny, well-observed diaries made readers out of more than a few Little Leaguers who grew up to be writers, present company included. Quoted from *Ball Four: My Life and Hard Times Throwing the Knuckleball in the Big Leagues,* edited by Leonard Shecter (New York: World Books, 1970).

BRACKETT, CHARLES Screenwriter-producer, longtime writing partner of Billy Wilder's earlier, less raunchy, more urbane comedies. Quoted from *It's the Pictures That Got Small: Charles Brackett on Billy Wilder and Hollywood's Golden Age,* edited by Anthony Slide (New York: Columbia University Press, 2015). Used by permission.

BRADBURY, RAY Author of *Fahrenheit 451* and *The Martian Chronicles;* screenwriter of *Moby-Dick.* Among Bradbury's ancestors was a Salem, Massachusetts, woman tried for witchcraft in the seventeenth century. His parents drove across the country to Los Angeles in 1934, with young Ray piling out of their jalopy at every stop to plunder the local library in search of L. Frank Baum's *Oz* books. Two years later, Bradbury experienced a rite of passage familiar to most early science-fiction readers: the realization that he was not alone. At a secondhand bookstore in Hollywood, he discovered a handbill promoting meetings of the Los Angeles Science Fiction Society. Thrilled, he joined a weekly Thursday-night conclave that would grow to attract such science-fiction legends as Robert A. Heinlein, Leigh Brackett, and the future founder of Scientology, L. Ron Hubbard. Bradbury wrote *Fahrenheit 451* on a rental typewriter in the basement of UCLA's Lawrence Clark Powell Library, one invaluable dime at a time. Quoted from *The Bradbury Chronicles: The Life of Ray Bradbury* by Sam Weller (New York: William Morrow, 2005).

Brecht, Bertolt Author of, among other plays, *Galileo, Mother Courage,* and *The Resistible Rise of Arturo Ui.* Fled Europe for Santa Monica. After World War II, fled Joseph McCarthy for Europe again. Quoted from *Bertolt Brecht Journals, 1934–1955* (London: Methuen, 1993).

Bremer, Sylvia Strum Newspaper columnist. Visited L.A. as a junketeer and, only occasionally starstruck, filed stories for the folks back home. Her reports were published in the Davenport, Iowa, *Daily Times,* in 1956.

Brewer, William H. Botanist on the first California Geological Survey; first chair of agriculture at Yale. Quoted from *Up and Down California in 1860–1864: The Journal of William H. Brewer* (New Haven, Conn.: Yale University Press, 1930).

Briggs, L. Vernon Pioneering forensic psychiatrist. Quoted from his *Arizona and New Mexico, 1882; California, 1886; Mexico, 1891* (Boston: Privately printed, 1932).

Britten, Benjamin British composer of *Peter and the Wolf, The Young Person's Guide to the Orchestra,* and *Peter Grimes,* the latter inspired by his discovery of George Crabbe's poems in a maddeningly unspecified Los Angeles bookstore. At the time, he was staying with Peter Pears at the Escondido home of a patron, working against the imminent world premiere in L.A. of his first string quartet. Published in *Letters from a Life: Selected Diaries and Letters of Benjamin Britten,* edited by Philip Reed and Donald Mitchell (Berkeley: University of California Press, 1991).

Bryant, Edwin Quoted from his *What I Saw in California, Being the Journal of a Tour by the Emigrant Route and South Pass of the Rocky Mountains, Across North America, the Great Desert Basin in the Years 1846, 1847* (New York: Appleton, 1849).

BUKOWSKI, CHARLES Poet, novelist, and "Notes of a Dirty Old Man" columnist for the *Los Angeles Free Press.* Quoted from *Screams from the Balcony: Selected Letters, 1960–1970* (Santa Rosa, Calif.: Black Sparrow Press, 1993).

BURMAN, JENNY Erstwhile author of the Echo Park blog *Chicken Corner.* Quoted by gracious permission of the author.

BURROUGHS, EDGAR RICE Imaginatively gifted and lavishly prolific novelist, creator of *Tarzan of the Apes* and *Princess of Mars,* founder of Tarzana. All quotations from Edgar Rice Burroughs © 1975, 2017 Edgar Rice Burroughs, Inc. All rights reserved. Trademarks TARZAN® and Edgar Rice Burroughs® Owned by Edgar Rice Burroughs, Inc., and used by permission.

BURTON, RICHARD Brilliant Welsh actor. Played Hamlet for Gielgud, married Elizabeth Taylor, costarred with her in *Who's Afraid of Virginia Woolf?* for Mike Nichols, and enjoyed a long career in roles both great and awful. In L.A. occasionally for film work, doomed award nominations, and, improbably, to brush up his Spanish before shooting *The Night of the Iguana* in Mexico. Quoted from *The Richard Burton Diaries,* edited by Chris Williams (New Haven, Conn.: Yale University Press, 2012).

BUTLER, OCTAVIA E. MacArthur Fellowship–winning author of, among other works, *Kindred* and *Parable of the Sower.* Born and raised in Pasadena, which appears in disguised form in some of her work. Labored in solitude until she found camaraderie among other science fiction and fantasy writers, especially Harlan Ellison. Years after her death from a fall, her reputation continues to rise. Octavia E. Butler papers, The Huntington Library, San Marino, Calif.

BUTLER, OCTAVIA M. Mother of Octavia E. Butler.

Cabrillo, Juan Rodríguez Mariner, explorer.

Cage, John Composer, musician, Joycean. Born in Los Angeles. His mother wrote about society and classical music for the *Los Angeles Times* back when they were often the same thing. Studied under Arnold Schoenberg. His experimental "silent" sonata, *4′33″*, was the first of his pioneering works to be influenced by random chance. Absquatulated. Returned to L.A. late in life for a production of his Joyce-inspired "composition for museum," *Rolywholyover*. Quoted from *The Selected Letters of John Cage*, edited by Laura Kuhn (Middletown, Conn.: Wesleyan University Press, 2016).

Calvino, Italo Author of *Invisible Cities* and *If on a winter's night a traveler*. Taught at UCLA for a semester. Did not go native. Quoted from *Hermit in Paris: Autobiographical Writings* (New York: Farrar, Straus and Giroux, 2007).

Campbell, Julia Student at UCLA. Quoted from class diaries by gracious permission.

Carr, Harry Carr saw the city as it was, and L.A. loved him for it. The forgotten patron saint of Southland journalists, he scooped the world on the San Francisco Earthquake and rode with Zapata during the Revolution. Among the first telecommuting journalists, he was writing from home in Tujunga when he warned, apropos of Thelma Todd and John Gilbert's recent passings, that "Death cuts down the famous by threes in Hollywood." Hours later, Carr's heart attack supplied the third. Quoted from *Los Angeles, City of Dreams* (New York: D. Appleton-Century Company, 1935).

Carr, William American immigrant to California in 1849. Witness to the Colorado River massacre at the heart of Cormac McCarthy's novel *Blood Meridian: Or the Evening Redness in the*

West. Testimony published in *Southern California Quarterly,* vol. 6 (Los Angeles: Geo. Rice & Sons, 1904).

CATHER, WILLA American author of novels including *My Antonía, Death Comes for the Archbishop,* and *The Song of the Lark.* Stayed in Long Beach and commuted to Pasadena to care for her ailing mother. Not predisposed to love the place, and didn't. Quoted from *The Selected Letters of Willa Cather* (New York: Alfred A. Knopf, 2013).

CHANDLER, RAYMOND Author of *The Big Sleep,* creator of detective Philip Marlowe, co-screenwriter of *Strangers on a Train.* Directly or indirectly, Chandler has colored Angelenos' perceptions of their city more than any other writer. Quoted from *Selected Letters of Raymond Chandler,* edited by Frank MacShane (New York: Columbia University Press, 1981).

CHAVEZ, CESAR Co-founder of the United Farm Workers. Wielding the power of the hunger strike and the boycott, he fought for and won the first binding farmworker contracts ever negotiated in California. Apprenticed and flourished as a community organizer in Boyle Heights alongside *Grapes of Wrath* dedicatee Fred Ross, under the auspices of Saul Alinsky. Born in Yuma, he is buried at the National Chavez Center in Tehachapi, in the mountains that divide the state he did so much to unite. Quoted from *The Crusades of Cesar Chavez: A Biography,* by Miriam Pawel (New York: Bloomsbury, 2014).

CHÁVEZ-SILVERMAN, SUSANA Los Angeles–born Spanglish writer, scholar; author also of *Killer Crónicas.* Quoted from *Scenes from la Cuenca de Los Angeles y Otros Natural Disasters* (Madison: University of Wisconsin Press, 2010).

CHEEVER, JOHN Novelist and short-story writer, author of the *Wapshot* novels, *Bullet Park,* and *Falconer.* Passed through L.A. en route to Manila in 1945 for the Signal Corps. Returned periodically, staying with friends John Weaver (q.v.) and his wife. Published in *Glad Tidings: A Friendship in Letters. The Correspondence of John Cheever and John D. Weaver, 1945–1982* (New York: HarperCollins, 1993).

Churchill, Winston British politician, hero. As prime minister, rallied his countrymen to victory in World War II. Turfed out soon after. Awarded the Nobel Prize in literature for his history of the war. Visited L.A. a month before the 1929 Crash. Met Hearst, Chaplin, and a swordfish, to the latter's cost. Published in *Speaking for Themselves: The Personal Letters of Winston and Clementine Churchill,* edited by Baroness Mary Soames (née Mary Spencer Churchill) (New York: Doubleday, 1998).

Coleman, Wanda Fearsome doyenne of the L.A. poetry scene for decades. Fugitive from TV soap opera writing. Author of the National Book Award–nominated *Mercurochrome.* Quoted from *The Riot Inside Me: More Trials & Tremors* (Boston: David R. Godine, 2005).

Cooke, Alistair Broadcaster and author, best known for his long-running, only partly catalogued BBC Radio essays explaining the ways of Americans to the British. Returned to L.A. frequently to visit friends and file observations for the Beeb, including the horrific one quoted here. *Letter from America* scripts © Cooke Americas, RLLP.

Copland, Aaron Composer of *Fanfare for the Common Man, Billy the Kid,* and *A Lincoln Portrait.* Wrote scores for *The Heiress, The Red Pony,* and *Of Mice and Men.* A delightful photo survives of him poolside in Palm Springs, in shorts, at a typewriter, mountains looming behind him. Quoted from *The Selected Correspondence of Aaron Copland* (New Haven, Conn.: Yale University Press, 2006).

Coppola, Eleanor Writer-director of *Paris Can Wait.* Eloquent diarist of, among other experiences, the descent into genius of the screenwriter-director Francis Ford Coppola on the set of *Apocalypse Now.* Quoted from *Notes on a Life* (New York: Nan A. Talese, 2008).

Corwin, Norman Writer, radio scenarist of *On a Note of Triumph,* screenwriter of *Lust for Life.* Quoted from *Norman Corwin's Letters,* edited by A. J. Langguth (New York: Barricade Books, 1994).

Costansó, Miguel Catalan cartographer and cosmographer. Quoted from *The Portola Expedition of 1769–1770: Diary of Miguel Costansó* (Berkeley: University of California Press, 1911).

Coward, Noël Playwright, actor, songwriter. Returned to L.A. periodically to see friends and perform for films and onstage. Quoted from *The Noël Coward Diaries,* edited by Graham Payn and Sheridan Morley (New York: Little, Brown, 1982).

Craft, Robert Boswell to Igor Stravinsky's Johnson. Quoted from *Dialogues and a Diary,* by himself and Stravinsky (New York: Doubleday, 1963).

Crane, Hart Poet. Stayed over the winter from 1927 to 1928 visiting family, acting as companion to a wealthy Altadenan. Met Chaplin, drank with E. E. Cummings, was gay-bashed in San Pedro. Quoted from *The Letters of Hart Crane, 1916–1932,* edited by Brom Weber (Berkeley and Los Angeles: University of California Press, 1965).

Creason, Glen Map librarian at the Los Angeles Central Library. Quoted by gracious permission of the author.

Crespi, Fray Juan Expedition chaplain. Quoted from *Fray Juan Crespi, Missionary Explorer on the Pacific Coast 1769–1774,* edited by

Herbert Eugene Bolton (Berkeley: University of California Press, 1927).

CUMMINGS, E. E. American poet. Accepted Eric Knight's entreaties to visit. Stayed two months and angled for Hollywood money, to no avail. Quoted from *Selected Letters of E. E. Cummings* (New York: Harper, 1972).

DALTON, HENRY Rancher and newspaper publisher. Papers of Henry Dalton, Huntington Library, San Marino, Calif.

DANA, RICHARD HENRY Author of the first bestseller about California, *Two Years Before the Mast,* an account of his hitch as a midshipman up and down the Pacific Coast. Most editions contain his shorter account of a return visit twenty years later, when he found the state utterly transformed. Quoted from *Two Years Before the Mast* (New York: Library of America, 2005).

DEAN, JAMES Actor, star of *Rebel Without a Cause, Giant,* and *East of Eden.* The letter quoted was sent to his sometime girlfriend Barbara Glenn and published at lettersofnote.com, edited by Shaun Usher.

DE BEAUVOIR, SIMONE Author and groundbreaking feminist. Toured America, including Los Angeles. Liked what she saw of it. Quoted from *America Day by Day* (Berkeley: University of California Press, 2000).

DE LA ASCENSIÓN, FATHER ANTONIO Missionary. Quoted from *Spanish Exploration in the Southwest, 1542–1706,* edited by Herbert Eugene Bolton (New York: Scribners, 1916).

DEL OLMO, FRANK Newspaperman, longtime *L.A. Times* editor, columnist. Well remembered for a continuing series about his autistic son, Frankie. Inspiration to a generation of journalists. There's a school named after him on First Street. It's not enough. Quoted from *Frank Del Olmo: Commentaries on His Times* (Los Angeles: Los Angeles Times Books, 2004).

De Mille, Agnes Dancer, choreographer, UCLA English major. Niece of the director Cecil B. DeMille (the silent *and* sound versions of *The Ten Commandments*) and granddaughter of the great California social economist Henry George ("What the Railroad Will Bring Us"). Quoted from *No Intermissions: The Life of Agnes de Mille,* by Carol Easton (Boston: Little, Brown, 1996).

De Portolá, Gaspar Explorer. Quoted from *The Official Account of the Portolá Expedition of 1769–1770,* edited by Frederick J. Teggart (Berkeley: University of California Press, 1909).

Dick, Philip K. Massively influential science fiction writer. Where Jules Verne predicted inventions, Dick foresaw entire societies. He didn't just anticipate such modern amenities as robotic pets and Prozac, he imagined a future alienated enough to want them—a future that doesn't look as comfortably like science fiction as it used to. The screenwriters Hampton Fancher and David Webb Peoples transplanted Dick's 1968 novel *Do Androids Dream of Electric Sheep?*—set in San Francisco—into 2021 Los Angeles to create the classic film *Blade Runner.* When he died of stroke-related heart failure at fifty-three (weeks after pronouncing himself thrilled with a rough cut of *Blade Runner*), he was living in Orange County, lured there a few years earlier by an admiring academic at Fullerton to donate his archive and original sci-fi pulps to the library. Maybe Dick wrote so convincingly of marginalized alternate worlds in part because he worked in two of them: the cultish shadowlands of pre–*Star Wars* science fiction, and the literary Siberia that is writing for the East Coast from California. Quoted from *The Exegesis of Philip K. Dick,* edited by Pamela Jackson and Jonathan Lethem (Boston: Houghton Mifflin Harcourt, 2011).

DOHENY, E. L. Oil millionaire. With his partner Charles Canfield, struck a gusher at the corner of Patton and West State streets near Echo Park, inaugurating L.A.'s black gold rush. Homeowners rushed to sink wells in their backyards, but Doheny cornered much of the market and became ludicrously wealthy. Later implicated in the Teapot Dome scandal. Quoted from *Hearst's: A Magazine with a Mission* (New York: International Magazine Company, 1919).

DOS PASSOS, JOHN Novelist, epoch-making author of the *USA Trilogy,* which concludes with the centennial-ready, partly Hollywood-set *1919.* Visited awhile to work unsatisfyingly with Josef von Sternberg and make mock. Quoted from *The Fourteenth Chronicle: Letters and Diaries of John Dos Passos,* edited by Townsend Ludington (Boston: Gambit, 1973).

DREISER, THEODORE Author of *Sister Carrie* and *An American Tragedy.* Lived here lustily in the twenties with his beloved bride, Helen, while starting *American Tragedy.* Returned in the late thirties. Suffered fatal heart attack on December 28, 1945, after driving to the beach to watch the sunset. Buried at Forest Lawn. Quoted from *The American Diaries, 1902–1926,* edited by Thomas P. Riggio and James L. W. West III (Philadelphia: University of Pennsylvania Press, 1982).

DRISCOLL, CHARLES B. American journalist and editor. Quoted from his "New York Day by Day" column. New York: McNaught Syndicate, 1939.

DU BOIS, W.E.B. Pioneering African American writer and editor. Drawn here briefly by rumors of a post-racial paradise. Quoted from "Colored California," the *Crisis,* 1913.

DUNNE, PHILIP Well-regarded screenwriter, activist, son of the "Mr. Dooley" columnist, Finley Peter Dunne. Quoted from *The*

Best of Rob Wagner's Script, edited by Anthony Slide (Lanham, Md.: Scarecrow Press, 1985).

EINSTEIN, ALBERT Physicist, discoverer of the theory of special relativity. *Time* magazine's "Man of the Century" for his involvement in the two most important cataclysms of the twentieth century: the splitting of the atom, to which his discoveries led, and the rise of Nazi Germany, from which, as a Jew, he sought refuge in America. Earlier, he'd spent a term at Caltech. Quoted from *A Lone Traveler: Einstein in California,* by William M. Kramer and Margaret Leslie Davis (Los Angeles: Skirball Cultural Center, 2004).

ELIOT, T. S. Poet, author of "The Wasteland," *Four Quartets.* The poet traveled to America briefly as a guest lecturer at, among other campuses, Pomona. Quoted from the *Letters of T. S. Eliot,* vol. 6, edited by Valerie Eliot and Hugh Haffenden (London: Faber & Faber, 2016).

FANTE, JOHN Author of, among other novels, *Ask the Dust* and *Wait Until Spring, Bandini.* Discovering Fante is like tasting garlic for the first time. Quoted from *John Fante: Selected Letters, 1932–1981,* edited by Seamus Cooney (Santa Rosa, Calif.: Black Sparrow Press, 1991).

FAULKNER, WILLIAM Nobel Prize–winning author of, among other novels, *Absalom, Absalom!, The Sound and the Fury,* and *As I Lay Dying.* Co-adapted *The Big Sleep* and *To Have and Have Not* for Howard Hawks. Reputedly asked the studio if he could work from home, then took a favorable answer as permission to return to Mississippi. Wrote one great short story about L.A., "Golden Land." Quoted from *Selected Letters of William Faulkner,* edited by Joseph Blotner (New York: Random House, 1977).

FERLINGHETTI, LAWRENCE Poet and founder of San Francisco publisher and bookstore City Lights. Quoted from *Writing Across the Landscape: Travel Journals 1950–2010,* edited by Giada Diano and Matthew Gleeson (New York: Liveright, 2015). Used by generous permission of the author.

FEYNMAN, RICHARD Nobel Prize–winning physicist affiliated with the Manhattan Project and Caltech. Quoted from *Perfectly Reasonable Deviations from the Beaten Track,* edited by Michelle Feynman (New York: Basic Books, 2005).

FISHER, M.F.K. Essayist, cook, novelist, author of *Consider the Oyster* and *How to Cook a Wolf.* Like her friend and admirer Julia Child, a Californian. She grew up surrounded by citrus groves in Whittier, a few miles southeast of Child's native Pasadena. Her erudite father ran the local newspaper with every good small-town editor's mix of intelligence, boosterism, and cheerful overqualification. Early culinary influences included a grandmother who regarded all flavor as sinful and an aunt who steamed fresh mussels in seaweed on their weekend jaunts to Laguna. Fisher wrote about the pleasures of the table with all the sensuous urgency of someone for whom other pleasures came less often and rarely lasted long. Lovers came and went, and she ruthlessly considered her own talent second-rank, but happiness was always just a good meal away. Quoted from *M.F.K. Fisher: A Life in Letters,* compiled by Marsha Moran, Patrick Moran, and Norah K. Barr (Berkeley: Counterpoint Press, 1998).

FITZGERALD, F. SCOTT Author of *The Great Gatsby, Tender Is the Night,* and *The Last Tycoon.* If you want your child to be a writer, go bankrupt. Failing that, at least suffer a severe financial reversal, obliging your son or daughter to endure the social opprobrium of changed schools and dropped friendships. Do all this, and you may yet join an impecunious fraternity of writers' parents that includes John Shakespeare, John Joyce, John Clemens, John Dickens, John Ernst Steinbeck—and F. Scott Fitzgerald's father, Edward. (You might also want to consider changing your name to John.) Scott Fitzgerald's early literary successes made him and his charming, mercurial wife, Zelda, celebrities of the Jazz Age—a term he coined. In 1925 the publishers Charles Scribner's Sons came out with *Gatsby,* his most enduring work. Fitzgerald relocated in 1937 to write screenplays for Hollywood, where he began sustained work on his novel *The Last Tycoon* (1941). Tragically, his end came before the book's did. Several chapters shy of finishing, Fitzgerald died of a heart attack in the apartment of his Hollywood companion, columnist Sheilah Graham, while listening to Beethoven's *Eroica* symphony, eating a Hershey bar from Greenblatt's, and reading the Princeton alumni magazine. Quoted from *The Letters of F. Scott Fitzgerald,* edited by Andrew Turnbull (New York: Scribners, 1961).

Flores, Gen. José María Mexican general in the Mexican-American War (www.lrgaf.org/journeys/flaco.htm).

Font, Pedro Franciscan missionary. Quoted from *Font's Complete Diary: A Chronicle of the Founding of San Francisco,* edited by Herbert Eugene Bolton (Berkeley: University of California Press, 1933).

Foster, Stephen Clark Mayor, 1854–56. Los Angeles has a weak-mayor system, and sometimes it seems Angelenos prefer them that way. You could call Stephen Foster a lot of things—vigilante, murderer, Yalie—but "weak" didn't really enter into it. Think of the millions saved in liability costs if more mayors would kindly take a sabbatical like him before committing their felonies. Such was the case with Foster, a Yale-educated machine politician who abdicated the mayoralty just long enough to lead the lynch mob that strung up Dirty Dave Brown for murder. His responsibility as a private citizen thus fulfilled, his constituents voted him back into office two weeks later. Electing Foster got to be something of a habit with Los Angeles voters. In addition to a term apiece as a city councilman and state senator, he served as mayor as many as four times, depending how you count his post-vigilante reelection and the term he served before cityhood. He declined to write his memoirs after leaving office, preferring to serve as county supervisor for *another* four terms. Quoted in *Eternity Street: Violence and Justice in Frontier Los Angeles,* by John Mack Farragher (New York: Norton, 2015).

FOWLES, JOHN Author of *The Collector* (whose film adaptation occasioned his skeptical visit here), *The French Lieutenant's Woman,* many others. Quoted from *The Journals, Volume I: 1949–1965* by John Fowles, edited by Charles Drazin (New York: Knopf, 2005).

FRANKAU, GILBERT Author, poet, verse novelist. Quoted from his *My Unsentimental Journey* (London: Hutchinson & Co., 1926).

FRÉMONT, JESSIE BENTON Co-author of several books either with or for her husband, the explorer and first Republican presidential candidate John Frémont. Quoted from *The Letters of Jessie Benton Frémont,* edited by Pamela Lee Herr and Mary Lee Spence (Champaign: University of Illinois Press, 1992).

FRYE, JACK President of TWA. Quoted in *What They Say About the Angels* (Pasadena, Calif.: Val Trefz Press, 1942).

GARCETTI, ERIC Half-Jewish, half-Latino, half-Italian mayor of Los Angeles. Former city councilman, son of the photographer and former city attorney Gil Garcetti. The entry here was originally published in *Slate* and later included in *The Slate Diaries,* edited by Jodi Kantor, Cyrus Krohn, and Judith Shulevitz, with an introduction by Michael Kinsley (New York: Perseus Book Group, 2000). Copyright 2000 by Michael Kinsley. Reprinted by permission of PublicAffairs, a member of the Perseus Book Group.

GARLAND, HAMLIN Glum midwestern Pulitzer-winning author of *A Son of the Middle Border.* Retired here. Hated every minute. Quoted from *Hamlin Garland's Diaries,* edited by Donald Pizer (San Marino, Calif.: Huntington Library Press, 1968).

GARRETT, GARET Isolationist, anti–New Deal newspaper columnist. Quoted from "Los Angeles in Fact and Dream," *The Saturday Evening Post,* in *What They Say About the Angels* (Pasadena, Calif.: Val Trefz Press, 1942).

GERSHWIN, IRA American lyricist, long in partnership with his brother George. Quoted from *The George Gershwin Reader,* edited by Robert Wyatt and John Andrew Johnson (Oxford, U.K.: Oxford University Press, 2004).

GIANNINI, L. M. Son of A. P. Giannini, founder of S.F.-based Bank of America. Quoted from *What They Say About the Angels* (Pasadena, Calif.: Val Trefz Press, 1942).

GIELGUD, JOHN Distinguished British actor on stage and latterly in films, including his early turn as Cassius in *Julius Caesar, Arthur* with Dudley Moore, and Peter Greenaway's *The Tempest.* Quoted from *Sir John Gielgud: A Life in Letters,* edited by Richard Mangan (New York: Arcade, 2004).

GILLESPIE, ARCHIBALD American officer in the Mexican-American War.

GILMAN, CHARLOTTE PERKINS Writer and feminist, known best for her short story "The Yellow Wallpaper," published in *The New England Magazine* but written in California. Fled here from an unhappy marriage, began a writing career, returned often in later years. Suffering from breast cancer, she came back one last time to Pasadena, where she took her own life. Correspondence quoted from *The Selected Letters of Charlotte Perkins Gil-*

man, edited by Denise D. Knight and Jennifer S. Tuttle (Tuscaloosa: University of Alabama Press, 2009).

Ginsberg, Allen Poet, author of "Howl." Active mostly in his native New York and the Bay Area, but visited family near Los Angeles in the 1950s, most memorably for a 1956 reading/disrobing, here recounted from three different perspectives. Quoted from his *Journals Mid-Fifties, 1954–1958,* edited by Gordon Ball (New York: HarperCollins, 1995).

Gish, Lillian The first great actress of the screen. Who invented the close-up? D. W. Griffith? Or the woman he was filming? Quoted from *The Best of Rob Wagner's* Script, edited by Anthony Slide (Lanham, Md.: Scarecrow Press, 1985).

Gold, Jonathan Writer, most influentially for the *LA Weekly* and the *Los Angeles Times.* Author of *Counter Intelligence: Where to Eat in the Real Los Angeles.* The first food critic to win the Pulitzer Prize, and—with apologies to Eloise Klein Healy, Luis J. Rodriguez, and Robin Coste Lewis—the everlasting poet laureate of modern Los Angeles.

Grant, Richard E. Sleek-haired, combustible British actor, familiar from *Withnail & I* and *How to Get Ahead in Advertising.* In Los Angeles to shoot the canonical L.A. pictures *The Player* and *L.A. Story,* among others. Quoted from his *With Nails: The Film Diaries of Richard E. Grant* (Woodstock and New York, N.Y.: The Overlook Press, 1998).

Graves, Jackson Alpheus Banker, orange grower, and oilman. Quoted from his *My Seventy Years in California* (Los Angeles: Times-Mirror Press, 1927).

Griffin, Dr. John S. Military physician turned early settler. Quoted from *A Doctor Comes to California: The Diary of John S. Grif-*

fin, Assistant Surgeon with Kearny's Dragoons, 1846–1847 (San Francisco: California Historical Society, 1943).

GRIFFITH, GRIFFITH J. Journalist, industrialist, philanthropist, would-be uxoricide. Shortly before his death, Tolstoy actually answered Griffith's letter as follows: "Dear sir: Thank you heartily for sending your book. I have only looked it through and I think it is a book that is most necessary in our time. I will read it with the greatest attention and will then express to you my more thorough opinion on it." Quoted from the *Los Angeles Herald,* vol. 33, no. 91, 1910.

GUTHRIE, WOODY Folksinger-songwriter. Born Woodrow Wilson Guthrie, he wrote a great song that too many people know only at the expense of his hundreds of other tunes almost as good: America's folk national anthem, "This Land Is Your Land." The composer he most recalls may be Mozart, with whom he shared a boundless immaturity—he once dried a dish with the nearest soiled diaper that came to hand—and a graphomanically prodigious rate of production. Fellow tunesmith Pete Seeger once said, "I can't stand [Woody] when he is around, but I miss him when he's gone." Him and America both. (Found at https://www.loc.gov/resource/afc1940004.afc1940004_007/?sp=2&st=text)

HAMILTON, JAMES GILLESPIE Merchant. Quoted from *Notebooks of James Gillespie Hamilton, a Merchant of Old Westport, Missouri (1844–1858)* (Fresno: privately printed, 1953).

HAMMETT, DASHIELL Author of *The Maltese Falcon* and other brilliant American crime fiction. His was a style like nobody else's, least of all that of his perennial yokemate in publicist's hyperbole, Raymond Chandler. A Hammett sentence is stingy with ornamentation, suspicious of sentiment but by no means immune to it, and facetious down to its very serifs. As one might expect of a guy who never named his most frequent alter ego—the San Francisco detective agency operative called, by default, the Continental Op—Hammett guarded his emotional life as if it were a flight risk. He wrote one paramour, "I, in a manner of speaking, love you, or words to that effect." It's playful, but not exactly unbuttoned. Hammett wrote most of his letters either to his wife—from whom he separated after the birth of their second daughter, but with whom he kept up a healthy, affectionate correspondence—his two beloved girls, or his lovers, chiefly the playwright Lillian Hellman, whom he'd met here during one of his periodic bouts of screenwriting. But he seemed happiest when thousands of miles away from any of them, stationed with a U.S. Army company in the Aleutian Islands after volunteering for World War II at the age of forty-eight. There he edited the base's paper, turning a bunch of jarheads into journalists—some of them for life. Hammett returned to L.A. over the years to visit his children and grandchildren, by generous permission of one of whom these letters are gratefully excerpted. He died in 1961. Once interned in federal prison for contempt of Congress, he was interred at his request in Arlington National Cemetery for service to his country. Quoted from *Selected Letters of Dashiell Hammett, 1921–1960,* edited by Richard Layman with Julie M. Rivett (Berkeley: Counterpoint Press, 2001).

HANNA, PHIL TOWNSEND L.A. journalist, historian, wag. Longtime editor of the Auto Club magazine *Westways.* Quoted from his *California Through Four Centuries: A Handbook of Memorable Dates* (New York: Farrar & Rinehart, 1935).

HARPER, HARRIET Paid a six-month visit to California with another young woman and privately printed an account of their travels. Quoted from her *Letters from California* (Portland, Me.: B. Thurston & Co., 1888).

HARTWELL, DICKSON Author, executive with the public relations firm Hill & Knowlton. Quoted in *What They Say About the Angels* (Pasadena, Calif.: Val Trefz Press, 1942).

HAWTHORNE, JULIAN Journalist, son of the writer Nathaniel Hawthorne. Convicted of mail fraud, later a crusader for the abolition of penal imprisonment.

HAYES, BENJAMIN Lawyer, judge, memoirist of the city's early years, and, like many a frontier judge before and after him, among the most learned men in town. He had arrived in Los Angeles via the Mormon Trail through San Bernardino with all the saddlebags full of lawbooks that two mules could carry. As a judge, a year before the U.S. Supreme Court got the Dred Scott decision wrong, Hayes got the Biddy Mason decision—effectively the same case—dead right. Quoted from *Pioneer Notes from the Diaries of Benjamin Hayes: 1849–1875*, edited and published by Marjorie Tisdale Wolcott (Los Angeles: Privately printed, 1929).

HAYES, EMILY Wife and partner of jurist Benjamin Hayes. Quoted from *Pioneer Notes from the Diaries of Benjamin Hayes: 1849–1875*, edited and published by Marjorie Tisdale Wolcott (Los Angeles: Privately printed, 1929).

HEROLD, DON American humorist, writer, and cartoonist. Quoted from *The Best of Rob Wagner's* Script, edited by Anthony Slide (Lanham, Md.: Scarecrow Press, 1985).

HERRIMAN, GEORGE Pioneering newspaper cartoonist behind the *Krazy Kat* comic strip. Herriman lived most of his life between downtown L.A. and the Hollywood Hills, though few knew it at the time. (Nobody realized Herriman was a mixed-race Creole, either, and he took pains to keep it that way.) Beloved for both his wordplay and his draftsmanship by everybody from T. S. Eliot to Stan Lee, Herriman worked out his racial ambivalence in the anarchic continuing saga of an immortal black-and-white cat and his unrequited love for a brick-throwing mouse, Ignatz. Quoted from the *Los Angeles Herald*, 1912.

Heston, Charlton Actor, star of *The Ten Commandments, The Omega Man, Will Penny,* and *Planet of the Apes*. Quoted from *The Actor's Life: Journals, 1956–1976,* edited by Hollis Alpert (New York: E. P. Dutton, 1978).

Hill, Jeremiah Indian fighter. Quoted from "Origin of the Trouble Between the Yumas and Glanton. Deposition of Jeremiah Hill," *The Quarterly* (journal of the Historical Society of Southern California), vol. 6, p. 62 (1904).

Hisa, Aoki Wife, mother, World War II internee, writer. Quoted from *White Road of Thorns,* edited by Mary Y. Nakamura (Los Angeles: Xlibris, 2015).

Hollingsworth, Lieutenant John McHenry A Baltimore-born great-grandson of Justice Samuel Chase, one of the signers of the Declaration of Independence. Later the superintendent of George Washington's Mount Vernon home for many years. He left a widow, no children, and perhaps our best record of life in Los Angeles on the verge of statehood. Quoted from *Journal of Lieutenant John McHenry Hollingsworth of the First New York Volunteers [Stevenson's Regiment] September 1846–August 1849. Being a recital of the voyage of the Susan Drew to California; the arrival of the regiment in 1847; its military movements and adventures during 1847-1848-1849; incidents of daily life, and adventures of the author in the gold mines* (San Francisco: California Historical Society, 1923).

Hopper, Hedda Gossip columnist. Longtime rival of Louella Parsons. When she typed, Hollywood quaked. Quoted from her column, "Hedda Hopper's Hollywood." New York: Hearst Newspapers, 1941.

HUGHES, LANGSTON Poet, vital contributor to the Harlem Renaissance. In and out of Hollywood before World War II, working on songs and sketches for liberal revues. Was picketed at a Pasadena Hotel by the evangelist Aimee Semple McPherson and her congregants, then ungently escorted out of a potentially lucrative book luncheon by police. Quoted from *Selected Letters of Langston Hughes,* edited by Arnold Rampersad, David Roessel, and Christa Fratantoro (New York: Knopf, 2015).

HURSTON, ZORA NEALE Author of the epochal novel *Their Eyes Were Watching God,* with its ageless opening line, "Ships at a distance have every man's wish on board." Born in Notsaluga, Alabama, in 1891, Hurston wanted to write great literature about African American lives, and she succeeded. Came to Hollywood in 1941 as a story consultant for Paramount. Lived in West Adams, almost across the street from the William Andrews Clark mansion, later home to some of the UCLA Library's rarest collections. Quoted from *Wrapped in Rainbows: The Life of Zora Neale Hurston,* by Valerie Boyd (New York: Scribners, 2003).

HUSTON, JOHN Great adapter and director of literature from *The Maltese Falcon* through *The Dead.*

HUTTON, WILLIAM RICH Artist and surveyor. Quoted from *Glances at California, 1847–1853: Diaries and Letters of William Rich Hutton,* with a Brief Memoir and Notes by Willard O. Waters (San Marino, Calif.: Huntington Library Press, 1942).

HUXLEY, ALDOUS British author of *Brave New World, After Many a Summer Dies the Swan,* and *The Doors of Perception.* Relocated to Los Angeles originally for eye treatment and eventually for enlightenment, both chemical and not. Quoted from *Selected Letters of Aldous Huxley,* edited by James Sexton (Chicago: Ivan R. Dee, 2007).

IDLE, ERIC Writer, lyricist, performer, Python. Long resident in Southern California. Quoted from his *The Greedy Bastard Diary: A Comic Diary of America* (New York: HarperCollins, 2005).

IKEDA, TOMOKO Japanese American schoolgirl, internee. Quoted courtesy of the Japanese American National Museum (2000.378).

IMMEN, LORAINE Elocutionist and clubwoman. Visited California in the winter and spring of 1896. Quoted from *Letters of Travel in California* (Grand Rapids, Mich.: Privately published, 1896).

ISHERWOOD, CHRISTOPHER Author of *The Berlin Stories* and *A Single Man,* screenwriter, with Don Bachardy, of *Frankenstein: The True Story,* pioneering chronicler of gay life. Even a cursory reading of his work discloses a master stylist whose undeniable importance to gay literature, California literature, and the literature of pre–World War II Germany tends to obscure his contribution to literature, full stop. He caught this place as few have. Quoted from the three volumes of his *Diaries* (New York: Harper, 1996, 2010, 2012); and *The Animals: Love Letters Between Christopher Isherwood and Don Bachardy* (New York: Farrar, Straus & Giroux). All edited and introduced by Katherine Bucknell.

JACKSON, HELEN HUNT Author of *Ramona,* advocate for Native American rights. Quoted from *The Indian Reform Letters of Helen Hunt Jackson, 1879–1885,* edited by Valerie Sherer Mathes (Norman: University of Oklahoma Press, 1998).

JACKSON, WILLIAM HENRY Saddle tramp, later an influential Western photographer. Quoted from *The Diaries of William Henry*

Jackson, Frontier Photographer, edited by LeRoy R. Hafen and Ann W. Hafen (Cleveland: Arthur H. Clark, 1959).

James, Clive Critic, literary essayist, polymath. Here on a visit, filmed for broadcast. Quoted from *Flying Visits* (London: Jonathan Cape Ltd., 1984).

Jarrell, Randall Poet, critic, novelist. Lived here in the twenties with his paternal grandparents. Quoted from *Randall Jarrell's Letters: An Autobiographical and Literary Selection,* edited by Mary Jarrell (Boston: Houghton Mifflin, 1985).

Jeffers, Robinson "The great poet of the American West Coast," per California's poet laureate, Dana Gioia. Went to Occidental, where he wooed his beloved Una away from her husband, and cribbed the idea for his dramatic Tor House from writer-stonemason Charles Lummis's "El Alisal." Quoted from *Collected Letters of Robinson Jeffers, with Selected Letters of Una Jeffers,* edited by James Karman (Palo Alto, Calif.: Stanford University Press, 2009).

Jeffers, Una Kuster Wife of above; muse, mainstay. An Angelena until she and Jeffers fled scandal to Carmel. Quoted from *Collected Letters of Robinson Jeffers, with Selected Letters of Una Jeffers,* edited by James Karman (Palo Alto, Calif.: Stanford University Press, 2009).

Johnson, Nunnally Screenwriter-producer best known for *The Grapes of Wrath.* Quoted from *The Letters of Nunnally Johnson,* edited by Dorris Johnson and Ellen Leventhal (New York: Knopf, 1981).

Johnston, Alva Pulitzer-winning, Sacramento-born, New York–employed, California-posted journalist. Biographer of, among others, Samuel Goldwyn, Erle Stanley Gardner, and, more to the point, Edgar Rice Burroughs (q.v.). He numbered among the generations of East Coast correspondents who really *corresponded,* writing descriptive letters home to their readers (and editors), taking care not to sound as if they were having too good a time. Quoted in *Edgar Rice Burroughs: The Man Who Created Tarzan,* by Irwin Porges (Provo, Utah: Brigham Young University Press, 1975).

JONES, JAMES Author of *From Here to Eternity* and *The Thin Red Line.* Caught his breath here after finishing *Eternity.* Quoted from *To Reach Eternity: The Letters of James Jones,* edited by George Hendrick (New York: Random House, 1989).

JOYCE, JAMES Author of *Dubliners, Ulysses,* and *Finnegans Wake.* Never visited Los Angeles, but it's my book. Quoted from *Finnegans Wake* (New York: Viking Press, 1939).

KAPLAN, SAM HALL Urban planner, first ever architecture critic of the *Los Angeles Times.* Quoted from his *L.A. Follies: Design and Other Diversions in a Fractured Metropolis* (Malibu, Calif.: Cityscape Press, 1989).

KAZAN, ELIA Stage and film director of *On the Waterfront, East of Eden,* and *A Face in the Crowd.* Quoted from *The Selected Letters of Elia Kazan,* edited by Albert J. Devlin with Marlene J. Devlin (New York: Knopf, 2014).

KELLOGG, CAROLYN Book editor, *Los Angeles Times.* Kellogg works in a large for-profit company, the *Los Angeles Times,* and does a job not commonly thought to be all that creative, i.e., assigning and editing book coverage. But she finds young, raw writers and somehow turns them into cogent, graceful critics. Her matchmaking skills between reviewer and material are impeccable. The indicator species for literary culture, and quite possibly American daily journalism, is book coverage. Kellogg keeps it alive and lively. Quoted by gracious permission.

KEROUAC, JACK Author of *On the Road* and *The Dharma Bums.* Rode a northbound freight through town. Quoted from *Windblown World: The Journals of Jack Kerouac 1947–1954,* edited by Douglas Brinkley (New York: Viking, 2004).

KIP, WILLIAM INGRAHAM Yale-educated first bishop of California. Great-great-grandfather of the political financiers the Koch brothers. Quoted from his *The Early Days of My Episcopate* (New York: T. Whittaker, 1902).

KIRSCH, ROBERT Book critic, novelist. Patriarch of the Kirsch book-reviewing dynasty that includes son Jonathan and grandson Adam. He reviewed a book every morning in the *Los Angeles Times* for decades and, like his opposite number at the *San Francisco Chronicle,* Joseph Henry Jackson, read himself into an early grave. Quoted from his *Lives, Works & Transformations* (Santa Barbara, Calif.: Capra Press, 1978).

KNIGHT, ERIC This Yorkshire-born screen- (and brilliant letter-) writer of the 1930s, after almost losing his sanity doing thankless hackwork for the studios, walked away one day and built a farmhouse with his bare hands in what's now the San Fernando Valley. His equilibrium gradually restored, he started writing again and wound up turning out an unsung classic noir, *You Play the Black and the Red Comes Up,* and another novel that became one of the most beloved kids' movies of all time. Few realize that the Yorkshire-born title character was really based on Toots, the lovable best friend he found in Northridge. We know her better as Lassie. Knight also wrote acclaimed patriotic documentaries for Frank Capra before dying tragically in a World War II plane crash. Quoted from *Down and Out in Hollow-*

Weird: A Documentary in Letters of Eric Knight, by Geoff Gehman (Lanham, Md.: Scarecrow Press, 1985), and *Portrait of a Flying Yorkshireman: Letters from Eric Knight in the United States to Paul Rotha in England,* edited by Paul Rotha (London: Chapman & Hall, 1952).

L'Amour, Louis Beloved, prolific author, primarily of westerns, including the influential *Hondo,* and some early L.A. crime fiction. Lived and wrote here later in life, finally coming to rest at Forest Lawn. Quoted from *The Best of Rob Wagner's* Script, edited by Anthony Slide (Lanham, Md.: Scarecrow Press, 1985).

Lawrence, D. H. Groundbreakingly frank British novelist. Author of *Women in Love, Lady Chatterley's Lover, The Rainbow,* many others. Cruised through L.A. during his New Mexico years. Subject of Geoff Dyer's terrific reluctant biography, *Out of Sheer Rage.* Quoted by Carey McWilliams in "Tides West," the books column for *Westways,* the magazine of the Automobile Club of Southern California.

Lecouvreur, Frank Prussian immigrant, later a county clerk, surveyor, and businessman. Quoted from *From East Prussia to the Golden Gate,* translated by Julius C. Behnke (New York and Los Angeles: Angelina Book Concern, 1906).

Lennon, John Musician, poet, Beatle. A regular visitor for concerts, with and without the Beatles. Quoted from *John,* by Cynthia Lennon (New York: Crown/Archetype, 2010).

Leovy, Jill Author of *Ghettoside,* versatile *Los Angeles Times* journalist, especially about crime. Inaugurated the paper's acclaimed murder blog, memorializing each new homicide victim in the city. Diary entry originally published in *Slate,* later included in *The Slate Diaries,* edited by Jodi Kantor, Cyrus Krohn, and Judith

Shulevitz and with an introduction by Michael Kinsley (New York: Perseus Book Group, 2000). Copyright 2000 by Michael Kinsley. Reprinted by permission of PublicAffairs, a member of the Perseus Book Group.

Lewis, Sinclair First American to win the Nobel Prize for Literature. Author of *Babbitt, Main Street, Elmer Gantry, Dodsworth.* Debated publicly in L.A. whether fascism could happen here, at the Philharmonic Auditorium for Rabbi Herman Lissauer's sadly unremembered Modern Forum. Quoted in *The War Between the State,* by Jon Winokur (Seattle: Sasquatch Books, 2004).

Lindsay, Vachel Major American poet, also author of *The Art of the Moving Picture.* Wrote his most famous poem, "General William Booth Enters into Heaven," in Los Angeles. Quoted from *Letters of Vachel Lindsay* (New York: Lenox Hill Publishing, 1979).

Liveright, Horace Publisher and co-founder of the Modern Library. Tried to reinvent himself in L.A. late in life, alas without success. Quoted from *Firebrand: The Life of Horace Liveright,* by Tom Dardis (New York: Random House, 1995).

London, Jack Author of *The Call of the Wild, Martin Eden,* and *The People of the Abyss.* Used to come down to watch prizefights and duck creditors. Quoted from *The Letters of Jack London: 1913–1916,* edited by Earle Labor, Robert C. Leitz, and Milo Shepherd (Palo Alto, Calif.: Stanford University Press, 1988).

Lopez, Steve Newspaper columnist, novelist. Maybe Northern Californians get L.A. better than the natives do. First there was Joan Didion, blowing south out of Sacramento like some neurasthenic tule fog, writing the books that color how we see Los Angeles even today. Now Angelenos have Steve Lopez, a bread-truck-driver's son from Pittsburg, California, whose city-side column may be the best thing to appear in the *Los Angeles Times* since Nixon's hometown op-ed page demanded his impeachment. Quoted from "A Bright Future Bought with Hard Work and Lots of Tacos," *Los Angeles Times,* May 30, 2003.

LOVE, MIKE Beach Boy; songwriting partner and cousin of Brian Wilson. Lyric from "The Warmth of the Sun," published by Irving Music, affiliated with BMI.

LOWENSTEIN, MANNIE Shopkeeper. Quoted from *Mannie's Crowd: Emanuel Lowenstein, Colorful Character of Old Los Angeles, and a Brief Diary of the Trip to Arizona and Life in Tucson of the Early 1880s,* by Norton B. Stern (Cleveland: Arthur H. Clark, 1970).

LOWRY, MALCOLM Author of *Under the Volcano.* Met his wife here. Worked on *Under the Volcano* at the Normandie Hotel—later a cannabis hostel, now a boutique inn with the storied Cassell's Hamburgers grilling again on the ground floor. Quoted from *Selected Letters of Malcolm Lowry,* edited by Harvey Breit and Margerie Bonner Lowry (Philadelphia: Lippincott, 1965).

LUBITSCH, ERNST Director of *Ninotchka* and other sophisticated comic romances. Quoted from *The Best of Rob Wagner's* Script, edited by Anthony Slide (Lanham, Md.: Scarecrow Press, 1985).

LUMMIS, CHARLES Newspaperman, city librarian, archaeologist, and founder of the Southwest Museum. Also a booster, self-promoter, windbag, mountebank, and rapscallion. Diaries in the Charles Fletcher Lummis Papers, 1850–1929. Braun Research Library Collection, Autry Museum of the American West; MS.1.

MACDONALD, ROSS Author of *The Chill,* the surprisingly contemporary *Black Money,* and other novels featuring detective Lew Archer. Quoted from *Meanwhile There Are Letters: The Correspon-*

dence of Eudora Welty and Ross Macdonald, edited by Suzanne Marrs and Tom Nolan (New York: Arcade, 2015).

Magaña, Benedicta M. Eastside Angelena. Personal letter to her brother.

Magon, Ricardo Flores Mexican revolutionary and journalist, briefly resident in Edendale. Lived near Red Hill in Echo Park while on the lam from the Mexican government. Did time as a guest of the local constabulary. Quoted from *Dreams of Freedom: A Ricardo Flores Magon Reader,* edited by Chaz Bufe and Mitchell Cowen Verter (Oakland, Calif.: AK Press, 2005).

Mailer, Norman Novelist, journalist, filmmaker, author of *The Naked and the Dead* and *The Armies of the Night*—and a Palm Springs–set Hollywood novel, *The Deer Park.* Covered the 1960 Democratic Convention at the Sports Arena when JFK won the nomination. Returned on book tours, granting voluble interviews to journalists including this one. Quoted from *Selected Letters of Norman Mailer,* edited by J. Michael Lennon (New York: Random House, 2014).

Mann, Thomas Nobel Prize–winning German author of *The Magic Mountain, Buddenbrooks,* and *Doktor Faustus.* Fled Hitler for Pacific Palisades, where the modernist home he built now houses a cultural center dedicated to democracy. Quoted from *Letters of Thomas Mann, 1889–1955,* selected and translated by Richard and Clara Winston (New York: Knopf, 1971).

Marchesseault, Damien Mayor of Los Angeles. Wrote the note quoted here and then fatally shot himself in City Hall. *Los Angeles Semi-Weekly News,* January 21, 1868.

Marquis, Don Creator of the newspaper feature "archy and mehitabel." Came to L.A. to write scripts. Hated it. Went home.

Quoted from *Selected Letters of Don Marquis,* edited by William McCollum, Jr. (Stafford, Va.: Northwoods Press, 1982).

MARX, GROUCHO Comedian and star, with his brothers, of, among others, *Animal Crackers, Horsefeathers,* and the immortal *Duck Soup.* Quoted from *The Groucho Letters* (New York: Simon & Schuster, 1987).

MCCARTHY, BRANDON Ex-Dodger pitcher, aphorist, and heir to Jim Bouton (q.v.). From his delightful Twitter feed (https://twitter.com/bmccarthy32/status/877412303209021440?lang=en).

MCCOY, ESTHER Architecture critic, author of the indispensable *Five California Architects.* In Reyner Banham's words, "No one can write about architecture in California without acknowledging her as the mother of us all." Quoted from *Piecing Together Los Angeles: An Esther McCoy Reader,* edited and with an essay by Susan Morgan (Valencia, Calif.: East of Borneo Books, 2012).

MCGRAMA, G. Diarist during what then-Angeleno Woody Guthrie's great ballad memorialized as L.A.'s "New Year's Flood" of 1934. Quoted at http://oldmcgramasmohairfarm.blogspot.com/2014/01/memory-is-elusive-capture-it-grandmas.html.

MCKINLEY, WILLIAM President of the United States, assassinated in 1901, succeeded by Theodore Roosevelt (q.v.). Passed through L.A. four months before the anarchist Leon Czolgosz murdered him and elevated Theodore Roosevelt to the presidency. Quoted from the *San Francisco Chronicle,* May 9, 1901.

MCLUHAN, MARSHALL Public intellectual, professor, philosopher futurist. Courted his future wife, Corinne, while living in Pasadena and researching the Elizabethan pamphleteer Thomas Nashe at the Huntington Library. Quoted from *Letters of Mar-*

shall McLuhan, edited by Matie Molinaro, Corinne McLuhan, and William Toye (New York: Oxford University Press, 1987).

McPherson, Sister Aimee Semple Evangelist, broadcaster, faith healer. For years perhaps the most famous Angeleno this side of Mickey Mouse. Tarnished by her disappearance and subsequent discovery in a beachfront love nest. Once, no out-of-towner could call a trip here complete without a visit to her Angelus Temple, across the street from Echo Park. Buried at Forest Lawn, supposedly with a telephone for communication from the beyond. Quoted from *This Is That: Personal Experiences, Sermons and Writings* (Los Angeles: McPherson/Bridal Call, 1921).

McWilliams, Carey Historian, journalist, activist, author of *Southern California: An Island on the Land* and *California: The Great Exception.* McWilliams reported and editorialized on California's most important battles for social justice of the last century. He also helped organize committees that won several of them. Other fights, such as the one to get the government to admit its mistake in interning Japanese Americans during World War II, were won only after his death. A contagiously jovial writer, McWilliams found the stupidity of politicians not only unconscionable but risible. His merry takeouts on California's water wars and ecology have left writers as varied as Robert Towne and Mike Davis in his debt. Diaries preserved in the UCLA Library Special Collections, Charles E. Young Research Library, and published here by gracious permission of his scholar granddaughter.

Mencken, H. L. Newspaperman and author of a series of gleeful ragbags titled *Prejudices,* the much-revised landmark *The American Language,* even a youthful translation of Ibsen. Mencken's biliously quotable prose is the culmination of all the Twain and Wilde that Mencken ingested from childhood—Twain for sand, Wilde for silk—and the disappointment he must have felt when nobody else measured up. He said such wonderful things as "A horse-laugh is worth ten thousand syllogisms. It is not only more effective; it is also vastly more intelligent." Enjoyed his brief reporting visit here like a mountain lion enjoys a mule deer. Quoted from *Mencken and Sara: A Life in Letters: The Private Correspondence of H. L. Mencken and Sara Haardt,* edited by Marion Elizabeth Rodgers (New York: McGraw-Hill, 1987).

MERRITT, RUTH WOLFFE Douglas Aircraft worker here in World War II. Quotation published by gracious permission of her granddaughter-in-law.

MILLER, HENRY Author of *Tropic of Cancer, The Cosmological Eye,* and *The Air-Conditioned Nightmare.* Relocated from the cliffs of Big Sur to the bluffs of Pacific Palisades to spend his last years here. Quoted from *Letters by Henry Miller to Hoki Tokuda Miller,* edited by Joyce Howard (New York: Freundlich Books, 1986).

MILLIKAN, ROBERT Caltech president, Nobel Laureate for measuring the charge of an electron, and eventual anticommunist informer for the FBI. Quoted from "The Creation of LA's 'Most Recognizable and Beloved' Building," by Hadley Meares, posted at https://la.curbed.com/2014/12/17/10011026/the-creation-of-las-most-recognizable-and-beloved-building-1 (2014).

MINGUS, CHARLES Pathbreaking black–Chinese–German–Native American jazz composer and musician. Raised in Watts playing classical cello, then found the double bass and jazz. Quoted from his memoir *Beneath the Underdog: His World as Composed by Mingus* (New York: Knopf, 1971).

MIX, TOM Movie cowboy, valiant hero to a generation of American boys. Quoted from *The Best of Rob Wagner's* Script, edited by Anthony Slide (Lanham, Md.: Scarecrow Press, 1985).

MONROE, MARILYN Actress and star of *Some Like It Hot* and *The Misfits.* Quoted from *Marilyn Monroe Day by Day,* by Carl Rollyson (Lanham, Md.: Rowman & Littlefield, 2014).

MOORE, ERNEST CARROLL Co-founder of UCLA. Quoted from *UCLA: The First Century,* by Marina Dundjerski (Los Angeles: Third Millennium Publishing, 2011).

MORA, BISHOP FRANCIS Bishop of Los Angeles. Personal letter at http://www.jmaw.org/bernard-cohn-jewish-la/.

MOTLEY, WILLARD F. African American author of the social-protest novel *Knock on Any Door,* adapted into the Humphrey Bogart film. Later moved to Mexico. Nephew of the artist Archibald Motley. Didn't stay long, but plenty of journalists have stayed longer and seen less. Quoted from "Small Town Los Angeles," *Commonweal* (June 30, 1939).

MUIR, JOHN Writer, naturalist. There had been California writers before Muir, just as there had been American writers before Emerson. But not until Muir met Emerson on a Sierra mountaintop did he find his own voice. Muir's first published essay, "Yosemite Glaciers," appeared just seven months after they met. Returned often to visit family and to hike and write about the San Gabriel Mountains, most memorably in "The Bee-Pastures," chapter 16 of *The Mountains of California.* Quoted from *John Muir in Southern California,* by Elizabeth Pomeroy (Pasadena, Calif.: The Castle Press, 1999).

NABOKOV, VLADIMIR Russian-born author of *Lolita, Pnin,* and *Pale Fire.* Nabokov's prose is beautiful—and often uproarious—in ways that no native English speaker would think to write. He knew English from lessons and books, but his arrival in the United States in 1940 may have marked his first real opportunity to hear English spoken badly. The evidence suggests that he found the sound intoxicating. Always oblique yet never obscure, Nabokov sounds like English on the morning of its birth, with every word equally available to him, and all ruts of habit gone suddenly smooth. In 1960, he took a rented villa at 2088 Mandeville Canyon in Los Angeles to work on a screenplay of *Lolita* for the young director Stanley Kubrick. Not much of Nabokov's work remains in the finished film, but he liked the unorthodox screenplay he wrote enough to publish it later. Graciously, he also spoke well of Kubrick's version, but retained sole screen credit for himself. According to biographer Brian Boyd, "He and Vera would have been ready to settle permanently in 'charming semitropical' California if their son had not been singing in Milan." In 1963, the Academy of Motion Picture Arts and Sciences nominated Vladimir Nabokov in the Best Adapted Screenplay category. There's no indication that he returned to Los Angeles for the Oscar ceremony, alas. Nabokov lost to Horton Foote for *To Kill a Mockingbird.* Quoted from *Dear Bunny, Dear Volodya: The Nabokov-Wilson Letters, 1940–1971,* edited, annotated, and with an introductory essay by Simon Karlinsky (New York: Harper & Row, 1979).

NASH, OGDEN Poet and wit. Came for the movies, missed his family too much to stay long. Quoted from *Loving Letters of Ogden Nash,* edited by Linell Nash Smith (Boston: Little, Brown, 1990).

NIN, ANAÏS Frenchwoman of letters, author of *Delta of Venus.* Led parallel lives with her husband in New York and her longtime paramour in Sierra Madre. Quoted from *The Diaries of Anaïs Nin,* vols. 6, 7, edited by Gunther Stuhlmann (New York: Harcourt Brace Jovanovich, 1976, 1980).

NISHIDA, J. W. Jailed Communist bookseller. Quoted from *Gentle Rebel: Letters of Eugene V. Debs,* edited by J. Robert Constantine (Champaign: University of Illinois Press, 1995).

ODETS, CLIFFORD Pioneering playwright and screenwriter of American social drama. Author of plays including *Waiting for Lefty, Awake and Sing!, Golden Boy,* and several films, among them *Sweet Smell of Success* and *The Big Knife,* from his play about compromise in Hollywood. In 1940 he kept his only journal, which he himself called "the daily diary, often naïve, sometimes crude, occasionally pompous, prejudiced, mannered, unfair, even conceited and arrogant. Its pages cover almost a full year in the personal life of a 'successful' writer living in a very 'successful' country." He died on August 14, 1963, on the same day and in the same hospital where I was born. Quoted from *The Time Is Ripe: The 1940 Journal of Clifford Odets,* with an introduction by his son, Walt Whitman Odets (New York: Grove Press, 1988).

OJEDA, EVELYN Gold medalist in the 1932 Olympic Games. Quoted in Andrew Bell, "Female Gold Medalist from 1932 Olympics Turns 100," *USA Today.*

O'MELVENY, HENRY Lawyer, city father, founder of O'Melveny & Myers. Quoted from *History of the Law Firm of O'Melveny & Myers,* by William W. Clary (Los Angeles: Privately printed, 1966).

PALEY, AARON As much as anybody, Paley is the urbanist most responsible for L.A.'s recent renaissance. Co-creator of CicLAvia, the quarterly Sunday happening during which all automobile traffic is banished from some of this city's most traffic-choked boulevards. Every three months—monthly, if Paley ever gets his way—Angelenos now reclaim their streets on foot, on bicycles, on rickshaws, you name it. The result has fairly transformed the way L.A. thinks of itself. Quoted by gracious permission.

PALIN, MICHAEL Author, actor, Python, screenwriter of *A Fish Called Wanda.* Has slithered into Los Angeles whenever his career obliged him, including for the Pythons' triumphant stand at the Hollywood Bowl. Quoted from his *Diaries, 1969–1979: The Python Years* (New York: Thomas Dunne Books, 2007).

PARKER, DOROTHY Witty, tragicomic writer of magazine feuilletons, book reviews, poems, and short stories including "Big Blonde." Lived here off and on writing scripts, including her Oscar-nominated, delightful adaptation, with S. J. Perelman, of *Around the World in 80 Days*. Quoted from *You Might as Well Live: The Life and Times of Dorothy Parker,* by John Keats (New York: Simon & Schuster, 1970).

PARTCH, HARRY Avant-garde composer. Lived here in the twenties and thirties. Dropped out of USC to compose. Ushering for the Philharmonic helped keep body and soul together. Designer of irreproducible musical instruments. Alumnus of the WPA's Federal Writers Project in California. Quoted from *Bitter Music: Collected Journals, Essays, Introductions, and Librettos,* edited by Thomas McGeary (Champaign: University of Illinois Press, 2000).

PATTON, GEORGE Attorney, father of General George S. Patton. Descended from pioneer Don Benito Wilson. Quoted from *General Patton: A Soldier's Life,* by Stanley P. Hirshson (New York: HarperCollins, 2002).

PEARS, PETER Opera singer, partner of the composer Benjamin Britten. Quoted from *The Travel Diaries of Peter Pears, 1936–1978,* edited by Philip Reed (London: Boydell & Brewer, 1999).

PEGLER, WESTBROOK Newspaper columnist. Stopped here to file the once-obligatory hatchet job. Quoted from his column "Fair Enough," *The Washington Post,* etc., King Features Syndicate, 1939.

PERCIVAL, OLIVE Writer, regional historian, and botanist. Olive Percival Papers (Collection 119), UCLA Library Special Collections, Charles E. Young Research Library.

Perelman, S. J. Dyspeptic writer, satirist, screenwriter. He and Nathanael West married sisters and lived here in the thirties. Visited L.A. periodically to write scripts, including his Oscar-nominated adaptation with Dorothy Parker of *Around the World in 80 Days.* Returned later in life as writer-in-residence in sadly knish-less Santa Barbara. Quoted from *Don't Tread on Me: The Selected Letters of S. J. Perelman,* edited by Prudence Crowther (New York: Viking, 1986).

Perkoff, Stuart Poet, beatnik. Stuart Z. Perkoff Papers (Collection 1573), UCLA Library Special Collections, Charles E. Young Research Library.

Phillips, D. L. Diarist who brought his consumptive son to California. Quoted from his *Letters from California* (Springfield: The Illinois State Journal, 1877).

Pickering, Edward Charles American astronomer. Published as "Edward Charles Pickering's Diary of a Trip to Pasadena to Attend a Meeting of Solar Union, August 1910," edited by Howard Plotkin, *Southern California Quarterly* (Spring 1978).

Plath, Sylvia American poet (*Ariel*) and novelist (*The Bell Jar*). If only Sylvia Plath could have married Leonard Woolf, and Virginia Woolf could have married Ted Hughes, maybe everybody would have lived happily ever after. Plath visited California on a road trip to see her aunt in Pasadena, whose bountiful garden made a strong impression—though not as strong as an ornery bear she met in Yosemite. Quoted from *Letters Home: Correspondence 1950–1963,* edited by Aurelia Schober Plath (New York: Harper & Row, 1975).

Powell, Anthony British novelist, author of the towering "Dance to the Music of Time" dodecalogy. Summoned from England to L.A. as a consultant on *A Yank at Oxford.* Quoted from *To Keep the Ball Rolling: The Memoirs of Anthony Powell* (New York: Penguin, 1984).

POWELL, DAWN Great "lost" writer of the mid-twentieth century, championed into rediscovery largely by Gore Vidal. Happy to visit here, but her heart was in New York. Quoted from *The Diaries of Dawn Powell,* edited with an introduction by Tim Page (South Royalton, Vt.: Steerforth Press, 1995).

PRATT, ORVILLE C. Jurist, traveler. Quoted from *The Journal of Orville C. Pratt, 1848* (Utah: Hafen & Hafen, 1954).

PYNCHON, THOMAS RUGGLES, JR. American writer, born May 8, 1937, in Glen Cove, Long Island. Between the 1960s and the 1980s, spent some time in California, where three of his novels are set. Others range all over the globe and throughout history, often in the same book. Many pit a plucky heroine or poor, priapic, paranoid schnook against some bureaucratic, merciless conspiracy. The voice in his occasional nonfiction is postdoctoral yet cheerfully sophomoric, sad yet undespairing, as expressive in its alternation of long notes with short as an SOS. It's an instrument tuned and retuned in more than half a century of occasional essays, reviews, and liner notes—forming one of the great uncollected anthologies in American letters. In fiction or nonfiction, Pynchon's underlying verbal music stays ever recognizable, unique as a great reed player's embouchure. He remains the archpoet of death from above, comedy from below, and sex from all sides, ringing endless fresh variations on the same two questions: What happened to the country we wanted? And can its original promise ever be redeemed? No one rivals Pynchon's range of language, his elasticity of syntax, his signature mix of dirty jokes, dread and shining decency. (Letter quoted from the Stephen Michael Tomaske Collection of Thomas Pynchon, Huntington Library, San Marino, Calif., by gracious permission.)

Ramirez, Francisco P. Pioneering prodigy of bilingual Los Angeles journalism, lovingly resurrected in *A Clamor for Equality: Emergence and Exile of Californio Activist Francisco P. Ramirez,* by Paul Bryan Gray (Lubbock: Texas Tech University Press, 2012). Translations by Gray and me.

Reagan, Ronald President, actor. Quoted from *The Reagan Diaries,* edited by Douglas Brinkley (New York: HarperCollins, 2007).

Reid, Hugo Early Scotch settler, author in the *Los Angeles Star* of the "Indian Letters," calling attention to wretched conditions for Native Americans in post-statehood L.A. Quoted from the *Los Angeles Star,* 1852.

Renoir, Jean Screenwriter-director of *The Rules of the Game* and *Grand Illusion.* Directed *Swamp Water* and *The Southerner* for Hollywood. Unfailingly amused by his sojourn here. Died in Beverly Hills. Quoted from his *Letters,* edited by Lorraine LeBianco and David Thompson (London: Faber & Faber, 1994).

Rexroth, Kenneth San Francisco–based poet, critic, translator, and radio commentator. Occasionally came down from San Francisco to L.A. for public appearances and broadcasts, and to disparage the restaurants. Later taught in Santa Barbara, where he died of a coronary so massive that his heart monitor blew a fuse. Published by permission of the Kenneth Rexroth Trust. With thanks to the Bureau of Public Secrets, Berkeley, 2017.

Reynolds, Ryan Actor, known for *Buried* and *Deadpool,* among others. Witty tweeter (https://twitter.com/vancityreynolds/status/817799908937736192?lang=en).

Reznikoff, Charles Poet. Worked as a script reader. *Selected Letters of Charles Reznikoff, 1917–1976,* edited by Milton Hindus (Santa Rosa, Calif.: Black Sparrow Press, 1997).

RICE, HARVEY Ohio newspaper publisher, father-in-law of Orange County patriarch James Irvine, Sr. Stayed a week at his son-in-law's Rancho San Joaquin. Quoted from his *Letters from the Pacific Slope* (New York: Appleton, 1870).

RICHARDSON, ROBERT A *Times* man. Shared a Pulitzer Prize for coverage of the Watts riots while still the classified advertising messenger, venturing where police officers, firefighters, and staff reporters feared to tread. That was his last night in the ad department. Quoted from "'Get Whitey,' Scream Blood-Hungry Mobs," the *Los Angeles Times,* August 14 and 15, 1965.

RIVERS, JOAN Self-deprecating, insult-reliant, pioneering comedian. Quoted from her *Diary of a Mad Diva* (New York: Berkley, 2014).

ROCH, ROGERIO Dispossessed Californio. Quoted from *The Condition of Affairs in Indian Territory and California: A Report,* by Charles Cornelius Painter (Philadelphia: Indian Rights Association, 1888).

RODDENBERRY, GENE Beloved creator of *Star Trek,* former driver for LAPD chief William Parker. "Star Trek" Collection, UCLA Library Special Collections, Charles E. Young Research Library.

RODERICK, KEVIN Newspaperman, founding editor of LAObserved.com. Quoted by gracious permission.

RODRIGUEZ, JOSÉ Guatemalan American classical music impresario. Went to Manual Arts High School in L.A. Studied music. Found a mentor in the left-wing editor Rob Wagner, the editor of a magazine in the 1920s and 1930s called *Script,* which some East-Coast-centric people called a West Coast version of *The New Yorker.* Rodriguez wrote mostly about music and wound up programming for both the Hollywood Bowl and the L.A. Philharmonic. He also became a host and music director for local radio stations, especially KFI, driven by a democratic, leveling, truly Angeleno vision for the potential of radio. Commissioned a striking Neutra house that still stands in Glendale. Quoted from *The Best of Rob Wagner's* Script, edited by Anthony Slide (Lanham, Md.: Scarecrow Press, 1985).

ROGERS, HARRISON Member of the Jedediah Smith expedition through California. Quoted from *The Ashley-Smith Explorations and Discovery of a Central Route to the Pacific 1822–1829,* edited by Harrison Clifford Dale (Cleveland: Arthur H. Clark, 1918).

ROGERS, WILL Humorist, entertainer, and newspaper columnist. Lovingly published at willrogers.com/writings.

ROOSEVELT, ELEANOR First Lady of the United States, shoulder to shoulder with her husband, Franklin, in the White House from 1933 to 1945. Peace advocate and social activist. Visited Los Angeles several times on goodwill tours to benefit the less fortunate. Champion of the New Deal, which paved roads and built bridges that Angelenos still drive every day. The Eleanor Roosevelt First Street Bridge, anybody? "My Day," *The Eleanor Roosevelt Papers Digital Edition* (2017), accessed Oct. 29, 2017 (https://www2.gwu.edu/~erpapers/myday/displaydoc.cfm?_y=1946&_f=md000295).

ROOSEVELT, THEODORE President of the United States and uncle of the above. The fatal shooting of President William McKinley on September 6, 1901, may well be the only political assassination in history that actually worked out for the best. In McKinley's place, we got the indefatigable Teddy Roosevelt. It's startling to realize just how many strains in contemporary American political thought trace their origins, under different names, to Roosevelt. His unprecedented efforts to conserve the country's natural resources, inspired by his naturalist friends John Muir (q.v.) and John Burroughs, we now recognize as federal environmentalism in embryo. His trustbusting of Big Oil, Big Sugar, and Big Coal we wouldn't hesitate to call anti-corporatism today. And Roosevelt's overall progressive agenda looks uncannily like what people used to call modern liberalism, until the stigma attached to that word now has us calling it progressivism all over again. Amid all the nostalgia for Roosevelt the statesman—coupled with some revulsion against Roosevelt the imperialist—it's easy to overlook Roosevelt the writer. But TR, as his hardy band of acolytes generally call him, worked at writing as he did at so much else in his life: prodigiously, brilliantly, tirelessly, and probably more than was good for him. Quoted from *A Compilation of the Messages and Speeches of Theodore Roosevelt,* vol. 1, edited by Albert Henry Lewis (New York and Washington: Bureau of National Literature and Art, 1906).

Ruess, Everett Free-spirited young man who left L.A. and wandered into the California wilderness, never to be seen again. Quoted from *Everett Ruess: A Vagabond for Beauty,* by W. L. Rusho (Salt Lake City: Gibbs Smith, 1983).

Ruiz de Rodriguez, Doña Bernarda Uncredited contributor and compromise broker for the Treaty of Cahuenga, which ended the Mexican-American War. Quoted in "In a State of Peace and Tranquility," by Hadley Meares, https://www.kcet.org/history-society/in-a-state-of-peace-and-tranquility-campo-de-cahuenga-and-the-birth-of-american (accessed May 28, 2018).

Russell, Bertrand British philosopher, pacifist, anti-nuclear campaigner. Taught at UCLA for a term. Like most professors, left few traces of his sojourn. Someday someone will compile a roster of all the distinguished visiting faculty to grace Southern California campuses over the years, and what they said and did here. The list isn't short. The talent is phenomenal. Quoted from *The Selected Letters of Bertrand Russell, Volume 2: The Public Years, 1914–1970,* edited by Nicholas Griffin (New York: Routledge, 2001).

SAITO, SANDIE Japanese American schoolgirl, internee. Quoted at http://ddr.densho.org/ddr-janm-1-10/.

SALVATOR, LUDWIG Archduke of Austria, son of the Duke of Tuscany. Visited Los Angeles in the winter of 1876, not long after the city was linked directly by rail to the East. While most of the ballyhooers in town were falling all over themselves comparing L.A. to Italy, an actual Italian princeling visited L.A. and saw that it was good. Quoted from his *Los Angeles in the Sunny Seventies: A Flower from the Golden Land,* translated by Marguerite Eyer Wilbur (Los Angeles: Bruce McCallister and Jake Zeitlin, 1929).

SANDBURG, CARL American poet, Lincoln biographer, pioneering film critic. Sandburg went to Hollywood in 1960 for a year and a half to work on the script for *The Greatest Story Ever Told,* which fell well short of becoming the greatest movie ever made, but paid perhaps the best-loved poet in America $125,000. Quoted from *The Letters of Carl Sandburg,* edited by Herbert Mitgang (New York: Harcourt Brace, 1968).

SANDERS, GEORGE Urbane, insinuating British actor, familiar from *Rebecca, All About Eve,* and scores more. Quoted from his *Memoirs of a Professional Cad* (New York: Putnam, 1960).

SANDERS, SUE A. Traveler, correspondent. Quoted from her *Journey to, on and from the "Golden Shore"* (Delavan, Ill.: Times Printing Office, 1887).

Saroyan, William Armenian American writer, son of Armenian immigrants. In his twenties, he romanticized a deprived childhood into the bestselling short-story collections *The Daring Young Man on the Flying Trapeze* and *My Name Is Aram.* Within a few years, he added a similarly beloved semiautobiographical novel, *The Human Comedy,* and, in 1939, a play set in a San Francisco waterfront saloon: *The Time of Your Life,* which won the Pulitzer Prize. There's a little bit of William Saroyan in every fine writer, but aggressive therapy can usually keep it in remission. Where most writers differ from Saroyan is that they also have at least some vestigial sense of proportion, or, failing that, a renewable lithium prescription. Sadly, the talented, versatile Saroyan had neither. Quoted from *The Best of Rob Wagner's* Script, edited by Anthony Slide (Lanham, Md.: Scarecrow Press, 1985).

Sayle, Alexei British stand-up comedian, actor, writer. Parachuted in to perform a less-painful-than-usual version of the obligatory Hollywood diary for *The Guardian.* Published as "Los Angeles Diary," *The Guardian,* 1991.

Schallert, Edwin *L.A. Times* critic, father of the beloved character actor William, grandfather of the educator-writer Brendan. Quoted from the *Los Angeles Times.*

Scheyer, Galka Refugee, educator, pioneering art dealer for the European painters, including the Blue Four group—Wassily Kandinsky, Lyonel Feininger, Paul Klee, and Alexej von Jawlensky. Client of architect Richard Neutra. Quoted from *Galka E. Scheyer and the Blue Four: Correspondence 1924–1945,* edited by Isabel Wünsche (Salenstein, Switzerland: Benteli Verlags, 2006).

Schickel, Erika Gifted essayist, author of *You're Not the Boss of Me: Adventures of a Modern Mom* (New York: Kensington, 2001). Quoted from LAObserved.com, 2012.

Schindler, Rudolf Architect of landmark L.A. buildings including his namesake house on Kings Road. Quoted from *Vienna to Los Angeles: Two Journeys: Letters Between R. M. Schindler and Richard Neutra + Letters of Louis Sullivan to R. M. Schindler,* by Esther McCoy (Santa Monica, Calif.: Arts + Architecture Press, 1978).

Schoenberg, Arnold Modernist "serial music" composer of, among others, *Moses und Aron* and *Verklärte Nacht.* Later a fairly acclimated refugee here, like his occasional tennis partner Stravinsky. When they were on the outs, the Brentwood Country Mart wasn't big enough for both of them. Schoenberg taught at UCLA, where the music building is, at least for now, still named after him. Quoted from *Schoenberg Remembered: Diaries and Recollections,* by Dika Newlin (New York: Pendragon, 1980).

Seaborg, Glenn T. Nobel Prize–winning physicist, co-discoverer of plutonium. Grew up in Southern California. "Glenn Theodore Seaborg Diaries, 1927–1946," Box 951575, UCLA Library Special Collections, Charles E. Young Research Library.

Selznick, David O. Producer. *Gone with the Wind* had sixteen co-writers and several directors, but not a single co-producer. His memos are marvels of perspicacity and megalomania. Quoted from *Memo from David O. Selznick,* edited by Rudy Behlmer and Roger Ebert (New York: Grove Press, 1972).

Serling, Rod Television writer, producer, playwright. Wrote landmark teleplays for live television in New York, decried its move west, then followed it and created *The Twilight Zone,* the first television series that completely realized the medium's potential. His writings are published by the Rod Serling Memorial Foundation at https://www.rodserling.com/letter032064.htm.

Shellhorn, Ruth A celebrated landscape architect whose projects included, frustratingly for her, Disneyland. "Ruth Patricia Shellhorn Papers, 1909–2006," UCLA Library Special Collections, Charles E. Young Research Library.

Shippey, Lee Columnist. Quoted from "The Lee Side o' L.A.," in the *Los Angeles Times.*

Silliman, Benjamin Yale-based scientist, first to distill petroleum. Quoted in *What They Say About the Angels* (Pasadena, Calif.: Val Trefz Press, 1942).

Sirhan Sirhan Assassin of Robert F. Kennedy. At the time, a student at Pasadena City College. The line appears in his published notebooks, including in *RFK Must Die* by Robert Blair Kaiser (Woodstock and New York, N.Y.: Overlook Press, 2008).

Slonimsky, Nicolas Longtime editor of *Baker's Dictionary of Musicians.* Lived to be 101, updating his invaluable compendium right to the end. Quoted from *Dear Dorothy: Letters from Nicolas Slonimsky to Dorothy Adlow,* edited by Electra Slonimsky Rourke (Rochester, N.Y.: University of Rochester Press, 2012).

Smith, Jack *Los Angeles Times* columnist, author of *God and Mr. Gomez* and *Spend All Your Kisses, Mr. Smith.* His longtime good-natured rival Herb Caen was the Jack Smith of San Francisco. Originally published in the *Los Angeles Times.*

Smith, Jedediah Explorer. A cartographer of the West. Furrier, too. Finally killed by Native Americans. Quoted from *The Travels of Jedediah Smith: A Documentary Outline. Including the Journal of the Great American Pathfinder,* edited by Maurice S. Sullivan (Santa Ana, Calif.: Fine Arts Press, 1934).

Smith, Joseph B. Record executive. Handled the Grateful Dead. Briefly. Published at lettersofnote.com, edited by Shaun

Usher, http://www.lettersofnote.com/2011/02/grateful-dead-has-many-problems.html.

SONTAG, SUSAN Critic, essayist, novelist, author of *Against Interpretation, Illness as Metaphor,* and *The Volcano Lover.* Consummate New Yorker, but also the sweetheart of North Hollywood High. "Papers of Susan Sontag," UCLA Library Special Collections, Charles E. Young Research Library.

SPALDING, WILLIAM ANDREW Los Angeles newspaperman. Quoted from *William Andrew Spalding: Los Angeles Newspaperman,* edited by Robert V. Hine (San Marino, Calif.: The Huntington Library Press, 1961).

SPENDER, STEPHEN British poet, contemporary of Christopher Isherwood and W. H. Auden. Stopped for tea with the Hollywood Raj, including Isherwood. Quoted from his *Journals 1939–1983,* edited by John Goldsmith (London: Faber and Faber, 1985).

STANDAGE, HENRY Member of the Mormon Battalion in the Mexican-American War. Quoted from *The March of the Mormon Battalion from Council Bluffs to California Taken from the Journal of Henry Standage,* by Frank Alfred Golder with Thomas A. Bailey and J. Lyman Smith (New York: The Century Co., 1928).

STEELE, THE REV. JOHN Quoted from *Echoes of the Past in California: In Camp and Cabin* (Chicago: The Lakeside Press, 1928).

STEIN, BEN Columnist, actor, game show host. Quoted from his *Hollywood Days, Hollywood Nights: The Diary of a Mad Screen Writer* (New York: Bantam Books, 1988).

STEINBECK, JOHN Nobel Prize–winning author of *The Grapes of Wrath* and other novels. Lived for a time in a house uphill from the present-day Eagle Rock Plaza mall. Quoted from *Steinbeck: A Life in Letters,* edited by Elaine Steinbeck and Robert Wallsten (New York: Viking Press, 1975).

STEINMAN, LOUISE Author of three books, including *The Souvenir: A Daughter Discovers Her Father's War,* dancer, founding curator of the Library Foundation of Los Angeles's long-running ALOUD literary series. Quoted by gracious permission.

STENDAHL, EARL Art gallerist, chocolatier. It's just possible that no one now alive visited Stendahl's modest but elegant L.A. art gallery under a candy factory for the unveiling of the most important painting of the twentieth century, Picasso's *Guernica,* brought to town by European exiles like Fritz Lang and art dealer Galka Scheyer (and New York exiles like Dorothy Parker) as a fund-raiser for Spanish Civil War orphans. Quoted by gracious permission of the family.

STOCKTON, ROBERT F. Military commander of California. Signed but didn't write the Treaty of Cahuenga ending the Mexican-American War. (See Ruiz de Rodriguez, Doña Bernarda.)

STRAVINSKY, IGOR Illustrious twentieth-century composer of *The Firebird, The Rite of Spring,* and the *Symphony in Three Movements,* among other masterworks. Based in Los Angeles from the World War II years until his death. Quoted from *Dialogues and a Diary,* by himself and Robert Craft (New York: Doubleday, 1963).

TAYLOR, BENJAMIN FRANKLIN Chicago-based war and travel correspondent. Quoted from his *Between the Gates* (Chicago: S. C. Griggs and Co., 1878).

THOMAS, DYLAN Welsh poet, author of "Do Not Go Gentle into That Good Night," *A Child's Christmas in Wales,* and the story collection *Adventures in the Skin Trade*—the little-remarked titular precursor to William Goldman's classic screenwriter's-eye-view of Hollywood, *Adventures in the Screen Trade.* Lurched through Los Angeles on the American tour immortalized by Peter DeVries and Julius J. Epstein in the novel and film *Reuben, Reuben.* Quoted from *Dylan Thomas: The Collected Letters,* edited by Paul Ferris (London: J. M. Dent & Sons, 2000).

THOMPSON, HUNTER S. Journalist, political columnist, author of *Fear and Loathing in Las Vegas* and *Fear and Loathing on the Campaign Trail.* For the hard-living or the famous, somebody's always ready to spin suicide into a cautionary tale. It's too easy to forget what a brilliant writer Thompson was. The signature Thompson speedball mixes grandiosity, paranoia, and pure poetry. He wrote about his nemeses, especially Nixon, with an invigorating lack of gentility. Met Oscar Zeta Acosta (q.v.), the inspiration for Dr. Gonzo in *Fear and Loathing in Las Vegas,* while reporting his firsthand account of the Chicano Movement and Moratorium. Quoted from "Strange Rumblings in Aztlan," *Rolling Stone,* April 1971.

THORNTON, HAZEL Juror, diarist. Quoted from *Hung Jury: The Diary of a Menendez Juror* (Philadelphia: Temple University Press, 1995).

THURBER, JAMES Writer and cartoonist, long at *The New Yorker,* author of *My World and Welcome to It* and the short story "The Secret Life of Walter Mitty." Thurber didn't hate L.A. as much as he let on. He hated it more. Quoted from *The Thurber Letters: The Wit, Wisdom, and Surprising Life of James Thurber,* edited by Helen Thurber and Edward Weeks (Boston: Little, Brown, 1981).

TRILLIN, CALVIN Journalist, long associated with *The New Yorker* and *The Nation,* author of *Alice, Let's Eat; Killings; Deadline Poet;* and the underrated *Floater.* Much of the story of the Watts

Towers comes down to us via variations on his May 29, 1965, *New Yorker* "Reporter at Large" feature. Quoted from that article.

TRUMBO, DALTON Screenwriter, novelist, and the man who broke the blacklist. Author of the antiwar classic *Johnny Got His Gun.* In *Spartacus,* Trumbo has Kirk Douglas shout "I am Spartacus!" to reclaim his identity—just as Trumbo would reclaim his own, by securing screen credit after a decade on the blacklist. Quoted from the canonical *Additional Dialogue: Letters of Dalton Trumbo, 1942–1962,* edited by Helen Manfull (New York: M. Evans and Company, 1970).

TYNAN, KENNETH Critic and author of *Oh, Calcutta!* Alongside Laurence Olivier, a presiding intelligence behind the birth of Britain's National Theatre. Latterly, critic at large for *The New Yorker.* Moved to Southern California and revived his reputation with trenchant profiles of everyone from Louise Brooks to Johnny Carson for *The New Yorker.* Called himself "a climatic émigré," but died of emphysema in Santa Monica. His daughter Roxana runs the Los Angeles Alliance for a New Economy. Quoted from *Diaries of Kenneth Tynan,* edited by John Lahr (New York: Bloomsbury, 2001).

VALENTINER, WILLIAM R. Pivotal curator of the Los Angeles County Museum of Art during its pre–Wilshire Boulevard, Exposition Park era. Quoted from *The Passionate Eye: The Life of William R. Valentiner* (Detroit: Wayne State University Press, 1979).

VANCOUVER, GEORGE British explorer of the Pacific Coast. Named Point Dume after his friend Francisco Dumetz, a Franciscan padre. Quoted from *Captain George Vancouver* (London: G. G. and J. Robinson, 1798).

VENEGAS, DOLORES Quoted from *Letters Home: Mexican Exile Correspondence from Los Angeles, 1927–1932,* by María Teresa Venegas

(Los Angeles: María Teresa Venegas, 2012). Department of Archives and Special Collection, William H. Hannon Library, Loyola Marymount University.

VENEGAS, JOSÉ MIGUEL Quoted from *Letters Home: Mexican Exile Correspondence from Los Angeles, 1927–1932,* by María Teresa Venegas (Los Angeles: María Teresa Venegas, 2012). Department of Archives and Special Collection, William H. Hannon Library, Loyola Marymount University.

VILLARD, OSWALD GARRISON Journalist and civil libertarian. Quoted from "Los Angeles Kaleidoscope," *The Nation,* 1934.

WAGNER, ROB This 1930s L.A. radical edited *Script,* the magazine some called a West Coast *New Yorker,* and published everybody from Chaplin to the unsung L.A. classical music writer José Rodríguez (q.v.). Quoted from *The Best of Rob Wagner's* Script, edited by Anthony Slide (Lanham, Md.: Scarecrow Press, 1985).

WALLACE, EDGAR Prolific novelist, today best known for conceiving, with Merian C. Cooper, the idea for *King Kong.* Four days after confiding to his diary that he again felt "quite gay and bright now," he died here of double pneumonia. Quoted from his *My Hollywood Diary: The Last Work of Edgar Wallace* (London: Hutchinson & Co., 1932).

WALLACE, IRVING Novelist, USC undergrad, author of *The Prize, The Man, The Plot, The Word,* and the rest. Quoted from *The Best of Rob Wagner's* Script, edited by Anthony Slide (Lanham, Md.: Scarecrow Press, 1985).

WARD, JOHN SHIRLEY Tennessee-born, San Bernardino–based newspaperman and alfalfa farmer. Gloriously described in his 1905 obituary as "Chesterfieldian in his intercourse with the weak and the poor as with the rich and the strong." Beats "Services pending" any day. Quoted from "Death of a Prominent Resident of Southern California," *Los Angeles Herald*, January 5, 1905.

WARNER, JACK Co-founder with his brothers of the Warner Bros. film studio. Quoted from a company-wide memo in *Warner Bros: The Making of an American Movie Studio*, by David Thomson (New Haven, Conn.: Yale University Press, 2017).

WARREN, ROBERT PENN Poet, novelist, author of *All the King's Men*. Stayed briefly in Santa Monica, later returned to sit in on the editing of Robert Rossen's film of *All the King's Men*. Quoted from *Selected Letters of Robert Penn Warren: The Apprentice Years, 1924–1934*, vol. 1, edited by Randy Hendricks (Baton Rouge: Louisiana State University Press, 2000).

WAUGH, EVELYN Author of *The Loved One, Brideshead Revisited, Scoop*, and the *Sword of Honour* trilogy. Visited Los Angeles in 1947, essentially to keep *Brideshead* from being made into a movie, and succeeded beyond his fondest dreams: He came away with the material for *The Loved One*, his merciless dissection of Forest Lawn and, by extension, the embalmed lives of the expats around him. Quoted from *The Diaries of Evelyn Waugh*, edited by Michael Davie (Boston: Little, Brown, 1976).

WAXMAN, AL Columnist and editor of the *Eastside Journal* in Boyle Heights; uncle of Congressman Henry Waxman. Quoted in *Southern California: An Island on the Land* by Carey McWilliams (New York: Duell, Sloan, & Pearce, 1946).

WEAVER, JOHN D. Author, magazine editor. Occasionally some editor will lift his eyes to the heavens and wish for a good single-volume history of Los Angeles, unaware that Weaver already wrote one, *The Enormous Village*. A little outdated, but so is any single-volume history after a decade. The first two hundred years of it are golden. Quoted from *Glad Tidings: A Friendship in Letters. The Correspondence of John Cheever and John D. Weaver, 1945–1982,* edited by John D. Weaver (New York: HarperCollins, 1993).

WEST, NATHANAEL Author of the novella *Miss Lonelyhearts* and the great Hollywood novel *The Day of the Locust.* Found L.A. a nice place to write about, but he didn't want to live here—until he did. His unexpected happy marriage might well have ruined him for satire, but the couple perished in a car crash that same year, just a day after the death of his friend and admirer F. Scott Fitzgerald. Quoted from *Nathanael West: Novels and Other Writings,* edited by Sacvan Bercovitch (New York: Library of America, 1997).

WESTON, EDWARD Celebrated photographer best known for his Western landscapes and nudes. Early in his career, Weston set up shop in Glendale. He wooed a prodigious cavalcade of women, squiring many to the Philharmonic of an evening. Finally he shacked up with his beloved Charis—all the while refining, and redefining, modernist photography. Diaries published in *The Daybooks of Edward Weston; Two Volumes in One: I. Mexico, II. California,* edited by Nancy Newhall (New York: Aperture, 1991).

WILDER, LAURA INGALLS Author of *Little House on the Prairie, Farmer Boy,* and other beloved, underrated books about her childhood homesteading on the South Dakota plains. Quoted from *The Selected Letters of Laura Ingalls Wilder,* edited by William Anderson (New York: HarperCollins, 2016).

WILLIAMS, LIZA Sadly under-remembered, coolly neurasthenic columnist for the *Los Angeles Free Press.* Quoted from her *Up the City of Angels* (New York: Putnam's Sons, 1971).

WILLIAMS, TENNESSEE Playwright, author of *A Streetcar Named Desire* and *The Glass Menagerie,* the latter more or less begun in Santa Monica during an otherwise unproductive—albeit highly sociable—screenwriting stint. Deflowered years earlier in Laguna Beach, to his mortification. Quoted from *The Selected Letters of Tennessee Williams, Volume 1, 1920–1945,* edited by Albert J. Devlin and Nancy M. Tischer (New York: New Directions, 2000).

WILSON, BENJAMIN DAVIS "DON BENITO" City father and L.A.'s second mayor. Arrived with the first party of overland settlers. Owned land from Westwood to Riverside, from Altadena to Wilmington. Led U.S. Army troops in the Mexican-American War, as would his grandson, George S. Patton, in World War II. Quoted from *Don Benito Wilson: From Mountain Man to Mayor, Los Angeles 1841 to 1878,* by Nat B. Read (Santa Monica, Calif.: Angel City Press, 2008).

WILSON, BRIAN Presiding genius of the Beach Boys. Quoted lyrics published by Irving Music, affiliated with BMI.

WILSON, CHARIS Author, model, diarist, and once the wife and muse of photographer Edward Weston. Quoted from "Charis Wilson journal, letters and notes documenting the Whitman trip with Edward Weston, 1936–2009," Huntington Library, San Marino, California.

WILSON, EDMUND Critic, historian, essayist, man of letters. Like Mencken and many other great American critics, he gave up on American fiction (except his own) too soon and pursued other curiosities. The rest of his career consistently altered the world's understanding of whatever caught his fancy, from the history of Communism to the Dead Sea Scrolls. Visited Southern California once. Unimpressed. Stayed in L.A. only long enough to write about the evangelists Aimee Semple McPherson and Bob Shuler, then decamped south to file "The Jumping-Off Place" about San Diego, then among the suicide capitals of the world. Quoted from his *The Twenties: From Notebooks and Diaries of the Period,* edited by Leon Edel (New York: Farrar, Straus & Giroux, 1975).

WILSON, WOODROW President of the United States celebrated for his worst achievement, humiliating Germany in World War I, and ridiculed for one of his best, trying to bring about world peace. Glimpsed in his biography by Palisades High's own A. Scott Berg actually *clicking his heels* aboard the presidential sleeping car on the morning after his second wedding night. Most of us picture Wilson, provided we can even keep him and the mediocrities who succeeded him straight, as a picklepuss, a hypocrite who ran on a peace platform and within months took us to war, a racist who threw a black civil-rights activist out of the Oval Office, a sap who bet his presidency on a gossamer sand castle called the League of Nations and lost. How to reconcile that Wilson with the virile, adoring husband who wrote from the road to his doomed first wife, "I am madly in love with you.... Are you prepared for the storm of love making with which you will be assailed?" Wilson's best biography is Berg's, his weirdest by Sigmund Freud. He whisked through L.A. on a campaign tour just long enough to give an anti-corporate speech to the since-disappeared Jefferson Club and, wistfully, look up an old flame. Quoted from *A Day of Dedication: The Essential Writings and Speeches of Woodrow Wilson,* edited by Albert Fried (New York: Macmillan, 1965).

WINCHELL, WALTER Terrifyingly influential newspaper gossip and political columnist. Quoted from "Hollywood Americana." *New York Daily Mirror,* among others, 1941.

WINTERS, YVOR Underappreciated poet and professor. Quoted from *Selected Letters of Yvor Winters,* edited by R. L. Barth (Athens, Ohio: Swallow Press, 2000).

WODEHOUSE, P. G. Comic author of the Jeeves and Wooster novels. Wodehouse passed through and wrote the Hollywood-set novel *Laughing Gas,* nine short stories, and many mostly unused scenes for reputedly unmemorable movies. He also cleared

$104,000 and complained about it in an *L.A. Times* interview, thus killing the golden goose for himself and not a few other screenwriters too. Quoted from *A Life in Letters,* edited by Sophie Ratcliffe (New York: W. W. Norton & Co., 2013).

WOODS, REV. JAMES The first Presbyterian pastor in L.A. Lasted less than a year. Diaries published in *The Reverend James Woods, Recollections of Pioneer Work in California* (San Francisco: Joseph Winterburn & Co., 1878).

WOOLLCOTT, ALEXANDER Waspish actor and wit. Quoted from *The Letters of Alexander Woollcott,* edited by Beatrice Kaufman and Joseph Hennessey (New York: Viking Press, 1944).

WPA GUIDE TO LOS ANGELES, THE Idea bin for historical novelists, cribsheet for fact-checkers, God's gift to narrative historians, *Los Angeles: The City and Its Environs* is a wayback machine for retrophile Angelenos everywhere. Also not above the occasional April Fool's joke that eluded the D.C. office, as seen here. Quoted from *Los Angeles in the 1930s: The WPA Guide to the City of Angels,* introduced by this volume's author (Berkeley: University of California Press, 2011).

WRIGHT, FRANK LLOYD Architect of Hollyhock House, La Miniatura, and other landmark buildings in Los Angeles and around the country. His reputation has aged better than his buildings, as anyone over six feet tall can tell you. But he improved American architecture even more than L.A. improved him, and that's saying plenty. Quoted in *What They Say About the Angels* (Pasadena, Calif.: Val Trefz Press, 1942).

WYLER, WILLIAM Film director of *The Best Years of Our Lives, Roman Holiday,* and the Great World War II documentary *Memphis Belle.* As detailed in Mark Harris's landmark book *Five Came*

Back, Wyler went to war a light entertainer and came back a tragedian. Quoted at http://starsandletters.blogspot.com/2013/12/.

ZANUCK, DARRYL Head of 20th Century-Fox, once a story man on Rin Tin Tin silents. Quoted from *The Grove Book of Hollywood*, edited by Christopher Silvester (New York: Grove Press, 1998).

ZORINA, VERA Dancer on stage and film, a muse of the choreographer George Balanchine. Quoted from her *Zorina* (New York: Farrar, Straus & Giroux, 1986).

Acknowledgments

As someone who's not above sheepishly glancing at the acknowledgments of my friends' books in search of my own name, I know that the next couple-three pages count. I've worked on *Dear Los Angeles* for seven years, and I daresay the acknowledgments below will leave *some*body out—surely a cause of relief in certain cases, but maybe knocking a nose or two out of joint elsewhere. I apologize to anybody who might look at these acknowledgments and find their own name unfairly missing. Whether below or not, numberless souls have helped me bring this book in for a landing. I so, so, thank you all.

Libraries have always been my Jerusalem, and if I forget thee, O librarians, may my laptop lose its memory. As always, I bow down before all dozen outposts of the mighty UCLA library system. From the day I first ransacked its endless-seeming shelves as a high school student right up to my current dependence, bordering on the chemical, as a member of the faculty, it has never failed me. I thank its dedicated full-time staff for never de-accessioning all the books that I never knew I needed until I did.

The guardians of the arcane mysteries housed in UCLA Special Collections, especially Genie Guerard, deserve special mention. One floor up, David Poepoe showed compassion, if not mercy, for my many crimes against due dates. He also helped run the late, keeningly lamented library book sales that once helped feed my appetite for Californiana. And that steely pair, Victoria Steele and Ginny Steel, the former Curator Emerita & Distinguished Librarian and the latter Norman and Armena Powell University Librarian, have helped make and keep UCLA libraries the envy of the academic world—just as Norman's dad, the great Lawrence Clark Powell, intended.

Reader, are you starting to skip past all these librarians? I wish you wouldn't. Everything good in the world comes from either librarians or their patrons. I also thank my capable friend the USC archivist and manuscripts librarian Claude Zachary and the redoubtable Ned Comstock of the USC Cinema Arts Library—even if they do work at the wrong university. There's a reason every book on film history for decades has Mr. Comstock's name in the acknowledgments, and it's not because he knows where all the confidential studio memos are kept.

USC also hosts the Los Angeles Institute for the Humanities, which has given me a sense of unearned legitimacy for almost eight years now. The friendships I've made or deepened at LAIH have nourished this book in ways beyond counting. Hats off to ringmasters Louise Steinman, Allison Engel, and Clifford Johnson—and to Louise, especially, for introducing me to the one book I'll never finish reading. Oh, and to Catherine Quinlan, dean of the USC Libraries, graceful sitter in the Valerie and Ronald Sugar Dean's Chair, for courtesies and cookies of many kinds.

USC's hospitality also extends to hosting L.A. as Subject, the indispensable association of smaller organizations all dedicated to as quixotically heroic a mission as I can think of: preserving, archiving, and sharing the history and culture of the Los Angeles region. If this book sends a reader googling nowhere else, let it send you here: https://laassubject.org.

I hope my next book gives me even more excuses to hang out at the Margaret Herrick Library, where Howard Prouty puts his encyclopedic knowledge of movies, books, and Los Angeles to work in the service of the Academy of Motion Picture Arts and Sciences. Every serious student of L.A. should have Howard's contact info as a *vade mecum.*

At my home away from home, the Huntington Library, my friend Dave Mihaly, curator of Graphic Arts and Social History; the Western American History curator, Peter Blodgett; Christopher Adde, wizardly keeper of the library; retired Collections curator Sue Hodson; and Natalie Russell, Sue's deserving inheritor, have all made the creation of this book both possible and congenial.

And to all the stalwart librarians of the Los Angeles Public Library, a deep and lifelong bow.

This book was also made possible by a generous, if finite, grant from the Department of Labor, i.e., unemployment insurance—and from Franklin Delano Roosevelt and Frances Perkins, too, while we're at it. There's no payroll tax I pay more proudly.

And, less directly but just as indispensably . . .

To the Sycamore Street book group, for all the California savvy, good books, conviviality, and truly stupendous food you've brought into my life. If you ever pick *Dear Los Angeles* for a Tuesday night, be gentle with me.

To the bookstores of Southern California, which have nourished me for as long as I've known how to read: If I'd bought every book I ever browsed among your shelves, there'd be even more of you left. I wish I had.

To this region's journalists, past and present, under good management and bad, who never stop teaching me how to write. You're forever in my heart, and in my driveway.

To my friends, especially the ones who've helped out when I needed an assignment or an attaboy. I haven't forgotten.

To three bosses who gave me the most fulfilling work I've ever known: Paul Wilner, Dana Gioia, and Bruce Beiderwell. If I could see you all in one room, I would levitate for joy.

To Kevin Starr, who taught me most of what I know about California, and Jeffrey Lustig, the founder of the California Studies Association, who introduced me to Kevin and so much more. I picture them both, strolling the strand at Carey McWilliams's favorite beauty spot, Point Sal, north of Santa Barbara, the only state park closed for repairs all but permanently. Save me a towel, guys.

To the staff of Libros Schmibros, the nonprofit lending library we've built over the years—shelve this one under "gratitude."

To all the people in all the permissions departments who cut me some slack, thank you. I know you were only looking out for the rights of two groups I revere: authors and publishers. Sorry for all the guilt trips.

To Fred Courtright, permissions dude extraordinaire, who gave me my first inkling of what I was in for.

For Teresa Carpenter, in whose slushy footsteps I walk. Her book *New York Diaries* does the impossible: It makes New York almost as interesting as Los Angeles.

To my agent, Sandy Dijkstra, who called me with the idea for this book just as I was thinking of it. That's what I call simpatico.

To Rachel Ake, who designed the book jacket. It's weird but great to see, for the first time, the amorphous book I've had in my head for years and suddenly know—thanks to someone I've never met—exactly how I'll picture it forever after.

To my editor, Sam Nicholson, for winkling *Dear Los Angeles* out of me, and to Modern Library and the whole Penguin Random House team I'm just getting to know. If Albert Boni and Horace Liveright could see you, they'd be proud. Let's do it again.

And did you hear the one about the neurotic Jewish author who asks his mother, "How'd you like my book?" Mom says, "Meh. You might at least say something nice for your mother in the acknowledgments." The author says, "But, Mom, I did! Didn't you see where I said, 'All errors are my own'?"

And they are.

Finally, to all the diarists, correspondents, and their families, this book is the party I wish I could throw for you. Please drop me a line and at least let me send you a book.

And to Angelenos everywhere, homesick or still here: I'd love it if you'd at least consider sharing a personal or family diary entry or a letter with me for possible future publication via kipend@gmail.com. This pointillist history of Los Angeles has more blind spots than a Camry with a busted mirror. Let's fill them in together. There's always the paperback. . . .

Index

Page numbers beginning with 475 refer to contributor biographies.

PERMISSIONS ACKNOWLEDGMENTS

Grateful acknowledgment is made to the following for permission to reprint both previously published and unpublished material:

Oscar Acosta: Excerpt from letter to Hugh Hefner from *Oscar "Zeta" Acosta: The Uncollected Works* edited by Ilan Stavans, copyright © 1996 by Marco Acosta (papers), copyright © 1996 by Ilan Stavans (introduction, chronology, bibliography). Reprinted by permission of Arte Publico Press. **Louis Adamic:** Excerpts from *Dynamite* by Louis Adamic, copyright © 1931, 1934 by Louis Adamic. Reprinted by permission of AK Press, Chico, CA. **Theodor Adorno:** Excerpts from *Letters to His Parents 1939–1951* by Theodor W. Adorno, English translation copyright © 2006 by Polity Press. Reprinted by permission of Polity Press, Cambridge, UK. **James Agee:** Excerpt from *Letters of James Agee to Father Flye* edited with an introduction by James Harold Flye. Reprinted by permission of Melville House Publishing, Brooklyn, NY, and London. **Ed Ainsworth:** Excerpt from "Along El Camino Real" by Ed Ainsworth (*Los Angeles Times*, January 30, 1936). Reprinted by permission of the *Los Angeles Times*. **Ellen Alperstein:** Excerpt from "The Enduring Fragments of 9/11" by Ellen Alperstein (*LA Observer*, 9/9/2011). Reprinted by permission of the author. **Heather B. Armstrong:** Excerpts from the writings of Heather B. Armstrong. Reprinted by permission of the author. **Amy Asbury:** Excerpts from *The Sunset Strip Diaries*. Reprinted by permission of the author. **Brendan Behan:** Excerpts from a letter by Brendan Behan displayed in the Dublin Writers Museum. Reprinted courtesy of Failte Ireland/the Dublin Writers Museum. **Valeria Belletti:** Excerpts from *Adventures of a Hollywood Secretary* edited and annotated by Cari Beauchamp, copyright © 2006 by Cari Beauchamp (Berkeley, CA: University of California Press, 2006). Reprinted by the kind permission of editor Cari Beauchamp and Margery Baragona. **Stephen Vincent Benét:** Excerpts from *Selected Letters of Stephen Vincent Benét* by Stephen Vincent Benét (New Haven, CT: Yale University Press, 1960). Reprinted by permission of Brandt & Hochman Literary Agents, Inc. All rights reserved. **Alan Bennett:** Excerpt from *Writing Home* by Alan Bennett, copyright © 1995 by Forelake Ltd. Reprinted by permission of The Zoë Pagnamenta Agency. **Sergei Bertensson:** Excerpts from *My First Time in Hollywood* edited and annotated by Cari Beauchamp, introduction, annotations, and volume compilation copyright © 2015 by Cari Beauchamp. Reprinted by permission of Asahina and Wallace, Los Angeles. **Jim Bouton:** Excerpts from *Ball Four* by Jim Bouton, copyright © 1970, 1981, 1990, 2000 by Jim Bouton. Reprinted by permission of the author. **Charles Bukowski:** Excerpts from pp. 132, 294, 353 from *Screams from the Balcony: Selected Letters, 1960–1970* by Charles Bukowski, edited by Seamus Cooney, copyright © 1993 by Charles Bukowski. Reprinted by permission of HarperCollins Publishers. **Edgar Rice Burroughs:** All quotes from Edgar Rice Burroughs © 1975, 2017 Edgar Rice Burroughs, Inc. All rights reserved. Trademarks TARZAN® and Edgar Rice Burroughs® owned by Edgar Rice Burroughs, Inc. and used by permission. **Richard Burton:** Excerpts from *The Richard Burton Diaries* by Richard Burton, edited by Chris Williams (New Haven: Yale University Press, 2012), copyright © 2012 by Swansea University. Reprinted by permission of Richard Burton Archives, Swansea University, United Kingdom. **Octavia Butler:** Various quotes by Octavia Butler, copyright © by Octavia E. Butler. Reprinted by permission of Writers House LLC acting as agent for the Estate. **John Cage:** Letters from John Cage to Pauline Schindler. Reprinted by permission of the John Cage Trust. **Italo Calvino:** Excerpts from *Hermit in Paris: Autobiographical Writings* by Italo Calvino, translated from the Italian by Martin McLaughlin, copyright © 2003 by the Estate of Italo Calvino. English translation copyright © 2003 by Jonathan Cape. Reprinted by permission of Houghton Mifflin Harcourt Publishing Company. All rights reserved. **Raymond Chandler:** Excerpt from *Selected Letters of Raymond Chandler* by Raymond Chandler, edited by Frank McShane (New York: Columbia University Press,

1981), copyright © 1981 by College Trustees, Ltd.; introduction, selection, editorial matter copyright © 1981 by Frank McShane. Reprinted by permission of the Estate of the author c/o Rogers, Coleridge & White Ltd., 20 Powis Mews, London, W11 1JN. **Cesar Chavez:** Excerpts from the writings of Cesar Chavez, TM/© 2018 the Cesar Chavez Foundation www.chavezfoundation.org. Reprinted by permission of the Cesar Chavez Foundation. **Susana Chávez-Silverman:** Excerpt from *Killer Crónicas* by Susana Chávez-Silverman. Reprinted by gracious permission of the author. **John Cheever:** Excerpts from *Glad Tidings: A Friendship in Letters, The Correspondence of John Cheever and John D. Weaver, 1945–1982* by John Cheever and John D. Weaver (New York: HarperCollins Publishers, 1993). Reprinted by permission of Harold Ober Associates Incorporated. **Winston Churchill:** 427 words from a letter from Winston S. Churchill to Clementine Churchill dated September 29, 1929, copyright © The Estate of Winston S. Churchill. Reproduced with permission of Curtis Brown, London on behalf of The Estate of Winston S. Churchill. **Wanda Coleman:** Excerpts from *The Riot Inside of Me: More Trial & Tremors* by Wanda Coleman, copyright © 2005 by Wanda Coleman. Reprinted with the permission of Black Sparrow Books, an imprint of David R. Godine, Publisher. **Alistair Cooke:** Quotes by Alistair Cooke © Cooke Americas, RLLP. Reprinted by permission of the Alistair Cooke Estate. **Aaron Copland:** Letter from Aaron Copland to Leonard Bernstein dated February 21, 1943. The words of Aaron Copland are reproduced by permission of The Aaron Copland Fund for Music, Inc., copyright owner. **Eleanor Coppola:** Excerpts from *Notes on a Life* by Eleanor Coppola, copyright © 2008 by Eleanor Coppola. Used by permission of Nan A. Talese, an imprint of the Knopf Doubleday Publishing Group, a division of Penguin Random House LLC. All rights reserved. **Norman Corwin:** Letters by Norman Corwin housed in the Norman Corwin Collection. Reprinted by permission of the Thousand Oaks Library Foundation. **Noël Coward:** Excerpt from *The Noël Coward Diaries* edited by Graham Payn and Sheridan Morley, copyright © 1982 by NC Aventales AG. Reprinted by permission of Alan Brodie Representation Ltd., www.alanbrodie.com. **Glen Creason:** Diary entries by Glen Creason. Reprinted by permission of the author. **Simone de Beauvoir:** Excerpt from *Letters to Sarte* by Simone de Beauvoir, translated by Quintin Hoare, published by Vintage, an imprint of Penguin Random House UK, copyright © 1992. Reprinted by permission of The Random House Group Limited. **Frank del Olmo:** "Perspective on Autism: Facing Loss by Keeping Hope" by Frank del Olmo (*Los Angeles Times,* December 27, 1998). Reprinted by permission of the *Los Angeles Times.* **John Dos Passos:** Writings by John Dos Passos. Reprinted by permission of Lucy Dos Passos Coggin. **Theodore Dreiser:** Excerpts from three letters from Theodore Dreiser to John Steinbeck (1940), Eleanor Roosevelt (1942), and Edward G. Robinson (1940), copyright © 1940, 1942 by the Dreiser Trust. Reprinted by Curtis Brown, Ltd. All rights reserved. **Philip Dunne:** Quotes from Philip Dunne from *Script Magazine.* Reprinted by permission. **William Faulkner:** Excerpts from eleven letters from *Selected Letters of William Faulkner* by William Faulkner, edited by Joseph Blotner, copyright © 1977 by Jill Faulkner Summers. Reprinted by permission of Random House, an imprint and division of Penguin Random House LLC. All rights reserved. **Richard Feynman:** Excerpts from *Perfectly Reasonable Deviations from the Beaten Track* by Richard Feynman, copyright © 2005, 2006, 2006. Reprinted by permission of Basic Books, an imprint of Hachette Book Group, Inc. **M.F.K. Fisher:** Excerpts from the writings of M.F.K. Fisher. Reprinted by permission of InkWell Management on behalf of The Literary Trust u/w/o M.F.K. Fisher. **F. Scott Fitzgerald:** Excerpts from letters dated March 11, 1938, March 19, 1940, October 23, 1940, and December 15, 1940, from *The Letters of F. Scott Fitzgerald* by Andrew Turnbull, copyright © 1963 by Frances Scott Fitzgerald Lanahan. Copyright renewed 1991. Reprinted by permission of Scribner, a division of Simon & Schuster, Inc. All rights reserved. **Sir John Gielgud:** Excerpts from five letters by Sir John Gielgud. Reprinted by permission of the Sir John Gielgud Charitable Trust. **Allen Ginsberg:** Excerpts from *Journals: Early Fifties, Early Sixties* by Allen Ginsberg, copyright © 1977 by Allen Ginsberg. Reprinted by permission of Grove/Atlantic, Inc. Any third party use of this material, outside of this publication, is prohibited. **Lillian Gish:** Quotes from Lillian Gish from *Script Magazine.* Reprinted by permission. **Don Herold:** Quotes from Don Herold from *Script Magazine.* Reprinted by permission. **Langston Hughes:** Excerpt from *Selected Letters of Langston Hughes* edited by Arnold Rampersad and David Roessel with Christa Fratantoro, copyright © 2015 by The Estate of Langston Hughes. Reprinted by permission of Alfred A. Knopf, an imprint of the Knopf Doubleday Publishing Group, a division of Penguin Random House LLC. All rights reserved. **Aldous Huxley:** Excerpt from *The Selected Letters of Aldous Huxley* edited with an introduction by James Sexton, copyright © 2007 by James Sexton (Chicago, IL: Ivan R. Dee, Publishers, 2007). Reprinted by permission of Rowman & Littlefield. All rights reserved. **Eric Idle:** Excerpt from *The Greedy Bastard Diary* by Eric Idle, copyright © 2005 by Eric Idle. Reprinted by permission of HarperCollins Publishers. **Helen Hunt Jackson:** Excerpt from *The Indian Reform Letters of Helen Hunt Jackson, 1879–1885* edited by Valerie Sherer Mathes, copyright © 1998 by the University of Oklahoma Press, Norman, Publishing Division of the University. Reprinted by permission of the University of Oklahoma Press. **Una Kuster Jeffers:** Two quotations from Una Jeffers appearing on pp. 169-170 of *Collected Letters of Robinson Jeffers with Selected Letters of Una Jeffers,* Volume One, 1890-1930 edited by James Karman, copyright © 2009 by the Board of Trustees of the Leland Stanford Jr. University. All rights reserved. Used by permission of the publisher, Stanford University Press, sup.org. **Nunnally Johnson:** Excerpts from *The Letters of Nunnally Johnson* by Dorris Johnson, copyright © 1981 by Dorris Johnson. Reprinted by permission of Alfred A. Knopf, an imprint of the Knopf Doubleday Publishing Group, a division of Penguin Random House LLC. All rights reserved. **James Jones:** Excerpt from *To Reach Eternity: The Letters of James Jones* edited by George Hendrick, copyright © 1989 by George Hendrick and Gloria Jones. Reprinted by permission of Random House, an imprint and division of Penguin Random House LLC. All rights reserved. **James Joyce:** Excerpt from *Finnegans Wake: Centennial Edition* by James Joyce, copyright © 1939 by James Joyce, copyright renewed 1967 by Giorgio Joyce and Lucia Joyce. Reprinted by permission of Viking Books, an imprint of Penguin Publishing Group, a division of Penguin Random House LLC. All rights reserved. **Elia Kazan:** Excerpts from *The Selected Letters of Elia Kazan* edited by Albert J. Devlin and Marlene J. Devlin, copyright © 2014 by Frances Kazan. Reprinted by permission of Alfred A. Knopf, an imprint of the Knopf Doubleday Publishing Group, a division of Penguin Random House LLC. All rights reserved. **Carolyn Kellogg:** Excerpts from personal journals from 1986–1987. Reprinted by permission of the author. **Jack Kerouac:** Excerpts from *Windblown World: The Journals of Jack Kerouac 1947–1954* by Jack Kerouac, edited by Douglas Brinkley, copyright © 2004 by The Estate of Stella Kerouac, John Sampas, Literary Representative. Reprinted by permission of Viking Books, an imprint of Penguin Publishing Group, a division of Penguin Random House LLC. All rights reserved. **Eric Knight:** Quotes from Eric Knight from *Script Magazine.* Reprinted by permission. **Louis L'Amour:** Quotes from Louis L'Amour from *Script Magazine.* Reprinted by permission. **John Lennon:** Excerpts from *John* by Cynthia Lennon, copyright © 2005 by Cynthia Lennon. Reprinted by permission of Crown Books, an imprint of the Crown Publishing Group, a division of Penguin Random House LLC. All rights reserved. **Steve Lopez:** "Points West: A Bright Future Bought with Hard Work and Lots of Tacos" by Steve Lopez (*Los Angeles Times,* May 30, 2003). Reprinted by permission of the *Los Angeles Times.* **Mike Love and Brian Wilson:** Excerpt from "The Warmth of the Sun," lyrics and music by Mike E. Love and Brian Douglas Wilson, copyright © 1964 by Irving Music, Inc. Used by permission of Hal Leonard Corporation. All rights reserved. **Ernst Lubitsch:** Quotes from Ernst Lubitsch from *Script Magazine.* Reprinted by permission. **Charles Lummis:** Excerpts from Charles Fletcher Lummis Papers, 1850–1929. Braun Research Library Collection, Autry Museum; MS.1. Reprinted by permission. **Ross Macdonald (pseudonym of Kenneth Millar):** Excerpts from two letters from Ross Macdonald to Eudora Welty. Reprinted by permission of the Margaret Millar Charitable Remainder Unitrust. **Ricardo Flores Magon:** Excerpts from *Dreams of Freedom: A Ricardo Flores Magon Reader* by Ricardo Flores Magon, edited by Chaz Bufe and Mitchell Cowen Verter. Reprinted by permission of AK Press, Chico,

CA. **Norman Mailer:** Excerpts from *The Selected Letters of Norman Mailer* by Norman Mailer, edited by J. Michael Lennon (New York: Random House, 2014), copyright © 2014 by the Estate of Norman Mailer. Reprinted by permission of The Wylie Agency LLC. **Thomas Mann:** Excerpts from five letters by *Letters of Thomas Mann* by Thomas Mann, selected and translated by Richard and Clara Winston, copyright © 1970 and copyright renewed 1998 by Penguin Random House LLC. Used by permission of Alfred A. Knopf, an imprint of the Knopf Doubleday Publishing Group, a division of Penguin Random House LLC. All rights reserved. **Groucho Marx:** Excerpts from *The Groucho Letters* by Groucho Marx, copyright © 1967 by Groucho Marx and copyright renewed 1995 by Miriam Marx, Arthur Marx, and Melinda Marx. Reprinted by permission of Simon & Schuster, Inc. All rights reserved. **H. L. Mencken:** Excerpts from two letters by H. L. Mencken. Reproduced by permission of Enoch Pratt Free Library, Maryland's State Library Resource Center, in accordance with the terms of the will of H. L. Mencken. **Henry Miller:** Excerpts from two letters by Henry Miller, copyright © 2018 by the Estate of Henry Miller. Reproduced by permission of Curtis Brown Ltd. on behalf of the Literary Estate of Henry Miller. **Tom Mix:** Quotes from Tom Mix from *Script Magazine*. Reprinted by permission. **Marilyn Monroe:** Excerpt from *Marilyn Monroe Day by Day: A Timeline of People, Places and Events* by Carl Rollyson, copyright © 2014 by Rowman & Littlefield. Reprinted by permission of Rowman & Littlefield. **Willard F. Motley:** Excerpt from an article in *Commonweal* from 1939. Reprinted by permission of *Commonweal*. For more information, visit www.commonwealmagazine.org. **Vladimir Nabokov:** Excerpts from *Dear Bunny, Dear Volodya: The Nabokov-Wilson Letters 1940–1971* by Vladimir Vladimirovich Nabokov and Edmund Wilson, letters of Vladimir Nabokov copyright © 1979 by Vera Nabokov, executrix of The Estate of Vladimir Nabokov; additional letters copyright © 2001 by Dmitri Nabokov. Reprinted by permission of University of California Press via Copyright Clearance Center. **Ogden Nash:** Excerpts from *Loving Letters from Ogden Nash* by Ogden Nash, edited by Linell Nash Smith (Boston, MA: Little, Brown & Co., 1990) copyright © 1990 by Linell Nash Smith. Reprinted by permission of Curtis Brown, Ltd. **Anaïs Nin:** Excerpts from *The Diary of Anaïs Nin*, Volume Six, 1955–1966 by Anaïs Nin, copyright © 1966, 1976 by Anaïs Nin. Reprinted by permission of Houghton Mifflin Harcourt Publishing Company. All rights reserved. **Clifford Odets:** Excerpts from *The Time is Ripe: The 1940 Journal of Clifford Odets*, copyright © 1988 by Walt Whitman Odets and Nora Odets; introduction copyright © 1988 by William Gibson. Used by permission of Brandt & Hochman Literary Agents, Inc. All rights reserved. **Aaron Paley:** Excerpts from Aaron Paley's personal diaries. Reprinted by permission of the author. **Michael Palin:** Excerpts from *Halfway to Hollywood: Diaries 1980–1988*, copyright © 2009 by Michael Palin and *Diaries 1969–1979: The Python Years* copyright © 2006 by Michael Palin. Reprinted by permission of The Orion Publishing Group, London. **George S. Patton:** Excerpt from *General Patton: A Soldier's Life* by Stanley P. Hirshson, copyright © 2002 by Stanely P. Hirshon. Reprinted by permission of HarperCollins Publishers. **S. J. Perelman:** Excerpts from *Don't Tread on Me: The Selected Letters of S. J. Perelman* edited by Prudence Crowther. Reprinted by permission of Harold Ober Associates Incorporated. **Dawn Powell:** Excerpts from *The Diaries of Dawn Powell: 1931–1965* by Dawn Powell, copyright © 1995 by the Estate of Dawn Powell, introduction copyright © 1995 by Tim Page. Reprinted by permission of Steerforth Press. **Ronald Reagan:** Excerpts from *The Reagan Diaries* by Ronald Reagan, edited by Douglas Brinkly, copyright © 2007 by The Ronald Reagan Presidential Library Foundation. Reprinted courtesy of HarperCollins Publishers. **Jean Renoir:** Excerpts from *Letters* by Jean Renoir, copyright © 1994 by the Estate of Jean Renoir. Reproduced by permission of Faber & Faber Ltd. **Kenneth Rexroth:** Excerpt from a *San Francisco Chronicle* column by Kenneth Rexroth. Reprinted by permission of the Kenneth Rexroth Trust. **Charles Reznikoff:** Excerpts from *The Selected Letters of Charles Reznikoff: 1917–1976*, copyright © The Estate of Charles Reznikoff. Reprinted by permission of David R. Godine, Publisher, Inc. **Robert Richardson:** "'Get Whitey' Scream Blood-Hungry Mobs" by Robert Richardson (*Los Angeles Times*, August 14, 1965). Reprinted by permission of the *Los Angeles Times*. **Joan Rivers:**

Excerpts from *Diary of a Mad Diva* by Joan Rivers, copyright © 2014 by CCF Productions, Inc. Reprinted by permission of Berkley, an imprint of Penguin Publishing Group, a division of Penguin Random House LLC. All rights reserved. **José Rodriguez:** Quotes from José Rodriguez from *Script Magazine*. Reprinted by permission. **Sandie Saito:** Excerpts from letters between Sandie Saito and Molly Wilson archived at Densho: The Japanese American Legacy Project, www.densho.org. Reprinted by permission. **Carl Sandburg:** Excerpts from *The Letters of Carl Sandburg*, copyright © 1968 by Lillian Steichen Sandburg. Reprinted by permission of Houghton Mifflin Harcourt Publishing Company. All rights reserved. **William Saroyan:** Quotes from William Saroyan from *Script Magazine*. Reprinted by permission. **Edwin Schallert:** "New Orchestra Is Organized" (*Los Angeles Times*, June 11, 1919) and "Philharmonic Makes Debut" (*Los Angeles Times*, October 25, 1919). Reprinted by permission of the *Los Angeles Times*. **David O. Selznick:** Two memos. Reprinted by permission of Daniel Selznick. **Ruth Shellhorn:** Excerpt from the Ruth Patricia Shellhorn Papers (Collection 1757) UCLA Library Special Collections, Charles E. Young Research Library, University of California, Los Angeles. Reprinted by permission. **Nicolas Slonimsky:** Excerpts from *Dear Dorothy: Letters from Nicolas Slonimsky to Dorothy Adlow*, edited by Electra Slonimsky Yourke. Reprinted by permission of Boydell & Brewer, Inc., University of Rochester Press. **Jack Smith:** "Fantasy Land of Films Doomed by Big Project" by Jack Smith (*Los Angeles Times*, January 13, 1958). Reprinted by permission of the *Los Angeles Times*. **Susan Sontag:** Excerpts from "1948" and "1949" from *Reborn: Journals and Notebooks, 1947–1963* by Susan Sontag, edited by David Rieff, copyright © 2008 by The Estate of Susan Sontag. Reprinted by permission of Farrar, Straus & Giroux. **Stephen Spender:** Excerpt from *Journals: 1939–1983*, edited by John Goldsmith (London: Faber & Faber Limited, 1985), copyright © 1985 by The Estate of Stephen Spender. Reprinted by permission of Curtis Brown Ltd. on behalf of the Literary Estate of Stephen Spender. **Ben Stein:** Excerpt from *Hollywood Days, Hollywood Nights: The Diary of a Mad Screenwriter* by Ben Stein, copyright © 1988 by Ben Stein. Used by permission of The Wallace Agency. **John Steinbeck:** Excerpts from a letter by John Steinbeck to Robert Ballou dated February 11, 1933, and excerpts from a letter by John Steinbeck to Elizabeth Otis dated December 15, 1939, from *Steinbeck: A Life in Letters* by John Steinbeck, edited by Elaine Steinbeck and Robert Wallsten, copyright © 1952 by John Steinbeck, copyright © 1969 by The Estate of John Steinbeck, copyright © 1975 by Elaine Steinbeck and Robert Wallsten. Reprinted by permission of Viking Books, an imprint of Penguin Publishing Group, a division of Penguin Random House LLC. All rights reserved. **Igor Stravinsky and Robert Craft:** Excerpt(s) from RETROSPECTIVES AND CONCLUSIONS by Igor Stravinsky, copyright © 1969 by Igor Stravinsky and Robert Craft. Copyright © 1965, 1966, 1967, 1968, 1969 by Igor Stravinsky. Copyright © 1966, 1968, 1969 by Robert Craft. Used by permission of Alfred A. Knopf, an imprint of the Knopf Doubleday Publishing Group, a division of Penguin Random House LLC. All rights reserved. **Hazel Thornton:** Excerpts from *Hung Jury: The Diary of a Menendez Juror*. Reprinted by permission of the author. **James Thurber:** Two excerpts from James Thurber's correspondence with *The New Yorker*, copyright © 1939 by James Thurber. Reprinted by arrangement with Rosemary A. Thurber and the Barbara Hogenson Agency, Inc. **Dalton Trumbo:** Excerpts from *Additional Dialogue: Letters of Dalton Trumbo 1942–1962* by Dalton Trumbo. Reprinted by permission. **Kenneth Tynan:** Excerpts from the diaries of Kenneth Tynan. Reprinted by permission. **Dolores Venegas:** Excerpts from letters published in *Letters Home: Mexican Exile Correspondence from Los Angeles 1927–1932*. Reprinted by permission. **José Miguel Venegas:** Excerpts from letters published in *Letters Home: Mexican Exile Correspondence from Los Angeles 1927–1932*. Reprinted by permission. **Rob Wagner:** Quotes from Rob Wagner from *Script Magazine*. Reprinted by permission. **Irving Wallace:** Quotes from Irving Wallace from *Script Magazine*. Reprinted by permission. **Robert Penn Warren:** Quotes from the writings of Robert Penn Warren. Reprinted by permission of the heirs of Robert Penn Warren. **Evelyn Waugh:** Excerpts from *The Diaries of Evelyn Waugh* by Evelyn Waugh, copyright © 1976 by The Estate of Evelyn Waugh. Reprinted by permission of The Wylie Agency LLC. **Nathanael West:** Excerpt from letters from *Nathanael West: Novels and Other Writings*. Reprinted by permission of Harold Ober Associates Incorporated. **Edward Weston:** Excerpts from Edward Weston's *Daybooks*. Reprinted by permission of Weston Photography. **Laura Ingalls Wilder:** Excerpt from *The Selected Letters of Laura Ingalls Wilder* by Laura Ingalls Wilder and William Anderson, copyright © 2016 by William Anderson; letters copyright © 2016 by Little House Heritage Trust; introduction, annotation, footnotes, explanatory text, photograph captions copyright © 2016 by William Anderson. Reprinted by permission of HarperCollins Publishers. **Liza Williams:** Quotes from three articles by Liza Williams, staff writer, *Los Angeles Free Press*. Reprinted courtesy of LAFreePress.com. **Tennessee Williams:** Excerpts from *The Notebooks of Tennessee Williams* by Tennessee Williams, copyright © 1975 by The University of the South. Reprinted by permission of Georges Borchardt, Inc. on behalf of the Tennessee Williams Estate. **Charis Wilson:** Excerpts from Charis Wilson, *Guggenheim Journal*. Reprinted by permission of Rachel Harris. **Edmund Wilson:** Excerpt from *The Twenties: From Notebooks and Diaries of the Period* by Edmund Wilson, edited by Leon Edel, copyright © 1975 by the Estate of Edmund Wilson (New York: Farrar, Straus & Giroux, 1975). Reprinted by permission of Farrar, Straus & Giroux and The Wylie Agency LLC. **Yvor Winters:** Excerpts from *Selected Letters of Yvor Winters* by Yvor Winters edited by R. L. Barth. Reprinted by permission of Swallow Press/Ohio University Press. **P. G. Wodehouse:** Excerpts from *A Life in Letters* by P.G. Wodehouse edited by Sophie Ratcliffe (New York: W. W. Norton, 2013), copyright © 2011 by Trustees of the Wodehouse Estate; introduction, selection and other editorial matter copyright © 2011 by Sophie Ratcliffe. Reprinted by permission of the Estate of the author c/o Rogers, Coleridge & White Ltd., 20 Powis Mews, London, W11 1JN. **Alexander Woollcott:** Excerpt from *The Letters of Alexander Woollcott* by Alexander Woollcott, copyright © 1944 and copyright renewed 1972 by Penguin Random House LLC. Reprinted by permission of Viking Books, an imprint of Penguin Publishing Group, a division of Penguin Random House LLC. All rights reserved.

ABOUT THE EDITOR

DAVID KIPEN was born in Los Angeles. Author of *The Schreiber Theory: A Radical Rewrite of American Film History* and translator of the Cervantes novella *The Dialogue of the Dogs,* he teaches on the full-time UCLA writing faculty. For seven years Kipen was book critic of the *San Francisco Chronicle* and now serves as critic-at-large for the *Los Angeles Times.* As literature director of the National Endowment for the Arts, he co-created the permanent federal literary, still-thriving initiative The Big Read. In 2010 he founded the nonprofit lending library Libros Schmibros in the working-class L.A. neighborhood of Boyle Heights.